Applied Conversation Analysis

Palgrave Advances in Linguistics
Consulting Editor: **Christopher N. Candlin, Macquarie University, Australia**

Titles include:

Charles Antaki (*editor*)
APPLIED CONVERSATION ANALYSIS
Intervention and Change in Institutional Talk

Mike Baynham and Mastin Prinsloo (*editors*)
THE FUTURE OF LITERACY STUDIES

Noel Burton-Roberts (*editor*)
PRAGMATICS

Susan Foster-Cohen (*editor*)
LANGAUGE ACQUISITION

Monica Heller (*editor*)
BILINGUALISM: A SOCIAL APPROACH

Martha E. Pennington (*editor*)
PHONOLOGY IN CONTEXT

Barry O'Sullivan (*editor*)
LANGUAGE TESTING
Theories and Practices

Ann Weatherall, Bernadette M. Watson and Cindy Gallois (*editors*)
LANGUAGE, DISCOURSE AND SOCIAL PSYCHOLOGY

Palgrave Advances
Series Standing Order ISBN 978-1-4039-3512-0 (Hardback)
978-1-4039-3513-7 (Paperback)
(*outside North America only*)

You can receive future titles in this series as they are published by placing a standing order. Please contact your bookseller or, in the case of difficulty, write to us at the address below with your name and address, the title of the series and the ISBN quoted above.

Customer Services Department, Macmillan Distribution Ltd, Houndmills, Basingstoke, Hampshire RG21 6XS, England

Applied Conversation Analysis

Intervention and Change in Institutional Talk

Edited by

Charles Antaki
Loughborough University, UK

Selection and editorial matter © Charles Antaki 2011
Chapters © their individual authors 2011

All rights reserved. No reproduction, copy or transmission of this publication may be made without written permission.

No portion of this publication may be reproduced, copied or transmitted save with written permission or in accordance with the provisions of the Copyright, Designs and Patents Act 1988, or under the terms of any licence permitting limited copying issued by the Copyright Licensing Agency, Saffron House, 6–10 Kirby Street, London EC1N 8TS.

Any person who does any unauthorized act in relation to this publication may be liable to criminal prosecution and civil claims for damages.

The authors have asserted their rights to be identified as the authors of this work in accordance with the Copyright, Designs and Patents Act 1988.

First published 2011 by
PALGRAVE MACMILLAN

Palgrave Macmillan in the UK is an imprint of Macmillan Publishers Limited, registered in England, company number 785998, of Houndmills, Basingstoke, Hampshire RG21 6XS.

Palgrave Macmillan in the US is a division of St Martin's Press LLC, 175 Fifth Avenue, New York, NY 10010.

Palgrave Macmillan is the global academic imprint of the above companies and has companies and representatives throughout the world.

Palgrave® and Macmillan® are registered trademarks in the United States, the United Kingdom, Europe and other countries.

ISBN 978–0–230–22995–2   hardback
ISBN 978–0–230–22996–9   paperback

This book is printed on paper suitable for recycling and made from fully managed and sustained forest sources. Logging, pulping and manufacturing processes are expected to conform to the environmental regulations of the country of origin.

A catalogue record for this book is available from the British Library.

A catalog record for this book is available from the Library of Congress.

10 9 8 7 6 5 4 3 2 1
20 19 18 17 16 15 14 13 12 11

Printed and bound in Great Britain by
CPI Antony Rowe, Chippenham and Eastbourne

Contents

List of Figures and Tables		vii
Series Editor's Preface		ix
List of Contributors		xi
Notation		xii
1	Six Kinds of Applied Conversation Analysis *Charles Antaki*	1
2	'Some' versus 'Any' Medical Issues: Encouraging Patients to Reveal Their Unmet Concerns *John Heritage and Jeffrey D. Robinson*	15
3	Changing Interactional Behaviour: Using Conversation Analysis in Intervention Programmes for Aphasic Conversation *Ray Wilkinson*	32
4	Improving Response Rates in Telephone Interviews *Douglas W. Maynard, Nora Cate Schaeffer and Jeremy Freese*	54
5	Improving Ethnic Monitoring on a Telephone Helpline *Sue Wilkinson*	75
6	Working with Childbirth Helplines: The Contributions and Limitations of Conversation Analysis *Celia Kitzinger*	98
7	Simulated Interaction and Communication Skills Training: The 'Conversation-Analytic Role-Play Method' *Elizabeth Stokoe*	119
8	Should Mandatory Jobseeker Interviews be Personalised? The Politics of Using Conversation Analysis to Make Effective Practice Recommendations *Merran Toerien, Annie Irvine, Paul Drew and Roy Sainsbury*	140
9	Giving Feedback to Care Staff about Offering Choices to People with Intellectual Disabilities *W. M. L. Finlay, Chris Walton and Charles Antaki*	161

10 Reflecting on Your Own Talk: The Discursive Action Method at Work *Joyce Lamerichs and Hedwig te Molder*	184
11 Conversation Analysis Applied to User-Centred Design: A Study of Who 'The User' Is *Maria Egbert*	207
12 A Psychoanalyst's Reflection on Conversation Analysis's Contribution to His Own Therapeutic Talk *Anssi Peräkylä*	222
References	243
Author Index	265
Subject Index	270

List of Figures and Tables

Figures

2.1	First page of patient pre-visit survey	27
3.1	Handout example	45
7.1	Participants at a mediation training workshop	127
7.2	PowerPoint presentation of DC call (a)	128
7.3	PowerPoint presentation of DC call (b)	130
7.4	PowerPoint presentation of HC call	130
7.5	PowerPoint presentation of DC call (a)	132
7.6	PowerPoint presentation of DC call (b)	133
7.7	PowerPoint presentation of DC call (c)	134
7.8	PowerPoint presentation of DC call (d)	134
7.9	PowerPoint presentation of DC call (e)	135
7.10	PowerPoint presentation of EC call	136
9.1	Staff member Tim (right) picks out a bag	168
9.2	Resident Alec (right) taps the mixed veg. bag	170
9.3	Staff member Tim (left) holds on to the green beans	170
9.4	Making hot drinks in the kitchen	177
9.5	Pouring out the coffee	178
9.6	A staff member guides a resident on to the scales	179
10.1	The cyclical approach to analysis	196
10.2	The play as it was performed by secondary school pupils in 2004 at a symposium addressing health prevention initiatives (Photo courtesy of Jurriaan Balke)	202

Tables

2.1	Projected distribution of cases in the study	25
2.2	Patient multiple concerns by geographic area	28
2.3	Model building for unmet concerns	29
4.1	Continuum of cautious and presumptive requests	63

Series Editor's Preface

The *Advances in Linguistics Series* is part of an overall publishing program by Palgrave Macmillan aimed at producing collections of original, commissioned articles under the invited editorship of distinguished scholars.

The books in the Series are not intended as an overall guide to the topic or to provide an exhaustive coverage of its various sub-fields. Rather, they are carefully planned to offer the informed readership a conspectus of perspectives on key themes, authored by major scholars whose work is at the boundaries of current research. What we plan the Series will do, then, is to focus on salience and influence, move fields forward, and help to chart future research development.

The Series is designed for postgraduate and research students, including advanced level undergraduates seeking to pursue research work in Linguistics, or careers engaged with language and communication study more generally, as well as for more experienced researchers and tutors seeking an awareness of what is current and in prospect in adjacent research fields to their own. We hope that the some of the intellectual excitement posed by the challenges of Linguistics as a pluralistic discipline will shine through the books!

Editors of books in the Series have been particularly asked to put their own distinctive stamp on their collection, to give it a personal dimension, and to map the territory, as it were, seen through the eyes of their own research experience.

There are many ways in which this ground-breaking collection of chapters on the application of CA meets these aims.

Firstly, that it signals how the delicate descriptions of talk characteristic of CA can be realised in a range of institutional sites of engagement, thus reinforcing CA's inter- and intra-institutional capacity as a key research methodology. Secondly, as Charles Antaki argues in his initial chapter, that the well-recognised descriptive and interpretive powers of CA can, and indeed need, to be linked to an equivalently powerful explanatory capacity which takes account of the situated interaction order but does so in relation to the affordances and constraints of the institutional order. This is in itself quite novel in relation to much of the CA tradition. Thirdly, there has been something of a breakthrough development in CA research, supported and reinforced in this volume, whereby qualitative analyses of conversational data, perhaps especially those that focus on critical moments in crucial sites, can usefully be supported, and indeed substantiated, by the deployment of appropriate quantitative analytical method. This is again an innovative landmark in that it opens CA to contributing strongly to collaborative mixed methods research now advocated in a range of fields in discourse analysis and applied linguistics more generally. Finally, the emphasis in the title and the chapters on intervention and change not only point to a social and institutional responsibility on CA researchers but suggest that jointly problematising and collaborative work with institutional members, complex and difficult though this can be in practice, is now as much a CA objective as it is in other discourse and talk/gesture-related methodologies. "Making CA matter" could well be a guiding principle underlying this aspect of this exciting and authoritative collection, and in ways in which we need not be at all reticent. After all, current interest in professional and organisational communication is not just sourced from language and communication specialists, whether from CA or other methodological persuasions. There is ample evidence that such communities of practice are themselves intensely interested in their discursive practices and seeking just the powerful accounts that CA is characteristically able to provide.

There are other foci in this book, however, which contribute to its originality, and where Antaki's construction of CA, supported by the illuminative array of chapter themes, has quite significant messages for research and practice. One of these touches on the issue of values and ethical research behaviour. CA researchers, as with other analysts of talk and gesture, have long accustomed themselves to submitting research proposals to Ethics Committees for a warrant to conduct human-focused research. Notwithstanding this quite general procedure, there are other ethical constraints, perhaps not adequately adumbrated in the literature, which touch on whether there are some sites and some discourses which, despite all consciousness, may lead researchers, as it were innocuously, to take sides with particular proponents in the context of sites of contested discourses. Moreover, and more nearly now in data collection terms, especially in the context of researcher-participant interactions, how can we guard against lines of questioning which by their very nature impose, breach and even encourage ethically sensitive disclosures? CA, like any other talk and gesture-focused methodology, cannot be innocent of such pressures of power. It is a tribute to Charles Antaki and his authoritative gathering of contributions from senior researchers in CA that such issues emanate and are highlighted in this exciting volume.

Chris Candlin
Macquarie University, Sydney

List of Contributors

Charles Antaki, Loughborough University, Loughborough, UK.

Paul Drew, University of York, York, UK.

Maria Egbert, University of Southern Denmark, Sønderborg, Denmark.

W. M. L. Finlay, Anglia Ruskin University, Cambridge, UK.

Jeremy Freese, Northwestern University, Evanston, USA.

John Heritage, University of California at Los Angeles, USA.

Annie Irvine, University of York, York, UK.

Celia Kitzinger, University of York, York, UK.

Joyce Lamerichs, Vrije Universiteit, Amsterdam, the Netherlands.

Douglas W. Maynard, University of Wisconsin, Madison, USA.

Anssi Peräkylä, Helsinki University, Helsinki, Finland.

Jeffrey D. Robinson, Portland State University, Oregon, USA.

Roy Sainsbury, University of York, York, UK.

Nora Cate Schaeffer, University of Wisconsin, Madison, USA.

Elizabeth Stokoe, Loughborough University, Loughborough, UK.

Hedwig te Molder, Wageningen University, Wageningen, The Netherlands.

Merran Toerien, University of York, York, UK.

Chris Walton, Lancaster University, Lancaster, UK.

Ray Wilkinson, University of Manchester, Manchester, UK.

Sue Wilkinson, Loughborough University, Loughborough, UK.

Notation

The notation symbols that readers will see in the book are based on the system invented by Gail Jefferson and now well established in Conversation Analysis.

(.)	Just noticeable pause
(.3), (2.6)	Examples of timed pauses, in seconds
word [word] 　　　[word]	Square brackets aligned across adjacent lines denote the start and end of overlapping talk
.hh, hh	In-breath (note the preceding full stop) and out-breath respectively
wo(h)rd	(h) shows that the word has aspiration, possibly hearable as laughter or crying, bubbling within it
wor-	A dash shows a sharp cut-off
wo:rd	Colons show that the speaker has stretched the preceding sound
↑word ↓word	Up and down arrows indicate a marked intonation shift
((word))	A guess at what might have been said if unclear
(　　)	Unclear talk
word= =word	The equals sign shows that there is no discernible pause between two speakers' turns or, if put between two sounds within a single speaker's turn, shows that they run together
wo<u>r</u>d, WORD	Underlined sounds are louder, capitals louder still
°word°	Material between 'degree signs' is quiet
>word word< <word word>	Inwards arrows show faster speech, outward slower
→	Analyst's signal of a significant line
((*snort*))	Transcriber's attempt to represent something hard, or impossible, to write phonetically

1
Six Kinds of Applied Conversation Analysis

Charles Antaki

Conversation Analysis is the study of how social action is brought about through the close organisation of talk. It can be applied, but the term 'Applied Conversation Analysis' has various shades of meaning. The two most familiar are that the application of Conversation Analysis (CA) to the talk of an institution like the school or the medical clinic can shed light on its workings; and that the CA researcher can suggest improvements in the service that such an institution provides. Those two senses of the term (which Richards, 2005, calls 'discovery' and 'prescription' respectively) capture a great deal of what is called applied CA, but not all. A survey of the literature suggests four more senses of the term, making six in all.

The full set of applied Conversation Analyses is probably this: *foundational*, where Conversation Analysis is applied to established areas of scholarship, with the intention of respecifying its foundations; *social-problem oriented*, where its micro approach is applied to the understanding of macro-social issues; *communicational*, where it offers complementary or alternative analyses of communication problems; *diagnostic*, where it reveals correlations between features of talk and underlying organic or psychological disorders; *institutional*, where it illuminates the workings of society's institutions; and – more recognisably as an applied discipline in the style of applied physics or applied maths – *interventionist*, where CA can be applied to a practical problem as it plays out in interaction, with the intention of bringing about some sort of change.

I shall say something about each of these in this chapter, but it is the last, most interventionist, of these senses that this book as a whole is concerned.

Conversation Analysis

Before I describe those senses of 'application' in more detail, a capsule account of Conversation Analysis (CA) is in order. CA is the close examination of language in interaction. It answers these concrete questions: How do you and I bring off the business we transact with each other? How do I design my turns at talk to perform some action, and to make your next turn and next action fit a certain range of possible shapes? How, in short, does any pair or group of people use language to conjure up the social world of which they're a part?

By asking those kinds of question about people's everyday methods for conducting their lives – as opposed to theorising more abstractly about society in general, or using summary categorising of what went on in it – Harvey Sacks and a small band of colleagues started a revolution in sociology in the 1960s.[1] The questions could only begin to be answered by recording human conduct and replaying it under inspection. Repeated playing of a recording of a given social scene had the same effect as Eadweard Muybridge's slow-motion photographs had on the science of movement: to reveal a level of subtle organisation that demanded a new set of concepts, and a new vocabulary to express them in. Detailed capture of talk, Harvey Sacks and his pioneering colleagues discovered, revealed that people perform the actions of everyday life by the way they *design their turns* in the *sequential organisation* of talk; those turns set up *normative expectations* on what is to follow, which fellow-interactants abide by or flout; and the analyst's job is to find evidence for varieties of turn-design, sequences and the *actions* they perform by looking to the *internal construction of turns* and the way in which the next speaker *orients to* the talk that has gone before.

The reader will turn to the chapters of this book to put the flesh on those dry terminological bones, and we may leave the description of CA's details at that, for the moment. The point to be made here is that CA provided a new and more microscopic way of thinking about social exchange. Its concepts and vocabulary have now become established not only in its mother discipline, but also in linguistics, psychology and communication studies, among others. Forty-plus years' worth of microscopic inspection of the social world has accumulated an impressive encyclopaedia of findings. CA provides a detailed, coherent, integrated catalogue of the normative sequences of language in interaction, and the actions that such regularities (and their exploitation) bring off.

Applied CA: a range of meanings

How might CA be applied? Its pioneer Harvey Sacks was himself unmoved by the prospect of CA having any sort of instrumental application, as Silverman points out (Silverman, 1998, p. 194) and as is clear from his own lectures. But once the base had been established by him and the other founders, and consolidated by further converts, subsequent generations were free to look outwards, and begin to see that CA might usefully find application elsewhere. Over the years many different sorts of application have developed, which I shall try to capture in a list before concentrating on the interventionist kind that is the theme of this book.

Foundational applied CA: respecifying an intellectual field of study

The most ambitious sense of the phrase 'applying CA' is that it refer to what people in some neighbouring field of study do when they look across to CA, are attracted by it, and try to import it into their own field in the hope of encouraging their colleagues to rethink some basic intellectual foundations and (in consequence) solve some problems in the superstructure. Just as Sacks and colleagues' enterprise was meant to shake up sociology, the same spirit inspires those who want to 'apply' CA to other disciplines and respecify their fields of study, chalk off old problems as meaningless, and identify new and more interesting ones, with a CA solution.

Stephen Levinson's importation of CA into pragmatics to clear up worries about speech-acts (Levinson, 1983) is perhaps the clearest early example. Since then we have seen similar attempts in linguistics, psychology, anthropology and speech sciences. CA-inspired linguists may, for example, want to respecify the understanding of syntax, to start not from the proposition that culturally fixed rules determine the syntactical coherence of a given stream of words, but that syntactical structures may, on the contrary, develop contingently and in real time (see, for example, the collection edited by Ochs, Schegloff and Thompson in 1996, and subsequent developments which repaid the optimism of that volume). Or, in psychology, the discursive psychologists Edwards and Potter may promise to shake up such apparently entrenched concepts as 'memory' by respecifying it as a communicative act rather than a pre-existing faculty, part of people's ethno-methods as opposed to their internal mechanisms (see, for example, Edwards and Potter, 1992; and subsequent work collected in Hepburn and Wiggins, 2007)).

Social-problem applied CA: a perspective on macro-societal issues

An early sense of 'applied CA' which, still survives today, is its promise to throw light on what are thought of, among sociologists at least, as social problems. As Maynard put it in his introduction to the special edition of the journal *Social Problems* he edited in 1988, CA promises to 'offer a different standpoint for a social organizational understanding of such traditionally-identified social problems as subcultures, conflict, power, troubles, and institutional processing' (Maynard, 1988, p. 311).

If one looks carefully at the topics of the papers in that special issue, one sees that what counts as social problems is varied. Few are canonical large-scale macro issues like poverty, class and inequality, or crime and delinquency. Indeed, the papers which are furthest from such social problems (on complaining, by Drew and Holt, 1988, or troubles-telling, by Jefferson, 1988) turned out to be probably the ones which had the most impact, as measured by their subsequent citation. However, one paper does stand out, and that is Mehan and Wills's (1988) study of the undeniably 'macro' problem of nuclear deterrence. Here, however, they don't analyse the practices of deterrence itself, in the sense of the activities of governments, the military or political analysts: they analyse the discourse of an activist group who have a view on the subject. Inspection reveals that Mehan and Wills's methods were conversation analytic less in the sense of sequential analysis, and more in the sense of an analysis of the terms and forms of speech used by the parties in the debate, shading into a more generalised discourse analysis.

Seventeen years after Maynard's Special Issue of the journal *Social Problems*, the journal published, in one of its 2005 issues, a special section devoted to 'Language, interaction and social problems'. In his introduction, Zimmerman (2005) reiterated Maynard's (1988) claim that the study of the interaction order would contribute to the understanding of social problems. Among the three papers published, perhaps the only really self-evident case of a macro problem being addressed by CA was Kitzinger's (2005) engagement with the broad issue of societal assumptions about sexuality. This emerged from Kitzinger's broader feminist project (Kitzinger 2000), and here Kitzinger uses the sequential analysis of calls to the doctor to argue that the handling of such calls (in terms of the questions posed and the allusions made) is a site in which society reproduces the 'standard' heterosexual nuclear family. To this may be added the earlier work by Kitzinger and Frith (1999) on rape myths, which demonstrated, using the insights of CA, the invalidity of the claim that a sexual advance was permissible if the woman does not actually say 'no'. That is comparatively direct confrontation of a social issue.

Such confrontation is rare. More typical is CA's contribution to such classic social issues as race and gender in a more indirect way, by examining how they are handled in interaction (e.g., Antaki and Widdicombe, 1998a; Speer and Stokoe, 2010; Stokoe and Edwards, 2007; and see Sue Wilkinson, Chapter 5 in this volume). On the whole, it is probably true to say that the number of applied CA projects directly engaging with what sociologists would recognise as macro issues is, with the notable exception of the feminist perspective advocated by Kitzinger and colleagues (see the influential call to develop a feminist conversation analysis, Kitzinger, 2008a), still relatively limited.

Communicational applied CA: a complementary or alternative analysis of 'disordered' talk

One of the most compelling strands of applied Conversation Analysis has been its application to allegedly disordered talk about which there is an existing body of educational, medical or psychological expertise. The promise is either to help understand the features of such talk, if it is remediable (as it would be in the case of second language learning) or, more ambitiously, to challenge the picture of disorder and deficiency – in, for example, the communication of people with aphasia, autism, dementia or learning disability. The two sets of problems are different, but in both cases there is an established body of knowledge with a set of diagnostic and assessment criteria for communication problems under test conditions, and a weaker set of expectations and predictions about how the condition will manifest itself in everyday life.

Conversation Analysis takes an interest here because the nature of the phenomenon is – at least arguably – interactional. CA has certainly established itself as a viable and productive aid to understanding the difficulties that people have with learning (and teaching) second languages, and how they cope both in the classroom and outside (see, for example, the chapters in Part IV of Richards and Seedhouse, 2005). In clinical conditions, CA can disregard the organic or other causes of the disorder, and look dispassionately at how the person with the condition actually engages with the world. In doing so, CA applies its armoury of concepts from 'ordinary' conversation and offers new insights into the person's capabilities. Indeed, CA was used as early as 1989 to find that the conversational competencies of people with a learning impairment (mental retardation, in US terms) was competent in 'patterns of turn-taking, the response to adjacency pairs, and the reflexive monitoring of speech in interaction' (Yearley and Brewer, 1989, p. 100). The tone of the accumulated research since then as been cautiously positive; while not denying the severe problems faced by people with communication problems, researchers have pointed up their ingenuity and determination in bringing off their aims – or trying to, with success often dependent on attentive and cooperative interlocutors.

The pioneering work of Charles Goodwin has been especially influential. His series of publications on the single case of one aphasic man (see, for example, Goodwin, 1995, 2003a) documented how it was that someone who, by exploiting the sequential structure of conversation, and the variability of intonation, could make the most out of tiny fragments of normal speech (*yes, no* and *and*). Goodwin's work is very explicitly on the aphasic sufferer's experiences and competences outside the confines of the clinic and the deliberately neutral exchanges of the language test. But as Schegloff graphically shows, even here the aphasic can demonstrate competences that would elude the formalities of the test. In the example he gives (Schegloff, 2003, pp. 28–37), the patient is able to regulate, to a microscopic degree, his part in the interactional unfolding of the test, even though he is unable to provide the required standard answers to test questions.

The treatment of communication problems is probably the applied area where there has been the closest uptake by practitioners of the spirit and the findings of CA. At its most direct, it shades into direct intervention by speech and language therapists, as the chapter by Ray Wilkinson (Chapter 3) in this volume records. But even at its more dilute form, the take-up of CA by clinicians has added a complementary view of what people with aphasia and other language problems can do, and how they use the affordances of conversational sequence to do it (see, as well as Wilkinson's chapter, the collection of chapters on aphasia in Goodwin, 2003b; and for work on dementia, Shakespeare, 1998, Mikesell, 2009).

Diagnostic applied CA: correlating sequential features of talk with clinical disorders

One of the more contentious applications of CA has been the attempt to correlate features of the organisation of a person's speech with some underlying organic or psychological disorder. So far there is little activity in this area of research, but the correlation of speech features with real and pseudo-epileptic seizures (Schwabe et al., 2007; Reuber et al, 2009) stands out. Apparently 'true' epileptics – those whose later EEGs reveal to have unusual electrical discharges in the brain – volunteer detailed narratives of their seizures, while those who turn out to suffer 'non-epileptic' seizures are disfluent, resist focusing on individual seizure episodes and provide a detailed seizure description only if the clinician persists in pursuing it. Whether this sort of analysis really does exploit CA's insights into the sequential structure of language in interaction is not uncontroversial, but the potential of correlating speech features to medical diagnosis is an attractive one for clinicians when other means are elusive (for an ambitious collection of such work on frontotemporal dementia, see Mates et al., 2010).

Institutional applied CA: an illumination of routine institutional work

A very large volume of CA is done to shed light on routine 'institutional talk' – the way that the business of the doctor's clinic, the classroom, the interview and so on is carried out. As Drew and Heritage (1992a) say, these places are roped off from casual life not only by physical barriers and by the presence of certain furniture and props, but by different rules of, and entitlements to, talk. Understanding this talk is sometimes referred to as 'applied CA', but the application is not usually to solving institutions' problems as such (in the sense of failed medical procedure, unsuccessful teaching practice and so on). Usually the CA analyst goes in curious to see how the institution manages to carry off its work so smoothly and successfully. 'Application' here is more a redirection of the analyst's gaze – away from the ordinary conversation which made up the raw data of much of CA's early work, and towards the worlds of work and social institutions which impose their own imperatives on the exchange of talk.

Turning the CA spotlight onto institutional talk was an attractive project at quite an early stage in CA's development. Landmark research done in the late 1970s and the 1980s is still influential today, including studies of the work of the courtroom (Atkinson and Drew, 1979), the classroom (McHoul, 1978), the doctor's clinic (Heath, 1981, 1986), the mental illness hearing (Holstein 1988) and the news interview (Clayman and Whalen, 1988; Greatbatch, 1988). A vivid example of an early and highly successful application of CA in this sense is the work of Max Atkinson on political speeches (1984). Atkinson's minute study of speechifying produced a very accessibly written book, with detailed analyses of, among other rhetorical devices, practices which generated applause. The analyses, though not meant to be prescriptive, were so clear as to allow politicians to use the book as a manual: in a recent commentary, Drew remarks that 'it was widely believed that [British Members of Parliament] all bought copies of Atkinson's book' (Drew, 2005, xix) – and, no doubt, learnt a thing or two.

That use of the CA by practitioners was unintended – Atkinson did not (at the time) intend to be solving anyone's problems.[2] His project was institutional CA, where it remains an unusually colourful landmark. The years since then have seen a steady and growing stream of work on institutional talk, extending from mainstream service and employment sites (clinics, classrooms, offices, shops). The recent collection of this popular and general sense of applied CA is the volume *Applying Conversation Analysis* (Richards and Seedhouse, 2005) which gathers together very accomplished recent work on interaction in the classroom, in the doctor's clinic, the seminar room or the shop[3]. There is also a growing willingness to take on complex, difficult-to-access locations and highly demanding tasks: the London Underground control room (Heath and Luff, 1992), the surgical theatre (Hindmarsh and Pilnick, 2002, Mondada, 2003), the aircraft cockpit (Nevile, 2004), and so on.

At some point the analyst's focus shifts from illuminating the routine work of the institution to how its members solve snags and tangles that come up during the day. Early moves are visible in the work of Whalen and Zimmerman (1987) on time-wasting calls to an emergency service, and Clayman (1988) on the management of neutrality in news interviews.

In both those cases the researchers have in their sights demanding or challenging episodes at work, and their interest is in explicating how it is that the practitioners themselves manage the problem and find its solution. This is still neutral: the analyst might be (and usually is) simply interested, as it were, sociologically, where the institution's problem is just one more part of the social scene, to be understood with the same sentiments as the analyst brings to understanding the institution's smooth running. Even such a pair of closely targeted research projects as Peräkylä's and Silverman's studies of AIDS counselling (Peräkylä, 1995, Silverman 1997) were devoted to explication rather than, in the first place, change in the counsellors' habits. Although Silverman was at pains to explain (not always optimistically) how the implications for counselling might benefit from the findings, that was not his principal motivation.

In general, the kind of applied CA researcher we have seen in this section, who puts institutional activity under the microscope, is revealing how the way the world (and its problems) works. But one step more can be taken.

Interventionist applied CA: solving pre-existing problems collaboratively

This is the sense of applied CA that the reader will find represented in this book. Interventionist applied CA has these characteristics: it is applied to an interactional problem which pre-existed the analyst's arrival; it has the strong implication that a solution will be identified via the analysis of the sequential organisation of talk; and it is undertaken collaboratively, achieved with people in the local scene.

The promise of intervention usually comes late to a given field of study. At some point the scholar becomes confident enough to claim that their knowledge might bring about change. They might then undertake projects which are 'applied' in the sense shared with, say, applied physics. Theory is used to make sense of a practical problem which is not actually part of its intellectual framework, with no guarantee of theoretical return: physics can help solve the problems of – for example – radiography, even though the reverse is not the case. The radiographer wants a way of calculating the safe dosage of X-rays; such practical matters are of no concern to the physicist, and, equally, the radiographer will not be interested in physics theory as such. But the calculation of trajectory, energy and radiation are of interest to both parties. The radiographer's pre-existing practical problem of reducing risk to patients can be helped by the application of the physicist's theoretical expertise. The physicist departs, having helped solve the dosage issue; and also having learnt more about energy and radiation, and refined theory accordingly.

The analogy with CA can best be illustrated with a real case, taken from this collection. In Chapter 6, Kitzinger describes her engagement, as a CA analyst, with a service that provides telephone advice and support for women about to give birth. That service has nothing to say to CA as such, but is ready to hear how CA might help it solve its own concerns about how well the call-takers deal with the many troubles and worries with which women call. Kitzinger makes a collection of telephone calls, analyses them with her CA techniques, and, in close collaboration with the service managers, offers some help in how the calls might be better dealt with. She can depart the scene having done some good in a practical way, having added to her stock of data, and having refined her theories accordingly. The project has been set and brought off in collaboration with an outside agency which has a given problem, and has been willing to let a conversation analyst try to lend a hand.

That last feature makes the application of CA significantly different from the application of something so culturally familiar as physics. CA is not yet in the phone book, and has not reached the point where calls come in from outside agencies wanting CA help. Rather, it is the CA researcher who sees the possibility of working in collaboration with others to solve a problem, and do some funded social science in the process.

Themes in interventionist applied CA

Over its short history certain themes can be seen in CA's engagement with practical problems. Where the problem is in a person's everyday communication – because of aphasia or dementia, for example – then the CA researcher may be able to work directly with the person and her or his close conversational partners (as described in Ray Wilkinson, Chapter 3). Otherwise, and more commonly, the researcher will be engaging with an institution, where the practitioner is experiencing some difficulty in bringing off a part of the service they offer a client. The perspective is usually that of the institution, not of the client. The evidence will often be qualitative rather than quantitative. The analyst generally has no powers, him or herself, actually to make changes, and may never know whether those changes have in fact been made. There may be tensions between those who commissioned the analyst (usually, staff at higher managerial levels) and the less powerful grades of staff whose interactions are being studied, and who may be instructed to change their practices. The project will usually require the analysis of documents and other ethnographic records (possibly including the physical layout of the scene), as well as the more familiar audio- and video-records. Let us take each of these in turn.

A problem in the delivery of a recurrent institutional service

An intervention project is more liable to succeed if two conditions can be met: that the problem be an example of a recurrent phenomenon, and that there be agreement over what it is that the problem stops the interactants doing. Both these criteria are more readily met in institutional than casual talk. Doctors often encounter difficulties in soliciting full health histories from their patients, teachers regularly have to deal with unsatisfactory answers from their pupils, pilots and control towers routinely have to cope with difficulties of intelligibility, and so on; these are all regular and frequent occurrences, allowing a collection of data to be built up. And the aims of what the doctors, teachers and pilots are trying to achieve are well-known and agreed by all parties, and so there is an independent way of assessing how well any change in a given practice has worked.

The institution's perspective rather than the client's

There is no compelling reason why the analyst should not take the client's point of view, and ask – for example – how the patient can resist medical advice, or how the customer can negotiate a better price at sale, and so on. Most interventionist CA effectively takes the practitioner's side, for four reasons: commissioning, access and funding; the identifiability of staff-side as opposed to client-side routines; and shared values.

Access and funding. The analyst is usually commissioned by the managerial levels of an institution, not by its clients. So far in CA's short history, the general case is that the commission is held by a non-profit making body (usually a university, or a research centre) at which the analyst is employed, so the economic imperative is perhaps not so forceful as if the analyst had been a freelance consultant (though, c.f. the activities of Max Atkinson, mentioned above, and locatable on his website); still, it is usually the institution, and not those it serves, which nominates the problem that wants solving, or that has the final say in the matter. One example of a study which attempts to give the client an equal say is Williams's efforts to include as collaborative researchers the people with learning disabilities whose communication she studies (see Williams et al., 2005). Such efforts are, however, rare.

Identifiable routines. One of the features that Drew and Heritage (1992b) identified as separating institutional from ordinary talk is that in the former, especially in the case of practioner-client encounters, the practitioner is working to a given agenda which repeats for each client; but the client does not, typically, come into the encounter with a practised set of routines he or she can run off to achieve pre-given goals. So the CA analyst, with an eye to regularities in the data, is more likely to be drawn to the recurrent features of the practitioner's activities than the more contingent responses of the client. Moreover, even if clients can develop identifiable routines (as might long-term users of psychotherapy services, for example), the agenda they are working to is not likely to be as uniform or as identifiable, *a priori*, as those of the institution whose services they seek.

Shared values. The student of interventionist CA will not often come across researchers explicitly making the case for siding with the given institution's values, usually because they work with what can be taken to be socially positively valued services: medicine, education, non-commercial helplines and so on. The objectives of such institutions can be taken to be consensually acceptable, so any intervention which speeds their progress seems uncontroversial. But even within these generally consensual services, there are practices on which a citizen may have a stance. Not all citizens, for example, will agree with religious instruction at school, or the provision of contraceptives to children under the legal age for sex. Should a CA researcher be called in to help make these services more effective, then they would be caught up in a controversy, and accused of 'taking sides' by at least some people.

Nothing remotely so contentious has yet arisen in applied CA, but there is an instructive example which does raise the question. Stivers (2007) identified practices which might help physicians resist their patients' inappropriate demands for antibiotics. On the one hand, this might be seen as 'taking sides' against the patient, and their rights to get medication that they think (falsely or not) is good for them or their children. On the other hand, the extensive prescription of antibiotics is of doubtful benefit to an individual but of certain disadvantage to the community (in so far as widespread use promotes resistance). Here the defence would be that although any one patient's perceived interests may be compromised, the wider community's health prospects are protected. Whether one agrees with this stance or not, it does show that on certain issues at least, the CA researcher may need explicitly to offer a social justification for their work.

Qualitative and quantitative evidence

Every CA study will have at its core a qualitative analysis in which the researcher identifies some practice that seems significant. The questions then become: how often does that practice happen, and how good is the evidence that it affects what happens next? If the researcher has discovered some key practice that is self-evidently significant (for example, a way in which pilot and control-tower fail to understand each other), then it cries out for attention, whatever its statistical frequency. If the conversational move is subtler, then the researcher may need to establish that it is recurrent, frequent and causally significant. The use of quantification in CA is controversial, but here it may be inescapable, certainly in the researcher's efforts to persuade collaborators to be more comfortable with survey data (for the generality and representativeness of the phenomenon) and experimental methods (for the link between cause and effect).

The analyst usually has little or no power to make changes

The analyst may identify practices which are contributing to the institution's given problem, and may make recommendations, but it will be up to the institution itself to accept them or not. Here CA researchers can, and have, encountered a series of obstacles, as do any applied researchers: the staff who commissioned the research may not agree to the changes (they may have what Peräkylä and Vehviliainen, 2003, call their own 'stocks of interactional knowledge' which are proof against new perspectives), or, even if they do agree, may not have the power to implement them (e.g., they may hold no sway over the institution's training department); there may have been a turnover in personnel such that the original staff who sponsored the research have left their posts; the changes might be too costly, or interfere with some other aspect of the institution's business; the particular staff who deliver the service, and who are instructed to change, may have their own reasons to resist; and so on.

The need for ethnographic background

Canonical CA tends to privilege word and gesture. The use of multi-modal evidence has nevertheless long been a feature of some strands of CA work – see, for example, the ethnographically influenced work of Charles and Marjorie Goodwin, ranging from Goodwin and Goodwin (1990), where such local detail as the manufacture of children's slingshots is important for the analysis, through to the programmatic argument in favour of multi-methods in general (Goodwin, 2007). This openness to the use of non-language data becomes critical in projects which call for the analysis of some physical, documentary or situated task, which is common in applied CA of the interventionist kind.

The fact that participants will be bringing off some recordable institutional achievement means that the analyst will have to get a grip on what the institution counts as an achievement and as a record. Only ethnographic background – gleaned from documents, interviews and observation of the site will provide that. In the work reported in Finlay, Walton and Antaki, Chapter 9 in this volume, for example, it was crucial to understand the local history of the everyday arrangements in the homes in which the recordings were made – the staff rota, the health and safety duties, the 'mission statement' of the agency which provided the service and so on. Equally, in Toerien, Irvine, Drew and Sainsbury's chapter (Chapter 8), the business conducted between interviewer and interviewee would be unintelligible without background knowledge of the UK welfare agency's criteria for the eligibility for unemployment benefit. The list can be extended to cover all the work reported in this book. Such reliance on ethnography has the promise of flowing back into 'basic' CA, and join up with the stream of multi-modal work which champions a more situated kind of analysis (see, for example, Mondada, 2009); this is probably one of the closest points of fruitful contact between applied CA and its more foundational work.

Concluding comments

There are limitations to what the researcher, armed with CA, can offer in addressing practical institutional problems. In medicine, for example, Drew (2010) makes the observation that advances are, and will continue to be, largely made by applications of the established bio-medical sciences and epidemiology; CA's contribution will be to medical communication, and is likely to have a comparatively modest effect on medical outcomes *per se*. That is a salutary reminder that, where problems arise in the provision of services which are primarily physical (as they would be in medicine, architecture, manufacturing industry and so on), then there may be a disinclination to look, in the first instance, to communicative practices as routes to the solution. But, as Drew also notes, that said, the contribution of CA in medical communication has been significant, and is likely to grow as the medical establishment gives greater value to understanding the ways in which medical personnel and patients interact.

Where the practices under scrutiny are more fully realised in talk – as in the case of interviewing, soliciting information, offering choices, giving advice, teaching, mediating, providing psychotherapy or speech therapy, each of which is covered in a chapter in this book – then the obstacles in the way of an interventionist CA are less daunting. Although Drew (2005, p. xx) cautiously observes that not everyone in CA is sure of CA's applicability to training and practice, there is, never the less, ample evidence to show that once the researcher has engaged with people in the local scene, negotiated access and agreed a feasible research project (none of which are easy matters, of course), then they can work towards identifying how it is that that institution brings off its services through talk. The next step, working out how actually to bring about change, is admittedly not easy, and brings with it moral and political, as well as technical, considerations. But to the extent that it makes the social scientist engage with practitioners, and makes her or him articulate exactly what the benefits are of their academic analysis, then the application of Conversation Analysis is to the benefit of the discipline as a whole.

Notes

1. For fuller accounts, see Heritage (1984b); Schegloff (1992); Silverman (1998); and Lerner (2004).
2. He did go on to become a successful consultant doing just that; see http://maxatkinson.blogspot.com/
3. The volume also includes work on language impairment which are examples of applied CA as 'communicational', described above.

2
'Some' versus 'Any' Medical Issues: Encouraging Patients to Reveal Their Unmet Concerns

John Heritage and Jeffrey D. Robinson

In this chapter we reconsider the design, implementation and dissemination of an NIH-funded study of unmet patient concerns that we conducted in 2005–6 and published in 2007 (Heritage et al., 2007). The study took an aspect of preference organisation that has, to our knowledge, never been systematically studied, and applied it to a well-known problem in primary-care visits: the fact that patients frequently do not voice the full range of their concerns. We review the decisions we made about the design and implementation of the study and about the interpretation of its results. We also contrast this study with 'regular' CA studies and conclude with an appeal for eclecticism in the application of CA to real-world problems. We begin with some comments on the distinction between conversation-analytic studies and their applied counterparts.

What is applied CA?

The fundamental assumption of conversation analysis is that social action and interaction are methodically produced by and for one another (Garfinkel, 1967; Sacks, 1992; Schegloff, 2007). Conversation analysis, as we understand it, is the study of the practices through which persons engage in this process of methodical production and recognition (Heritage and Atkinson, 1984; Heritage, 2010a). Although ordinary conversation constitutes a more general and fundamental layer of interactional practices than 'institutional' domains of interaction, such as primary care visits (Drew and Heritage, 1992; Heritage and Clayman, 2010), we regard studies of interaction in institutional contexts as just as conversation analytic as any other. A finding about how patients address the different formats that physicians use to open medical consultations (Robinson, 2006) is just as much a CA finding as one about how telephone calls are opened (Schegloff, 1968, 1986), or about cell-phone openings (Arminen and Leinonen, 2006; Hutchby and Barnett, 2005; Schegloff, 2002). In short, a CA finding is not 'applied' because it arises from a study of an institutional context.

Applied CA, as we understand it, uses CA for purposes other than the investigation of practices of talk in interaction (see also Antaki's account in Chapter 1 of this volume). These purposes generally involve the causes and consequences of actions (Robinson, 2007; Stivers et al., 2003) and practical interventions in fields of action. Applied CA studies often begin with a problem defined in non-CA terms. For example, what are the causes of inappropriate antibiotics prescribing (Stivers et al., 2003), and what interactional changes might reduce such prescribing (Mangione-Smith et al., 2006; Heritage et al., 2010)? How do the openings of interactions influence noninteractional outcomes (Boyd, 1998; Robinson and Heritage, 2006)? How do economic trends influence the type and tenor of questions asked of an American president by the White House Press Corps (Clayman et al., 2007)? These are evidently not 'CA questions' but they are all questions for which CA has provided the basic conceptual ingredients for compelling answers.

Applied CA, as the very name suggests, does not end with arriving at findings, but also implies using them in concert with professionals or other practitioners to solve practical problems, and this ordinarily means dissemination of some kind. Dissemination and use can vary enormously. Many of us have participated in 'ground up' approaches that use 'hands on' data sessions to prompt reflection among professionals, or have used these as part of a more systematic training process that might also include reports of systematic findings and role-play training in larger groups convened as professional education courses. At the other end of the spectrum are 'top down' approaches in which CA results trigger organisational change (as in Drew's work for the British 999 emergency service), or form part of a curriculum change in medical textbooks (such as the Calgary-Cambridge guide to communication skills for medical patients [Silverman, Kurtz and Draper, 2005]), or prompt other kinds of changes in skills training (Drew et al., 2010), and work organisation (Vinkhuyzen and Whalen, 2007; Whalen and Bobrow 2010).

Our study was very much in this latter group. In previous conversation-analytic research, we had already described the structure and dynamics of problem presentation (Heritage and Robinson, 2006a, b; Robinson, 2006, Robinson and Heritage, 2005), including how physicians and patients manage its transition to the next medical activity of information gathering (Robinson and Stivers, 2001). We then identified a healthcare problem – patients' unmet concerns (see below) – and an institutionalised solution (i.e., one provided by medical textbooks on interviewing) that is virtually never implemented by physicians in 'natural' practice – soliciting patients' unmet concerns immediately after the problem presentation phase of the visit. We then developed a study to 'intervene' in physicians' natural practice by having them solicit unmet concerns immediately after patients present their problems, and designed the intervention questions using CA findings focused on preference organisation in question design (Sacks, 1987). In sum, we identified a communicative practice in primary care that we had good reasons to think could be improved. We developed a study to show that this is indeed the case, and provided evidence of how it could be improved. And we have hopes that primary-care textbook writers and curriculum designers will take note of our results.

The problem

According to the National Ambulatory Medical Care Survey (2005), which is based on physician reports, about 40 percent of patients bring more than one discrete concern to their primary care visit (e.g., cold and infected toenail). However, physicians' opening questions (e.g., 'What can I do for you today?') normally elicit a single concern. Recognising this, medical school curricula and textbooks of medical interviewing recommend that, after patients present their initial concern, physicians solicit additional concerns by asking questions such as: 'Is there anything else we need to take care of today?'

The benefits of looking for additional concerns early in the visit are straightforward: patients get the opportunity to voice additional concerns, and physicians learn about them early enough in the visit to manage them effectively within the confines of a visit lasting about 11 minutes in the case of American family physicians (Callahan et al., 2004). In practice, however, physicians rarely ask for additional concerns (Beckman and Frankel, 1982; Marvel et al., 1999) and tend to do so close to the ends of visits (Robinson, 2001) when the additional concerns are less likely to be dealt with in an effective and timely fashion (White, Levinson and Roter, 1994; White et al., 1997). The larger costs of concerns that go unmet are considerable: patients are left to worry (perhaps unnecessarily) about a concern for which they could have received advice and reassurance; conditions for which treatment is necessary go untreated and potentially worsen; and patients and their doctors spend additional time and money on visits scheduled to deal with concerns that might have been dealt with in the initial visit.

We were interested in showing that asking about additional concerns early in the visit is an effective and time-saving strategy for physicians. However, we also believed that the question recommended by medical textbooks – 'Is there anything else we need to take care of today?' – might be ineffective as a means of eliciting additional concerns. Our reasons stemmed from fundamental CA research on the design of questions and answers.

The CA background

It is a well-known feature of polar ('yes/no') questions that they are almost unavoidably built for, tilted towards or prefer either a 'yes' or 'no' response. In fact, it is very difficult to pose a question in English that does not prefer a 'yes' or a 'no'. In a classic paper first presented in 1973, Sacks (1987) made several fundamental observations about these questions and their responses. The first was that responses that are aligned to the preference of the question, and that affirm its primary proposition, are more frequent than disaligned responses, and also occur earlier than disaligned responses. This finding subsequently received strong empirical support from a recent ten-language study of polar questions (Stivers et al., 2009). A second observation was that questioners can and do exploit the emerging delays associated with disaligned responses to redesign their questions to enable answerers to produce aligning responses. For example, in Extract 1, A understands the emerging silence as indicative of a 'No' answer and redesigns the question – reversing its polarity (line 3) – to permit the 'No' to happen as an aligning response.

Extract 1   (Sacks, 1987, p. 64)

```
01  A:         They have a good cook there?
02             ((pause))
03  A:    ->   Nothing special?
04  B:         No, everybody takes their turns
```

And in the following case, also discussed by Sacks (1987), Nancy has called to ask her friend Emma to go shopping, but there is an obstacle: Emma has just had a toenail surgically removed and is apparently in some pain.

Extract 2   (NB:II:IV, pp. 23–35)

```
01  Nan:                            [.hh-hh-hh W'l ↑I
02           wz gunnuh call ↓en a:sk you'f you (.) Buh wz playing ↑golf
03           th's aft'↑noon 'f you wandih go over tuh ↑↑Ro:bins'ns with
04           me.I've got to uh .hhh I have goT.hh t[o g e]t.h .hhh
05  Emm:                                           [Aah ha]
06  Nan:     a couple of things tuh wear Emma I (.) jus'don't have enough
07           clothes tuh: (.) t'go duh work in.
08  Emm:     Mm m[: .
09  Nan: ->      [.t.hhh at a*:ll. .hhhh Ken yih wa↑:LK?hh
10           (0.3)
```

```
11   Nan:   ->  °W'd be too ha:rd for yu [h?° ]
12   Emm:                                [.t  ]  °Oh::::: darling I don'kno:w°
13                 uh it's bleeding a lid'l 'e dis took the bandage o:ff
```

Perhaps registering the lack of uptake to her suggestion at line 8, Nancy investigates with a question: *Ken yih wa↑:LK?hh* (line 9). This question entertains Emma's inability to walk as a possibility, but it is framed to prefer the 'yes' response that would advance her proposal to go shopping. After the delay in response at line 10, she redesigns her inquiry so as to invite a 'yes' response targeted at Emma's inability to walk (line 11), and this attracts an immediate affirmative response. Polar questions, then, take up a stance towards the state of affairs they inquire into and invite aligning responses that affirm that stance (Bolinger, 1978; Pomerantz, 1988a; Heritage and Raymond, frth). As Sacks (1987) showed, questioners will reverse the polarity of their questions, thus enabling aligning responses to emerge.

Sacks's final observation was that, in addition to basic temporal delay, responses that turn out to be disaligned tend to be built to be as aligning as possible. For example, in the following case, the recipient (who lives in California), affirms what he can from the question, rather than responding in the negative.

Extract 3   (Sacks, 1987, p. 62)

```
01      A:   That where you live? Florida?
02      B:   That's where I was born.
```

And in Extract 4, the recipient initially aligns with the polarity of the question and then disaligns in a series of incremental moves,

Extract 4   (Sacks, 1987, p. 62)

```
01      A:   How about friends. Have you friends?
02      B:   I have friends. So called friends. I had friends.
03           Let me put it that way.
```

In sum, polar questions are ordinarily designed so as to permit recipient affirmation of the state of affairs they describe, and recipients will work to find ways of avoiding disaffirming responses and to build them with as many elements of affirmation as possible.

Returning to the textbook 'anything else' question with which we started, we can note that questions containing the word 'any' have negative polarity (Bolinger, 1957; Borkin, 1971; Horn, 1978): they are designed for, and tilted towards, 'no' as the grammatically preferred response (Schegloff, 2007). This is because the word 'any' is negatively polarised: it ordinarily occurs in declarative sentences that are negatively framed (e.g., 'I haven't got any samples'), and is normally judged to be inappropriate in positively framed declarative sentences (e.g., 'I've got any samples.'). The negative polarity of 'any' is easily observable in primary-care well visits involving 'systems review'. Here physicians review a wide variety of possible conditions with the optimised presumption that the patient is not experiencing any of them. This presumption is encoded in the design of their questions (Boyd and Heritage, 2006).

Extract 5   (Torn Roto Cuff: 3)

```
01  DOC:   ->  An' do you have any other medical problems?
02  PAT:       Uh: no.
03             (7.0)
04  DOC:       No heart disease,
05  PAT:       #Hah:.# ((cough))
06  PAT:       No.
07             (1.3)
08  DOC:   ->  Any lung disease as far as you know:,
09  PAT:       No.
10             (.)
11  PAT:       Not that I know of.
12             (.)
13  DOC:   ->  Any diabetes,
14  PAT:       No.
15  DOC:   ->  Have you ever had (uh) surgery?
16             (0.5)
17  PAT:       I've had four surgeries on my left knee:.
```

In this sequence, every one of the physician's questions is built to favour a 'no' response, and this is matched in the patient's responses which are prompt, brief and type-conforming (Raymond, 2003) when they are aligned to the preference for a 'no' answer, but not (as in line 17) when the response is disaligned.

The possibility that we were prepared to entertain was that disaligned responses – that is, the raising of additional medical concerns – to questions like 'Is there anything else we need to take care of today?' (which are tilted toward preferring a 'No'-concern answer) might not merely be delayed, but actually suppressed altogether, thus negating the question's purpose in eliciting additional concerns.

Designing the study: the necessity of multiple methods

At the core of our study is a conversation-analytic observation about question polarity and preference. Yet, it was obvious that we could not pursue the study's aims using standard conversation-analytic methods involving the collection, and straight sequential analysis, of naturally occurring data. There were several reasons for this. First, we knew from our earlier corpora of naturally occurring, primary-care openings that doctors rarely (perhaps less than 1 per cent of the time) perform the follow-up question (e.g., 'Is there anything else we need to take care of today?') at the recommended time (i.e., after problem presentation vs. at the closing of the visit). This meant that we would have to train our doctors about when and how they would ask the follow up question, thus intervening in the very production of the data we were planning to collect. Second, we would have to build in a comparison to the standard 'any' follow-up question if we were to demonstrate its deficiencies. This meant we would have to develop a field experiment and train different physicians to ask different questions to see if there were different outcomes. Third, in order to ground the claim that patients' concerns were (possibly) unmet during visits, it was necessary to obtain a measure of the range of concerns that patients had as they came into the visit. We could only know this by surveying patients, in the waiting room before the visit, about what they wanted to talk to the doctor about. Finally, because our research question was fundamentally distributional (i.e., would different question designs result in different patient outcomes?), we needed to use statistical methods. These methods would allow us to 'control for' a range of variables that are exogenous to interaction yet may independently influence whether patients concerns will all be addressed. These variables eventually included age, sex, education, income, practice setting, severity of presenting concern and so on. Statistical modelling also allowed us to adjust for the fact that differences between individual physicians might also influence our outcome.

In our study, then, a CA finding about preference and negative polarity would be the central explanatory variable of interest, but it would require a field experiment, coupled with survey data and statistical modelling to determine its significance.

The experimental questions

As we thought about the question comparisons we might work with, several alternatives presented themselves. First, there was the textbook recommendation that we operationalised as:

(i) Are there *any* other concerns you'd like to address during this visit?

And we came up with several plausible alternatives including:

(ii) Are there other concerns you'd like to address during this visit? (Question (i) without the word 'any')

(iii) Are there *some* other concerns you'd like to address during this visit? Question (i) with the word 'some' substituting for 'any')
(iv) *What* other concerns would you like to address during this visit? (Builds in the assumption that the patient definitely has additional concerns)

In the end, we quickly dismissed question (iv). While we felt it would be successful in eliciting additional concerns, we were worried about the patients (perhaps 50–60 per cent) who did not have such concerns. In particular, the question seemed too presuming, and patients who did not have additional concerns might feel that they had 'come up short'; that their presenting concern was not sufficient to justify the medical visit and that their decision to make the visit was effectively delegitimated (Heritage and Robinson, 2006a). In addition, such a presuming question might seem to convey that the physician has negative health expectations about the patients to whom it was addressed. Moreover, we also entertained the notion that the primary care physicians in the study would feel that the question was 'too strong' and would decline to use it. For all these reasons, we dropped question (iv) as a possible study question.

This left questions (i)–(iii). We would ideally have liked to include all three questions in the study. However, three questions would increase the size and cost of the study by a factor of 50 per cent over a two-question study. Since our study might strike National Institutes of Health reviewers as strange and unlikely to yield a positive result, we thought it would be more likely to be funded if we kept costs down, and that meant a two-question study.

If the 'any' version of our question is negatively polarised, the 'some' version (question (iii)) is positively polarised. This is because 'some' ordinarily occurs in positively framed declarative sentences (e.g., 'I've got some samples'), and is normally judged to be inappropriate in negatively framed ones (e.g., 'I haven't got some samples'). We reasoned that the question, 'Are there some other concerns you'd like to address during this visit?' would provide positive incentives for aligning responses conveying additional concerns, counterbalancing the negative incentives for these responses in the 'any' version of the question. At the same time, we had reservations about the question. It takes up a less optimised position about the patient's health status (Boyd and Heritage, 2006), and intuitively felt less 'natural' as a question to ask. We were worried that it might be difficult to teach physicians this form of the question, because they were already habituated to its 'any' counterpart. By contrast, question (ii) – containing neither 'some' nor 'any' – invites additional concerns, but without the additional incentives that those words supply. Question (ii), we reasoned, might garner more positive responses than the 'any' version of the question, but surely less than the 'some' version. Since we were looking to maximise the expression of additional concerns, we decided on the 'some' version of the question.

Secondary study goals

While the primary focus of our study was getting patients' multiple concerns on to the conversational floor of the medical visit, at least two other countervailing practical dilemmas emerged. One of these was the possibility of, as Michael Wilkes (a practising physician and co-author) put it, 'opening Pandora's box'. By this he meant that asking for additional concerns – regardless of the question's polarity – would provide patients with an interactional slot in which they would raise a whole range of medical concerns that they did not otherwise plan to deal with before the visit. We saw this as a serious problem. Physicians are not going to ask for additional concerns if they fear this kind of reaction. In order to test for a Pandora's Box effect, we measured 'unanticipated' concerns, or those that patients raised in response to intervention questions that were not included in patients' self-generated, pre-visit list of concerns. As part of this process, we also decided to measure whether the pre-visit survey itself would cause more concerns to be brought up during the visit.

The second practical dilemma was the possibility that any intervention question, even if it generated 'anticipated' biomedical concerns, would increase visit length, minimally through its very production, and maximally through its generation of additional concerns. We believed that, if physicians were able to identify additional concerns early – that is, shortly after problem presentation, rather than after diagnosis and treatment – they would be able to efficiently manage visit time. By and large, the doctors who agreed to be studied accepted this argument ... in principle. However, it was important for us to know by the end that our intervention would not significantly extend visit times, and we included this as a secondary goal of the study.

Designing the study parameters

As we began to think about the nuts and bolts of the study, we started by considering its geographical location. We knew that studies that were more broad-based geographically had more credibility, and we were worried that the study's natural home, Los Angeles, might be considered an atypical location. At the same time, we would be unlikely to have the resources to go to multiple sites. However one of us (JR) had good contacts in Pennsylvania and, usefully, outside of its major metropolitan areas, giving us some of the geographic dispersion we needed, a non-metropolitan contrast with Los Angeles, and a somewhat different, more relaxed culture of doctor-patient interaction than the more pressured and hectic context of Los Angeles.

Deciding how many patients to include in the study was much more difficult. We knew we needed equal numbers of patients to be exposed to the 'some' and 'any' forms of the experimental intervention, and we knew we needed control cases to compare these with. But we also knew that the National Ambulatory Medical Care Survey showed that, according to physicians, only 40 per cent of patients would show up with multiple concerns. Even allowing that this was conservative (the unmet concerns that we were interested in would not have come up and so would not have registered with the physicians who participated in the survey) and we could estimate a larger population with multiple concerns, this still meant that around 50 per cent of our sample would arrive at the doctor's office with only one concern which, presumably, would emerge in response to physicians' opening questions. These patients would not factor into our central investigation at all. In short, our overall sample of patients would have to be around double the number we needed to work with who had multiple concerns. A power analysis performed by our statistician to determine how many cases of multiple concerns we would need to see if our questions would have a measurable impact was an important deciding factor in deciding how many patients we would have to recruit.

Third, we had to decide how many physicians to include in the study. We reasoned that the more physicians we had, the less idiosyncratic our results would be. But each physician would have to have a reasonable number of trials, and so the number of physicians we could enrol would be limited by the number of patients we could handle given the funding we could hope to attract.

In the end, we settled for the following configuration. There would be two study areas: Los Angeles and Pennsylvania. Within each area, we would recruit ten physicians, and we would collect data on 11 patients for each physician. For each physician, the first four patients would be 'control' patients, for whom there would be no intervention; physicians would proceed with visits as they would normally. After the fourth patient, we would intervene, and train physicians to ask either the 'some' or the 'any' question after the main problem presentation was over with, for the next seven of their patients. As a result we would end up with a roughly even distribution of controls, 'some' cases, and 'any' cases (Table 2.1).

Finally, in 20 of the control cases, we planned not to administer a pre-visit survey; comparing these cases with survey-present control cases would allow us to determine if the very administration of the pre-vist survey was a factor in patients' topicalisation of additional concerns. This removed 20 cases from our control comparison.

Table 2.1 Projected distribution of cases in the study

Control Cases	20 doctors × 4 patients	80 cases
'Any' Cases	10 doctors × 7 patients	70 cases
'Some' Cases	10 doctors × 7 patients	70 cases

This meant that, if our projections were correct, we would end up comparing about half the cases (the ones with multiple concerns) in something like a 30 control (80 − 20 = 60; 60/2 = 30) to 35 'any' (70/2 = 35), to 35 'some' (70/2 = 35) comparison.

Implementing the study

Implementing the study required a means of training the physicians. We decided to use a training video that could be put on a CD or DVD that could be played on physicians' office computers. Part of our thinking was that the intervention should be 'scaleable' – that is, the intervention could ultimately be implemented on a widespread basis at low cost, for example, by being placed on the internet. Accordingly, we made a five-minute video training tape. The video included: (1) information about the problem of patients leaving visits with unmet concerns; (2) a discussion of the importance of soliciting the full range of patients concerns early in visits; (3) information about the importance of specific words in questions; (4) instruction about the intervention (i.e., the 'some' or 'any' question; based on Heath's (1986) findings about body behaviour and recipiency, we instructed physicians to 'gaze directly at the patent [and to] avoid looking at the patient's record' while asking the intervention question; (5) two vignettes, involving standardised physicians and patients, that modelled the intervention behaviour (i.e., physicians were shown using the desired question, in the desired format, at the desired moment for two patients, one of whom raised additional concerns, and one of whom declined to do so); and (6) a brief reinforcement of the intervention (the video also told physicians that they would be reminded of the particular question wording by a Post-it note that would be placed in patients' charts).

The tape needed to be presented with some authority, and we were lucky to have the video moderated by Dr Michael Wilkes, who was Assistant Dean for Medical Education at UCLA at the time, and was (and is) a broadcaster on medical affairs on National Public Radio in the United States. This training video was withheld from the participating physicians until they had completed their four 'control' cases.

In all cases, research assistants verified that physicians had watched the video prior to their first 'intervention' visit; research assistants had to confirm physicians' intervention condition (i.e., 'some' or 'any') prior to placing appropriate Post-it notes in patients' charts. Perhaps the most common physician question about the intervention involved the precise placement of the experimental question, with physicians confirming that it should be asked before information gathering. Only one physician explicitly expressed scepticism about the intervention, saying that he would 'try it', but if it 'caused problems' he would withdraw from the study. By 'cause problems' he was referring to both Pandora's Box and visit length. In the end, though, no physician withdrew from the study.

In general the doctors had few problems with the 'any' intervention. Most of them completed their quota of seven cases without difficulty, though one or two occasionally forgot to ask the question. In those instances, we simply recruited an additional patient to complete the intervention quota. When it came to the 'some' intervention, there was more difficulty. In addition to cases of forgetfulness, one or two of our study physicians tended to substitute the word 'any' for 'some', reinforcing our pre-study anxieties that the 'some' intervention might be harder to implement. In these cases, we also recruited new study patients until each doctor's quota was complete.

The patients were asked to complete two surveys. The pre-visit survey asked patients to give their 'primary reason' for the visit, and then to list 'other concerns' they wanted to talk about (Figure 2.1).

In general, patients had little difficulty in separating a primary concern from others, though some listed their multiple concerns as equal in significance. Some also listed what looked like multiple symptoms of a common condition (e.g., headache, sore throat, runny nose), and we were forced to examine the interaction to see if they were treating these as part of the same concern, or as issues to be dealt with separately. In practice, we had no problem in making this determination. The survey also contained a four-item health-status scale, and asked for a range of demographic information, including age, ethnicity, gender, education, income and medical insurance type.

The post-visit survey assessed patients' satisfaction with visits, using a well validated instrument (Wolf et al., 1978) for this purpose.

Analysing the results

Some of the results of the study emerged from simple tabulations of outcomes. As it turned out, 49 per cent of our patients listed more than one concern on the pre-visit survey but, as Table 2.2 shows, geography made a difference. More Los Angeles patients came in with multiple concerns by comparison with their Pennsylvania counterparts. Significantly, however, the Los Angeles patients left with less unmet concerns than the Pennsylvanians.

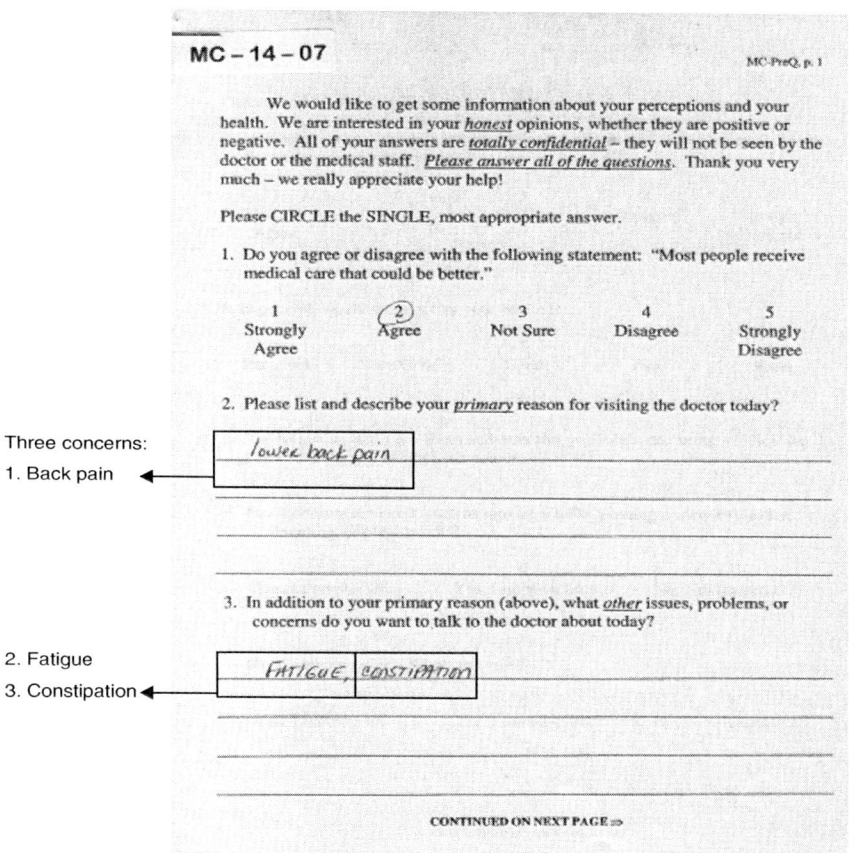

Figure 2.1 First page of patient pre-visit survey

About 50 per cent of the concerns that remained unmet in the control cases were potential acute care conditions (e.g., chest pain, heartburn, neck/shoulder/back pain, skin conditions, etc.), 40 per cent were questions about ongoing conditions (e.g., angina, uterine fibroids, blood pressure, weight loss, etc.), and 10 per cent were questions about medications.

Our examination of the control cases confirmed that examples of our physicians following the textbook recommendation of soliciting additional concerns before the ends of visits were very rare indeed (2/80 or 2.5 per cent). However, when it came to raising unanticipated concerns (not listed in the survey), something that patients did 27 per cent of the time, neither the 'some' nor the 'any'

Table 2.2 Patient multiple concerns by geographic area

	Patients with two or more concerns (complete sample)	Patients who left with unmet concerns (control cases with 2+ concerns only)
Pennsylvania	40%	44%
Los Angeles	58%	32%
Total	49%	37%

intervention significantly altered patients dispositions to introduce such concerns, thus allaying the 'Pandora's Box' worry. Finally, comparison of the first control cases (who did not complete the survey) with the remainder (who did) revealed that the survey did not 'prime' patients to introduce more concerns.

Turning to the primary focus of the study, we quickly saw that the polarity of our intervention question had a remarkable effect on patients' responses. Focusing just on the cases where patients had two or more concerns, and therefore on patients who could have responded affirmatively to the intervention question, we found that, while 53 per cent responded affirmatively to the 'any' version of the question, a full 90 per cent responded affirmatively to the 'some' version. At this elementary level, our conversation analytic hypothesis was supported to a degree that was well beyond our expectations.

But simply comparing percentages does not adequately answer our research question. We needed to be able to isolate the relative influence of the intervention questions themselves, recognising that a range of other variables (e.g., age, sex, education) might have had some influence, and recognising that unmet concerns may have emerged later in visits for a variety of reasons. Other things may have happened during the course of the visit: patients may volunteer their concerns at a later point; physicians may find other ways of introducing and focusing on those additional concerns. We could hardly suggest that physicians change their behaviour without determining the 'bottom line' efficacy of our intervention.

This final analytic hurdle required us to compare both our 'any' and 'some' intervention cases with the control cases to determine the efficacy of both interventions. We also needed to factor in our demographic variables (age, gender, education, etc.) to see what impact they might have and to correct our results for differences between individual doctors. These variables are listed in Table 2.3.

As it turned out, not one of the demographic covariates had any statistically significant influence on whether the patient left the doctor's office with unmet concerns.

Table 2.3 Model building for unmet concerns

We screened bivariately for eight potential covariates, in addition to the SOME/ANY intervention, for inclusion in our model

1. Number of pre-visit concerns expressed (2 versus 3–4).
2. Patient age in decades.
3. Patient gender
4. An indicator that the patient was non-Hispanic white.
5. An ordinal measure of educational attainment.
6. Household income.
7. Physician gender.
8. Location: Los Angeles vs. Pennsylvania

Covariates were retained in multivariate models if they passed a significance threshold of $p. < 0.20$.

In the end, although the 'any' intervention did tend to reduce the number of unmet concerns compared to the control cases, when the reduction was compared with the control cases in a regression analysis, it was not statistically significant: the recommended textbook intervention turned out to be statistically ineffectual. The 'some' intervention (relative to 'control' cases), by contrast, was significantly effective, reducing the odds of a patient leaving the medical visit with an unmet concern by a factor of nearly seven. At the same time, there was a countervailing influence. While the 'some' intervention successfully elicited nearly all the concerns of those patients who had listed two concerns, it did not readily solve the problems of those who had listed three or more. These latter patients were highly likely to leave the visit with unmet concerns.

Finally there was the question about visit time. Surely addressing all those additional concerns would expand visit time? Our result was genuinely surprising. While the 'any' intervention visits were on average 55 seconds longer (a result that was not statistically significant), the 'some' intervention visits were on average one hundredth of a second shorter! Here, it would appear, the 'some' question was getting additional concerns out early in the visit, which allowed for effective time management such that additional concerns could be dealt with within the confines of normal visit length.

Estimating the effectiveness of the intervention

Assuming that our sample was representative of the population of doctor-patient interactions, what was the general effectiveness of our five-minute, video-based intervention? We estimated its effectiveness while, first, allowing for the influence of covariates. In this calculation, it emerged that the 'some' intervention eliminated more than three-quarters of unmet concerns, reducing the rate at which patients left the doctor's office with concerns outstanding from 37 per cent to 8 per cent. However, we also had to factor in the fact that our doctors were able to follow the training correctly only 75 per cent of the time. When this is taken into account, the final tally suggests that our five-minute training tape alone could eliminate more than half the cases of unmet concerns, reducing the rate from 37 per cent to 15 per cent.

Disseminating the study

Our study was a relatively small-scale and inexpensive investigation that emerged with a result that was unexpectedly clear and definite. To use a boxing metaphor, it punched above its weight. It provided solid, evidence-based findings that showed that a small change in physician behaviour could yield a large change in patient outcomes. The paper was first presented at the European Association for Communication in Healthcare (EACH) Annual Meetings in 2006 and attracted a good deal of interest from the healthcare professionals and trainers there – one audience member even raised her hand and asked 'Why didn't we know about this before?' The following year, the paper was published in the *Journal of General Internal Medicine*. It has been cited to a moderate degree and attracted a brief mention in the *Wall Street Journal* and in the newsletter of the funding body – the *Agency for Healthcare Research and Quality*.

It is not difficult to persuade practising clinicians that the word 'any' has negative polarity and will tend to exert a chilling effect on patient response. Many will pick up on even a throwaway reference to it in training devoted to some entirely different medical goal. It was not difficult either to persuade the doctors participating in our study that the intervention could be valuable to them. In fact, most physicians spontaneously volunteered that they planned to use it in their future interactions with patients, and one even requested additional Post-it notes to remind him to keep up the intervention question. Yet, even a small change in behaviour – perhaps *especially* a small change in behaviour – can require a wrenching period of self-conscious struggle with habit: the habit of not asking the question, or of asking it in the 'any' form.

In this case, habit is supported by the underlying pragmatics of the question. A bare majority of patients come to physicians' offices with a single concern. If patients do not mention more than one concern in response to the question 'What can I do for you today?', is it appropriate for the physician to follow-up with a question that is tilted towards the possibility that they in fact have more? And is it desirable to ask a question that, no matter how subtly, hints that patients may have more health concerns than they initially disclose? Of course it is desirable in the clinic. But in the world of everyday life that informs the underlying pragmatics of these question designs, this kind of presumption is often not desirable. And it is the pragmatics of the everyday world that imperceptibly seep into medical questioning and contribute to the patients' concerns remaining unmet. In the end, then, habits and pragmatics conspire to hold negative polarity as the putatively dominant modality of our question (Heritage, 2011). It is a formidable combination, and one that will only be overcome if the results of our study and others like it are included within medical textbooks and the communication training curriculum for medical students. This training curriculum has taken an increasingly clear shape in recent years, due in part to the ascendancy of the Calgary-Cambridge model of communication skills training on both sides of the Atlantic (Silverman, Kurtz and Draper, 2005). It is in this arena that the real process of dissemination will take place.

Concluding comments

We conclude this chapter with a plea for eclecticism in applied conversation-analytic studies. It is clear that our study is based in conversation-analytic findings of a relatively fundamental kind. But it is also clear that we could not have arrived at our conclusions without the use of patient surveys, an intervention in the form of a field experiment and statistical analysis of our findings. None of these techniques are typically used in the field of conversation analysis because they are ineffective as resources in the primary goal of conversation analysis: identifying and delineating fundamental practices involved in the production and recognition of actions and sequences of actions (but see Robinson, 2007).

However, in the applied domain where the effort is to determine the efficacy of interactional practices in shaping some outcome, these kinds of methods are most definitely necessary. In this, and a number of other studies we have participated in, conversation analysis supplies details of turn design and, just as important, a refined sense of the context in which these turn designs are implemented. Its supplementation by surveys, statistical analysis and, where appropriate, experimental intervention essentially serve to demonstrate how powerful the world of interactional practice can be, and how valuable our field can be in uncovering it. We subtitled out study 'the difference one word can make'. Indeed it can, and we can only hope that our study will have made a difference too.

3
Changing Interactional Behaviour: Using Conversation Analysis in Intervention Programmes for Aphasic Conversation

Ray Wilkinson

For over forty years, Conversation Analysis (CA) has been producing findings about the orderly nature of talk-in-interaction, and the methods used by people to produce and make sense of interactional contributions as orderly and meaningful (see, for example, Schegloff, 2007). In this chapter I shall report a CA-based intervention programme which has, since the late 1990s, been used to change interactional behaviour in mundane conversation where one or more speakers has aphasia (Wilkinson et al., 1998; Lock, Wilkinson and Bryan, 2001; Burch, Wilkinson and Lock, 2002; Wilkinson, Bryan, Lock and Sage, 2010; Wilkinson, Lock, Bryan and Sage, 2011). Much of the focus of the intervention has been on the non-aphasic participant in the dyad, in most cases the spouse of the person with aphasia. An overarching aim has been to assist the dyad, and in particular the non-aphasic participant, by making them aware of choices they have in how they produce talk together, and providing them with opportunities of trying out some of these choices.

The approach described here differs in significant ways from other work which has used CA as part of intervention programmes (including work described elsewhere in this volume; see also Antaki's overview in Chapter 1). Such interventions tend to be within institutional settings (schools, doctors' clinics, helplines and so on) whereas the approach described here focuses on changing behaviour within mundane conversation (albeit mundane conversation where one of the participants has aphasia). A second difference is this. Examples such as Heritage and colleagues (2007) on soliciting information from patients, or Atkinson (2004) on making speeches, describe *generalised* advice or training. In the Heritage and colleagues' (2007) study, for example, all the physicians in each of the two groups were given the same instructions – to use either the 'some' or 'any' form of the question (see Heritage and Robinson, Chapter 2 in this volume). This generalised form of advice/training is obviously useful in situations where professional practice can be changed across a group of practitioners by, as here, changing one particular interactional practice (indeed, in this case one word). In many other situations, however, it will be the case that those receiving the intervention will benefit from that intervention being individualised to their particular needs or circumstances. This is the case, for example, with the people with aphasia and their partners described in this chapter.

The problems evident in the conversations of each dyad, as well as the methods developed by those particular participants to adapt to those problems may be quite different to that evident in another dyad (although this is not to say that similar patterns do not recur across some dyads). This means that the most effective intervention is likely to be one which addresses the individual patterns of problems and attempted solutions to those problems evident in the conversation of each dyad.

The analytic and intervention data presented in this chapter is a summarised version of two published case studies (Wilkinson et al., 1998, and Wilkinson et al., 2010) which emerged out of a project focusing on intervention for people with aphasia and their main conversation partners. Details of the project are provided in Lock, Wilkinson and Bryan (2001). In each case study, the intervention was designed, carried out and evaluated based on the particular patterns of conversational interaction seen in the recorded data of the dyads taking part. Here, the two studies will be compared and features of how CA was used to target and evaluate the intervention in both cases will be discussed. The process of intervention in each study will also be described. The aim here is to use the two case studies to display some of the general principles involved in this form of interaction training.

The chapter also includes details of how the general principles of designing, implementing and evaluating intervention to change conversational behaviour which were developed during the research project were subsequently used as the basis for the publication of a resource pack entitled *Supporting Partners of People with Aphasia in Relationships and Conversation* (*SPPARC*) (Lock et al., 2001). *SPPARC* was developed in order that speech and language clinicians (the main professionals involved in managing the communication difficulties of people with aphasia) might be provided with an introduction to conversation-analytic research findings about normal and, in particular, aphasic conversation, and to the practical processes of collecting, transcribing and analysing aphasic conversation data. *SPPARC* also includes assessment and intervention materials which allow speech and language therapy clinicians to begin to use this approach in their everyday clinical practice with people with aphasia and their significant others such as family members. As such, one aim of the *SPPARC* is to facilitate change in the institutional practices of speech and language therapy clinicians by providing them with information and resources which allow them to assess and treat aphasic conversation.

Before discussing the use of CA for intervention programmes targeting aphasic conversation, I will give some background on aphasia, including the main forms of intervention which have been traditionally employed to ameliorate its effects, and the recent application of CA as a method of investigating the impact of aphasia on conversation.

Aphasia, intervention, Conversation Analysis

Aphasia is a language disorder acquired following brain damage such as that caused by stroke (Code, 2010). People with aphasia primarily display grammatical and/or lexical impairments in the context of, in most cases, relatively intact pragmatic skills. For most of these speakers, therefore, it is not the case that they have lost knowledge of the conventions of talk-in-interaction, but rather that their impaired system of linguistic resources may affect the way in which talk-in-interaction is conducted.

Intervention for aphasia can take a number of main forms. One main form is impairment-focused intervention, that is, treatment which attempts to facilitate people with aphasia to regain at least some of the linguistic resources which they lost following the onset of aphasia (Nickels, 2002). A second main form is communication-focused intervention, where intervention focuses on giving training/advice to the person with aphasia and/or a significant other in order to achieve greater use of intact/available verbal and non-verbal resources and through these means to improve the conveying of information (e.g., Lawson and Fawcus, 1999). A third form is psychosocial-focused intervention, where a central focus is on treatments which will enhance the psychosocial wellbeing of the person with aphasia (e.g., Kagan et al., 2001).

A consequence of the application of CA within aphasiology since the mid-1990s onwards has been that a distinct, interaction-focused, intervention approach has begun to emerge. These studies are 'interaction-focused' in that they have used conversational data as a primary source of pre- and post-intervention data collection, and have drawn on CA methods and findings in order to investigate the effects of aphasia on the particular dyad's talk-in-interaction, to choose targets for that particular intervention and to evaluate its effects. These studies have also been able to draw on an accumulated body of work which has used CA to investigate the nature of aphasic talk-in-interaction. Two collections of papers on aphasic talk-in-interaction are Goodwin (2003b) and a Special Issue of *Aphasiology* (1999). What follows is a very brief summary of some of the main findings which have influenced interaction-focused therapy studies, in particular the two studies discussed below.

One area of aphasic talk-in-interaction which has been the focus of much analytic attention is repair. While repair attempts in normal talk are usually brief and successful (Schegloff, Jefferson and Sacks, 1977), in aphasic talk they can regularly be long and, despite the prolonged attempt, may be unsuccessful (Laakso and Klippi, 1999; Wilkinson, 2007). This is particularly the case for self-repair attempts by the person with aphasia since the same types of linguistic deficits which lead to repair being initiated can also make it difficult for the person with aphasia to achieve the outcome of self-repair, which is the preferred outcome for repair attempts (Schegloff et al., 1977). A distinctive type of repair-related sequence seen in aphasic talk is the 'correct production sequence' (Lock, Wilkinson and Bryan, 2001). This is a sequence where, following one or more unsuccessful attempts at the production of a word/words by the person with aphasia, a conversation partner encourages further attempts at correct production, even though it is evident that the partner understands what the target of the mis-produced attempt was. The aphasic speaker's attempts are regularly accepted or rejected as being correct, or at least good enough, by the conversation partner in the next turn, highlighting the pedagogic nature of these sequences.

Another major area of analytic work has been turn and sequence organisation in aphasic talk. Drawing on findings from research into normal (non-communication disordered) conversation such as that of Schegloff (1996a, b, 2007), this work has emphasised the importance of analysing the utterances of speakers with aphasia, including the linguistic forms used to construct the utterance, in relation to the sequential context within which it is produced (Auer and Rönfeldt, 2004; Heeschen and Schegloff, 1999, 2003; Wilkinson, Beeke and Maxim, 2003; Wilkinson et al., 2007). One aspect of context here is the sequence-organisational relationship between the turn of the speaker with aphasia and the prior turn of the conversation partner. For example, Goodwin (1995) analysed conversations involving a man with severe aphasia whose lexical output was largely limited to 'yes', 'no' and 'and'. He described ways in which interlocutors designed their turns to the man as guesses, making relevant responses from him such as 'yes' or 'no'. These 'guess sequences' could extend over numerous turns, with the conversation partners of the man with aphasia taking the role of providing relevant guesses, and the man with aphasia in the role of accepting or rejecting the guesses.

While accepting the guess closes down the guess sequence, a rejection keeps the sequence open leading to another guess (often as an alternative from the category which has previously been used by the guessing participants). These first pair parts (Sacks, Schegloff and Jefferson, 1974) in the form of guesses provide a sequential framework in which a turn such as 'yes' or 'no' can be used by the person with aphasia to take a focal role in the conversation and present himself as an able interlocutor despite the paucity of linguistic resources at his disposal. One other way in which non-aphasic partners can use first pair parts is in the form of 'test questions' (see Lock, Wilkinson and Bryan, 2001). Here, the partner asks a question in the role of a 'knowing' rather than 'not-knowing' participant (Goodwin and Goodwin, 1987). These questions can be used to elicit talk from the person with aphasia and are typically used for pedagogic purposes, such as encouraging the person with aphasia to produce certain linguistic items, and allowing the partner to monitor, and perhaps correct, the person with aphasia's effort.

Using Conversation Analysis in intervention programmes for aphasia

The two single case studies I shall present emerged from a research project which focused on new ways of providing support for the significant others (usually spouses or other family members) of people with aphasia. Details of the overall project are provided in Lock, Wilkinson and Bryan (2001). A major part of the project involved collecting and analysing conversational data from the person with aphasia and a significant other, and designing, implementing and evaluating intervention to assist the dyad in coping with the effects of aphasia within everyday conversation. CA was the main method used for this part of the project.

Within the project I was responsible for overseeing the data collection and transcription of the conversation data and for carrying out CA analysis of that data. I also had the main responsibility for working out, both in general terms for the project and for the individual couples, how to move from analysis to choosing targets for intervention for conversation, what intervention principles might be used, and how evaluation of conversation post-intervention might be carried out. In these tasks I drew on my experience both as a conversation analyst and as a qualified speech and language therapist with a number of years of clinical experience of working with people with aphasia in the UK National Health Service. For the planning and implementing of the intervention for individual dyads I worked closely with Sarah Lock, the speech and language therapist who managed the data collection process and who carried out the intervention with the dyads, either in groups or as individual couples. For example, Sarah and I worked together in turning intervention ideas into tasks and materials (such as information sheets and handouts) to use with the dyads. Many of these tasks and materials were later re-worked and published as part of the *SPPARC*.

Participants and methodology

The two dyads discussed here, Connie and Sam and Len and Jane,[1] were both married couples where one partner had aphasia following a cerebro-vascular accident (CVA) in the left cerebral hemisphere. Both people with aphasia had a non-fluent, Broca-type aphasia. Also, at the time of their intervention both people with aphasia were more than 12 months post-onset and, as such, were beyond the period when changes in linguistic and communicative performance might be due to spontaneous recovery of neural function.

Connie was 36 when she became aphasic, 14 months prior to when the analysis and intervention reported here was carried out. In conversation Connie presented with good comprehension, simplified syntactic structure, and phonemic and semantic paraphasias (i.e., sound and meaning word errors). She also had a mild dysarthria (motor problems linked to the speech production apparatus, such as problems with the clear articulation of words).

At the time of the study Len was 66 and had become aphasic 18 months previously. He presented in conversation with simplified syntactic structure and sound production errors. He had a right hemiplegia and was able to walk with care and write with his non-preferred (left) hand. Jane, his wife, was 63. Both were retired teachers.

In both cases, there were three assessment points, two pre-intervention and one post-intervention. At each assessment point, the couple video-recorded at least 20 minutes of conversation (this could be made up of more than one continuous conversation) using a video camera which the non-aphasic partner had been trained to use.

Choosing targets for intervention

As noted in the Introduction, when using CA as part of an intervention programme one question which arises is how one might move from having a series of analytic findings about the data (as might be the case in a standard CA study) to deciding which features of the interaction, if any, might be the focus of an intervention. Lock, Wilkinson and Bryan (2001) describe three features of aphasic conversation data which might lead to that aspect of the dyad's conversational style becoming a target of intervention. These are:

- conversational behaviours which appear to be causing obvious discomfort, distress or noticeable problems for the dyad, as visible through their display of emotions (such as anger or tearfulness) or verbal comments;
- a pattern of occurrences which displays that the dyad are over-relying on a particular method, such as the non-aphasic partner habitually using questions;

- a pattern of occurrences in which the non-aphasic partner in particular can be seen to be reacting to the presence of aphasia by adopting a pedagogic role and speaking in the 'institutional' style of a professional such as a teacher or clinician

Between them, the case studies presented here display these three features.[2] In each case, the behaviour can be seen to be one aspect of the conversational style adopted by the dyad, and in particular by the non-aphasic conversation partner, in response to the linguistic limitations and/or errors of the speaker with aphasia. It is the fact that one or more of these behaviours is not working well for the dyad (e.g., through causing noticeable problems or particular emotional reactions, or being over-used at the expense of other possible behaviours) that results in them becoming targets for intervention in the programme.

Connie and Sam: pre-intervention

The talk of Connie and Sam contains correct production sequences with Sam (the non-aphasic partner) adopting a pedagogic role of either accepting Connie's attempt as acceptable or rejecting it and requesting her to produce another attempt. Also, as on the occasion shown in Extract 1, the correct production sequence can be seen to lead to Connie twice becoming upset and tearful.

Extract 1   Connie and Sam pre-intervention

```
01  Connie:   yes (0.4) uhm (0.3) whee:l ba:rrow,
02  Sam:      yeah
03  Connie:   uhm (.) I can't (0.3) paint its
04  Sam:      why's that?
05  Connie:   eh lef hands.
06  Sam:      what hand?
07  Connie:   lef hands.
08  Sam:      lef:T
09  Connie:   lef [    ] hands
10  Sam:          [/t/]
11  Sam:      you're saying- you're saying lef: you're not putting the 't' at the end
12  Sam:      (0.2) left.
13  Connie:   lef:
14  Sam:      /t/
15  Connie:   lef:
16  Sam:      /t/
17  Sam:      you're missing the 't' (0.3) left
18  Connie:   lef (.) hands (0.3) [I    ] can't (hear) it ((sounds and looks tear-
            ful))
```

```
19   Sam:                        [right]
20   Sam:      yes but you tried didn't you? you try.
21   Connie:   mm ((laughs))
22             (1.5)
23   Sam:      you didn't say left you said lef. lef. 'l' 'e' 'f' ((spells))
24   Connie:   l:ef (.)
25   Sam:      /t/ (.)
26   Connie:   han [ds
27   Sam:          [like you spit at the end. /t/ (0.3) say /t/.
28   Connie:   't'
29   Sam:      't' (.) lef:T
30   Connie:   lef:
31   Sam:      lef:t,
32   Connie:   lef,
33             (0.3)
34   Sam:      hand.
35   Connie:   hand.
36             [( 5.5 )
37             [((Connie looks tearful))
38   Sam:      so's your hand tired (.) been doing the exercises?
39   Connie:   yeah
```

The source of the correct production sequence is Connie's attempt at 'left' which in line 5 she produces as *lef*. In aphasiological terms, this is a phonemic paraphasia, a sound error due to Connie's aphasic phonological problems (Goodglass, Kaplan and Barresi, 2001). In response to the production of this phonemic error, Sam's other-initiation of repair (*what hand?*) in line 6 is hearable as pedagogic, requesting from Connie a further attempt to produce the word in the correct phonemic form and achieve the preferred outcome of self-repair. There is evidence that Connie indeed treats it this way as she produces her next attempt, in line 7, more slowly and carefully. This attempt too is unsuccessful. Now, following Connie's failed attempt to successfully use the opportunity for self-repair offered by his other-initiation of repair, Sam produces an explicit other-initiated other-repair (*lef:T* in line 8). This correction is hearable here as a model for Connie to copy, but due to her aphasic phonemic problems she is unable to do so (line 9). This form of sequence consisting of attempts by Connie and non-acceptance of the attempts by Sam continues over a number of rounds (lines 9–12, 13–14, 15–17) before Connie follows a try by commenting that she *can't* (*hear*) *it*. At this point she sounds and looks upset and tearful. A couple of turns later, Sam again makes relevant an attempt by Connie to produce the word correctly by feeding back her previous attempts to her and breaking up her incorrect production into its constituent sounds (line 23). After a further series of tries, the attempt is abandoned by the couple (lines 32–38). At this point Connie again appears noticeably tearful.

Despite the couple focusing on Connie's error over a number of turns (lasting around 50 seconds), Connie has been unable to achieve the preferred outcome of a self-repair of her error. At the same time, over these turns the conversational focus has been on Connie's incompetence (both her original inability to produce the word 'left' correctly and her subsequent inability to repair her incorrect attempts). For his part, Sam has here taken a pedagogic role, repeatedly correcting his wife and providing her with models and advice on how to produce the word correctly. On two occasions during this sequence Connie has become noticeably tearful. It was these factors which motivated us to focus our intervention on Connie and Sam's correct production sequences.

Len and Jane: pre-intervention

In the case of Len and Jane, the non-aphasic conversation partner, Jane, recurrently relies on questions, particularly in the form of yes-no interrogatives (Raymond, 2003), when talking with Len. This can be seen in Extract 2, where, in a transcript of 25 lines, yes/no interrogatives are used in lines 1, 3, 5, 7, 10, 16, 21 and 23. Other questions are also used which make relevant the production by Len of specific information such as the name of one or more persons (line 18) or of an action (line 25).

Extract 2   Len and Jane pre-intervention

```
01 Jane: did you have a good walk?
02 Len:  (4.5) ((Len turns from Jane and looks forward; goes as if to speak then
         stops))
03 Jane: did you enjoy your walk?
04 Len:  °yes°
05 Jane: was it very hot?
06 Len:  yes.
07 Jane: did you see anybody?
08 Len:  (0.5) uh: no. yeah, (1.9) (man) with a dog.
09 Jane: you saw the man with the dog uhm (.) °whats his name. not Bill. cant
10       remember what his name is°. right. was he going for a walk with the dog?
11 Len:  no
12 Jane: oh [(right)
13 Len:     [(he's) coming (down).
14 Jane: he was coming down, [right.
15 Len:                      [yeah
16 Jane: and uhm you didn't see Glen or Ellen?
17 Len:  (0.2) y:es,
18 Jane: oh right. who did you see?
19 Len:  (hh) (1.5) [(two) uh
20                  [ ((holds up two fingers))
21 Jane: you saw them both.
```

```
22  Len:   yeah
23  Jane:  oh right. and what was- was Ellen going to the shops?
24  Len:   no,
25  Jane:  what was she doing?
```

It is also notable that in the turns following Len's answers, Jane regularly produces another question. This may constitute the whole turn (lines 3, 5, 7, 21, 25) or follow some other action earlier in her turn such as a news receipt (lines 9–10, 18, 23).

As a result of Jane's questions, Len is recurrently allocated a turn (Sacks, Schegloff and Jefferson, 1974) and thus can make regular contributions to the conversation. Indeed, this may have been an interactional motivation for Jane which led her to adopt this style of talking to Len (a style which is evident throughout the nearly 25 minutes of pre-intervention conversational data). At the same time, however, it is evident that Jane's adopted style of recurrently relying on questions is restricting Len's contributions to the conversation. It is notable, for example, that he uses few sentences or attempted sentences in his talk. In Extract 2 he produces one sentence ((*he's*) *coming* (*down*)) in line 13. This is despite the fact that he is able to produce, or attempt to produce, sentences in other types of speech activity, such as on a picture description task carried out around the same time as this conversation was recorded (see Wilkinson et al., 2010).

Most typically, Len's utterances are answers to Jane's questions which use a minimal form sufficient to produce an answer. Thus, he regularly answers yes/no interrogatives with a *yes* or a *no* alone (lines 4, 6, 15, 17, 22, 24). Where he does elaborate, it is typically where there is an expectation to do so, such as when his answer differs from that anticipated by the polarity of the question design (see Raymond, 2003). For example, in line 10, Jane's question 'was he going for a walk with the dog?' anticipates a positive response. It is produced in what can be termed, following Heritage (2010b), a positively polarised form (compare *he wasn't going for a walk with the dog, was he?*). Len, however, responds to the question with a *no* (line 11). Following Jane's *oh* (part of *oh right*) in line 12 displaying her stance of having been informed of something she did not previously know (Heritage, 1984b), Len elaborates and produces a sentence (line 13).

While there is evidence that Len can produce more complex, sentential, structures than the lexical (in particular 'yes' and 'no') and phrasal constructions he is predominantly using here, these are used only rarely, and typically in particular sequential environments such as in responses which do not align with the polarity of the preceding question. Linked to this, Len's role in terms of determining the content, direction and topical development of the conversation is a minimal one. Rather, his role in conversation at this stage is passive and responsive, with Jane constantly taking the initiating actions (such as asking questions and initiating and developing the topics of talk).

In the case of Len and Jane, therefore, intervention was motivated by the fact that the couple's (and, especially, Jane's) adopted style of talking resulted in them over-relying on particular turn formats (yes-no interrogatives from Jane and lexical, especially 'yes' or 'no', responses from Len). This resulted in Len's contributions to conversation being noticeably limited, and his linguistic abilities (evident in certain parts of the conversation, and in other types of speech activity such as language testing) being under-utilised.

Intervention

Once certain interactional behaviours have been identified as possible targets for intervention, a next question is: what form might that intervention take? In the case of the two studies presented above, the approach used was what has been termed 'interaction therapy' (Wilkinson et al., 1998; Wilkinson, 1999). A basic feature of this approach is that it aims to make participants more aware of certain features of their current interactional behaviours as a precursor to possible change. Many of the interactional behaviours of participants in conversation appear to occur below their level of conscious awareness, and one feature of the intervention approach described here is that it aims to make participants more conscious of these behaviours. Change takes the form of, for example, giving one or more of the participants greater choice about whether they might perform a certain action in a certain sequential context, and/or what form that action might take. The aim, therefore, is often not to replace one practice with another, but to provide a participant with a wider range of options in relation to that practice.

While this intervention approach was developed for targeting behaviours in aphasic conversation, it can be thought of as a general form of interaction training which can be applied to various types of interactant, not just those with communication disorders. As will be seen in the case studies discussed below, many of the behaviours targeted are in fact those of the non-aphasic partner.

Within this approach, participants' awareness is raised by the therapist/facilitator playing them video clips from their conversations and discussing with them certain features of their interactional behaviours in these conversations. In discussing the behaviours, the therapist/facilitator may draw on relevant concepts from conversation-analytic research and familiarise the participants with these concepts in a simplified form (e.g., the term 'problem' may be used rather than 'trouble source', and 'solving the problem' used instead of 'repair completion'). To raise participants' awareness of aspects of conversation in general, and features of their own conversational style in particular, various means may be used, including using video and audio recordings (of the participants and of others), transcripts of conversational excerpts, handouts about aspects of conversation (such as turns and sequences, repair and topic), written exercises and role plays. As part of reflecting on their interactional behaviours, participants are encouraged to discuss how common these interactional behaviours may be in their everyday conversations together, and how they feel about them (e.g., whether they see them as problematic or not).

Based on the viewings of the video clips and the discussions around them, certain interactional behaviours are agreed on by the participants and the therapist/facilitator as the focus of intervention. The target behaviours are tried out by the participant(s) with the therapist/facilitator in exercises and role-plays and/or by the participants themselves in their everyday conversations. These target behaviours are themselves reflected upon through means such as video-feedback and discussion or the participants keeping a record of the use and effectiveness of the target behaviours within their everyday conversations during a specified period.

Connie and Sam: intervention

In the case of Connie and Sam, we worked to raise their awareness of repair activity through the use of handouts about repair (see Lock, Wilkinson and Bryan, 2001, for examples of the type of handouts used). These were used as the basis for discussion during which the therapist (SL) introduced concepts about repair in general before moving on to discuss Connie and Sam's patterns of repair activity. She played the couple the video-clip of the sequence shown in Extract 1 as a means of promoting discussion about Sam's patterns of initiating correct production sequences following Connie's production of phonemic errors. The couple said they engaged in correct production sequences regularly in their everyday conversations. They did this because they felt it would improve Connie's speech, but at the same time both felt these sequences disrupted conversation and Sam said he found them tiring to do. After discussion with the therapist, it was agreed that an aim for Sam would be not to initiate correct production sequences on Connie's errors during conversation since the resulting attempts at self-repair by Connie could often be prolonged and unsuccessful and could lead to upset and frustration. Rather, if he could understand the word Connie was saying despite it containing one or more phonemic errors, Sam was to continue the conversation without initiating repair on the error. In CA terms, this meant that an error was not being treated as a trouble source (for this distinction, see Schegloff, Jefferson and Sacks, 1977) and in these cases Sam, the recipient, was to 'let pass' the error. Errors could be mentally noted when they occurred and worked on at a later time if the couple wished. The therapist used handouts during the intervention sessions to reinforce the ideas being discussed. Figure 3.1 is an example of the type of handout discussed with both partners. Both (especially Sam) were encouraged to consider using a 'let it pass' strategy. The aim was not blanket prescription, but rather to show them interactional choices. The couple were also given a handout to fill in between sessions which required them to reflect on the success or otherwise of not initiating correct production sequences on Connie's phonemic errors.

Len and Jane: intervention

The intervention for Connie and Sam thus involved a certain type of behaviour (correct production sequence) not being carried out in a certain sequential environment (in response to the production of a phonemic paraphasia by Connie). For Len and Jane, our focus was primarily on changing the nature and type of certain of Jane's actions in order to provide more opportunity for Len to contribute to conversation. The therapist played Jane selected video clips of Jane's questioning behaviours, such as that seen in Extract 2. Using handouts, she discussed with Jane some basic findings about question-answer sequences and discussed different types of question (such as the distinction between yes/no interrogatives and less constraining forms of question). Handouts were also made for Jane which included examples of her different types of questions and their effect on Len's responses. In discussion with the couple, it was agreed that Jane would make greater use of forms to initiate sequences other than yes/no interrogatives and 'closed' wh-type questions. Another decision was that Jane would try to respond to some of Len's turns with a paraphrase or repeat of his turn, or with a continuer such as 'mm hm' (Schegloff, 1982) rather than with another question. With both of these suggested changes we were aiming to provide Len with greater opportunities to contribute to conversations through, for example, producing more sentential turn-constructional units (TCUs) (rather than his current reliance on lexical TCUs), and through developing the topic of talk by developing it across turns. Len was aware that Jane was aiming to change her style of talking to him, and that he could attempt to make use of the opportunities these changes aimed to create.

A number of methods were used in order to experiment with and practise these changes in conversational style between the couple. The therapist gave Jane handouts with written versions of a range of question types, including those she had used in the pre-intervention conversations, and Jane had to decide which type of question each was (i.e., whether yes/no interrogative or another type of question). She also provided Jane with

Handout C21a

Dealing with Problems Can Stop Conversation

You can choose not to deal with problems!

Problems in conversation can be dealt with by either you or your partner with aphasia, or by both of you working together, and by using a variety of strategies.

However, while some problems are solved quickly enough for the conversation to continue without disruption, some can take so long that the conversation grinds to a halt. This can happen if the person with aphasia cannot find the words she is looking for and takes a long time searching for them, or if you take a long time trying to work out her message. It can also happen if you highlight your partner with aphasia's mistakes every time she makes one, or if you encourage her to produce words correctly during conversation (like the man in the cartoon above).

Stopping the conversation to solve a problem means it can be difficult to pick up the threads of the conversation again. It may also make your partner feel or look 'incompetent' as a speaker, and could shake her confidence.

Figure 3.1 Handout example

practice at trying different types of turns to initiate sequences (i.e., different types of questions, and statement forms instead of question forms) and also different types of turns in response to Len's turns (i.e., minimal turns or paraphrases of what Len had said rather than a further question). Jane did this in role plays with the therapist (with the therapist taking the role of Len) and in a videoed role play with Len (followed by watching the video with the therapist and receiving feedback from her). She also practised this style of talking with Len on some occasions between the intervention sessions. The therapist provided her with a form in which to keep notes about what the effect of these different types of turn appeared to be on Len's talk.

Evaluation of possible changes post-intervention

After intervention, there is the question of whether the changes in interactional behaviours which were agreed upon by the participants and the therapist/facilitator, and have been practised during the intervention programme by the participants, are now evident in the dyad's naturally occurring conversations in daily life. This comparison of behaviour pre- and post-intervention raises a number of methodological issues for an approach such as CA, which has historically engaged in close qualitative analyses of single cases of a candidate phenomenon, and not in detailed comparisons of phenomena across, for example, two or more conversations involving the same participants (Schegloff, 1993; Heritage, 1995).

One set of issues relates to data collection. For instance, how much conversational data should be collected in order to ground claims that change has indeed occurred within the conversations of these participants? Another set of issues relates to data sampling and data analysis. For instance, in tracing a particular conversational phenomenon across conversations to see if it may have changed, what would constitute an 'environment of possible relevant occurrence' (Schegloff, 1993) where that phenomenon might be analysed in relation to its incidence or non-incidence? Also, what role, if any, may quantification have in allowing comparison of data and in making a case for change? A third set of issues relates to what other methods beyond CA, if any, may be brought to bear in providing some form of evidence that the participants have changed following the intervention. Is there a role, for example, for interviewing the participants about their views on their interactions and how they compare pre- and post-intervention? Or in using naïve raters to provide comparisons of aspects of the different conversations and the behaviours therein?

Discussing these methodological issues in the detail they deserve must be reserved for elsewhere. Here, a description will be given of how evaluation of possible changes post-intervention was carried out in the case of the two couples described above.

Connie and Sam: post-intervention

In the post-intervention conversation of Connie and Sam, there were no examples of correct production sequences in relation to Connie's talk. This was despite the fact that Connie was still producing the types of sound errors (for instance, phonemic paraphasias) which, pre-intervention, Sam had been treating in his next turn as a trouble source and as a target for Connie to self-repair within a correct production sequence. As such, one form of evidence for the effectiveness of the intervention was that within the type of sequential context (here, following a phonemic paraphasia produced by Connie) where previously Sam had, at least on occasion, initiated repair and a correct production sequence, he was now not producing this type of behaviour. This is not to say that Sam was not still initiating repair on Connie's talk, and indeed on some occasions correcting her, as can be seen in Extract 3.

Extract 3: Connie and Sam post-intervention

```
01   Connie:    this morning (0.2) (rain) (0.2) phone me (0.9) Australia
02   Sam:       yeah ((yawns))
03   Connie:    ehm guess what?
04   Sam:       what?
05              (1.5)
06   Connie:    you [and me          ]
07   Sam:           [she's moving back?]
08              (0.6)
09   Sam:       you and I yeah
10   Connie:    no (.) you and I,
11   Sam:       (you mean) you and me ((starts to smile))
12              ((both laugh))
13   Connie:    ehm (0.3) godparents
```

In this extract, which starts with Connie announcing that her friend Lorraine phoned from Australia that morning (line 1), Sam twice corrects Connie. He first (line 9) corrects her *you and me* (line 6) to *you and I* (line 9). Secondly, after Connie then picks up and uses the formulation which he has just used to correct her (line 10), he corrects her for a second time, here by flipping back to her original version (line 11). These corrections are obviously different in terms of target and import to that seen in the couple's pre-intervention conversation (Extract 1) where Sam corrected Connie's phonemic paraphasia *lef* to *lef:T* (Extract 1, lines 7–8). In Extract 3 the correction is related to English usage rather than aphasic error, and the effect is one of humour (see Sam's smile in line 11 and the laughter from both Connie and Sam following the correction).

It is also notable that in line 1 of Extract 3, Connie produces a phonemic error ((rain)) as an attempt to name her friend Lorraine). Sam, however, does not treat this phonemic paraphasia as a jumping off point for initiating repair and a correct production sequence as he did in the pre-intervention conversation. Instead, he produces a non-repair-related next turn, acknowledging the announcement.

Further evidence that the intervention focused on the correct production sequences in the couple's conversations had had an effect came from discussions and an interview with the couple. Sam said that he did not produce correct production sequences in conversation now and told the interviewer: 'Connie doesn't, or didn't, get the word correctly. And I would pick up on that. But really as long as I understand her, I'm not worried about it any more' (Lock, Wilkinson and Bryan, 2001).

Len and Jane: post-intervention

In the case of Len and Jane too, there was evidence in the post-intervention conversation that the couple were now producing interactional behaviours which differed from those seen anywhere in the pre-intervention conversations and which were in line with those which the therapist had discussed and practised with them. As with Connie and Sam, the primary form of evidence for change was that uncovered through the qualitative analysis of the sequential patterns of action and practices of action observable in the couple's behaviour. An example can be seen in Extract 4.

Extract 4:   Len and Jane post-intervention

```
01 Jane: tell me about your walk.
02 Len:  (2.0) I eh (1.9) I've eh (4.7) I (0.7) eh (walked) [(past the) (0.5) (cemetery)
03                                                          [ ((points outside))
04       (1.1) I (saw Glen)
05 Jane: (1.1) you walked (.) past the cemetery (.) you s [aw Glen
06 Len:                                                   [(saw Glen)
07       (0.5) and he [(was) (0.7) (coming down)
08                    [((gestures towards himself))
09 Jane: Glen was coming down.=
10 Len:  =yeah. (0.5) and he [have (bwocks) with him
11                           [ ((gestures carrying something))
12       (0.9) a (with) eh- (0.4) °(him)° (1.0)
13 Jane: [he had a box [with him
14 Len:  [NO::: a bag.
15 Jane: he had a [bag with him right?,
16 Len:           [°ye:s° (1.2) ((gestures carrying something)) and he was (2.1)
```

```
17          (going out) (0.5) t-to, (2.2) to eh, (2.6) ) oh (anyone oski) the (0.3) eh
18          (0.5) (kowers but eh lays), ((laughs)) and k-heh heh and ((laughing))
19          (0.5) he was (0.7)  eh s: saying (0.6) eh (par) (0.5) eh (.7) ooh ((waves
20          hand)) (0.9) (at) ((laughs)) eh (1.1) ooh ((makes gesture on lap-tray))
21  Jane:   (1.5) eh he had a bag with him was he going shopping?
22  Len:    No    [((pointing))
23  Jane:         [coming home from the [shops.
24  Len:                                 [no he was (0.9) he (wa) (ts)
25          (0.9) and he (wat) (.) talked to me about the (Wales)?
26  Jane:   he talked to you- he talked to you about Wales (.) right?
```

As was the case in Extract 2, Jane here initiates a conversation with Len by topicalising his daily walk (Jane used this topic recurrently through the data set as a means of eliciting talk from Len). Unlike in Extract 2 where this action was done in the form of a question, and specifically a yes-no interrogative which restricted Len's possible response (*did you have a good walk* in line 1 of Extract 2), here it is done in a non-question format which gives Len greater scope in terms of both the content and form of his response (*tell me about your walk*). In his response in lines 2–4, Len makes use of these increased opportunities and produces a turn made up of two sentential turn-constructional units (TCUs) (Sacks, Schegloff and Jefferson, 1974). This differs from Len's pattern of turn construction in the two pre-intervention conversations where there were no turns made up of two or more sentential TCUs. In her third turn response, Jane does not ask a further question but instead virtually repeats back to Len what he has just said (line 5).

In this episode Jane recurrently responds to Len's turns by providing some form of repeat (lines 9, 13, 15, 26). While this gives the conversation a somewhat stereotyped and unnatural feel compared to mundane, non-aphasic, conversation, it can be seen to have some positive consequences for this couple. One is that through doing a repeat of the prior turn rather than asking another question, Jane provides Len with the floor in a manner which leaves him significant freedom about how he might produce his next turn. Recurrently he uses this freedom to produce turns in the form of one or more sentences or attempted sentences (lines 7, 16–20, 24), a pattern which was not evident in the pre-intervention conversations where one word or one phrase TCUs were the norm. Second, by means of these sequential practices, Len directs the topical direction and content of the conversation in a way which was not evident anywhere in the pre-intervention conversations. For instance he tells Jane about where he walked and about meeting Glen (lines 2–4); that Glen was coming down and had a box with him (lines 7 and 10); and other facts about Glen including that he talked to Len about the Welsh rugby match (line 25). Third, by repeating back what she thinks Len has said, Jane provides Len with an opportunity to correct her hearing of his turn, an opportunity which Len can be seen to take in line 14. As such, Len is far more conversationally active in this episode than he was anywhere in the pre-intervention interactions.

As with Connie and Sam, feedback from the participants (in this case Jane) provided some evidence that the behavioural changes seen in the post-intervention conversation were also perceived by those taking part in the conversation and that these changes extended beyond that one set of recorded conversations. In a post-intervention letter to the research team and interview Jane said that Len was now using sentences daily, whereas before the intervention he had only used sentences in conversation 'on about five occasions'. She attributed this change to the advice and training she had been given in the intervention programme which encouraged her to (in her words) 'hang back a bit' in conversations with Len (see Wilkinson et al., 2010, for further details of the feedback).

In the case of Len and Jane further investigation of change was carried out (see Wilkinson et al., 2010). A section from the post-intervention conversation (this included, but extended beyond, the talk shown in Extract 4) was compared with a section from the pre-intervention conversations which was independently agreed by three naïve raters to be the 'best' section of conversation prior to intervention. 'Best' here meant the section which most appeared to display the behaviours of Jane and/or Len which were later to be chosen as the targets of intervention (e.g., Jane responding to Len with a non-question turn or Len using, or attempting to use, a sentential TCU). A quantitative comparison of these two sections (each of which consisted of 35 turns) showed, for example, that the number of turns which contained questions by Jane to Len decreased from 78 per cent in the pre-intervention conversation to 22 per cent in the post-intervention conversation. The number of Len's turns which contained at least one sentential TCU, or attempted sentential TCU, rose from 41 per cent to 59 per cent, while the number of his turns which contained two or more sentential TCUs and/or attempted sentential TCUs rose from 0 per cent to 17 per cent.

The video recordings of these two section were shown to 15 speech and language therapists who were naïve to the couple and the intervention. Without knowing what the intervention consisted of, 14 of the 15 correctly chose which section was pre-intervention and which post-intervention. The therapists were then told what the intervention consisted of and were asked to examine the video recordings and the transcripts of the two extracts and to note the occurrence of five specific intervention-related behaviours (three of Jane's behaviours: use of open questions; use of repeats or paraphrases of what Len had just said; and use of continuers such as 'mm hm'; and two of Len's behaviours: adding something new to the topic; and taking an active role in conversation in some other way, e.g., by correcting Jane). There was a significant change in the mean for all the behaviours (Wilcoxon matched pairs test: $W = 60$, 2 tailed $p = 0.0007$) suggesting that the targeted therapy behaviours were observed by the therapists in the post-intervention section more than in the pre-intervention section. This change was driven by both Jane and Len's change in conversational behaviours as both showed significant differences in their pre- and post-intervention means (Jane: Wilcoxon matched pairs test: $W = 60$, 2 tailed $p = 0.0007$; Len: Wilcoxon matched pairs test: $W = 52.50$, 2 tailed $p = 0.0011$). These results indicated that naïve raters were able to see changes between the pre- and post-intervention conversational sections both at an overall level and in terms of specific behaviours that made up the overall appearance of change between the two sections.

The application of CA within clinical practice

The type of intervention drawing on CA methods and findings described above has begun to be incorporated into the clinical practice of the speech and language therapy clinicians who have primary responsibility for clinically assessing and treating people with communication disorders such as aphasia.

One main way in which this has occurred is through the publication of *SPPARC* (Lock, Wilkinson and Bryan, 2001). *SPPARC* contains a manual providing an introduction to CA along with a step-by-step description of how to collect, transcribe and analyse conversational data, and how to plan and carry out interventions for people with aphasia and their conversation partners based on the analysis. A number of examples of conversational phenomena found in aphasic conversation are presented through video clips of these phenomena, with each clip accompanied by a transcript and a brief analysis. The pack also contains a set of handouts for the clinician to use and adapt with clients when carrying out an intervention programme.

Overall, the aim of the *SPPARC* is that by using it, a clinician unfamiliar with CA would be able to collect conversational data involving a person with aphasia, analyse it to a level whereby an individualised interaction-focused intervention programme can be devised, and then carry out that intervention. The publication of *SPPARC* has been supplemented by courses on this approach which we (Ray Wilkinson and/or Sarah Lock) have run for speech and language therapy clinicians and other interested professionals. These courses, which run over either one or two days, provide clinicians with the opportunity to carry out exercises on aphasic conversation data, plan interventions, and ask questions and discuss possible application of *SPPARC* in relation to their own clinical caseloads. To date over 20 of these courses have been run across a number of countries (England, Scotland, Wales, Northern Ireland, Republic of Ireland, Australia, Denmark, Norway and Slovakia). A Dutch resource pack based closely on the conversation sections of *SPPARC* is currently being developed (Wielaert and Wilkinson, in prep.).

There is evidence from the speech and language therapy professional literature that this interaction-focused intervention approach is being used by clinicians in their everyday clinical practice with people with aphasia and their significant others (Armstrong and McGrane, 2003; Niewenhuis, 2005). From these reports it seems that the approach is often modified in various ways to suit the particular circumstances and clinical caseload of the clinician. In particular, the time-consuming nature of transcription is often commented upon and regularly appears from the reports to be either omitted or significantly modified compared to standard CA research practice.

As such, the primary way in which CA has influenced the clinical practice of speech and language therapists, at least in the United Kingdom, is through therapists learning something of CA's methods and findings and using this knowledge in their clinical management of people with communication disorders and their significant others. This learning occurs through the use of clinical resources such as *SPPARC* and/or through face-to-face training and education, such as training days or classes in CA taught as part of undergraduate or graduate courses in speech and language pathology and therapy.

What is less developed at this stage is the investigation of speech and language therapy talk as a form of institutional interaction. There has, therefore, been virtually no work done using CA to inform changes to professional practices in ways which are reported in this volume for some other professions. However, as a body of work on the analysis of speech and language therapy talk grows (see Wilkinson, 2004; Simmons-Mackie, Elman, Holland and Damico, 2007) this becomes a possible focus of future work.

Concluding comments

In this chapter I have discussed the process and some results of an approach which draws on the method and findings of Conversation Analysis to implement and evaluate intervention programmes targeted at conversation. In the two case studies presented here, the conversations involved a person with aphasia interacting with their spouse in their home environment. In both cases, the intervention primarily targeted certain interactional behaviours of the non-aphasic partner. In both cases, the intervention aimed in particular to facilitate the non-aphasic partner to adapt their talk in order to cope more successfully with the effects of aphasia within conversation. Positive results have been reported for similar types of intervention targeted at aphasic conversation (Booth and Perkins, 1999; Booth and Swabey, 1999; Turner and Whitworth, 2006).

Future developments of the interaction training approach discussed here might involve its application beyond people with communication disorders to a wider range of interactants, with a focus on how they carry out certain actions and activities within either institutional interaction or mundane conversation.

Notes

1. The names used for these participants are pseudonyms and other names of people and places in the transcripts which might identify the participants have also been changed.
2. For reasons of space and clarity, only certain parts of the two couples' interaction-focused intervention programme will be described here. Details of other parts of Connie and Sam's programme are presented in Lock, Wilkinson and Bryan (2001).

4
Improving Response Rates in Telephone Interviews[1]

Douglas W. Maynard, Nora Cate Schaeffer and Jeremy Freese

Fewer people are responding to surveys than in the past, which is a problem of urgent importance for social science, government, business and other institutions that depend on this form of data gathering. In this chapter we report a study involving the Wisconsin Longitudinal Study (WLS), which was begun with a one-third sample of 1957 Wisconsin high school graduates and had follow-up waves in 1965, 1975, 1992 and in 2004. The WLS collects a wide range of economic, familial, health and other information and has been used in many different kinds of studies, most recently about the life course, intergenerational relationships, family functioning, and physical and mental health.[2]

In 2004, WLS telephone interviews were digitally recorded. The digital recordings provided an opportunity to study the organisation and detail of obtaining survey participation. We were interested both in the theoretical and empirical understanding of requesting as a social action, but we also wanted to know, as a practical matter, how participation rates could be improved not only for the WLS but also for other surveys. How might Conversation Analysis address this practical problem? Our CA studies are ongoing but we have made specific recommendations for interviewers to alter their practices, recommendations that are being reviewed for inclusion in interviewer training and that can be studied with our quantitative data and by designing additional experiments.

Our major recommendation, which we shall describe in detail later, is that interviewers should *tailor* their requests to how the talk has developed in the early moments of the call's inception, or what we call the interactional environment of requesting. Investigators (Campanelli and Sturgis, 1997; Couper and Groves, 2002; Dijkstra and Smit, 2002; Groves and Couper, 1996, p. 67) have already used the term 'tailoring' to refer to the strategies by which interviewers address the questions or concerns that potential respondents raise. We suggest, on the basis of our CA inquiry, that tailoring can be done in relation to the early interactional environment when the base sequences involved in answering the phone, getting the potential recruit (whom we call a sample person) on the line, and engaging in the tasks of identification and recognition and others associated with the WLS. During the opening moments when the sample person comes on the line, she or he provides signals that may be more or less encouraging for making a request and obtaining participation.

Tailoring is related to the conversation analytic concepts of recipient design and context sensitivity (Sacks, Schegloff and Jefferson, 1974), and another way of reporting our findings is to say that interviewers can engage in purposeful recipient design by using requesting practices that are sensitive to the cues provided by the vocal and non-vocal (e.g., silences, intonation, etc.) conduct of sample persons. However, we also find that often interviewers are not able to ask for participation because the person they are calling 'blocks' the production of a request.

The study: data and methods

Because we have considerable information about those who were approached to participate in the 2004 round of the survey, the WLS provides an exceptional opportunity for our investigation. We could estimate the propensity of sample persons to participate, their education, cognitive test scores from high school, health status and past record of WLS participation (Maynard, Freese and Schaeffer, 2010). For the present investigation using conversation analytic (CA) methods, we analyse a small subset of calls. The initial sample for our quantitative analysis of the impact of features of the interaction on participation consisted of 200 pairs of calls (400 total) matched in their propensity to participate, but differing in outcome; thus one call in each pair ended in participation and one did not. We selected a subset of these 400 calls for the CA investigation, approximately half acceptances and half declinations. The sample was selected unsystematically based on the order of cases in sample lists and the availability of recordings; the resulting sample for the CA study included 57 acceptances and 51 declinations (a total of 108). We transcribed these 108 cases using conversation analytic conventions. (We use pseudonyms for all personal names, locations and schools.) WLS has high continuing participation for a longitudinal study, and although the rate of acceptances versus declinations in 2004 was about 88.7 per cent, non-response bias remains a concern (Hauser, 2005).

The problem, then, is, how do callers from the WLS survey ask sample persons to take part? Do interviewers tailor the requests to the interactional environment? Are there patterns to be found in successful and unsuccessful deliveries of the request? If so, can the more successful delivery style be taught in training?

Analysing requesting actions

CA research on requesting, and especially the more generic practices or structures that requests involve, provide a resource for gaining new insights into survey interview requests. Although previous studies of survey introductions have used CA (Houtkoop-Steenstra and van-den Bergh, 2002; Maynard and Schaeffer, 1997, 2002), none has fully explicated the more generic practices of ordinary requesting as a backdrop for understanding the dynamics of asking for participation. There is, then, both an applied and a theoretical character to the research we report here.

With regard to the theoretical background, the act of requesting has a respectable history in the philosophical tradition of speech act theory and in the pragmatics area of linguistics (Grice, 1975; Searle, 1969, p. 69; Searle 1975, p. 61). In pragmatics, the politeness theory of Brown and Levinson (1987) suggests that requests are done in 'indirect' ways to avoid threatening the 'face' of a recipient. From a CA standpoint, Curl and Drew (2008) review and critique these approaches, suggesting that speech act theory analytically overemphasises participants' cognition and use of rules of inference to go beyond the literal meaning of utterances, while politeness theory – although interested in the actual design of utterances – either fabricates examples or abstracts examples of actual, spoken utterances from their contexts of production.

Like Curl and Drew (2008), and following Heritage's (1984b, pp. 19–22) critique of attempts to develop causal, abstract explanatory models of social action without analyses of the concrete conduct of actors, we study requests in their interactional contexts. As is well known, rather than denoting psychological states, the CA notion of preference refers to design features of the talk, the interactional accompaniments both to the turns of talk that initiate actions and to the subsequent or responsive turns. For example, as first or initiating turns in two-part sequences, offers are preferred over requests. One way this is visible is that requests may be deferred through preliminary moves including a turn or turns that provide background to a projected request, as when a caller leads up to a request with 'I have a big favour to ask you', and then mentions a broken 'buttonholer' (Schegloff, 1980). These preliminary turns project a request for help without explicitly making it. Then the call recipient interjects, 'Rita, I told ya when I made the blouse I'd do the buttonholes'. Thus, the potential recipient of a projected and dispreferred action – a request – pre-empts with a preferred action – an offer. Other features of requesting also attest to its dispreferred and delicate status: When a person telephones to make a request, co-participants may work through several casual topics before the request is finally performed (Schegloff, 2007, pp. 83–7).

Understanding that, interactionally, requests are dispreferred actions in ordinary conversation gives us some purchase on the structural difficulties of requests issued in the institutional context of the survey interview. Thus, in telephone surveys, interviewers are working *against* the usual pattern. Instead of occurring after preliminary topics and background as would happen in ordinary conversation, in an interview the requesting action is often the *first* order of business in a call whose sole purpose is to complete an interview. Furthermore, although preliminary identification and recognition activities may precede the request, it is extremely rare for sample persons themselves to offer to participate in the survey before being asked to do so. In the sub-sample of 200 acceptance calls we studied, only two result from offers made by the people being called. One of these is shown in Extract 1 (see line 20).

Extract 1   HP059_107012g.wav

```
01   FR:   Hello?
02         (0.3)
03   FI:   ↑Hi:↓could I speak to Brenda Caw please?
04         (0.4)
05   FR:   ↑Speaking.
06         (.)
07   FI:   ↓°Hi:° I'm calling about the Wisconsin Longitudinal S:tudy, .hhhhh
08         u:m: (0.2) d- (0.2) didju receive a letter? (.) from us recently
09         regarding (this) stu [dy?  ]
10   FR:                        [Yeah:]I ↓did an' I work nights and I've
11         gotten all kinds of hhhhh
12   FI:   ↑Oh↓:: o [kay:.]
13   FR:            [messa]ges an' crap,
14         (0.2)
15   FI:   [↑Oh(h) o↓k(hh)ay I'm s:(hh)orry.]
16   FR:   [How long is this gonna take.    ]
17         (0.3)
18   FI:   .hhhhh U:m: well it's hard tuh say becuz it varies from person tuh
19         person, .hhhh on average, it['s-]
20   FR:                                [Wel]l let's just ↓do it.
21         (0.4)
22   FI:   Oh: okay? (0.4) if: at any time you need tuh go ↑just let me ↓know,
23         ...
```

Preceding the offer, at lines 10–11, 13, this female respondent (FR) complains about the *messages an crap* she has got and initiates a sequence at line 16 (in talk that overlaps the turn at line 15) asking about the time involved for completing an interview. The female interviewer (FI) answers in a hedging way (lines 18–19), and then FR urges movement toward the interview

(*Well let's just do it*, line 20), proposing that the task be done immediately. If we consider the sample person's complaints, her offer may be rather begrudging, but it does pre-empt the need for the interviewer to request participation. Although pre-emptive offers can happen in the survey introduction, the overwhelming pattern is for call recipients to withhold offering participation and for interviewers to move toward producing a formal request. And often, as we shall discuss in the Conclusion, the lead-up not only fails to elicit an offer. It can yield a different kind of pre-emption – a declination that blocks the interviewer from making a request.

Features of requesting actions

One of the most prominent features of requesting actions is the degree to which they exhibit entitlement to make the request (Curl and Drew, 2008; Heinemann, 2006; Lindström, 2005). Researchers have studied requests in 'institutional' settings such as home health care (Heinemann, 2006; Lindström, 2005) and a 'copy' shop (Vinkhuyzen and Szymanski, 2005), while Curl and Drew (2008) compared requests in ordinary conversation with calls to institutional settings including doctors' offices and other organisations. Requests in the form of imperatives or interrogatives with modal verbs ('can you', 'could you', 'will you') are high on entitlement and predominate in conversation,[3] whereas requests to institution-based co-participants are regularly formed as declaratives prefaced with variants of 'I wonder if' and are thereby low on entitlement. A second dimension that requests can display is an assumption that granting or accepting the request does not face many contingencies – that the recipient of the request can fulfil it because there are few impediments. A third dimension on which requests vary is the use of mitigating and politeness terms such as 'please' (Heinemann, 2006). Their use or non-use may diminish or reinforce the displays of entitlement or contingencies just described. For example, the request (arrowed) at line 7 in Extract 2, with the modal form *Could you*, is an entitled request in which there are no mitigating items and displays a 'known contingency' (Curl and Drew, 2008, p. 143) when mentioning Leslie's upcoming trip (line 9).

Extract 2   Field SO88:2:8:1

```
01   Les;   Hello:?
02          (0.3)
03   Gor:   It's Gordon.
04   Les:   .hhhh Oh Gordon. Sh'l I ring you back darling,
05   Gor:   Uh:: ↓no y- I don't think you can,
06          (0.3)
07   Gor:   But uh: just to (0.3) say (.) Could you bring up a letter.  ←
```

```
08            (.)
09   Gor:  When you come up,
10              .
11              .         ((Discussion re: which form))
12              .
13   Les:  Okay
```

Compare this request with one that a caller makes to a doctor, and which uses an 'I-wonder' preface (Curl and Drew, 2008).

Extract 3   25:1:9

```
Doctor:   .hhHello:
Caller:   Hello I. I'm wonderin' if a doctor could call and see
          Robert Smith please
```

With such prefaces, requests to persons in institutional settings are formatted to display low entitlement and an awareness of the contingencies surrounding granting of the request. These displays may be general enough to be accomplished by the 'I-wonder' preface alone – what Gill (1998) has called a 'speculative' one – or there may be a more concrete naming of contingencies (Curl and Drew, 2008, p. 141).

As we examine survey requests, we will see that modal verbs and 'I-wonder' prefaces play a role in displaying entitlement but do so in relation to other aspects of the request, including those based on the scripted introduction. In addition, in a slight departure from Curl and Drew (2008), we distinguish 'contingency' as a separate dimension of requests from entitlement. Overall, we suggest that different formats for requesting, beyond displaying the 'stance' of speakers toward the projected 'grantability' of a request (Curl and Drew, 2008, p. 149), can respond to concrete features of the interactional environments in which the request is produced. Requests may be sequentially retrospective and take account of the interaction so far, in addition to projecting a type of next action. To adapt Heritage's (1984, p. 242) felicitous words, requests in various ways are often 'context-shaped' as well as 'context renewing'.

Before we consider requests for participation in the WLS interview, two matters require our attention because they are literally and materially prior aspects of the situation in which interviewers and call recipients talk to one another. One is the advance letter that is sent to sample persons, and the other is the computer script on which interviewers can base their introduction for requesting participation. It is crucial to take into account this kind of ethnographic context so as to make sense of the resources the institutional agents can call upon in designing their approach to sample persons (Maynard, 2003, ch. 3).

Advance letter

All calls in our CA collection are initial telephone contacts with the sample person for the 2004 survey. However, in the WLS, as in many surveys, the effort to secure participation begins with an advance letter. If sample persons read the letter, they may regard various attributes of the survey discussed in the letter positively and be more disposed to take part (Roose, Lievens and Waege, 2007, pp. 413–15). Overall, we speculate that an advance letter affects the context within which the initial contact takes place in several ways: It provides the interviewer with a resource to incorporate into her introduction, it may relieve the interviewer of needing to provide some details of identity or the purpose of the call, and some sample persons who have read the letter may become predisposed one way or another before getting the call.

Introductory script

For the phone call to a household, the WLS provides the interviewer with an introductory script in the form of a series of screens on the interviewer's monitor. The first screen of interest contains the following:

> Hello, my name is [SAY NAME]. I am calling from the University of Wisconsin Survey Center at the University of Wisconsin-Madison. May I please speak to [RESPONDENT'S NAME]? (IF NECESSARY: We're not advertising or selling anything.)

If the person who initially answers the phone appears to be the targeted sample person, the interviewer's script reads:[4]

> Is this the [RESPONDENT'S NAME] that was enrolled in [NAME OF HIGH SCHOOL] High School in 1957? [IF YES:] As you probably recall from our recent letter, we are doing a follow-up study of our sample of people who were Wisconsin high school seniors in 1957. We'd like to interview you now for this important study.

At this point, interviewers have identified themselves by name and institutional identity, and have mentioned the original survey in 1957 and the recent letter. With its last sentence – 'We'd like to interview you now for this important study', the screen also poses the official or formal request. Consistent with previous research, we find that, in their practices, interviewers engage in considerable 'analytic alternation' (Maynard and Schaeffer, 2000): they use the script in their talk, but then embellish or improvise as the occasion calls for, only to return to a close reading of that script when possible or necessary. We know that WLS interviewers were trained to consider the scripted introduction as 'flexible', meaning that they could use it as a guide rather than following it verbatim (Houtkoop-Steenstra and van-den Bergh, 2002; Morton-Williams, 1993).

Forms of requesting in WLS interviews

Our examination of practices indicates that interviewers show sensitivity to the interactional environment in which the survey request occurs, including the various kinds of detailed vocalisations as well as silences from the sample member and sometimes from a spouse or other informant who initially answers the phone. Depending on these detailed cues, we came to classify the actions of sample persons or informants when answering an interviewer's call as discouraging, encouraging or ambiguous, following how the interviewers themselves seemed to orient to the cues.

Past CA research offers a useful guide to understanding among non-professionals and requests where non-professionals appeal to staff members in particular institutional (e.g., health care) settings. Patients request attention from doctors, customers request services at shop counters and so on. However, in requests for survey participation, the roles are reversed. Here, institutional staff (interviewers) make requests of individuals who are approached solely because they were 1957 Wisconsin high school graduates and not in their occupational or other institutional identities. This means that while our study adapts the concepts of entitlement, contingency and mitigation described in earlier studies of institutional and ordinary interactions, we also add two relevant dimensions of survey requesting – task partitioning and pre-emption – into the analysis, as is shown in the list below:

1. Entitlement. Scripted requests in the WLS ('We'd like to interview you now for this important study') exhibit entitlement in the sense of claiming a right to the interview by taking participation for granted through the syntax and verb forms being employed. Spoken interviewers' requests nonetheless vary in the degree of entitlement. Those that are relatively high in entitlement, as compared with those that are not, employ modal verbs ('we *would* like to interview you now') or turn-initial copular verbs ('*is* this a good time to start the interview?'). Requests are relatively higher in entitlement when they use a declarative syntactic form as compared with an interrogative syntactic form, except when a declarative request contains a 'wondering' preface ('we were wondering if now is a good time to start the interview') or other prefacing phrase of speculation (Gill, 1998).

2. Contingency. WLS survey requests vary in when they suggest the interview could be done. Those that present only the option of doing the interview 'now' – what we call 'one option' requests – display a presumption that there are no obstacles or contingencies that stand in the way of current participation. Those that exhibit an orientation to a possible high level of contingencies pose multiple options, for example by saying that the interview could be done now or later (or that it could be postponed until a more convenient time, or after the survey centre sends additional information about the survey).

3. Task partitioning. Interviewers sometimes offer to break the interview into parts. When interviewers simply ask, for example, 'to interview' the sample person or 'to do the study', they imply that it would be completed in one sitting (low partitioning). In contrast, when an interviewer asks to 'start' or 'begin' the task, or offers to complete the interview 'in parts', the request can be heard as implying that the instrument could be administered incrementally (high partitioning).

4. Mitigators. WLS survey interviewers vary in their use of politeness markers and other hedges such as 'please', 'just', 'some', 'might', or 'trying' that can weaken the level of entitlement of a request (Brown and Levinson, 1987; Watts, 2003). For example, although one way a request can be high in entitlement is by use of modal verbs, such a request can also include mitigating terms that diminish the level of entitlement, as when an interviewer asks, 'Would you be able to work on that some this morning', and the 'be able to' and 'some' soften the request.

5. Pre-emption. Sometimes interviewers skip sections of the opening script prior to the request, including sections that verify whether the recipient is a 1957 graduate of a particular high school, ask about the advance letter or state the purpose of the call ('doing a follow-up study'). Because they omit this material, such pre-emptive requests get produced early in the call. In the contrasting category are requests that are preceded by most or all sections of the scripted opening and therefore occur later.

Using these five practices and analysing the interactional environments of 69 explicit requests in our sub-sample of 108 cases, we were able to classify requests as relatively cautious or presumptive, where these are ends of a continuum through which interviewers design their utterances. Table 4.1 depicts a continuum on which requests can be arrayed, with strongly cautious requests at one end and strongly presumptive requests at the other.

Table 4.1 Continuum of cautious and presumptive requests

Fully cautious requests	Requests that are ambiguous	Fully presumptive requests
Low entitlement ('I wonder if . . '. or comparable prefacing)	Low or high entitlement	High entitlement ('We would like' 'is' prefacing)
High contingency: two timing options ('now' or another time)	High or low contingency	Low contingency: only 1 timing option ('now')
Task partitioning ('start' or 'begin')	Possible task partitioning	No task partitioning
Use of mitigators	Some mitigators	No mitigators
All three preliminary sequences present: sample person verification, letter receipt, study description	One or two preliminary sequences pre-empted	Pre-emption of all three preliminary sequences: sample person verification, letter reference, study description

Fully presumptive requests are those in which at least three of the following are present: entitlement is high through the use of modal verbs ('would') or copular verbs ('is'); only one option is presented for the timing of the interview; there is no task partitioning; there is no mitigation; or there is pre-emption of at least one of the following scripted statements: sample person verification ('is this the [name of person] who graduated from [name of high school] in 1957?'), reference to the advance letter, or description of the study. Fully cautious requests are those in which there are at least three related practices – that is, entitlement is low, more than one timing option is presented, task partitioning is present, there is mitigation (at least two forms), and there is no more than one pre-emption. Some requests are in between, in that, for example, a request can be 'mostly' presumptive or cautious depending on which and how many of the practices that interviewers deploy.

Survey requests in their interactional environments

Discouraging environments and requesting

Sample persons or others who answer the telephone can create a discouraging interactional environment with the content of their statements, by failing to respond when an interviewer's talk provides an opportunity, responding at such points in a terse fashion, and imbuing their talk with various prosodic cues (pacing, intonation, volume) that show resistance. For example, in one of our calls (HP005), a female informant replies to an interviewer's request to speak to a male sample person by asking, 'Who's calling please?' This response presents at least a mild challenge to the interviewer because it is a dispreferred response to the request (the preferred response being 'yes' or something comparable), and it inserts a repair sequence before the request is actually answered, thus suggesting that there is trouble with the request (Schegloff, 1979:38). The interviewer then identified himself as calling from the WLS and reported that they had called 'a couple days ago'. The informant replied, 'Yep, many times', in what might be a mild rebuke. On some calls, it is possible to hear offline interaction between the informant and the sample person that exhibits a stance toward the interview, but in this case, the informant said she had to 'go down and let him know' and nothing was audible for about 25 seconds. That she had to retrieve him from elsewhere in the household, taking nearly a half-minute to do so, might also be relevant to the interviewer.

When the sample person (MR) comes to the phone and, in response to the interviewer (line 2), confirms his identity, it is with a terse, downward intoned *yes* at line 3.[5]

Extract 4   HP005

```
01  MR:  .hhh Hello?
02  MI:  tch .h ↑Hi Mister Martino? hh
03  MR:  Yes.
04  MI:  My name is Brandon Johnson. I'm calling from the Wisconsin
05       Longitudinal Study? .h Ah d- we sent you a letter ahu:::h probly   about
06       th:ree months ago. I don't know if it- do you remember what (0.4) th- ah
07       Wisconsin Longi↑tudinal ↑Study is?
08       (0.3)
09  MR:  No.
10       (.)
11  MI:  #No? .hh Um (0.3) es↑sentially what it is is back in nineteen fifty
12       seven when you gradu↑ated from uh Stockdale ↑High School I think it
13       ↑says. .hh Um (0.4) we did a s- we began a st↑udy with you and
14       we've talked with you about ↑ev'ry:: twelve years since then?
15       (0.4)
16  MI:  .hh Do you #re↑member ↑that at all?
17       (0.9)
18  MR:  Ye:ah I remember o::ne.
19       (.)
20  MI:  Okay. .hh well- (.) basically it's been a↑bout (0.2) n:: eleven
21       years, and so we're ↑doing another wa:ve of this study right now.
22       .hh um .h I was wonder↑ing if- do you have some t↑ime to maybe
23       begin it ↑now or would you like us to send you another letter to
24       remind you about what it is?
25       (0.2)
26  MR:  ↑I':::m not gonna ↓be innerested sir. hh
```

And, after the interviewer (MI) identifies himself by his name and the name of the study (lines 4–5), the possible complete turn, its questioning intonation and the subsequent in-breath (line 5) occasion an opportunity for acknowledgment by MR, but he bypasses this opportunity. The interviewer's claim of having *sent you a letter* (lines 5–6) also meets with no response, and when MI asks whether MR remembers the WLS, MR delays (line 8) and then answers in the negative (line 9), again tersely and with downward intonation. As MI begins to describe the study, he embeds an implicit confirmation request about the MR's high school (lines 11–12), but receives no response (notice the in-breath and other hesitations at line 13). After MI completes the study description and ends this utterance with rising intonation (lines 13–14), MR still withholds response. Subsequently MI asks again whether MR remembers the study (line 16). MR delays in answering, and then only does so with a weak confirmation token and with a vague reference that minimises his previous involvement (line 18). In a number of ways, then, this sample person, like the informant who answered the phone, shows a discouraging stance toward the possibility of participation in the interview.

In this discouraging context, after MI confirms MR's apparent remembrance by suggesting a time span since the last interview and identifies the study as *another wave* (lines 20–21), he produces a request with a number of cautious features. At line 22, there is hesitation before the request, a preface that is low in entitlement *(I was wondering if)*, a re-started utterance *(do you have some time to maybe begin it now...)* that is mitigated with the *maybe*, a suggestion of partitioning (with *begin*), and a version of two options for timing (*now* or later after re-sending the letter). None of the preliminary sequences are omitted: there is a reference to the advance letter at lines 5–6, MI's proposal to the recipient that he graduated from Stockdale High School in 1957 (which serves as sample person verification) at lines 11–21, and a description of the study accomplished over lines 13–21. The interviewer, operating in a discouraging interactional environment produces an earnestly cautious request that is, nevertheless, turned down (line 26).

In some cases – in similarly discouraging environments – interviewers' cautiously formed requests do succeed in gaining acceptance. Our point here, however, is to observe that interviewers may embellish their requests in a variety of ways that are tailored to unfolding signs of discouragement from the sample person they are trying to recruit.

Encouraging environments and requesting

When interviewers obtain early cues from sample persons that can be interpreted as encouraging, they are regularly more presumptive in their requesting practices. Encouraging environments include those in which the sample persons produce relatively immediate and explicitly agreeing responses ('right' or 'correct' instead of 'yes/no'), employ expansive (rather than terse or one-word) confirmations and acknowledgments, modulate the pitch within these utterances substantially (rather than using monotone), or offer unprompted displays that they recognise the study or the purpose of the call.

In Extract (5), after MI introduces himself and asks to speak to the sample person (lines 3–5), MR relatively quickly acknowledges being that person (line 7), in an utterance with an intonational contour that rises and then falls slightly toward the utterance's end (sounding 'affiliative', per endnote 5). MR also acknowledges his high school graduation (line 11) at an early juncture in overlap with MI's inquiry (lines 8–10). And, when MI mentions the letter that had been sent (lines 13–14), MR not only interrupts to acknowledge receipt but also offers a report about where the letter is (lines 15–16).

Extract 5   HP058

```
01   MR:   tch Hello:?
02         (1.2)
03   MI:   Hullo: my name is: (.) Marcus Beale an' I'm calling from the
04         University of Wisconsin Survey Center: at the UW Ma:dison:? May I
05         speak to Nathan?
06         (0.2)
07   MR:   This ↑is Na:than.=
08   MI:   =.hh (.) Hullo: Nathan? u:m:: (0.3) tch (0.2) is this the Nathan
09         Getz who wuz enrolled at Shellfish High School in nineteen
10         fif[ty seven?]
11   MR:      [Yeah:.   ]
12         (.)
13   MI:   .hh An' as you probably recall from uh recent letter
14         [we're (°goin' thru°) ]
15   MR:   [Yeah I got it        ] leh- (.) layin' on my ↑de:sk ↓in thuh
16         bedroom.
17         (0.4)
18   MI:   =Al↓right well is now a good time ↑for ya? sir? ←
19         (0.2)
20   MR:   Hah?
21         (.)
22   MI:   Is now uh good time to do the study?
23         (0.3)
24   MR:   ↑Oh yah.
```

MI, at line 18, then pre-empts the next scripted item – the study description ('we are doing a follow-up study of our sample of people ...') – and produces a request that, with an initial copula, is high on entitlement. Additionally, by posing only the option of *now* as *a good time*, the request is low in contingency, and MI does not offer to partition the task or use any mitigation. The repair that MR initiates at line 20 indicates that he had not heard the line 18 request, and after it is reproduced, he readily agrees to do the interview. The 'oh'-prefaced form he uses proposes that his doing the interview can indeed be presumed (Heritage, 1998). So even as this interviewer fashions a strongly presumptive request in line with an encouraging environment, with his acceptance the sample person then exhibits an orientation suggesting that such presumptiveness was warranted.

Ambiguous environments and requesting

So far we have seen clear examples of the recipient of the call being either encouraging or discouraging. The opening of each of these phone calls is comparatively brief. Extract 5 takes only 25 seconds from MR's answering *hello* to his acceptance, *Oh yah*, at line 24, while Extract 4 is about 47 seconds long. In these moments, nonetheless, interviewers may confront stances toward the interview that are strongly encouraging or discouraging. In reviewing the 69 requests in our sub-sample of 108 cases,[6] we identified 34 interview openings as predominately encouraging for those requests and 10 as predominately discouraging. But things were sometimes more ambiguous. Twenty-five environments show either a mixture of encouraging or discouraging forms of responsiveness or consistently neutral displays. To us, they seem ambiguous, and we assume that if they are that way for us as analysts upon repeated inspection, it is because they are ambiguous for interviewers in the first place. That is, in classifying ambiguous environments, we are suggesting that interviewers' own orientations exhibit this analysis.

Extract 6 is an example of an ambiguous environment. Ultimately the interview is completed. When, at line 16, MR says his time is *real flexible* it constitutes acceptance and the interview progresses from there. But up to the point at which he agrees to begin, MR is expansive in some ways but only tersely responsive in others.

Extract 6   HP001

```
01 MR:  .h Hello. h
02      (0.2)
03 FI:  tch tch ↑Hi: can I speak tuh Evan ↓Royal please?
04 MR:  °Yeah° thissiz Evan speakin.
05 FI:  tch Hi:: u:h my name is Linda I'm calling from thuh University of
06      Wisconsin ↑Sur:vey Center? .hh Um:: is this the Evan Royal who
07      wuz enro:lled at Belmont High School in nineteen fifty ↑seven?
08 MR:  Yuh. ↑huh
09      (.)
10 FI:  .h ↑Great um: (.) well as you probably re↓call from our re↑cent
```

```
11      letter .h we're doing a followup st̲udy of our s̲ample of p̲eople who
12      ↓were uh Wisc̲onsin high school seniors in nineteen fif↑ty ↑seven .h
13      An we'd j̲ust like to interview you now for this im↑portant ↑study if
14      you've g̲ot some ti:me?
15      (1.5)
16 MR:  H̲ow ↑long does this take.
```

After FI asks for the sample person (line 3), the call recipient identifies himself in an expansive way, but does so with uniformly falling intonation. Then, after FI's personal and institutional identification (lines 5–6), there is no acknowledgment even though FI ends with rising intonation and takes an in-breath. In answering the sample person verification question (lines 6–7), however, MR produces an acknowledgement with notable pitch movement within the utterance. But MR does not acknowledge either the letter reference (lines 10–11) or study description (lines 11–12), and FI goes on to produce the request for participation. The environment is ambiguous in having both encouraging indicators (expansive self-identification, upward intoned confirmation) and discouraging indicators (downward intonation on the self-identification, withheld acknowledgment at turn transitions).

FI's request appears oriented to this ambiguity. While it is high on entitlement *(we'd just like to interview you)*, presents just one timing option *(now)*, and does not offer to partition the task, there is no pre-emption (sample person verification, letter reference and study description are all present) and there are two mitigating terms *(just, some)*. Three features associated with presumptive requesting and two characteristic features of caution are present. This is consistent with a broader pattern: in our collection of 25 requests occurring in ambiguous environments, 18 have more presumptive than cautious features. That is, requesting practices in ambiguous environments are more often like those in encouraging environments, and the smaller number of requests in ambiguous environments that are cautious are not strongly so. For example, in one call identified as having an ambiguous environment, the interviewer's request was, 'And I was just wondering if now is a good time for you to start that study'. This displays facets of presumptiveness – no display of contingencies and only one mitigating 'just' in the preface – but otherwise it is marked by low entitlement, task partitioning, and no pre-emption, all practices associated with caution.

We attribute these patterns of interaction in ambiguous environments to a phenomenon documented in previous research on survey call openings, an interactional-structural tendency toward optimism in dealing with initial queries and other responses from the sample person (Maynard and Schaeffer, 2002). Presumption optimistically treats ambiguous signals from sample persons as foreshadowing acceptance of the request.

Context sensitivity: tailoring and not tailoring the request

We have seen that interviewers regularly design requests in ways that are sensitive to facets of the sample person's vocal and non-vocal feedback during the opening moments of the call. Often, however, interviewers do not know exactly what may prompt encouraging or discouraging signs on the part of sample persons – whether it is their regard (or lack thereof) for the study, the University of Wisconsin, the tone or content of the advance letter, events unrelated to the survey request, or because the sample person just generally likes or dislikes surveys as such. But even if interviewers cannot infer the exact concerns of sample persons, they can and do design their requests to reflect interactional signs that are interpretable as taking a positive or negative stance toward the survey task.

When sample persons express their concerns verbally (commonly, for example, by asking how long the interview will last), interviewers can tailor their remarks to deal with such concerns. However, the type of tailoring that we identify here, tailoring to the interactional environment, has not been previously examined. In conversation-analytic terms, interviewers can engage in recipient design (Sacks, Schegloff and Jefferson, 1974, p. 727), displaying orientations through their practices to the particularities of that environment and individualising their requesting approach through the dimensions of caution and presumption depicted in Table 4.1. Preliminary evidence indicates that small nuances might make a difference.[7] Requesting in well-tailored or context-sensitive ways to interactional environments means acting presumptively in encouraging environments, cautiously in discouraging environments, and perhaps slightly presumptively (or less cautiously) in ambiguous ones. However, in our data a small number of requests are ill-fitted in the sense that an interviewer may act presumptively when a sample person shows discouragement, or very cautiously when there are signs of encouragement. We found that eight of 34 requests in encouraging environments, and three of 10 requests in discouraging contexts, seemed ill-fitted. For each of these ill-fitted requests, we attempted to examine other cases in our sub-sample involving the same interviewer. This was possible for nine of the 11 ill-fitted requests, and we found that in seven of the nine instances, other requests for that interviewer were consistent with the ill-fitting ones.

An example of ill-fitted requests: the case of 'Tom'

Consistency in an interviewer's formulating of requests suggests that some interviewers may have a particular style of requesting, either idiosyncratic to the person or based upon a mechanical reading of the script. For instance, one interviewer whom we call 'Tom' used a presumptive style in four different interviews in our sub-sample. In an environment that was encouraging (HP057), his request was *we'd like to interview you now for this important study, is that all right?* Other than the tag question, this request follows the script appearing on his computer screen and is high on entitlement, low on contingency, contains only one timing option and does not offer to partition the interview. Another interview (LP052) also has an encouraging context, and Tom's request again follows the script. In yet another of Tom's interviews that have a more ambiguous environment (LP062), he performs no pre-emptions but still formats his request in a predominately presumptive way: *Ah is now a good time to start that?* And, in an interview that tended toward discouraging (LP008), Tom is even more presumptive than he was in encouraging or ambiguous environment. He pre-empts several matters to say simply, *Is now a good time er:::-*, at which point the sample person declines. Thus, across three different environments, Tom is presumptive in his requesting practices, exhibiting a contextually insensitive style that seems impervious to the cues of his individual sample persons.

Accordingly, Tom appears similar to interviewers who appear to engage habitually in less tailoring and are less successful than others (Morton-Williams and Young, 1987, p. 51). As it turns out, of the 66 WLS interviewers who had 50 or more completed or refused cases, Tom has the highest refusal rate (45 per cent, compared to 12 per cent on average), which is strong evidence that being insensitive to the interactional environment – that is, being stylistic rather than responsive in one's requesting practices – is counterproductive. Our analysis provides insight into an interactional dynamic that could underlie findings that interviewers who follow a script have lower response rates than interviewers who use a less formal agenda (Houtkoop-Steenstra and van-den Bergh, 2002; Morton-Williams, 1993; Morton-Williams and Young, 1987). From the very inception of the phone call, such interviewers may refrain from tailoring their talk to the discernable encouraging, discouraging, or even ambiguous cues from sample persons regarding their stance toward being interviewed. They engage in uniform if not mechanical requesting practices, whether by following the script or otherwise having a relatively rigid personal style.

Environments, requests, and participation

The interactional sequences that eventually result in participation or non-participation begin in the opening few seconds, continue through introductory sequences, and continue beyond the request until acceptance or declination is determined. We do not yet have definitive quantitative information about how interactional environments and requests are associated with acceptances and declinations – precisely how sample persons' cues and interviewers' requesting practices influence response rates – but one matter is clear. In our 34 instances of encouraging environments, nearly all have presumptive requests and *every* case results in an acceptance, whereas in our 10 interviews with discouraging introductory environments there are 4 acceptances and 6 declinations, and in our 25 ambiguous cases are 18 acceptances and 7 declinations. In encouraging environments, both the interviewer's request and the outcome are relatively constant, and these are all likely to be determined in such close coordination that any role the interviewer might play in producing an acceptance, rather than simply allowing its expression, would be difficult to observe. In negative and ambiguous environments, however, there is more variability in both interviewer behaviour and the ultimate outcome, making these environments a potentially fruitful site for interviewer influence on the requesting outcome.

Concluding comments

So far, drawing on previous research about requesting as a social action, we have described and analysed facets of the pivotal act of asking for participation in the survey interview. In our collection of calls, however, we found that interviewers often are not able to produce a request because a sample person refuses relatively early in the call. We call this a 'blocking' move, in that sample persons may orient to the survey introduction as a pre-request and halt progression to an anticipated requesting sequence (Schegloff, 2007, pp. 33–4). Blocking declinations are both firm and common. In our subsample of 200 calls that resulted in declination, 126 (63 per cent) are done using blocking moves – that is, the sample person declines before the request is made (Maynard and Hollander, 2010).

Where previous research has identified tailoring as the strategies an interviewer uses to answer questions or otherwise deal with information that sample persons appear to seek when deciding whether to participate in a survey – usually after a request has been made – we suggest that, from the very inception of the phone call, it may be possible for interviewers to custom fit their progression to, and the formatting of, the request in ways that are sensitive to cues from the sample person. That is, when interviewers actively engage practices for recipient design, the overall activity of requesting is alive to the interactional environments in which it occurs. Interviewers, we have said, can act presumptively and thus more efficiently in encouraging environments, and cautiously in discouraging environments by working through preliminary, scripted utterances, and then forming their requests by showing low entitlement, an awareness of temporal contingencies, the capacity for task partitioning, and with mitigating hedges or 'politeness markers'. In ambiguous environments, tailoring may mean being slightly presumptive or acting optimistically with regard to prospects for obtaining acceptance.

Sample persons, for their part, may seize interactional opportunities to issue refusals before the request has been made. That is, they block the interviewer's projected requesting action. Skilled tailoring, therefore, may not just facilitate having a request to participate accepted, it also may enhance the likelihood of making a request in the first place. Once a request is generated, the preference for agreement may lend a dynamic to the interview request that derives from the interaction order rather than attributes of the survey.

To what extent variation in interviewer practices, the interactional moves of sample persons, and the interrelation between these practices and moves have readily measurable effects on response rates awaits further, quantitative investigation. For example, our preliminary work has shown three patterns. Two of the patterns are documented in Schaeffer, Garbarski and Freese (2010). One is that when sample persons ask questions about 'who' is calling or 'what' the survey is about before the interviewer has requested participation, it is a likely precursor to a blocking declination. A second pattern is that when they ask about how long the interview will take, the request is associated with acceptance. A third pattern, examined in Maynard and Hollander (2010), is that when interviewers identify themselves (both personally by name and institutionally by designating the university or study from which calls originate) *before* asking for the sample person, this increases the odds of acceptance, whereas delaying self-identification until *after* asking for the sample person ('May I speak to Joe Smith?') decreases those odds.

Our research has meant reviewing how interviewers are trained to interact with respondents during the opening of calls at the University of Wisconsin Survey Center. One implication of our analysis for interviewer practice is clear. Given that the most consistent and presumptive interviewer in our data was also the least successful, mechanical styles of requesting participation and, for example, ignoring discouraging signals from the sample person are to be avoided. Tailoring, or showing context sensitivity, is something that can be done from the very beginning of the phone call, and our analysis suggests the need to find ways to train interviewers to recognise signs of encouragement and discouragement. In surveys where the sample person's name is known, our analysis indicates that interviewers should identify themselves before asking for that person (Hollander, 2008). The analysis in Schaeffer and colleagues (2010) suggests that when a sample person moves toward a blocking declination, a strategy of retreating quickly to avoid the delivery of the blocking declination is recommended. This leaves open the possibility of a later attempt at refusal conversion, whereas a blocking declination often forestalls any such call-back. Such a strategy, however, requires both being able to train interviewers to recognise that such a declination has been foreshadowed and experiments to demonstrate the viability of the strategy. Although further research, possibly involving experiments, will be useful in discerning further useful strategies, we believe that our recommendations may be helpful for designing requests and solicitations with different types of surveys (cross-sectional as opposed to longitudinal) and in other settings – calls for tissue donation (Weathersbee, 2009), for example – wherein organisational actors are approaching people in their everyday lives for purposes of eliciting altruistic contributions.

Notes

1. This research was supported by a grant (#0550705) from the National Science Foundation. The authors gratefully acknowledge Robert M. Hauser, Taissa Hauser and the Wisconsin Longitudinal Study (WLS) for digital data and data collection, which were obtained with support from the National Institute on Aging grants R01AG09775 and P01AG021079. The WLS is supported by National Institute on Aging grant R01 AG0123456, and by core grants to the Center for Demography and Ecology at the University of Wisconsin-Madison (R24 HD047873) and to the Center for Demography of Health and Aging at the University of Wisconsin-Madison (P30 AG017266). We are grateful for able research assistance from Dana Garbarski, Matt Hollander and Jason Nolen. Ceci Ford provided pivotal suggestions on the manuscript.
2. Information about the WLS can be found at http://www.ssc.wisc.edu/wlsresearch/
3. However, see Lindström's (2005) discussion of home health care as a kind of institutional interaction, where a patient, because of her role as a care recipient, often shows entitlement to make requests of home help assistants even while orienting to the dispreferred nature of requesting. Heinemann (2006) examines a similar setting – home health care – in Denmark, and suggests that low entitlement is exhibited in positive interrogatives with modal verbs (such as 'can', 'could', 'would', 'will', 'should', 'shall') addressing a recipient's willingness ('Would you please be kind enough to tuck it [a napkin] down to me?'), or with 'May I' prefaces asking permission to request ('May I ask to get a bit further into the chair?'). In contrast, negative interrogatives using modal verbs such as 'can' ('Can't you turn on the overhead light?') or 'shall' ('Shall I not get wiped?') or 'won't' display high entitlement, presupposing that the request will be fulfilled.
4. If the person answering the phone is not the WLS respondent, the interviewer is to ask for the respondent. If the respondent is available and comes to the phone, interviewers are scripted to again provide their name and that of the University of Wisconsin Survey Center before verifying the school from which the respondent graduated in 1957.
5. For a recent study of distinctive ways in which tokens and nodding can indicate affiliation or disaffiliation, see Stivers (2008). Müller's (1996) study of German tokens suggests that those which affiliate to prior turns are more varied within-utterance intonation and in length than those that disaffiliate, and we take his study as indicative for our English data, although systematic comparative research

between German and English remains to be done. What we hear as downward intonation, in our analysis, is taken as disaffiliation, while within utterance variable intonation on tokens is impressionistically affiliative. Although we do not more systematically investigate the prosody of the talk in these interview openings, in line with previous research (Groves and Couper, 1998), we recognise its importance and introduce observations regarding tone, pacing or emphasis at relevant points in our analysis.
6. In 39 cases, interviewers were unable to make the request, as discussed below (and see note 4).
7. For example, Nolen (2008) has shown that using two-option 'high-contingency' as opposed to one-option 'low contingency' requests is associated with more polite responses even when the response is a declination.

5
Improving Ethnic Monitoring on a Telephone Helpline[1]

Sue Wilkinson

How can Conversation Analysis be used to help an organisation handle sensitive questions over the phone? In this chapter, I describe my experiences with a telephone-based helpline service whose call-takers were experiencing real difficulties in asking callers to declare their ethnicity, as part of a call-monitoring process.

Ethnicity statistics are increasingly collected by organisations seeking to monitor their service provision. According to the UK Government Office for National Statistics (www.ons.gov.uk/census), more than 43,000 public bodies now use a Census-based ethnicity question for equal opportunities monitoring. The organisation with which I am working – a health-related charity (which will need to remain anonymous) – is not unusual, then, in having recently introduced ethnic monitoring of callers to its telephone helpline. Its reasons for so doing are both ideological and pragmatic: the charity aims to provide an inclusive, accessible service – and it needs to demonstrate to potential funders that it is meeting this aim.

When I began work with the charity (in mid-2007), it was already logging a number of aspects of its helpline calls on a fairly standard monitoring form and collating this information to provide a quarterly statistical summary to all volunteer call-takers. However, the addition of an ethnicity question to the form (just three months earlier) seemed to be posing a particular burden on call-takers. The organisation's statistical summary report for the quarter before I began data collection reported that:

> The ethnicity of callers was recorded for the first time this quarter, although not all monitoring sheets contained this information. At least two callers found it offensive that we should ask such a question. It may be necessary to explain that we need this information in order to gain funding.

76 *Applied Conversation Analysis*

It was partly to help the organisation figure out how to ask the ethnicity question without causing offence, and how to encourage all volunteers to collect the information (and collect it appropriately), that I focused an initial analysis of the recorded calls on the ethnicity question and callers' answers to it. On the basis of my analysis, it has been possible to develop advice to the organisation on how it might re-word the ethnicity question, and how call-takers might be trained to ask it (and other call-monitoring questions) in such a way as to reduce the problems they are encountering – and also increase the validity of the ethnic monitoring statistics. Based on recordings of 180 calls from six volunteers, this chapter will outline key aspects of that advice, reporting some of the ethnographic analysis and Conversation Analysis from which it derives.

The institutional task

When the ethnicity question was introduced, volunteer call-takers on the helpline now had to log, using write-in or tick boxes on a monitoring sheet, these five pieces of information for each call received:

(i) Type of caller (e.g., 'sufferer', relative/friend, health professional);
(ii) Main reason for call (e.g., information, dealing with health professionals, benefit advice);
(iii) Source of information about the organisation (e.g., a health professional, a friend, the internet, newspapers/magazines, TV/radio);
(iv) Location of caller (logged as first part of postcode);
(v) Ethnicity of caller (call-takers asked to select one of five ethnicity categories: 'White European', 'Black African/Caribbean', 'Asian', 'Chinese/Japanese' and 'Other').

The organisation's statistical summary for the quarter in which I was collecting data reports a total of 507 calls to the helpline. Not surprisingly for a health-related helpline, callers were mostly 'sufferers', calling for 'information' about the condition, and most had heard about the organisation either via 'a health professional' or 'the internet'. On the ethnicity question, 86 per cent of calls were coded as from 'White European' callers; 2 per cent as from 'Asian' or 'Black African/Caribbean' callers; and the remaining 12 per cent as having no information on ethnicity logged.

An initial look at how the ethnicity question is asked

Even on a cursory first listening to the recorded conversations, it was apparent that call-takers were struggling to ask the ethnicity question, and – as we will see in the next section – many never do. Some volunteers did not know how to pronounce the word: for example, rendering it as *ethnis-sicity* or *eth: nicicity*. Some were apparently unsure quite what 'ethnicity' means, and substituted (presumably more familiar) 'everyday' terms, asking, for example, *what's your nationality* or *were you born in this country*. Others displayed considerable difficulty in producing the question at all (e.g., *Uh: (.) could I also I ass:: .h uh:m (0.6) <what ethnic group> you're under*), and/or displayed an explicit orientation to the question as a delicate one (e.g., *I hope you're not offended*).

Call-takers, then, varied among themselves: a few were comfortable with the ethnicity question, but most were not, and the organization could usefully introduce training on this issue. To show some of the variability in the segments of interaction involving the ethnicity question, I will begin by contrasting a segment which runs off relatively smoothly with one which proves much more problematic. I will then focus more specifically on some of the particular difficulties volunteer call-takers display in asking the ethnicity question, together with some possible solutions to these difficulties.

First, then, here is one of the fairly rare cases in which the ethnicity question is asked – and answered – relatively unproblematically. It comes in the pre-closing phase of a 4-minute call, in which a newly diagnosed caller has asked to be sent an information pack. After the caller has declined the volunteer's offer of *a listening ear* (line 3), the volunteer moves towards closing with an invocation of future interaction (Schegloff, 2007) – an invitation to *contact us agai:n* (line 10) once the caller has received the information pack. She then collects the call monitoring details: first confirming the caller's source of information (lines 21–22), then asking her location (lines 24–25), and finally her ethnicity (lines 36–39). The sequence containing the ethnicity question is highlighted in bold typeface.

Extract 1 ('Marie')[2]

[C006]

```
01   Vol:   Uh:m >#w-# I mean< is there anything you: would like
02          to: (.) talk to me about >I mean I c'n n-n- you know
03          I'm a listening ear here if you would li:ke.
04          (.)
05   Mar:   Uh:m I do:n't think so=[not] at the moment n [o::. ]
05   Vol:                          [No.]                 [Ah ha]h.
06   Vol:   Fair enough:.
07   Mar:   But uhm you know as I say I can always phone you
08          ca:[n't I.]
09   Vol:      [Of cou]:rse. .hhh Well w- once you've got the
10          information pack by all mea:ns uhm do contact us agai:n.
11          A:nd .hh it's available- the helpline is available
12          Monday to Friday ten till fou:r [.hhh] and we'll be-=
```

```
13   Mar:                                    [yes ]
14   Vol:  =there's always someone available to speak to yo: [u.]
15   Mar:                                                    [Oh]
16         that's lo̱ve[ly.]
17   Vol:         [.hh]h uh:m but just before you go: uh:m
18         Ma̱rie (.) m-may I ask you: a kuh- one or two questions
19         plea:[se.=Is ] that alri:gh [t¿ .hh]
20   Mar:       [Yes.   ]              [Yes. ]
21   Vol:  Uhm so that was your doctor that gave you a lea:flet
22         you sai[:d.]
23   Mar:         [It w]a̱s. Ye[s. ]
24   Vol:                     [Ah ] hah. .hhhh uh:m and may I have
25         the first part of your po:stcode plea:se.=
26   Mar:  =It's R-R
27   Vol:  R-R
28   Mar:  seven two̱.
29   Vol:  seven two̱. .hh That's- it's only just for our re̱cords.=
30   Mar:  [ Yes. ]
31   Vol:  =[That's] a:ll. For our stati̱stics. [.hhh ]
32   Mar:                                      [D'you] want the re:st.
33   Vol:  No: that's alright.=It's just the first part.=It's just to
34         show us (.) you know roughly the (.) location as to where
35         people ca:ll from .hhhh An' one other question if I ma:y
36         .hh[hh uh]:m wha- we- we're looking at >you know< the=
37   Mar:    [Ye:s.]
38   Vol:  =ethni̱city of people who ca:ll.=Uh:m .hh are you white
39         Europe:an: black African [::]
40   Mar:                           [Oh] no I'm whi̱:te.
41   Vol:  You're white- white European. [.hhh That-]
42   Mar:                                [ Oh ye̱s. ]
43   Vol:  That's fine. <.hh It's only to- <.hh It's only just for uhm
44         our stati̱stics an:d you know [uh:m for r ]esea:rch as well.
45   Mar:                               [(No problem)]
46         (0.2)
47   Vol:  .hh But do feel free to contact us another ti:me [when- ]=
48   Mar:                                                   [( )   ]
49   Vol:  =when you get the informa:tion and you can discu̱ss it with
50         us.=
51   Mar:  =Tha̱nk you very mu:[ch.]
```

Although clearly not trouble-free, the way the ethnicity question runs off here is as good as it gets in any of the recorded calls. By contrast with other calls, the question does get asked; the volunteer uses the prescribed term (and pronounces it correctly), line 38; she begins to read out a list of the pre-designated response categories (although she only gets to the second of these), lines 38–39; when the response is a category not on the list, she does an understanding check (rather than presuming an answer), line 41; post-confirmation of the answer, she assesses it positively and provides a brief account for asking the question, lines 43–44; and she manages the transition into and out of ethnicity question sequence – and, indeed, the monitoring segment within which it is embedded – quite smoothly. Let us look in a little more detail at how these transitions are done.

First, the volunteer uses a formulation designed to forestall the imminent closing of the call (*just before you go*, line 17); she then issues a preliminary item[3] (Schegloff, 1980) – itself first repaired and then reissued for confirmation – seeking permission to collect the monitoring information (lines 18–19). After checking source of information (lines 21–22) and obtaining the caller's postcode (lines 24–29), the volunteer introduces the ethnicity question with another preliminary item (line 35), which is 'and-prefaced' – marking it as the next in a series of questions (Heritage and Sorjonen, 1994), followed by some information as to what *we're looking at* (lines 36 and 38), before asking the question itself and offering candidate response categories. Her post-response justification (lines 43–44) is similar to the one previously offered (at lines 29 and 31) for the postcode question. Once the monitoring segment is completed, the volunteer reissues the invitation (previously made at lines 9–10) to contact the helpline again after receiving the information pack (lines 47–50), thereby returning the call to the (pre-closing) trajectory it was on before she initiated the segment. She moves it on to closure shortly thereafter (data not shown).

Compare this with an instance in which the asking and answering of the ethnicity question does not run off smoothly (much more typical in my data set). Again, we are in pre-closing, and the volunteer has just asked the 'type of caller' question, presenting the category 'sufferer' for confirmation (lines 1–2). This is clearly not recognised as a monitoring question by the caller, who proceeds to topicalise her 'suffering' (lines 3–19). The volunteer asks the ethnicity question at line 26, and again the sequence containing it is shown in bold.

Extract 2 ('*Bella*')

[D012]

```
01  Vol:    .hhh Uhm (0.4) and u- y you're a fellow su- you're
02          a sufferer are yo [u.]
03  Bel:                     [Ye]ah I've j[ust      ] r:ecently
04  Vol:                                  [Yeah.    ]
05  Bel:    bee[n: ]
06  Vol:       [bee]n
07  Bel:    been:: very recently just been di[agnosed I've been
```

```
08   Vol:                              [Oh have you.
09   Bel:   suff]ering for quite some time but no [body p]ut
10   Vol:                                         [Yes.   ]
11   Bel:   (put their finger o   [n it and ] now they've put a name
12   Vol:                         [No.       ]
13   Bel:   to it.
14   Vol:   Good yeah. [hhhHHH ]hhh
15   Bel:              [So uh:m]
16          (.)
17   Bel:   So at least they know now.
18   Vol:   Yes[::. °heh°    ]
19   Bel:      [You know what ] s:teps to take
20   Vol:   Ye [s.]
21   Bel:      [( ] ¿)
22          (0.2)
23   Vol:   Yes. .h  [ h h ]h
24   Bel:            [(Mm.)]
25          (0.2)
26   Vol:   Um what- ↑what is your ethnicity. hh [hh  ]
27   Bel:                                        [I be]g
28   Bel:   your pardo[n,]
29   Vol:             [Wh]a- what is your ethnicity. Where
30          w- (.) where're you from- where were you born.
31          .hhhh
32          (1.4)
33   Bel:   I was actually born in Oxford but I grew up on the
34          west coast of Californi[a.]
35   Vol:                          [.h]hh I thought you a u- .h
36          I'm asking this for our s for statistics[:.]
37   Bel:                                           [Oh] [right.]
38   Vol:                                                [.hhh  ]
39          That's what it's for: but I thought you had an
40          £American ac  [cent anyway but£  ]
41   Bel:                 [(Yes) I was born i ]n Oxford
42          (I  [                            ]
43   Vol:      [but you were actually born]
44          [in Oxford so wh      ]ite yo- you're white European
45   Bel:   [( yes.)              ]
46   Vol:   .=It's ↑just we need       [to   ] keep recor:ds:.
47   Bel:                              [Yeah.]
48   Vol:   .h [hh A  ]nd it's for resear- it- it's for- (0.2)
49   Bel:      [Right.]
50   Vol:   more for funding things really: you know .hhh um
51          if we apply for funding they need to know the (0.4)
52          cross section of people that are actually
```

```
53              i-using the helpine and that's what it's for.
54              .h  [hh ]
55     Bel:         [Oh o]kay.
56     Vol:    Yeah.
57              (0.2)
58     Bel:    Right that's super.
```

Here, the volunteer launches the ethnicity question directly, without any kind of 'pre' – and also disjunctively from the prior sequence concerning recent diagnosis and long-term suffering. As is often the case with a turn which appears to the recipient to be 'topically disconnected' (Drew, 1997), this is met with an 'open class' repair initiation (*I beg your pardon*, lines 27–28) from her recipient. The repair solution produced by the volunteer consists of three different formulations of the ethnicity question in quick succession (the repeat of *what is your ethnicity*, followed by *where are you from*, and *where were you born*, lines 29–30). The caller's – not surprisingly, delayed – response addresses the third, then the second, of these, rather than providing a response to the repeated first question. None the less the volunteer takes the upshot of this (via 'so', line 44) to be that the caller may be considered *white European* (line 44), as well as, post-response, claiming already to have noticed the caller's accent (lines 35, 39–40) and accounting extensively for having asked the question (lines 36, 48–53).

In Extract 2, then, one key problem is that it is insufficiently clear to the caller that the ethnicity question is one of a series of monitoring questions – or, indeed, that call-monitoring is underway at all. One solution is to train volunteer call-takers to use 'pre's, both in introducing the bureaucratic task of call monitoring, and so marking it off from the rest of the call (as the call-taker does in Extract 1, lines 17–19); and in introducing each question in turn, including the ethnicity question, as the next in a series of questions (as in Extract 1, line 35). They can signal more strongly that each new question/answer pair is linked to the previous one and is part of a single ongoing activity by 'and-prefacing' each question (as the call-taker does for the ethnicity question in Extract 1, line 35). 'And-prefacing' can also serve to 'normalize or detoxify the question it prefaces', implying 'a routine, task-centred motivation for questions which might otherwise be treated as troublesome by virtue of their content' (Heritage and Sorjonen, 1994, p. 22).

A second key problem seen in Extract 2 is that, given the way the ethnicity question is asked (multiple formulations of the question, each targeting different information), it is insufficiently clear to the caller just what kind of response is required. Training volunteers how to formulate the question, in such a way as to promote clarity (just one formulation, as in Extract 1, line 38), and – as we will see – consistency in use of a single formulation across calls, will ameliorate this.

More broadly, these two extracts suggest there are two particular difficulties for volunteers in managing the sequential slot in which call monitoring takes place. The first is to effect the transition from the main business of the call to the monitoring questions; the second is actually getting to ask the ethnicity question itself. In what follows, I will focus mainly on the difficulties associated with asking the ethnicity question. I will examine: (a) how it comes about that volunteers don't ask the ethnicity question at all; (b) how they ask the ethnicity question in ways that get (or are likely to get) inaccurate answers; and (c) some of the (interactional) reasons why the ethnicity question is difficult to ask.

Volunteers don't always ask the ethnicity question

There is a huge discrepancy between the organisation's reported statistic of 12 per cent of calls for which no ethnicity information was logged (in the quarter in which I was collecting data) and the number of calls in my sample in which no ethnicity information was requested by the call-taker. My sample constitutes about a third of the total number of calls for the quarter, and *68 per cent* of these do not include (any version of) the ethnicity question. This discrepancy raises the possibility that call-takers may sometimes *presume* a particular ethnicity on the basis of contextual information, and tick an ethnic category box based on that presumption, without asking – and obtaining an answer to – the relevant question. The organisation could usefully add a tick box labelled 'Question not asked' to the response options for the ethnicity question. The availability of an option to record the data as 'missing' would be likely to reduce the incidence of reliance on presumption alone.

Within my data set I have instances of call-takers not asking the ethnicity question at all; of trying to ask the question but failing; and of avoiding or suppressing the question where it could have been asked. I will look at each in turn.

Not asking the question

One call-taker never requests information about ethnicity, and two others do so very infrequently. Presumably these volunteers are non-cooperative with the monitoring process because they find (or expect to find) it difficult or embarrassing, or because they cannot see the point of it. In order to encourage all volunteers to ask the ethnicity question, volunteer training could usefully include specific discussion of ethnic monitoring: both why it is important to do it and ways in which it can be done (see below for specific suggestions). While many volunteers display a general awareness that call monitoring is required by funding bodies, it might be useful to explain the goal of an inclusive service and how ethnic monitoring – in particular – fits into the practice of call monitoring more generally.

Another context in which the ethnicity question is regularly not asked (or in which the response may be recorded inconsistently) is when the call is made on behalf of someone else (e.g., a pharmacist on behalf of a client [D021], a mother on behalf of a daughter [B010]). In the first of these calls, the volunteer does not ask the ethnicity question (presumably she assumes it is not relevant to record this for a health professional); in the second, the caller gives both her own and her daughter's ethnicity – and it is unclear which of these the volunteer records. Volunteer training should be explicit that in every case it is the ethnicity of the *caller* which is required.

Trying to ask but failing

Here are two instances in which the volunteer call-taker tries, but fails, to ask the ethnicity question. In the first, the volunteer tries but fails to make the transition to (any of) the monitoring questions; in the second, the problem is specifically the ethnicity question itself.

Extract 3   ('Barbara')

[D011]

```
01   Vol:   I'm sure: there is help somewhere: in: the area
02          >where a< you're living:.
03          (0.5)
04   Bar:   (Y [es. )   ]
05   Vol:      [You kn ]ow.
06   Bar:   #Thank yo      [u so much#.]
07   Vol:                  [Uh:    I m]ean the citizens advice
08          bure-ee-au ('ve got) bureau 've got (.) .hh loads
09          of uhm: contacts and they you know they might even be
10          able to help hh .hhhh some- s: give you some
11          suggestions o-of any v- (.)voluntary organizations
12          in the area (0.2) you know that might be able to
13          help you. .hh[hh]
14   Bar:                [Ok][ay th]ank
15   Vol:                    [Uhm, ]
16   Bar:   you: I'll I'll try that.
17          (0.4)
18   Bar:   (Uh I-) I'll do that thank you
19          very much.
20   Vol:   Okay,
21   Bar:   Thank you.
22   Vol:   Uhm: (.) now before you [go:,          ]
```

```
23                              [((hanging up))]
24    Vol:   Hello?
25           (0.5)
26    Vol:   Aa:rghh
27           ((dialing tone))
```

The volunteer's *now before you go* (line 22) is identifiable as a common form of 'pre' often used before the monitoring questions (as in Extracts 1, 5, 8 and 10). However, she has left producing this too late, and the caller is already hanging up (line 23). We can notice that in this interaction, it is the *caller* who initiates pre-closing – with her thanks at line 6, repeated at lines 14–16, 18–19 and 21 – leaving the volunteer in second position, with much less control over the trajectory of the interaction. It is much harder from this position to create a slot in which to ask the monitoring questions. (Contrast this with Extract 1, where it is the *volunteer* who initiates pre-closing with her invocation of future interaction, and can then more readily create a call-monitoring slot; also Extract 8.) Many of the failures to ask the monitoring questions in general – and the ethnicity question in particular – occur when the volunteer attempts to do this from second position, when the caller has already initiated pre-closing. One solution is for training to show volunteers ways of initiating pre-closing themselves, rather than responding to the caller's initiation. (This is also likely to be of more general use in helping them to close lengthy calls: although the organization has a target maximum of 20 minutes, many calls are longer than this.)

In Extract 4 the volunteer is justifying asking the monitoring questions, and is hearably headed for the ethnicity question when she says *we've been asking people what origin they are* (lines 7–9). She never gets there.

Extract 4   ('Sandra')

[B005]

```
01    Vol:   But >as I say< we do want to kno:w if it's
02           prevalent sa:y .hh in an area that's got a
03           lo:t .h 'v electrical ac- activity a l-
04           a lot of [electri]cal py:lon[s.]
05    San:            [Yea:h. ]          [Ye]a:h. I know
06           what you're say:[in'. Mm.]
07    Vol:                   [.hh It's] the same we've
08           been asking people .hh u:h what origin they
09           a:re.=We want to find out if it's .hh u. the
10           illness is right throughout the wo:rld.
11           (0.2)
12    San:   Yea[h.]
```

```
13   Vol:      [.h]h u:hm we kno:w that Asians in this
14             country have it.   [Tch! But] we don't know if
15   San:                         [Ri:ght. ]
16   Vol:      people in India Africa .h living in these
17   Vol:      countries have it. .hh Does heat affect it.
18             Does cold affect it. .hh We know it's
19             throughout Eu:rop [e- ]
20   San:                        [Co:]ld does affect- Co:ld.
21             When it's da- when it's cold it does make it
22             worse.=I [(              ] .)=I work=
23   Vol:               [Well this is it. ]
24   San:      =outsi:de u:h I can tell you no:w that cold
25             does make it wor:se.
```

The problem here is too long a 'pre' justifying the upcoming ethnicity question (lines 7–19). The volunteer is still continuing with her pre when she is interrupted by the caller (line 20) with an answer to the research question she has posed (at lines 17–18). They get into a discussion of problems with temperature control (and whether this is a symptom of the illness or due to the menopause) – this segues into a discussion of other symptoms, then into what should be written on benefits application forms, and the call closes without any return to the issue of what origin the caller is. The advice for training here is that volunteers should not over-justify the monitoring questions, particularly in advance of asking them. A brief account, preferably post-response (as in Extract 1, lines 29–31 and 43–44) is all that is needed.

Avoiding or suppressing the question

Sometimes volunteer call-takers avoid asking or suppress the ethnicity question. Although the question is not hearably missing for the individual helpline caller, it is missing for the call-taker who has not asked it. And it is missing for us as analysts: most clearly so when the other monitoring questions are asked, but there is a relevant absence in the slot where the ethnicity question should be. As analysts we can identify such relevant absences by looking across a corpus of calls in each of which the same bureaucratic task is (supposed to be) performed, and with reference to the guidelines from the organization for performing it. Such 'top-down talk' (Cameron, 2008) is generally highly regulated and standardised. When asked, the ethnicity question is almost always the last of the monitoring questions, and it generally follows the postcode question (as in Extract 1). Here is the segment of a call which moves to closing directly after the postcode question, without the ethnicity question ever being asked.

Extract 5 ('Jenny')

[E015]

```
01    Vol:      =Just before you go: could I: ask you: .hh for the
02              first three letters of your po:stco:de='cause
03              we need to monitor where our <calls
04              c [ome from>.]
05    Jen:        [The first  ] three letters. C-F four.
06              (1.8)
07    Vol:      B.
08              (0.4)
09    Jen:      No C [:]
10    Vol:           [C]:
11    (Jen):    C [: for] c-
12    (Vol):      [F:   ]
13              (.)
14    Jen:      C for Colin,=
15    Vol:      =Right.
16              (0.2)
17    Vol:      F four. That's lovely.
18              (0.2)
19    Jen:      ( [ )]
20    Vol:        [Th]ank you very much indeed.=
21    Jen:      =And thank you for your help.
22    Vol:      O:ka [y: t      ]ake care n [ow.]
23    Jen:           [Thank you.]           [ Ye]s.
24    Jen:      Thank you. Thank you. Bye bye.
25    Vol:      B[ye b  ]ye.
26    Jen:       [Bye.  ]
```

We do not know for sure why the volunteer suppresses the ethnicity question here – but this caller has both a marked Welsh accent and a Welsh postcode. Given the ways in which – as we will see – the ethnicity question is often asked of callers with marked accents, we can speculate that the volunteer presumes she is Welsh (and therefore to be coded as 'white European'). We do not know, however, whether she is white, or even European – and the advice to call-takers here is not to presume, but always to ask (and not to code without explicitly asking).

In sum, then, although some volunteers may simply be non-cooperative with the monitoring process, there are also interactional reasons for not asking the ethnicity question. These include failure to make the transition to (any) of the monitoring questions, often when trying to do so from second position; and failure to ask the ethnicity question itself, sometimes because of over-justifying it in advance. Volunteers may also be uncertain whether it is appropriate to ask the ethnicity question, or presume that they already know the answer.

Volunteers ask the ethnicity question in ways that get inaccurate answers

When call-takers *do* ask the ethnicity question, the variability in the way they ask it – and consequently the kind of answer they get – has profound implications for the validity of the organisation's monitoring statistics. Some ways of asking the question produce more accurate answers than others. A key objective of volunteer training should be to improve consistency in the way the question is formulated; this might be achieved by asking volunteers to read out the question in a specified format, providing response options in the style of a survey questionnaire.

In a minority of cases, volunteers *do* start to read out the five pre-designated ethnicity categories from the monitoring sheet (as in Extract 1, lines 38–39: *are you white European, black African*). However, survey-type questions like this are vulnerable to interruption because they can be heard to implicate a response before all of the response categories are read out (Schaeffer, 1991, pp. 386–7), making presentation order and choice of response alternatives crucial (Schwartz and Hippler, 1991). Across my data set, not only is 'White European' always presented first, on no occasion is even as many as three of the five categories fully articulated before the caller interrupts to confirm their category membership. In Extract 1, the caller's response (*oh no I'm white*, line 40) overlaps the second candidate category offered, with the 'oh'-prefacing making this a particularly emphatic rejection of the possibility that she might be 'black African' and displaying her sense that the question itself was inapposite (Heritage, 1998). Although it seems that some callers are willing to endorse 'White European' if it is offered them, no-one ever spontaneously produces this category label, and many callers actively resist it (see Wilkinson, 2011).

A contributory problem here is that the response categories used by the organisation do not map exactly on to either the 1991 or 2001 Census categories, but are an amalgam of them. In particular, the category 'White European' does not appear on either Census (not does it appear on the 2011 Census).[4] A solution to this is for the organisation to adopt the categories used in the 2001 Census (with which volunteers and callers are likely to be most familiar) – in particular, replacing the category 'White European' with 'White'. I suggest that the question script indicates that five ethnic categories will be read out, and asks the caller to wait to hear them all before selecting the one that best 'fits'. This will not always happen, of course (and see below for some recipient design issues which militate against it), but it will massively increase consistency and, consequently, the validity of the organisation's monitoring statistics.

To use a survey-style question script is particularly far-reaching advice because, across my data set, the ethnicity question is far more often formulated in an open-ended way; and variously – as we have begun to see – as one of 'ethnicity' (as in Extracts 1 and 2), 'ethnic origin' (Extract 6), 'ethnic background' (Extract 8), 'ethnic group'; and sometimes 'nationality' (Extracts 11–12), where callers are 'from' (Extract 2), or where they were 'born' (Extracts 2 and 9).

When the ethnicity question is formulated in an open-ended way, callers typically self-categorise in terms of their nationality rather than their ethnicity. In Extract 6, the response to *may I ask your ethnic origin please* – a question design likely to orient the response backwards in time relative to using 'ethnic group' (Aspinall, 2001, p. 831) – is, after a delay, *I'm English* (line 4). This is transformed by the call-taker, via an understanding check, into the first of the pre-designated ethnicity categories, *So you're white European* (line 6) – which is treated (via *so*) as the upshot of being *English* (with whiteness simply presumed).

Extract 6   ('Carmel')

[C018]

```
01   Vol:      .hhh And: (.) may I ask you:r ethnic origin
02             please.
03             (0.5)
04   Car:      Yes:. [(It's-)] I'm- I'm Engli:sh.
05   Vol:            [You've-]
06   Vol:      You've- So you're white Europea: [n.]
07   Car:                                       [I']m
08             white Euro [pea:n.]
09   Vol:                 [Ye:s. ] That's lovely:.
```

Call-takers sometimes begin to provide the pre-designated response categories when there is some delay or problem in the caller's response to an open-ended question. We can see this in Extract 7, at lines 6–7.

Extract 7   ('Annie')

[D020]

```
01   Vol:       [<I-I just need to] know-=it's just for ou:r
02              [ uh:m stat-  ]statistics.=I=just need to know
03   Ann:      [That's fine. ]
04   Vol:      your ethnis-sicity.
05             (.)
```

```
06              You #u-u-u# you are (.) white European are you. .hh
07              [hhh ]
08     Ann:    [Yeh!]
09     Vol:    Yeah you sou:nd it! uh huh huh huh
10              [heh heh heh heh heh heh    ]
11     Ann:    [Yes. I'm- I'm white we:ll] uh (0.5)
12              Bri(h)tish s(h)ould I [(say)]
13     Vol:                           [[$Bri]tish yea:h.$
```

Here, although the caller initially confirms that she is *white European* (*'Yeh!*, line 8), she subsequently resists the category, revising her response (post-receipt) to *white well uh British should I say* (lines 11–12). In response to open-ended versions of the ethnicity question, callers typically select the category labels 'English' or 'British' (generally taking whiteness for granted). Call-takers' experience of this may even lead them to offer categories not in the pre-designated list, as in Extract 8, where (at line 16) *white British* is first offered, although repaired to *white European*, presumably in deference to the monitoring form (see also Extract 10):

Extract 8   ('Carrie')

[C013]

```
01     Car:   ( I reckon:) (.) I/you can't do anything about
02             (it/this) but um: (0.2) I'm sure my daughter will
03             [try:    ] [(              <very ha    ]rd.>)
04     Vol:   [pt      ] [It'd be nice if she could-  ]
05     Vol:   Yes if if she could b- help you in tha:t (.) that aspect.
06             =.hh ↑Just before you go Carrie may I just ask
07             you a couple of question[s:,    ]
08     Car:                            [↑Yes ]
09             (↑cert  [ainly.) ]
10     Vol:           [pt .hh u]m: .hh (.) You said you were from
11             Redtown may I have the first part of your postcode
12             please,
13     Car:   Ye:s it's R-T one.
14     Vol:   R-T one that's lovely .hh and u-the other thing we're
15             having to ask people it's only for statistics: .hh
16             um: pt .hh your ethnic background. Are you white British
17             white European:,
18     Car:   I'm white ↓Briti[sh.]
19     Vol:                   [ Wh]ite °Brit ( ) white European
20             that's fine:° that's lovely. .hh That's really all
21             I need to know.
22     Car:   O:ka[y (then.)]
```

In sum, inaccurate answers to the ethnicity question commonly result from asking it in an open-ended way, and from wide variation in how it is formulated. When it is presented in the style of a survey questionnaire, only one or two of the pre-designated response categories are generally presented – and the one that always comes first, 'white European', is unfamiliar and often resisted by callers (in which case volunteers may offer a category not on the list).

Why is the ethnicity question difficult to ask?

Ethnicity – like social class or sexual orientation – is generally understood to be a socially sensitive issue. From its statistical summary report (quoted earlier), the organisation is clearly aware that asking someone's ethnicity may be a 'difficult' task, in need of explanation; and the helpline volunteers themselves are manifestly oriented to the possibilities of being seen as improper or insensitive, or of causing offence to callers, particularly those from ethnic minorities. But social sensitivity alone does not account for their difficulties in asking the ethnicity question, and I will focus here on two more proximate interactional issues which also contribute: recipient design; and topicalisation.

Recipient design

In call monitoring, there is a tension between standardization of the question(s) and the principle of recipient design: i.e. that talk should properly be constructed 'in ways that display an orientation and sensitivity to the particular others(s) who are the co-participants' (Sacks, Schegloff and Jefferson, 1974, pp. 727; see also Wilkinson, 2010). On the one hand, the ethnicity question is a standard one that volunteers know they are supposed to ask of everyone who calls; on the other, in many cases they figure (rightly or wrongly) that they already have a pretty good idea of what the caller's ethnicity is, based on cues such as their accent, where they live, and (sometimes) their name. It may well seem to volunteers that it would be insensitive to ask a caller with a Irish accent who lives in Galway whether they are 'Black African', 'Asian' or 'Chinese'. It is massively unlikely that they would be (though of course not impossible). Such a question may seem to run counter to the principle of recipient design: to display an inattentiveness to the particular other they are interacting with, a failure to notice what they really should have picked up on over the course of what is often a fairly intimate and lengthy conversation.

So volunteers not infrequently design the monitoring questions to display a recall of earlier parts of the conversation, and an 'an orientation and sensitivity' to the particular caller. There is an instance of this in Extract 8, where the volunteer prefaces the postcode question with *you said you were from Redtown* (lines 10–11). Across my data set, volunteers regularly treat the 'sound' of callers' voices – in particular their accents – as a cue to their ethnicity (see Extract 7). This is particularly so with Scottish, Welsh and Irish accents, which are quite markedly different (at least to British ears) from regional English accents. We have already seen an instance in which the volunteer does not ask the ethnicity question of a caller with a Welsh accent (Extract 5). In other instances, the ethnicity question is recipient-designed to display attentiveness to such auditory cues, and their likely implications for the caller's ethnicity.

In Extract 9, a caller with a Scottish accent (and a Scottish postcode) is asked the ethnicity question (at lines 17–18) in the form *You were born in Sco- You're Scottish are you?* The caller confirms this, the volunteer receipts it, and then moves on. The question of whether the caller is black or white is never raised, and it is highly likely the volunteer ticked 'White European' in the monitoring box.

Extract 9   ('Florence')

[D022]

```
01   Vol:   I won't- I won't keep you a- much longer. What's
02          [your postcode.]
03          [((Dialling))  ]
04   Flo:   U:h L sixty nine
05   Vol:   L¿
06   Flo:   six nine.
07   Vol:   six nine. .hh
08   Flo:   Seven,
09   Vol:   #u-# >oh that's- I just ne[ed the first- =
10   Flo:                             [(            )=
11                                   =( )]
12   Vol:   =I only need the first part of it] jus:: so
13          we've got statis:tics of what- where people
14          are ringing fr [o:m. .hh]
15   Flo:                  [ Ye:s.  ]
16   Vol:   Uh:m (.) I think that's all I need to know.
17          =You-you were born in Sco- u-you're Scottish are
18          yo [u¿]
19   Flo:      [ Y]es.
20   Vol:   Yeah.hh That's all I need to know th[en.]
```

In Extract 10, the ethnicity question is preceded by a 'my side telling' (Pomerantz, 1988b), formulated as a compliment: the observation that the caller has *a nice Scottish accent* (lines 9–10). This is complicated because the volunteer also happens to have a Scottish accent, and this is part of what they are treating as laughable here. *You've got a nice Scottish accent* is built to claim

– in a manner attentive to their shared Scottishness – already to have some access to the caller's ethnicity, in advance of asking the question. The volunteer further delays the question itself by reporting that *we're having to ask people about their ethnicity* (lines 10 and 12), thereby claiming to be compelled to ask this question, despite already having a fair idea of what the answer will be. At lines 12–13, she launches the question with *I presume*, abandons this, and then asks it formally, in overlap with the caller laughing (I take it at the absurdity of the requirement to ask the question, and subsequently at the question itself). Although the volunteer's candidate ethnic category is (again) *white British*, the call would undoubtedly have been coded as from a 'White European'.

Extract 10 ('Hannah')

[C002]

```
01  Vol:   May I just ask you: a couple of other questions
02         just before you go:,=
03  Han:   =Ye::[s,]
04  Vol:        [.h]h uhm .hh (0.4) uhh- uHow uhh uhm >may
05         I just have< the first part of your postcode please,
06  Han:   W-X one three.
07  Vol:   <W-X one three.>=It's only for our statistics so
08         it doesn't go anywhere it's quite confidential,
09         .hh: uhm .hh an:d (.) $you've got a nice Scottish
10         a(h)cc(h)ent,    [ .hh    ] uhm .hh and we're having
11  Han:                    [hoh! hoh!]
12  Vol:   ask people about their ethnicity.=I presume: (.)
13         uhm I mean [are you whi:te] (.) white British? [O:r ]
14  Han:              [ huh huh huh  ]                    [Hah ]
15         hah hah. $.hh Ye:s de:fin[itely:(h) huh huh huh huh ]
16  Vol:                            [Yes.   hah-hah-hah hah hah!]
17         hah hah .hh: Well .hh um: .hh do feel free to
19         contact us: a[gai:n, ...
```

It is difficult to offer advice – such as standardising the question – which runs counter to the conversational principle of recipient design. Call-takers may very reasonably be expected to display their noticings of accent (and other cues to ethnicity) as part of a competent and sensitive engagement with a particular caller – and in a sense, to do so is also to attempt to 'humanise' a piece of bureaucratic business. My suggestion here is to make the monitoring questions more (rather than less) bureaucratic: to label them explicitly as an institutional requirement, and to divide them off from the rest of the call with a relatively formal 'pre'. In this way call-takers can display to callers that they are animating a question designed by others

(Houtkoop-Steenstra, 2000), rather than asking a question 'from me to you at this point in our interaction'. The objective is to encourage volunteers always to ask the ethnicity question – and for this to be possible, training should acknowledge that sometimes they will already know (or think they know) the answer, but emphasise the need to ask (formally) nonetheless.

Topicalisation

If social sensitivity alone were sufficient to explain difficulties with the ethnicity question, people would not be keen to talk about ethnicity. Yet I have a number of recorded calls in which the question is topicalised – by either the volunteer or the caller. These are always interactionally tricky. We have seen one example in Extract 4 – where the *caller* topicalises an aspect of the volunteer's preliminary to the ethnicity question, resulting in a failure to get the question itself asked.

In Extract 11 below, it is the *volunteer* who topicalises the caller's response. Having formulated the ethnicity question as one of *nationality* (line 1), the volunteer initiates repair on the caller's response, repeating it in interrogative form as an understanding check (line 4). Here she is using the technology of repair to display surprise (Wilkinson and Kitzinger, 2006), and she accounts for her surprise with a negative observation (Schegloff, 1988) about auditory cues (*You don't sound it*, line 4). Her follow-up question (lines 6 and 8) displays a candidate explanation for the caller's accent (confirmed at line 9). The volunteer then launches an elaborate post-response justification (lines 13–39) for asking the question in the first place, during the course of which she conveys a (commonly-held) lay theory of the cause of the illness (see Blaxter, 1983) – that it is to do with climate (as well as misrepresenting the country of origin of the caller's family, line 22). This sequence ends with the caller orienting to the caller's account as an apology (*Doesn't matter(s)*, line 44).

Extract 11   ('Laila')

[B008]

```
01   Vol:   Can I also ask you .hh what nationality
02          y'ar:e.
03   Lai:   Pak(h)ista(h)ni.
04   Vol:   You're Pakistani¿ You [don't ] sou:nd it.
05   Lai:                         [Yep!  ]
06   Vol:   Have [you been] in this country all your
07   Lai:        [huhhh   ]
08   Vol:   li:fe.
09   Lai:   Yep!
10          (.)
```

```
11   Vol:   °Pakistan°.
12          (.)
13   Vol:   .h Tha:t is also to try and find out .h
14          how many .h different (.) countries it's
15          hittin'. We   [kno:w ] that .hhh uh:m it's
16   Lai:                 [Right.]
17   Vol:   hittin' throughout Europe. Y [ou kn]o:w that
18   Lai:                                [Yes. ]
19   Vol:   European countries have it. [.hhh W ]hat we=
20   Lai:                                [Right.]
21   Vol:   =don't know is- is- (.) people like
22          yourse:lf if you were back in India    [.hh ]
23   Lai:                                          [Yep!]
24   Vol:   would you have ((the condition)) or is it more
25          to do with .hh weather and climate he:re.
26          (0.2)
27   Lai:   That's tru:e. [(              )]
28   Vol:                 [You kno:w.<I mean I'd] like
29          to find these thi:ngs out. .hh We haven't
30          heard if it's in China .hh or Japa:n.
31          (.)
32   Lai:   Ri:gh[t. ]
33   Vol:        [Or:] (.) >y'know< these Eas:tern
34          countries.
35          (0.4)
36   Lai:   [Ri:ght.]
37   Vol:   [(    )] We want to find this all out and
38          find out really what affe:cts it. .hh An'
39          [that's ] why we ask these ques:tions.
40   Lai:   [Ri:ght.]
41   Lai:   Ri:ght.
42          (.)
43   Vol:   [(                )]
44   Lai:   [It's all right.=Does]n't matters:.
```

In fact, this volunteer subsequently topicalises this particular call[5] in (at least) two later calls. For example, in one of these she tells another caller *I've had one girl on that's Asian ... but born and brought up in Britain*, and *I don't know if ((the condition)) 'd hit 'er .hhh if she was still in in: India* (again misrepresenting the caller's – or her family's – country of origin).

Explicit discussions of ethnicity are fraught with the potential for giving offence (however inadvertently). My advice to volunteers is (a) not to topicalise ethnicity (and also not to talk about other callers to the helpline);

and (b) not to engage with such topicalisation when it is initiated by callers. Extract 12 below shows how a volunteer can effectively manage a caller's topicalisation (and could usefully be employed in training).

Extract 12 ('Sonia')

[E004]

```
01  Vol:  An:d .hh (.) they want to know the nationality
02        of the people that we speak to:,=Are you white
03        European, .hh black African  [:,]
04  Son:                                [Ye]ah I'm whi:te.=White
05        (0.6) European British:
06  Vol:  R:ght.
07        (0.2)
08  Vol:  uhhh hah hah .hh $That's lovely:$.
09  Son:  $Distressi:ng$.=
10  Vol:     [uhhhh hah hah hah .hh       ]
11  Son: = [hah hah You j's never kno:w ] the:(h)se d(h)a:ys, hah
12        hah
13        (0.2)
14  Vol:  That's: (0.2) supe:r.=Thank you very much indeed and
15        if there's anything else that we can do to help please
16  Vol:  do get back to [us.]
```

After the volunteer's receipt and assessment of the caller's answer (*Right*, line 6; *That's lovely*, line 8), the caller produces (at line 9) what sounds like a counter-assessment. She says *Distressing*, apparently assessing the fact that her colour and nationality have been open to question (rather than 'white British' simply assumed). Her expansion at lines 11, *You just never know these days* is an idiomatic formulation that offers an account for her assessment that the ethnicity question is *distressing*, while also accepting the volunteer's need to ask it. It conveys something like: 'It's *distressing* that Britain "these days" is a multi-ethnic society such that you cannot simply assume that I'm white and British but have to ask'. The volunteer 'laughs along' (line 10) but does not otherwise engage with this assessment, then reissues a closing evaluation (line 14), and moves into closing the call. Laughter is often used in response to 'improprieties' (thereby constituted as such) as a way of showing alignment that 'stops short of outright affiliation' (Glenn, 2003, p. 122). By (politely) not engaging with the caller's assessment, or her account for it, the volunteer discourages a (potentially tricky) discussion of 'the state of Britain today'.

In sum, volunteers' adherence to the conversational principle of recipient design, and the election of volunteer and/or caller to topicalise ethnicity (for whatever reason) both powerfully shape the course of the interaction.

Ethnicity may be socially sensitive, but local interactional contingencies such as these also contribute to difficulties in asking the ethnicity question.

Concluding comments

In this chapter, I have shown how it has been possible to identify a number of problems with this organisation's ethnic monitoring process – ranging from the wording of the ethnicity question, to volunteers' difficulties in asking it, to the limited validity of the statistics derived from the coded responses – and to develop advice on how to address these problems. The key points of this advice are:

- To revise the wording of the ethnicity question to conform with the census question;
- To train volunteers (a) to ask – not presume – ethnicity (and not to code without asking); (b) to ask the ethnicity question clearly and consistently; (c) to avoid/discourage topicalisations of ethnicity;
- To revise the monitoring form to include a tick box for 'question not asked'.

More specifically, my suggestions are to include the following in volunteer training on how to ask the ethnicity question:

- Discussions of the concept of ethnicity; and the importance of ethnic monitoring;
- Strategies for making an effective transition to the call-monitoring questions as a distinct piece of organisational business (set off from rest of the call with a – short – 'pre'; in first position; not too late in call; not over-justified);
- Good practice in asking the ethnicity question (perhaps another 'pre'; 'and-prefacing'; consistent format: in style of a survey question, with response alternatives; possibly including a short post-response account).

One particular benefit of using Conversation Analysis in this work is the focus it mandates on the interactional aspects of asking – and answering – the ethnicity question. It would have been all too easy to assume that social sensitivity of the topic was responsible for the reported difficulties, and not to look at how call monitoring runs off in practice. And, of course, the particular interactional issues discussed here – recipient design and topicalisation – have a broader applicability to the call monitoring process across the range of information the organisation seeks to elicit. One limit of using CA alone, however, is that it offers little insight into non-cooperation with the monitoring process – and rather than speculate about any anticipated difficulties, it would probably be helpful to ask those volunteers who never (or rarely) request the information why this is so.

Finally, a brief note on the contribution this work makes to the field of 'applied' Conversation Analysis (for a wider survey of which, see Antaki's account in Chapter 1 of this volume). To my knowledge, there is no research on call-monitoring in the CA literature on helpline calls (e.g., Baker, Emmison and Firth, 2005; Edwards, 2007). Further, this analysis addresses an issue not hitherto considered in the CA literature on standardised survey interviewing (e.g., Houtkoop-Steenstra, 2000; Maynard et al., 2002; Schaeffer, 1991): the issue of navigating the boundary between one type of interactional task and another, very different, one. Because the whole of the job of survey research is done through asking and answering standardised questions, the issue of making the transition into this activity from another kind of task does not arise. In a helpline call, however, there is a stark contrast between the primary business of the call (an open-ended informational and/or empathetic task) and the very-much-subsidiary business of call-monitoring, such that a smooth transition between the two requires – as we have seen – considerable interactional skill. Having identified some components of this skill, in a way that can be used in training sessions, is a contribution whose applicability is not limited to the specific context of ethnic monitoring.

Notes

1. Thanks to Rowena Viney for transcription assistance, and to Celia Kitzinger for helpful feedback on an earlier draft of this chapter.
2. Pseudonyms are used for callers, and postcodes (and other possibly-identifying information) have been changed. The data tag indicates that this extract is taken from the sixth call recorded by call-taker 'C'.
3. On some occasions, these preliminary items appear to be *both* action projections (i.e., 'preliminaries to preliminaries' or 'pre-pres') *and* 'pre-delicates'. Schegloff (1980) also suggests that 'requests for permission' to ask a question may mark a particular type of delicateness: 'not the character of the projected question or other action, but the possibly violative or special character of the party in question talking at all' (pp. 144–5). It may be that the call monitoring sequence marks something of a role reversal relative to the rest of the call, with the caller 'helping' the call-taker by providing information, rather than vice versa. The form of the request is one that displays low entitlement to ask (Curl and Drew, 2008).
4. The 'level 1' ethnic group categories used in the UK Census are as follows (these were further sub-divided in the 2001 and 2011 iterations): 1991: White; Black-Caribbean; Black-African; Black-Other; Indian; Pakistani; Bangladeshi; Chinese; Any other ethnic group; 2001: White; Mixed; Asian or Asian British; Black or Black British; Chinese or Other ethnic group; 2011: White; Mixed/multiple ethnic groups; Asian/Asian British; Black/African/Caribbean/Black British; Other ethnic group.
5. This may have been a particularly noteworthy call for the volunteer, given that (according to the organisation's quarterly statistical summary) only 1.4 per cent of callers (N = 7) were categorised as 'Asian' in this monitoring period.

6
Working with Childbirth Helplines: The Contributions and Limitations of Conversation Analysis[1]

Celia Kitzinger

Pregnancy, childbirth and the post-partum period can be times of significant stress, anxiety, depression or trauma. In addition to the bodily changes involved in bearing and delivering a child and the social changes that motherhood brings, the challenges of navigating through the institutional politics of maternity care and seeking to make informed choices can be overwhelming (Davis-Floyd, 1992; S. Kitzinger, 2006; Oakley, 1980; Rothman, 1982). Various organisations involved in advocacy and/or education around childbirth advertise telephone helplines for women struggling with childbirth-related issues, including three from which I have recorded calls: a crisis network for women in trauma after childbirth; an information service for women seeking home births; and a charity for women with pelvic pain during or after pregnancy.

This chapter describes my experience of working with these three organisations. It shows examples of the kinds of analyses I offered back to the organisations and their uses of them to develop and improve their own work both on their helpline and in their broader educational/advocacy work. I use my experience to reflect on the contributions conversation-analytic work can make in 'applied' settings and also on its limitations. One important message of this chapter is that while CA can certainly make important contributions to workplace training and practice, our enthusiasm for CA should not override our willingness to acknowledge that other approaches may at times be more appropriate or more fitted to the aims of the organisations that have supplied us with data.

I did not initially set out to contribute to training and improving practice for childbirth helplines – or, in fact, even to engage in 'applied Conversation Analysis'. It so happened that when in 2001, as a newly trained conversation analyst, I wanted to collect my own data set, the first person to offer to make some recordings of naturally occurring interaction for me was my mother who – intrigued by what Conversation Analysis might reveal – volunteered to record a few of her own interactions on the birth crisis helpline she had founded a couple of years earlier (S. Kitzinger, 2006). This led to offers from other call-takers, first on the birth crisis helpline and then (as a result of call-takers' participation in workshops at which I presented findings from my birth crisis analyses) on other related helplines.

Having recorded and sent me their calls, call-takers began – not unreasonably – to ask what I made of them. Within a few weeks of receiving the first tapes, I began to receive burning questions – along the lines of *How am I doing? Did I handle that call okay? How can I do better?* – and queries about specific aspects of the interactions they believed they had 'screwed up' and could have handled better. After sending me several hundred recorded calls, the birth crisis organisation recognised the potential resource these offered and I was contacted with questions such as: *What percent of women who call the helpline have had their labours induced? How many of the induced labours end up as emergency caesareans? Can you send me some quotes in which women describe what was traumatic about their episiotomies?* In sum, my data-providers held me accountable for giving them feedback and information that would help them to do a better job as call-takers and/or in relation to their advocacy work in the childbirth field.[2]

For the most part call-takers' questions are not – or not without considerable 'translation' work on my part – conversation-analytic questions. As a *feminist* I admire and respect the work call-takers are doing and want to help them, on their terms. But as a *conversation analyst*, my primary interest in these data is not even in the 'applied' arena but rather as a resource for developing understandings of basic patterns of interaction – in the same way that Sacks drew on group therapy sessions and suicide prevention calls to uncover fundamental conversational practices such as turn-taking, adjacency pairs and story-telling. It is ironic that a data set that should surely have been ideal for a budding 'feminist conversation analyst' (C. Kitzinger, 2000) was actually pulling me in two different directions. On the one hand I could see how I could do analyses of direct value to the helplines – but much of what they needed (at least in the first instance) meant doing *thematic* (not CA) analyses of the data, and even the 'applied' CA that they might find useful is at best a 'CA-lite' approach which does little more than draw on established CA discoveries to explicate particular interactions. On the other hand, I could use the data sets they had supplied me with to pursue my own research passion in 'basic' Conversation Analysis – but this felt uncomfortably like a 'grab and run' approach to data collection, which failed to give anything back to the organisations whose values and commitments to making the world a better place for women I also share. Mostly, then, applied and basic analyses of my data pull me in different directions, and my solution has become to recognise it may be necessary for me to divide my time between the 'applied' and 'basic' research on the same data (with only some of the 'applied' work being CA) and without struggling overmuch to force them together.

So, on the one hand, I have used childbirth helpline data (without reference to the fact that it *is* 'childbirth helpline' data) in basic CA research dealing with, for example, reaction tokens (Wilkinson and C. Kitzinger, 2006), speaker self-reference (Land and C. Kitzinger, 2007; Lerner and C. Kitzinger, 2007), membership categorisation (C. Kitzinger and Rickford, 2007), and compound turn constructional units (C. Kitzinger, 2008c) – none of which are directly relevant to the goals of the organisations from which the helpline data were drawn.[3] On the other hand, in order to meet the expectations of the call-takers who provided me with data, and in order to fulfil my own feminist aspirations, I have also analysed these same data corpora using methods of analysis other than CA – in particular thematic analysis which has been helpful in two ways: (i) to systematise information about the callers and the way the call-takers handle the calls and to feed back to the organisations information they needed about the nature and scope of their work;[4] and (ii) to summarise key recurrent themes in what women were saying in the course of the calls in a way that might be used by the organisations in education and advocacy for policy change in the health services. Unlike Conversation Analysis, the results of thematic analysis take a form that is readily accessible to the educated general public, and results can be relatively quickly produced (thereby relieving the CA researcher of the impossible task of producing rapid CA findings). Given my close ongoing relationships with several of the call-takers, it is also important that thematic analysis is a 'useful method for working within participatory research paradigms, with participants as collaborators' (Braun and Clarke, 2006, p. 97). The thematic analyses provided an essential context for the 'applied CA' which I was also (eventually) able to offer.

Using thematic analysis

There are two different ways in which thematic analysis of the recorded calls was useful to the organisations. First, the organisations were keen to gain a better understanding of their client base and of their current practices in broad terms, that is, who was calling them, with what sorts of questions or concerns, and what kinds of information/referrals/help call-takers were providing. Understandably, call-takers give priority to their interactions with the women who call them, rather than to associated paperwork – and this means, given the constraints under which they are working, that their own record-keeping is either non-existent or insufficient. Call-takers' impressions of 'typical' questions and concerns are often skewed (when compared with the recorded data base) by vividly remembered but unusual interactions. Ironically, then, there is a real sense in which expert and knowledgeable call-takers do not know what their work involves, precisely because they are so immersed in actually doing it. Access to accurate information provided by an 'outsider' who can listen to the recorded calls and systematically code their content is useful to the organisations. It can help them to prepare new recruits for the kinds of calls they might be taking, to research and compile helpline handbooks with the kind of information call-takers need to be able access quickly if they are to answer common questions and concerns, and of course organisations can also use what they learn about their own work in publicity and fund-raising. During the main data collection periods I received mailed envelopes of audio-tapes (data collection just preceded widespread use of digital recorders) every week or so. I discovered that the best practice was to listen to them right away and to enter a summary of their contents on a log, something like this:

Call 147
'Lillian': Traumatic birth five years ago and now 28 weeks pregnant and 'petrified'. Induced labour, failed ventouse, forceps delivery, third degree tear, blood transfusion, son in intensive care for week. Flashbacks and sexual problems. Considering elective caesarean. Clt validates responses as 'normal under the circumstances' and raises: discussing concerns with lead midwife, avoiding induction, considering independent midwife and home birth. Or-prefaced repair about half way through.

Logging calls in this way made it relatively easy to answer questions from the organisations about how long after a traumatic birth women were calling, whether the traumatic birth involved particular interventions, whether or not callers are currently pregnant (and if so how many weeks) and so on,[5] and also to select out for analysis *only* that subset of callers who were (for example) considering elective caesareans, or whose babies had been in intensive care, or who talked about sexual problems. (As evidenced by the last sentence in this data log entry, I also recorded, for my 'basic' CA anything I spotted of interest!). I was also able to use this log to feed back a systematic list of the activities that call-takers regularly engage in (broadly specified). On one helpline, for example, call-takers commonly explain what causes pelvic pain in pregnancy; recommend getting hands-on physiotherapy treatment (and better pain medication); give contact information for physiotherapists who are 'good with pelvises'; advise about disability aids; offer to send out an information pack; discuss management of labour;

provide information about Disability Living Allowance; and validate women's experience by showing that they believe their accounts of pain and disability (C. Kitzinger, 2008b). These data logs made it possible to provide helplines with information about both about their callers and about their own work in a form they could use in training and in resource development. (For a parallel and much more worked-up thematic analysis of calls to the home birth helpline, see Shaw and C. Kitzinger, 2005.)

This kind of analysis is clearly **not** Conversation Analysis. It glosses complex actions (like 'giving information', 'offering', 'advising' and 'validating') using vernacular labels. Because it doesn't engage with the specificities of how these actions are composed as such, how they are positioned in an unfolding sequence, or how they are responded to by the persons to whom they are addressed, it risks mis-characterising them. This is the kind of analysis to which CA offers an important corrective. But when organisations do not (yet) have even this kind of systematised overview of their service provision, this is a helpful analysis which can be made available to them within a relatively short timeframe, in advance of the sophisticated in-depth Conversation Analysis of some particular aspect of their work that may take years to produce. As conversation analysts, it may be socially responsible for us sometimes to carry out thematic analyses (or to work with others who will) as a way of giving something back to our data providers relatively quickly.

Second, education and/or advocacy is an important part of the work of all three organisations. Many of the volunteer call-takers also work as educators in applied fields (e.g., in midwifery, antenatal care and physiotherapy). Many of them are in positions where they can represent the concerns of callers in the public domain (e.g., as lay members of professional committees, in interviews with journalists and in their own writing and speaking engagements) and many also have socio-political commitments to changing the policies and institutions that generate the problems they are dealing with in their helpline calls. Thematic analysis of the data corpora (either logged as shown or transcribed orthographically) is a resource for systematically representing the range and diversity of problems callers report.[6] So, for example, a thematic analysis of calls to the home birth helpline (Shaw and C. Kitzinger, 2005) reports common themes in the difficulties and obstacles that confront women planning a home birth: feelings of isolation and being the 'only one', negative reactions from friends and family, denial of midwifery cover, and scare tactics from medical professionals. A thematic analysis of calls to the birth crisis line (C. Kitzinger, 2005b) documents the extent to which women attribute the cause of their trauma to the predominant theme of uncaring, hostile or degrading treatment from medical staff, rather than to the physical experiences and medical interventions involved in giving birth. Each theme is illustrated with quotations from the recorded calls – for example, in relation to the 'degrading treatment' theme:

> He [the obstetrician] went out leaving the curtains open and me with my legs wide apart in stirrups was forced to lie like that while the hospital cleaners washed the floor. I felt completely humiliated.
>
> (C. Kitzinger, 2005b)

These thematic analyses (and my transcriptions of illustrative extracts) were used by the founder of the birth crisis helpline in her book, *Birth Crisis*, written for healthcare professionals and for women in trauma after childbirth (S. Kitzinger, 2006).

Thematic analysis treats what women say as (more or less) transparently reflecting the reality of their experience, that is, it treats a caller's report of being denied midwifery cover as evidence that she *was* denied midwifery cover; it accepts a woman's report of being left with her legs wide apart in stirrups while cleaners washed the floor as evidence that this is actually what happened. This approach to understanding what people say (whether in interviews, focus groups or naturally occurring data) is sometimes dismissed out of hand as naïve and simplistic by researchers with theories drawn from postmodernism, discourse analysis, discursive psychology or – indeed – Conversation Analysis. I acknowledge the critiques and have contributed to them and to discussions of their socio-political implications (C. Kitzinger and Wilkinson, 1997; C. Kitzinger, 2003). But in trying to support and facilitate the valuable work of these childbirth organisations, I cannot see that anything is gained by ironicising callers' accounts as 'discourses' or 'interpretive repertoires' or by treating their talk only in terms of the actions (e.g., 'complaining' or 'accusing') that it is doing in its current interactional context. Instead, I am disposed to treat this part of my work as what feminist sociologist Barbara Katz Rothman (1996, p. 53), describing her research on postnatal diagnosis, has called 'a project in bearing witness'. This approach is clearly not Conversation Analysis, but it does offer an important way of contributing to the work of these organisations by identifying and tackling the institutional and socio-political problems (e.g., lack of continuity of care in pregnancy, failure to implement home birth policies, inadequate provision of physiotherapy services) that cause the distress that leads women to contact them in the first place.

Using Conversation Analysis

It is increasingly common for communication training across a wide range of domains to include analysis of and feedback on recordings of actual interactions.[7] My reading of the literature strongly suggests that practitioners value having the opportunity to watch/listen to their interactions and to reflect on performance irrespective of which analytic approach is invoked or even without any formal analytic framework at all. In the field of communication in healthcare in particular, it is widely accepted that a practitioner who 'has an opportunity to receive feedback about how he or she communicates in real consultations will learn most' (Maguire and Pitceathly, 2002, p. 700). A range of different analytic and theoretical approaches underpin these educational interventions – the single most widely used of which is the Roter Interaction Analysis System (RIAS). a system for coding utterances into 39 predefined mutually exclusive categories, broadly divided into 24 task-focused (mainly asking questions and giving information or counselling) and 15 socio-emotional ones (e.g., 'shows disapproval', 'asks for reassurance', 'shows concern or worry', 'legitimises').[8] Positive correlations between particular categories of utterance and measures of patient satisfaction are routinely used to make practice recommendations (e.g., Mjaaland and Finset, 2009; Pieterse et al., 2006; Roter, 2008; Sandhu et al., 2009). Clearly, then the analysis of recorded interactions, and the use of these in training, does not in and of itself constitute a specifically 'conversation-analytic' application. In the rest of this chapter I focus on how conversation analysts *qua* conversation analysts can make a distinctive contribution, by describing my use of CA analyses to inform training via (i) group workshops and (ii) individual feedback to call-takers.

(i) Group training workshops

Along with others involved in the Birth Crisis Network, I run full-day workshops two or three times a year, each attended by 25–30 health workers in the childbirth field (midwives, doulas, breastfeeding counsellors, antenatal teachers and others). My contribution is based on a set of recordings of pre-analysed data extracts from the birth crisis calls, selected in order to shed light on typical concerns that arise in the course of the workshop. My analyses are based on CA's core theoretical precepts (language as action, actions as structurally organised, and sequentiality as a resource for intersubjectivity (Heritage, 1984a)) and on its cumulative empirical findings in the areas of turn-taking, action-formation, sequence organisation, repair and overall structural organisation (Schegloff, 2007, p. xiv). I introduce workshop participants to some of these findings as they become relevant in the course of the workshop.

Teaching CA concepts to these professional groups is comparatively challenging in that, although few are professional 'counsellors', most have completed counselling and/or communication skills courses as part of their professional qualification and already have access to a range of technical terms that characterise (or gloss) aspects of interaction from within other theoretical frameworks such as cognitive behavioural or Rogerian therapy (e.g., they regularly volunteer terms like 'open' vs. 'closed' questions, 'backchannel', 'challenging negative schema', etc.). Part of my job as a conversation analyst is to problematise these concepts and/or to find ways of 'translating' the observations they embody into a CA framework, and I have tried to illustrate how I do that below. A very positive aspect of the workshop is that participants' prior training in communication skills or counselling methods is always balanced by their own extensive experience of trying to put these models into practice in their own work – on the basis of which they have already developed critiques of them. They are generally resistant to, and sceptical of, mechanistic models of human interaction. Their background in a 'caring' profession – and the commitment to 'reflective practice' that led them voluntarily to attend the workshop – generally means that members of this self-selected group of healthcare workers already have outstandingly good interactional instincts and an excellent intuitive sense of how interactions run off. Part of what they get from the CA that I teach them is a language for describing what they can already 'see' in the data in ways not provided for in their training thus far – and, hence, ways of developing their interactional competences. Our collective work on the recorded calls is always a fully participative and energising session in which participants display enthusiasm for exploring the intricacies of human interaction in just the kind of detail that CA offers, and a readiness to apply new insights in their own work.

The workshop begins with a talk by the founder of the Birth Crisis Network about her own experience of working in this field (drawing in part on my thematic analyses of the calls) and introducing issues around distress after childbirth and the diagnostic category of postnatal post-traumatic stress disorder. This is followed by an open discussion session in which participants share their own experiences (both as caregivers and – sometimes – as women who have themselves experienced traumatic births). There is then a role-play exercise in break-out groups, which simulates the experience of counselling a woman in crisis after childbirth, and facilitates subsequent discussion of common issues and concerns that arise for caregivers. Usually participants are well acquainted with idealised descriptions of 'good practice' and have a wide *theoretical* knowledge of how they are supposed to behave (e.g., active listening, empathising, challenging self-blame, validating and empowering clients) but are less confident about how to put those principles into practice. On the basis of the role play and the discussion of their own professional experiences, they raise concerns including: opening and closing interactions; how to display empathy appropriately; how to strike a balance between 'professional' and 'woman-to-woman' care; and how 'empowering' and so on are actually *done* in action.

106 *Applied Conversation Analysis*

I explain that we are going to listen to and discuss real recorded interactions with these questions in mind.

I have a data bank of around 30 pre-analysed extracts that I can select to exemplify particular practice issues, but rarely play more than five or six (at most) in any one workshop. Each recorded fragment is paused at various places in the course of the unfolding interaction and participants are asked to say (out loud, in pairs) whatever they would say next if they were the call-taker at that point. The person with whom each participant is paired then gives feedback on what was said, the range of different responses are shared and discussed with the whole group, and then compared with what the call-taker actually *did* say and then how the caller responded. Drawing on CA principles, I emphasise that what really matters is not how *we* judge what was said (in terms of our professional counselling theories or personal values and preferences) but how the woman to whom it was addressed treats it. How does *her* response show her to have understood and received the previous turn? We then listen again to the extract, pausing each time the call-taker takes a turn (or makes a noise) to reflect on its import and effect for the unfolding interaction.

I will illustrate this process with just one extract. I have discovered it is best to require participants to work from the recordings and *not* to give them transcripts – since this more closely approximates the actual situation of counselling, and it also means that they listen more carefully and discover for themselves the importance of features of the interaction (such as in-breaths and out-breaths, pauses, gaps, laughter tokens, repairs and so on) that are otherwise already provided by the transcript as potential features of interest. For the reader, then, deprived of audio and reliant on a transcript and supplied unilaterally with a compressed summary of 'analysis' and its 'applications', this is unlikely to capture the spirit of the intensely interactive and passionate workshop discussions. You might want to pause in your reading and jot down your own analytic observations and thoughts about their possible applications after reading the transcript.

Extract 1   (Pam)[9]

[BCC 64]

((Call opening immediately following informed consent for taping. The caller (Pam) is crying when the call-taker (Clt) answers the phone and sniffs and sobs throughout this extract (e.g., '.shih' line 4 represents a 'wet sniff', Hepburn, 2004). All of Pam's talk here is delivered in what Hepburn has characterised as a 'wobbly voice' (2004, p. 261).)).

```
01    Clt:     [Oka:y  ]  .hh tell me what the problem
02             is. hh
03             (0.2)
```

```
04   Pam:    shih (.) I really really find it difficult
05           to come to terms with what happened to me.
06           .shih I had (.) a baby bo:y (.)
07   Clt:    mm hm
08   Pam:    ni:ne weeks ago now
09   Clt:    mm hm
10   Pam:    It was my thi:rd ba:by
11   Clt:    mm hm
12   Pam:    .hhhh a- and I just can't get- I just can't
13           get over what happened  [to me:..]  ('n him-)=
14   Clt:                            [A:::::h]
15   Pam:    =well 'e's fi:ne but (.) it was terrible it
16           was an awhfu:l expe:rience hhhshihh .hhh I mean
17           my fi:rst baby was hard enough because that
18           was the forceps delivery bu[t ]   [.hhh]=
19   Clt:                               [mm]  [hm  ]
20   Pam:    =(this was) terrible hhh .hhh d- j- I just
21           can't (.) come to terms with what happened
22           at all and [I fe ]el so (.) bad about it in=
23   Clt:               [No:hh]
24   Pam:    =myself. It was huh snhih
25   Clt:    .hhh Where was this¿
```

Building on workshop participants' spontaneous observations about this interaction (and others like it) I generally manage to convey the following key points – all derived from CA and all relevant to working with women in crisis after childbirth – without needing to be overtly didactic or explicitly 'technical'. Given my brief in this chapter to show the uses of 'applied CA', the succinct summaries that follow here focus on the ways in which observations related to counselling practice are rooted in the CA literatures. For an alternative version of some of these points (and others) addressing a midwifery readership, see C. Kitzinger and S. Kitzinger (2007).

1. Strategies used in the openings of interactions to elicit the caller's 'problem' can be more or less successful in so doing. These topic-proffering sequences, adapted from ordinary conversation (Button and Casey, 1984; Schegloff, 2007, ch. 8), have also been identified in research on doctors' elicitation of patients' presenting concerns (Gafaranga and Britten, 2005; Heath, 1981; Robinson, 2006). The topic proffer in Extract 1, *Okay, tell me what the problem is* (line 2), is successful in that the caller launches her story (line 4) with a slight delay caused only by the fact that she is crying. Other features of the delivery of this turn that contribute to its 'success' are the audible out breath at its end (indicating completion) and the short silence that the

speaker allows to develop afterwards. We compare this opening question and the response to it with differently formatted topic proffers in other calls: e.g. *Can I help you?* (to which the response is *Probably not. Nobody else has.*); *Why are you crying?* (to which the response in one call is an apologetic *Sorry, sorry,* and in another *I don't know*); *So you're feeling pretty rotten are you?* (to which the response is a long account of her feelings). Whatever we (as analysts) may think about the value of these differently designed questions, it is how the recipient hears the question, and responds to it, that tells us whether it is a 'good' question or not. The distinction between 'open' and 'closed' questions (with which workshop participants are already familiar – and which is also crucial to the RIAS coding scheme) is not sufficient to capture the differences between these topic proffers, which are more to do with the way in which question design is implicated in the actions that the questions are treated as performing (e.g., for those cited above, topic-proffer, a formulaic 'institutional' opening, a challenge, a candidate empathetic understanding).[10]

2. 'Active listening' and 'empathic understanding' are in part constituted by the appropriate use of continuers (Schegloff, 1982), response tokens (Gardner, 2001) and reaction tokens (Wilkinson and Kitzinger, 2006). In other analytic frameworks these small bits of behaviour are often combined (along with other features of talk-in-interaction) into a single category of 'back channel communication'; alternatively they may be omitted altogether from interactional analyses, as in much RIAS-based research. CA has documented how these tokens are differentially employed for different actions. So the *mm hms* in Extract 1 at lines 7, 9 and 11 are continuers that display the call-taker's understanding that the speaker is producing an extended turn which is not yet complete. Although *I had a baby boy* (line 6) is a complete sentence, and hence a grammatically possibly complete turn constructional unit (TCU), it cannot be considered, in this sequential context, to complete the response to *tell me what the problem is* (line 1–2); nor is it possibly complete as a description of *what happened to me* (line 5) in a sequential context in which *what happened* has already been flagged up as the *problem* (line 1) that she *find it difficult to come to terms with* (lines 4–5). This unit of talk is recompleted with an increment (line 8) and followed by another TCU (line 10), both of which extend the turn by providing background information without, as yet, having described the *problem*, and both are followed by continuers (*mm hm*, lines 9 and 10) that mark the call-taker's understanding of the turn as not yet complete.

The *Ah::* (line 14) does more than simply acknowledge that the speaker has more to say: without impeding the caller's ongoing talk by claiming a full turn, the call-taker produces a reaction token designed to convey a warm empathetic understanding of the speaker's predicament. Because they perform distinctive actions, continuers and reaction tokens can be *mis*placed and are not substitutable one for the other. In the workshop we try re-running the interaction above with *Ah::* in place of the continuers at lines 7, 9 or 11 or with *mm hm* at line 14 and it is easy to appreciate the difference this makes. We also examine other recorded interactions that use reaction tokens to convey empathetic understandings of pain (*euwww!*) surprise (*oooooh!*), disgust (*ugh!*) and disapproval (*tcht!*), and discuss how these compare interactionally with less economical articulations of empathetic understanding such as *That must have hurt, I guess you were pretty surprised at that* and so on. Participants also sometimes draw attention to the use of response tokens such as *right* and *okay* (and note the use of *okay* at Extract 1 line 2 which marks a reorientation of the interaction from the immediately prior sequence dealing with consent to record to the new sequence launched here). It is sometimes suggested either that we all already know how to use *mm hm*, *ah*, *right*, *okay* and the like – or that if we don't it cannot be taught. My feedback to one helpline call-taker – and her capacity to act on it – shows otherwise (see below).

3. Validating women's experience and confirming that their distress is recognisably of a kind that can be addressed by birth crisis counsellors is an important value for many workshop participants. These practices can be seen in Extract 1 at lines 23 (*No*) and 25 (*Where was this¿*) – neither of which utterance would be likely to be coded as such in the RIAS and neither of which is a self-evidently 'validating' expression of affiliation or support like others we identify and discuss in calls. In order to hear them as such we need a sequential analysis. The call-taker's *No* (line 23) is an acceptance of the caller's third and progressively upgraded reiteration of her problem as not being able to *come to terms with what happened* (lines 21–22), which she is advancing as her 'reason' for calling the helpline in a manner that bears comparison with patients' efforts to establish the legitimate 'doctorability' of their complaints (Heritage and Robinson, 2006, pp. 57–64), or with emergency callers' efforts to show that their reasons for calling are 'service-appropriate' (Raymond and Zimmerman, 2007).

The helpline advertises itself as available for women who want to talk about distressed or traumatic births and this caller *sounds* distressed and traumatised: she has been crying from the outset of the call, has a wobbly, sniffly voice quality throughout this episode (Hepburn, 2004) and occasionally breaks into sobs. In her first iteration (which also sounds like a 'banner headline' for the story she has been invited to tell about her 'problem'), the caller says that *com[ing] to terms with what happened* is *difficult* (lines 4–5). The second iteration upgrades the severity of what happened from something that is *difficult to come to terms with* to something that she *just can't get over* (lines 12–13) – and halts her turn to repair the prosody on *can't* to upgrade the force it conveys of having tried and failed. The third iteration is preceded by the caller's explicit assessment of what happened (still not yet described) as *terrible* and *awful* (line 16), even by comparison with another birth that was *hard enough* (lines 17–18), and further upgraded by this time including the extreme case formulation (Pomerantz, 1986) *at all* (line 23).

Through progressively upgrading her account of the severity of the problem without in any way advancing an account of what actually *did* happen, the caller presents herself as maximally needy for a service dedicated to helping women to *coming to terms* with an *awful experience* of birth. When the call-taker (with a simple *No*, line 24) accepts the caller's claim to be unable to *come to terms with what happened at all*, she both validates the caller's account of her experience and also thereby legitimises her reason for calling. Her response here is alternative to other possible responses – actualised in other extracts, and often volunteered by workshop participants if I stop the audio at the completion of the third iteration and ask for suggestions – such as questions about what has already been attempted by way of *com[ing] to terms with* her experience (e.g., *Have you spoken to your midwife about this?*) or reassurances that *coming to terms* will be possible (e.g., *It takes time and nine weeks isn't very long; You've called the right number – we're here to help you come to terms with traumatic births*). Comparison of different possible responses makes apparent the extent to which *No* is restricted only to accepting the caller's account without (yet) making anything of it.

The call-taker's subsequent question about the distressing labour (where it took place, line 25) – which follows a big sob from the caller – further embodies a tacit acceptance of the caller's problem as a worthy topic for counselling attention on the helpline: that is, it addresses the same concern as does a response like *You've called the right number*, but without explicitly stating that the problem is service-appropriate. The call-taker simply shows that she takes the problem seriously enough to ask a question about it: thereby underwriting and validating it as a justifiable reason for the call (compare the first history-taking question in medical interactions, see Heritage and Robinson, 2006, p. 64) – and also (as *You've called the right number* does not) advancing the interaction by producing a new first pair part. This question (*Where was this¿*, line 25) is rarely identified by workshop participants as a question that validates the reason for the call (it takes considerable analytic work to explain it as such) but it does usually provoke discussion for other reasons, since it is potentially hearable as interruptive (it does not sound as though the caller has completed a TCU at line 24), intrusive (violating the caller's anonymity by locating her geographically), and irrelevant (since traumatic births happen everywhere).

Observations like these lead to a useful discussion of what information-solicit questions can be used to do in addition to soliciting information, and the extent to which questions and the answers to them (and third-turn receipts of those answers etc.) need to be analysed as a *sequence* which displays how the recipient understood the question, what *she* took it to be doing, whether *she* treated it as interruptive, intrusive or irrelevant (and how, as analysts, we would know). Where time permits I have a small collection of other instances where a question about where a birth took place is raised and answered, and can use this to show how the sequential position of the 'same' question is profoundly influential on how it is understood and responded to. Continuing to play the recording on from the end of the transcript in Extract 1 *after* discussion of these issues is a helpful pedagogic exercise (for this and for other extracts) since it is then possible for participants to appreciate what is *actually* said next, and the particular understanding it displays of the prior talk, as an achievement from among possibilities, rather than 'standing in the splendid isolation of seeming inescapability' (Schegloff, 1982, p. 89).

(ii) Feedback to individual call-takers

Several individual call-takers (from all three organisations) have provided me with a sample of ten or more calls each, specifically for personal feedback on their performance. The main problem with this procedure is the (in their view, excessive) time lag between recording the data and receiving feedback. Its main value lies in the provision of individualised feedback tailored to the strengths and weaknesses of specific call-takers, and the opportunity it offers for creating change. I will describe two examples of the feedback I have given, both of which led callers to change their practice in ways that demonstrably helped them to achieve their stated aims.

The first instance is one in which I suggested that a call-taker might like to try using more reaction tokens and other ways of expressing empathy for or sympathy with her callers. This suggestion was based on my analysis of a series of calls in which, when callers described their pelvic pain, she regularly receipted these descriptions with response tokens as in Extract 2: *right* (line 4), *okay* (lines 6 and 11), and *mm* (lines 9 and 13).

Extract 2   (Dawn)

[PP 11]

```
01    Clt:    And what happens when you wa:lk.
02            (.)
03    Daw:    U:hm I get a lot of pai:n   [through my]=
04    Clt:                                [Right. So-]
05    Daw:    =my pelvis and my back
06    Clt:    Ok [ay]
07    Daw:       [My] hips get bad I get pain shootin'
08            up and down my legs
09    Clt:    Mm::.
10    Daw:    Uhm and that's pretty much permanently.
11    Clt:    Okay. [So-]
12    Daw:          [It']s really really bad.
13    Clt:    Mm.
14    Daw:    Like sometimes I'm in that much agony
15            I can't even get out of be:d.
16    Clt:    Oka:y. [So it sounds- ]
17    Daw:           [It's all swoll]en up around my hips...
```

These response tokens are affectively neutral, and contrast with the way in which call-takers respond to distressing experiences reported in many other calls – for example, the empathetic *A::::h* (Extract 1, line 14) or more developed responses such as *Oh dear, That sounds awful,* or *Poor you.* Across this particular call-taker's sample of calls there is tension between callers' extended accounts of their pain and suffering (apparently in search of an empathetic response that never comes) and the call-taker's readiness to move on (or back) to a different topic or activity. So in Extract 2, the call-taker treats the answer to her question (at line 2) as adequate when it reaches its earliest possible grammatical completion (after 'I get a lot of pain'): she receipts it with a token ('Right') designed to display recognition that what has just been said is building upon something that has been said earlier (Gardner, 2007), and is beginning (with *so*) to formulate its upshot (recycled at lines 11 and 16). The upshot she eventually produces – much later, after the caller's extended description of her pain (data not shown) – turns out to be that since that the caller experiences pain on walking, she may be eligible for a form of financial help for disabled people (which the call-taker has earlier referred to as *Disability Living Allowance,* data not shown). Since the purpose of the question at line 1 is to establish the caller's possible eligibility for financial assistance (and since this assistance is awarded to people with mobility problems), the caller's possible eligibility is established at the point at which the call-taker intervenes at line 4. The shift in response token from *right* (immediately after the relevant response to her question and preparatory to formulating its upshot) to *okay* ('a token that signals some degree of shift in topic or activity', Gardner, 2007, p. 322) in subsequent turns, marks the call-taker's orientation to the continued talk about pain as a topic in its own right from which her information about financial assistance will constitute a departure.

The misalignment played out across this sequence, then, derives from the call-taker's orientation to giving information about financial assistance (to which the extended description of pain is irrelevant) and the caller's orientation to conveying the extent of her pain. This is an instance of interactional asynchrony (Jefferson and Lee, 1981) in which one person is engaged in troubles-telling and the other does not align as a troubles recipient. By treating the trouble as a problem to be solved, and proffering information relevant to solving it, the call-taker shifts the focus away from the troubles teller and her experiences.[11]

I showed this call-taker transcripts of several interactions where women described their pain to her and she responded with *Right* or *Okay* and asked if she had any intuitions about why she did this, when so many other call-takers say things like *Poor you!*. She said that she herself had suffered with pelvic pain for many years and what changed her life was not sympathy but getting appropriate help. Part of her goal in working for the helpline is to ensure that women get physiotherapy and other services to which they are entitled, so that they get better. She expressed some frustration at the extent to which callers 'wallow' in pain and misery instead of getting help to recover. It is transparently clear from the recorded calls that this call-taker is extremely knowledgeable about the kind of practical help that women can access and she certainly achieves the very pragmatic aim of informing them about this – albeit at some interactional cost on both sides. She was very receptive to my suggestion that callers might appreciate the occasional *Poor you!* (or whatever equivalent seems 'natural' to her) in response to their reports of pain, before she delivers this information. I suggested that it might actually mean that they would more quickly and readily accept her advice to get physiotherapy and so on instead of pursuing – with lengthy accounts of their pain – the affiliation they experience her as withholding. She tried it, reported that it worked, and sent me recordings of the interactions which showed that her production of *Oh dear*s at appropriate places was having exactly the desired effect.

A second example of using CA to feed back to an individual call-taker is one in which I advised against pretending to remember repeat callers' stories. More than a third of the calls in the home birth corpus are repeat calls to the same call-taker as women call back to report on developments in their struggles to get midwifery cover for a home birth, or to report on their labours and new babies. The volume of calls (and the fact that women often don't give their names, and their call-taker rarely takes notes) means that – understandably – the call-taker often does not remember the previous call(s). Repeat callers commonly identify themselves as such and ask the call-taker whether she remembers them, providing memory prompts of dubious utility. In all of the recorded repeat calls (analysed in Shaw and C. Kitzinger, 2007) she claims so to do, but in relatively few is there any evidence that she does, and in several we found evidence that she does *not*. Moreover, our analysis showed that by claiming to remember she creates interactional difficulties for callers who then have to refrain from telling her, as if for the first time, whatever they should now properly suppose her to remember from the previous call (Schegloff, 2007, p. 38).

It sometimes becomes apparent that the claim to remember was fraudulent when the call-taker asks for information that the caller knows she has already conveyed in the earlier call, or when – in one case – the whole reason for the previous call has apparently been forgotten. This last rather dramatic case (for which the data, too long to reproduce in full here, are displayed in Shaw and C. Kitzinger, 2007, pp. 137–8) involves a repeat call from a woman who identifies herself as someone who had called previously because she had wanted to *have a home birth with a pool* but that something related to *getting a hoist* had stood in her way. The call-taker claims to remember (*Oh yes! Yes, yes.*). The caller has since given birth in hospital and most of the call is preoccupied with the reasons for this and her feelings about it. As part of moving towards closing the interaction, the caller returns to the reason for her previous call and offers to communicate with other would-be home birthers *if the hoist thing comes up*. The call-taker's response makes manifest that – despite her claim to have remembered the previous call – she has absolutely no recollection of *the hoist thing*.

Extract 3   (Belinda)

```
[HB 43, second call]

01      Clt:       .hhh Why: (.) they're not suggesting you
02                 have a hoist at home are the [:y?]
03      Bel:                                    [ Ye]s::=
04      Clt:       =Oh my god.
```

I showed the opening and closing of this call (and other less embarrassing instances) to the call-taker who readily appreciated the problems of fraudulent claims to remember but was dismayed at the prospect of having to admit to *not* remembering someone who had 'bared her soul' in a previous call. Given that a third of the calls involve a recognition solicit (something like *I called about two months ago when they said I couldn't have a home birth because they couldn't spare the midwives. I don't know if you remember me?*), she couldn't imagine what she could say in response. I searched out and discussed with her a few examples of responsive turns to recognition solicits from other call-takers (e.g., *Remind me again of the details*; *Uhm, it's probably best if you start at the beginning again*). Analysis showed that these are not the interactionally preferred responses (it *is* best to remember!), but that confessing to *not* remembering limits the interactional damage to this slot, whereas pretending to remember has unpredictable – and potentially much more damaging – reverberations across the entire interaction. In subsequent calls, this call-taker changed her practice and reported that she was pleased with the result.

These, then, are two examples in which CA 'falsifies and corrects' (Peräkylä and Vehviläinen, 2003) the assumptions of call-takers – that callers can be brought most efficiently to act to sort out their trouble (by seeking out appropriate help from a physiotherapist) if the call-taker avoids displays of emotional reciprocity and focuses on information-giving; and that it is better for the ongoing relationship to pretend to remember a repeat caller's story than to admit to having forgotten it. These 'corrections' were not based on abstract theory but on analysis of recorded data, and were compelling since call-takers could hear for themselves that their assumptions about best practice were not achieving the effects they wanted. In both cases, the call-taker's assessment was that the (CA-derived) alternative way of handling the interactional 'trouble' was more effective.

Concluding comments

This chapter contributes to existing CA work on helpline interaction (e.g., Baker, Emmison and Firth, 2005; Edwards, 2007) by using my research with three childbirth helplines to illustrate some of the 'applied' uses of this kind of research. I have tried to balance my presentation of the benefits of using CA in this way by also presenting some of its limitations.

In all three organisations, call-takers had never recorded and listened to their own calls before and this proved to be enormously helpful for reflective practice. Simply listening to calls together and discussing what was going on was revelatory. This alone, however, does not constitute 'applied CA'. The practice and training implications offered by applied CA are based on rigorous data analyses that are well-grounded in the empirical research literature. The length of time necessary to conduct CA analyses may mean managing organisations' expectations for rapid results. In addition, other methods may be more appropriate to address the issues and concerns of the organisation. We need to acknowledge this and be willing either to use other analytic methods ourselves (as I've illustrated here) or refer organisations to those who can.

In order to communicate CA analyses and their implications effectively, it is usually necessary to learn and engage with the professional stocks of knowledge (Peräkylä and Vehviläinen, 2003) held by members of the organisation. This enables CA researchers to ensure that any practice or training suggestions they make are relevant to the concerns and preoccupations of the organisation and that implementing recommended changes is something the organisation has an interest in doing. Researchers also need to demonstrate that any recommended changes are achievable, since it is sometimes suggested that many features of interaction studied by CA are not within the conscious control of speakers, or that altering them by an act of will as a result of research findings may sound 'artificial' or 'unnatural'.[12]

Finally, CA is descriptive, not prescriptive. There is nothing in CA's theory or method that gives the researcher a warrant for claiming that one way of interacting is 'better' than another. To answer call-takers' questions about which ways of talking are most effective, we need to establish what organisational goals they are hoping to achieve and then we can assess which ways of talking are likely to be most successful in achieving these goals. Such judgments are outside of the remit of CA as such. When we support an organisation's aims and objectives (as in the research reported here), applied CA can be personally and politically rewarding. When we do *not*, the ethics of applied CA can become problematic. (I would not want, for example, to give feedback to marketing representatives of a company producing infant formula feed on how to improve their interactions with healthcare workers in developing countries in order to maximise sales.) Since we cannot make ethical distinctions between different goals, or between different ways of achieving them, in our role as conversation analysts we must make them as human beings. Applied CA is likely to be most rewarding (for both parties) when the researcher supports (politically, socially, ethically) – or at least does not oppose – the goals of the organisation and the means by which it hopes to achieves them. Then, working with organisations like these three childbirth helplines can become a mutually beneficial partnership.

Notes

1. With thanks to Sue Wilkinson for helpful feedback on an earlier version of this chapter.
2. Despite four different grant applications, I have been unsuccessful in obtaining external funding for my research with any of these helplines. Had I been in a position

to hire research assistants (and to buy recording equipment, software, transcription services and so on), I would undoubtedly have been able to move forward much more rapidly in answering the needs of the organisations. What follows describes the relatively small-scale research that is feasible with minimal financial support and without buy-out from teaching responsibilities. I want to acknowledge the help of the University of York in allowing me a term of study leave and a small grant that enabled me to pay for digitising and transcribing some of the calls (and thanks to Rose Rickford, Clare Stockill and Rowena Viney for their help with this). I was also very pleased that an ESRC funded PhD research student, Rebecca Shaw, elected to work on the home birth helpline calls, and I draw on some of her analyses in this chapter.
3. Of course, all 'basic' research contributes to the core knowledge of the field from which 'applied' research draws, and in that sense it could be claimed that this work might at some point become indirectly relevant to the helplines – but that is not a claim I want to develop here, nor would it suffice as an answer to the call-takers who sent me their recordings.
4. This also involved some content analysis; e.g., to answer the question quoted above about the percentage of callers whose labours were induced.
5. I also discussed with the organisation how to develop appropriate coding sheets if they wanted to collect this data systematically and the problem of 'missing values'.
6. As a feminist I share these organisations' commitments to challenging and changing practice and policies around childbirth, and have used my thematic analyses of the calls in midwifery education (at my own university and elsewhere) and at the Royal College of Obstetricians and Gynaecologists (e.g., C. Kitzinger, 2005b).
7. This is sometimes called 'video-based self-assessment' (Zick, Granieri and Makoul, 2007). For examples of educational interventions in which practitioners (commonly nurses or doctors) record themselves in practice situations – e.g., delivering genetic counselling, administering chemotherapy, dealing with patients on an emergency ward, attending women in labour – and then examine the recordings and discuss their own strengths and weaknesses with a view to improving future performance, see McKay and Smith (1993); O'Baugh (2009); Pieterse et al. (2006); Sandhu et al. (2009); Yoo et al (2009). (Note that – although 'simulated' patients are often used, there are also many published reports, including all those cited here, which rely on 'real' interactions with actual patients.)
8. Unlike CA, this approach does not focus on the *interaction* between patient and doctor – i.e., how one responds to the other, in the CA sense of sequential analysis. For example, although analysis results in a numerical count of the different types of questions from the physician and different types of answers from the patient, it is not designed to relate questions and their answers to one another (Sandvik et al., 2002). Moreover, both the *content* (what the interactants are talking *about*) and the *context* of utterances (e.g., at what stage of the consultation) are expunged in the coding process (Heritage and Maynard, 2006, p. 7).
9. Callers gave consent for their recordings to be used for research and training purposes. Names of people, places, hospitals and any other identifying information in the transcripts are pseudonyms – and have been beeped out on the tapes.
10. According to Schegloff (2007, pp. 170–1) topic proffers are 'most often implemented by so-called 'yes/no'-type questions: two of the examples he cites are: *So are you dating Keith* and *So you're back*.
11. According to Jefferson and Lee (1981), call-takers in their 'limited institutional corpus' (p. 543) of troubles-tellings virtually never produce empathetic receipts.

They show one 'unique' instance in which a call-taker on the suicide prevention service line produces 'Oh my::' in what they describe as a misplaced attempt to 'humanise' the service with 'unwarranted affiliation' (p. 421). By contrast empathetic receipts are normative across my data corpora. This may reflect the way in which helplines have changed over the last 40 years and/or the nature of the helplines studied. The ethos of the childbirth helplines is very much 'woman to woman', and they are advertised more like 'self-help' groups than professional organisations.

12. These paragraphs, written to address CA researchers, can be inverted (as follows) to address members of organisations who may have been asked to cooperate with conversation-analytic research. You may wish to consider that the data corpus you will be providing (while of immense value to conversation analysts) is accessible to a range of different possible analytic approaches, and it is likely that, for some of the concerns and priorities you have as an organisation, approaches *other than CA* will be more appropriate. In exchange for handing your data over to conversation analysts, I strongly recommend that you request that analysis is not limited to CA alone but includes other approaches (e.g., thematic analysis, content analysis) that may be helpful in addressing live concerns within your organisation (as illustrated in this chapter). You may also want to consider requiring researchers to learn more about your organisation, its aims and objectives (perhaps via participant observation or ethnography).

7
Simulated Interaction and Communication Skills Training: The 'Conversation-Analytic Role-Play Method'

Elizabeth Stokoe

'Role-play' is a ubiquitous method for training people in workplace settings of all kinds to better interact with other colleagues and members of the public. Van Hasselt, Romano and Vecchi define role-play as 'simulations of real-world interpersonal encounters, communications, or events' (2008, p. 251). Typically, role-play methods involve the people being trained or assessed interacting with actors or other simulated interlocutors, using 'narrative adaptations' of hypothetical or actual scenarios as the basis for the simulated encounter (Van Hasselt, Romano and Vecchi, 2008, p. 254, see also Rosenbaum and Ferguson, 2006). In addition to its training function, role-play is used to assess 'communication skills' across numerous workplace settings. It is also used more generally as a pedagogical tool in educational contexts (e.g., Andresen, 2005; Rogers and Evans, 2007), and to assess other sorts of psychological competences (e.g., Leising, Rehbein and Sporberg, 2007; Palmieri et al., 2007).

My aims in this chapter are twofold. First, I describe and evaluate the existing literature on role-play, focusing particularly on the question of whether 'authentic simulation' is possible. Second, I describe and illustrate a different type of role-play training to traditional simulation based in a conversation-analytic study of neighbour disputes and mediation: the 'conversation-analytic role-play method' (CARM). I show how audio-visual technology, combined with conversation-analytic principles and practices, may be used effectively to train members of talk-based institutions. In contrast to more usual role-play methods, which presume that people already know 'how talk works' sufficiently to simulate interaction, the conversation-analytic approach uses actual interaction, turn-by-turn, to show participants how 'from close looking at the world you can find things that we couldn't, by imagination, assert were there' (Sacks, 1992, p. 420). I conclude by considering the context for, and shape of, 'interventionist Conversation Analysis' and the development of a new approach to role-play as an example of such an intervention in professional practice.

Role-play training as an empirical tool

Research about role-play can be grouped loosely into two domains of inquiry. First, role-play is compared to and evaluated against other forms of communication skills training, including theoretically-driven 'table-top' discussion, video-feedback and other forms of observation (e.g., Van Hasselt, Romano and Vecchi, 2008; Wannan and York, 2005). Second, the impact on trainees' communication skills scores of different categories of role-play participants has been studied extensively, comparing actors with both trainees themselves and 'real' parties (i.e., actual patients, clients, etc.) as interlocutors for the simulation. For example, in clinical settings, where role-play is used extensively to train doctors and other medical professionals, comparisons are made between using actors as 'simulated patients', versus getting clinicians themselves to play the patient role. In one study, Lane, Hood and Rollnick (2008) found no difference in health care professionals' communication competence 'regardless of whether they practised with an SP or a fellow trainee during training' (p. 637; see also Lane and Rollnick, 2007; Mounsey et al., 2006). Role-play participants are also asked regularly about their experiences, often regarding their assessment of different types of interlocutor (e.g., Bokken et al., 2009; Lim, Oh and Seet, 2008).

Simulating authenticity: problems with role-play

The guiding assumption of role-playing is that it sufficiently mimics an actual interactional event to be useful for rehearsing the same conversational moves that would comprise it. This assumption is implicit in most studies, but the issue of authenticity in role-play is debated in a substantial minority of papers. The main question is whether or not *authentic simulation* is possible. Some role-play practitioners and researchers discuss in detail the steps taken in order to make the role-play encounter as 'similar to real-life encounters' as possible (Van Hasselt, Romano and Vecchi, 2008, p. 254). In their evaluation of role-play training for hostage negotiators, Van Hasselt and colleagues use real-life cases as the basis for simulations. For example, they describe a 'family domestic' scenario in which a man abducts his wife and child and holds them hostage in an unoccupied farmhouse. Trainee negotiators then respond to the prompting first turn 'I'm not letting her take my son away from me'.

There are two related problems with Van Hasselt, Romano and Vecchi's method for initiating authentic interaction, and of role-play in general. The first is to do with the assumption, implicit in their and other people's studies, that plausible turns of talk can be invented on the basis of a normative understanding of how talk works. A common objection to the conversation analytic endeavour is that 'we', as native speakers, already know how talk works because it constitutes the very basis of our everyday social lives: talk 'just' is (Schegloff, 1996a). Indeed, much of linguistics uses unproblematically invented and hypothetical talk as the basis for generalising about language use. In response to both anecdotal complaints about CA's topic, and in more formal debate with linguists (e.g., Schegloff, 1992; Searle, 1986), conversation analysts have undermined arguments about the 'vernacular familiarity' people have about interaction, and shown how CA 'can yield empirically grounded results at variance with our commonsense intuitions about how some action is accomplished or what action some utterance is to be understood to have accomplished' (Schegloff, 1996, pp. 166–9). Similarly, Speer (2005, p. 54) argues that people's 'hypotheses about how talk works … caricature what happens in practice'. While any first turn at talk will initiate a second, it is impossible to know where and how a role-play prompt, as a first pair part, might be formulated and located in an actual interactional event.

There is some limited evidence that role-play interactions do differ from actual encounters, although there are no studies that make a direct comparison. In De la Croix and Skelton's (2009) study of simulated vs. actual doctor-patient consultations, they focused on features of 'conversational dominance' in both settings. They measured the amount of talk and number of interruptions by trainee doctors in role-play, and found that, in contrast to 'real' doctor-patient interaction, simulated patients interrupted and talked more than the doctors. Therefore, they argued that role-play interaction is at 'a similar distance from "reality" as a script to a play', and concluded that 'role-play is not, and should not seek to provide, a mirror to nature' (p. 701). However, there are several problems with this study. First, De la Croix and Skelton's definition of interruption was based on a flawed understanding of turn-taking as set out in Sacks, Schegloff and Jefferson (1974). Rather than take into account 'turn incursions' – overlaps that transgress transition relevance places – De la Croix and Skelton simply defined interruption by the occurrence of overlapping talk involving a change of speaker (see Kitzinger, 2008a, for a critique of 'interruption' studies more generally). Second, the literature on which they based their comparison, which treats talk time and interruption as indices of conversational dominance, has been heavily criticised by other researchers for inconsistent findings and various methodological flaws (see Cameron, 1997; James and Clarke, 1993; James and Drakich, 1993).

The second problem with role-play methods is precisely that the interactions are *simulations*, in which what is at stake for participants is necessarily different from what is at stake in any 'real' encounter. The issue of 'stake' in interaction echoes broader social science debates about the empirical value of interview accounts versus observations of 'real life', and of 'natural' vs. 'contrived' data (e.g., Griffin, 2007; Potter and Hepburn, 2005; Rapley, 2001; Speer, 2002). Because of the perceived problem of access to research sites, and perceived 'randomness' of conversation (e.g., Lakoff, 1973; Van Dijk, 1987), interview and focus group data are treated as 'surrogates for the observation of actual behaviour' (Heritage and Atkinson, 1984, p. 2). Similarly, role-play encounters are often used as surrogates for the behaviour of interest. For example, in their pursuit of understanding accountant-client interaction, Burns and Moore make the case for using role-play encounters between trainee accountants and simulated clients because 'access to actual workplace settings ... is unattainable ... difficult ... impracticable ... impossible' (2008, pp. 322–3).

Potter and Hepburn (2005) point out that the analysis of interview materials often disregards the researcher-saturated setting of the data's production. The data produced is a researcher-guided interaction that has *no other purpose* than being a research interview. The stakes are low, for the people being interviewed. Yet many interview-based researchers treat accounts as typical of accounts that may be produced in any other context. For example, Stokoe (2010) argues that, in the majority of work on male perpetrators of sexual violence, their accounts are analysed without considering how they may be designed differently for particular recipients (e.g., a social scientist, a police officer, a lawyer, a therapist, the victim's family and so on), or according to the differing institutional and interactional contingencies that are relevant to, say, minimising one's crime in a police interrogation, vs. being seen to 'accept responsibility' in an offender treatment programme.

Similar issues are relevant to role-play encounters and their treatment as equivalent to actual interactions between parties. It is hard to support a claim that participants in role-play are oriented to the same interactional contingencies as they would be in the actual setting; even if participants rate role-playing as 'authentic' after the event (e.g., Hillbrand et al., 2008). For those having their interactional skills evaluated, what is at stake is their performance and 'score' as trainees. For example, in Okada's study of foreign language proficiency testing, in which candidates role-play 'everyday' encounters as part of their assessment, he notes that the 'interviews are authentic high-stake tests whose results are used by corporations for decisions on employees' career advancement and overseas posting' (2010, p. 1653). De la Croix and Skelton tease out this argument more explicitly, concluding from their comparison of role-played medical interaction and previous studies of actual doctor-patient encounters, that 'the game of teaching ... overrides the game of medicine' (2009, p. 701).

This does not mean that role-play interaction is not interesting in its own right (Seale et al., 2007). Conversation analysts and discursive psychologists have long since made the case for, and conducted many studies of, research-generated interactions *as* interaction; as *topic*, not resource (Wieder, 1988). Indeed, as Seale and colleagues (2007, p. 178) suggest, 'understanding the particular linguistic dynamics of simulated encounters … seems long overdue'. We consider the small body of conversation analytic literature to date on role-play and simulated interaction in the next section.

Conversation analysis and role-play

The earliest studies that examined role-play encounters were conducted by ethnomethodologists and conversation analysts (Francis, 1989; Sharrock and Watson, 1985; Watson and Sharrock, 1988). Both sets of studies focused on the way participants accomplished their roles by performing the activities tied categorically to them. In so doing, they displayed their knowledge of category-bound activities and predicates. Role-play is therefore built from 'members' general, culturally based "reasoning procedures," procedures which of course are *not exclusively deployed in game contexts*' (Sharrock and Watson, 1985, p. 197, emphasis in original, see also Francis, 1989, p. 67). In Francis's study, he analysed role-play in business negotiation classes, in which participants negotiated the construction of both 'student' identities and the particular role-play identities. Similar observations were reported by Linell and Thunqvist (2003) in their analysis of role-play training for job interviews with unemployed teenagers. They noted that the participants shifted between different roles as, say, the tutor switched between being the 'tutor' to make pedagogic points and role-playing the 'employer' to conduct the simulated interview. These findings are relevant to our discussion above about what is at stake in role-play interactions, which includes being assessed or evaluated as a 'student' or 'trainee'.

Seale and colleagues take these findings about the different category incumbencies operating in role-play to raise 'the issue of the degree to which the experience of participants is comparable with that of the "real" events for which they are being trained' (2007, p. 179). However, answering this question is complex. On the one hand, 'one can ask whether the surface appearance of staying in the role-playing frame denotes "authenticity" if this involves a different inner psychological experience from that experienced by participants in the 'real' situations for which they are being prepared' (p. 179). On the other, Seale and colleagues suggest that being able to cope with 'the particular linguistic demands of simulations, which is probably related to a general facility with language in interaction, is the major factor in determining participants' capacity for learning new communication skills, quite aside from the degree to which simulations successfully mimic real clinical situations' (p. 179).

In a recent CA study, Okada (2010) examined role-play interaction in 'oral proficiency interviews' (OPI) that test potential employees' second or foreign language competence. He points out that previous studies of OPIs find that, when compared to ordinary conversation, one party – the interviewer – tends to determine turn-taking and the topic of talk. This is not surprising, given that tests are delivered in an interview format. In contrast, Okada studied oral proficiency tests that were designed to mimic everyday scenarios, role-playing a variety of domestic and consumer encounters. Okada found that

> although the role-play in OPIs is different from ordinary conversation in terms of the interactional structures, what candidates do in and for a role-play activity is highly similar to what s/he does in an ordinary conversation: s/he must understand what his/her interlocutors have said and display his/her understandings in their next turn. In this sense, the role-play activity is not unsuitable, but instead valid for evaluating a candidate's conversational competencies. In particular, the activity would work effectively to investigate how well a candidate can construct a social and discursive identity in interaction, which seems to be difficult to elicit in an interviewer-led interviewing sequence.
>
> (2010, p. 1666)

However, Okada's findings are not about whether or not the role-play looks more like ordinary talk than traditional OPI interviews, but more about candidates' abilities to engage in role-play in the first place. In any role-play, participants necessarily display their competencies in turn-taking, transition relevance, action formation, sequence organisation, repair – the basic machinery of talk-in-interaction. Whether or not turn design, action, sequence organisation and so on, are the same in role-play as its actual interactional partner are the same is an empirical question yet to be answered (and this is the subject of my own current research comparing taped police interrogations of suspects with taped, simulated interrogations of suspects conducted by both trainee and experienced police officers).

Having provided a critical overview of role-play research, I move on now to study a different approach to role-play. As discussed above, the main problems with role-play are, first, the assumption that simulated encounters mimic their real counterparts sufficiently to be of pedagogic or training use and, second, that interaction is actually *simulate-able*. Although role-play training often involves working with real-life cases, role-play has not, to the best of my knowledge, used such real encounters 'live'. While some conversation analysts use real materials with practitioners as a way of getting them to reflect on their practice (e.g., Heritage, 2009; Kitzinger and Kitzinger, 2007), such materials have not been used to replace or complement traditional role-play training itself. The rest of this chapter describes just such an approach, developed for and carried out with trainee and experienced mediators.

The conversation-analytic role-play method

As part of a UK research council-funded project on neighbour disputes I and my colleague on the project, Derek Edwards, collected a large corpus of interactional materials across a variety of institutional settings. The guiding rationale for data collection was to record people in the business of 'being neighbours' or formulating their own and other people's conduct as incumbents of that category (rather than, say, interviewing people about their neighbour relationships). The data corpus comprised over 120 hours of recorded and transcribed conversations, including face-to-face mediation sessions between mediators and clients, telephone calls to mediation centres, police interviews with suspects in neighbour-relevant crime, and telephone calls to council services; specifically, environmental health and antisocial behaviour units.

Because the primary aim of the research was to unpack the causes and trajectories of neighbour disputes, the practices of the institutional parties to these interactions (mediators, police officers and council workers) – or interventions in their practices – were not the main focus of the project. Nevertheless, in analysing the materials, we made numerous observations about the talk of both parties, and reported those that seemed pertinent to practitioners at regular feedback sessions. Most of the feedback has been delivered to mediators, who expressed strong interests in the findings of the project. Feedback sessions quickly became training workshops, and it was during these workshops that the role-play technique I report on here began to take shape. Over the past year, and in regular consultation with mediators, I have developed materials to use with groups of both experienced and novice mediators. I have also begun to work with the police in a similar way, focusing on suspect interviews.

The technique I set out below uses real, live calls from members of the public into mediation centres as the basis for role-play and discussion. I soon discovered that because mediation training is done via traditional role-play simulation, mediators seldom, if ever, study their own practice with real clients. This meant that the materials presented and method used were novel for participants. In one of the few studies of role-play training for mediators, White and Agne (2009) video-taped pairs of trainee mediators engaged in role-play, and then examined the reflection and discussion about these interactions that was provided by 'coaches', or experienced mediators. The aim of the study was to examine coaching as a method for experienced mediators to share their expertise with trainees, and their analysis focused on the coaches' behaviour and the advice and suggestions they gave to trainees. While White and Agne found that the coaches helped trainees to understand some of the problems of mediation, they did not 'identify or demonstrate for trainees the communication practices that would allow trainees to *enact* the communication behaviours considered central to the mediation process' (2009, p. 85). So, while on the one hand, coaches can help with trainees' knowledge of mediation in theory, they cannot, according to White and Agne, help develop trainees' 'procedural knowledge ... about *how to actually manage interaction*' (p. 85, emphasis added). Because the method I developed uses live interaction with real clients, mediators could begin to discuss their practice from a completely new perspective.

The method works as follows, using a laptop, portable data projection screen and projector, a sound system, and using PowerPoint software (Figure 7.1).

1. I identify a data extract, or series of extracts, in which a particular interactional problem seems to arise, or in which a 'successful' outcome (e.g., a client agrees to mediation) is accomplished.
2. The data is transcribed according to the usual conversation-analytic conventions (Jefferson, 2004) and both sound file and written transcript are anonymised.
3. The transcript is presented, line-by-line, synchronised with the audio file. This means that workshop participants 'live through' the call as it happens – they do not receive transcripts ahead of hearing the extract and do not know how the conversation unfolds beyond the lines I play to them.
4. Having played one or several lines, or turns, in a call, workshop participants then discuss possible trouble and perturbations in the call thus far, and begin to formulate candidate next turns.
5. The next turn of the conversation is then played, and participants discuss it as a possible solution to the trouble displayed earlier in the call.

The first step, then, is to identify the data on which to base the workshop. So far, this has worked in two ways: I select a set of extracts based on my analysis of them as possible 'trouble-spots' for mediators. I also ask workshop participants in advance to identify an issue they would like me to help them with. In the second half of the chapter, I describe one example from each dataset used in workshops with mediators.

Figure 7.1 Participants at a mediation training workshop

Case 1 Mediation as an unknown institution

Mediation, as an institutional setting, is a 'precarious institution', for two reasons. First, mediation centres often occupy either charitable status or are funded by local council authorities. This means that as an institution, and compared to, say, medical centres or police stations, mediation is not embedded 'solidly' in funding streams and is often set up and maintained only at the current political whim of governments, filtering down to local authorities. In the ten years I have worked with mediation services, I have seen many come and go, and have also seen the national mediation organisation fail. This lack of centralised, committed funding is relevantly tied to the second reason for mediation services' 'precarious' status as an institution in UK culture. It is an 'unknown institution'; something that most people have never encountered and do not know about. It was clear from the analysis of the materials that mediation services are not an obvious port of call for neighbour problems: people report first calling the council, police or environmental health services. When members of the public do call mediation centres, it often emerges that not only do they not know what mediation is, they do not know what to expect from mediators in response to their problem formulation, and often do not want the 'talking cure' on offer (Edwards and Stokoe, 2007; Stokoe and

Edwards, 2007). However, mediators must turn enough 'callers' into 'clients' in these initial calls to justify their funding.

Call openings, then, are places in which possible problems and misalignments between caller and mediator can and do emerge. As mentioned above, one reason for misalignments that callers do not automatically tie to the activity of 'solving neighbour disputes' to 'mediation services'. The example below comes from the start of a call to a mediation service. Figure 7.2 is a still image of the PowerPoint slide as presented to the participants. In the transcript, M is the mediator, and C is the caller.

The workshop participants' first task is to consider these five lines in 'slow motion', for several minutes. Having been presented with this interaction to this point, participants 'role-play' candidate next turns from the mediator in response to C's first turn. Therefore, as I draw their attention to emerging misalignments, they suggest and evaluate possible solutions. The points I draw their attention to start with are the way M initiates the interaction with an institutional self-identification, and C returns with a greeting but no identification, pointing out that already we can see that the parties to the interaction are both 'institutional' and 'ordinary' speakers. In other words, the parties are interacting from different interactional positions. Next, we note that following C's greeting she says 'I've ↑just been given this number↓'. This immediately signals potential alignment trouble: Despite the fact that the caller formulates her problem in terms of having 'really terrible neighbours.' (line 5), she shows that she has not associated her problem with

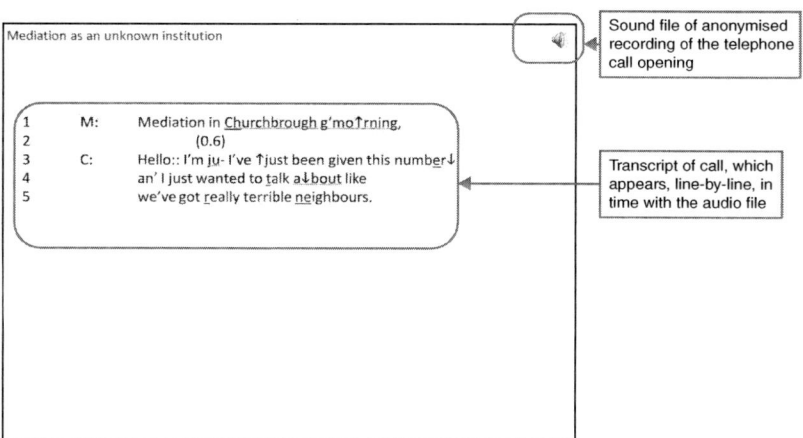

Figure 7.2 PowerPoint presentation of DC call (a)

the mediation service as the source of a possible solution. Such formulations were very common at the start of calls. It is a feature of neighbour mediation service calls, unlike calls to emergency services or doctors' receptionists, that callers did not always know much about the service. So misalignments between what the caller wants, and what is on offer, are a possible problem early in these calls. Furthermore, C's initial gloss on the problem: 'we've got <u>r</u>eally terrible <u>n</u>eighbours.' may look like a typical way of introducing and formulating a problem between neighbours, but I point out that it is more interesting than this. It does not define a problem *between* neighbours, such as not getting on with them, having an ongoing feud with them, or having broken off relations with them. Rather, C formulates a one-sided complaint: 'We've got <u>r</u>eally terrible <u>n</u>eighbours.' So, before the call has started, there are already signs of potential trouble for the service provider, which continues to be played out throughout the call.

By the end of this first task, which can easily take up 20 minutes or longer, participants are becoming familiar with the transcript layout and key, and have begun to appreciate the importance of thinking about each word selected and its function in the overall design of turns. Having spent several minutes role-playing possible responses, the next task is to evaluate what the mediator actually did next (Figure 7.3).

M's response comes after a short delay (line 7). The fact that C has used the category 'neighbours' is enough for M to see that this is the right type of call for her to deal with. She confirms that C has rung the right place, although not without some perturbation to the smooth progressivity of the call – that is, there is some delay (line 6), an audible in-breath, a repair initiator and a re-start on 'y've rung right place'. It might be that M is already picking up signs of trouble and her response symmetrically fits C's. These sorts of analytic observations are brought to bear in the discussion between me and the workshop participants. Having role-played various candidate turns that could have appeared at line 6, they can evaluate what the mediator did in response.

Before moving on to a second example, I want to explain briefly how participants come to understand the data and its presentation in the standard CA format using Jefferson transcription. It is perhaps surprising that, once they do understand it, they quickly see its benefits in understanding how, and where, troubles can arise in interaction. To 'train' mediators to understand the system, I use several examples, including the following clip (Figure 7.4) in which a caller is resisting a mediator's offer of mediation. There are numerous, uncomfortable gaps in the sequence, and participants readily come to understand the notion of turn construction units (TCUs), transition relevance and so on, although without necessarily using the technical language of CA to describe these phenomenon.

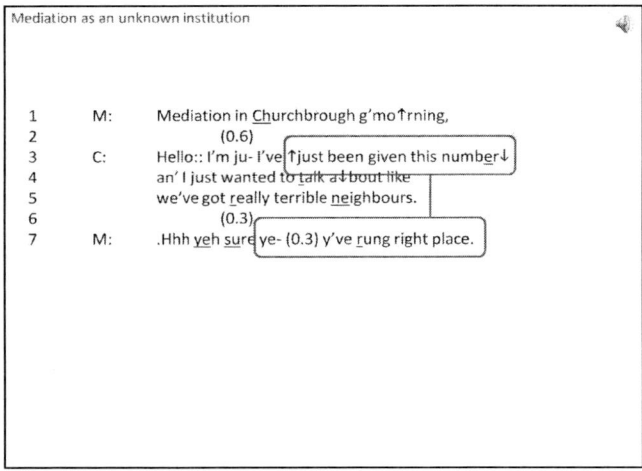

Figure 7.3 PowerPoint presentation of DC call (b)

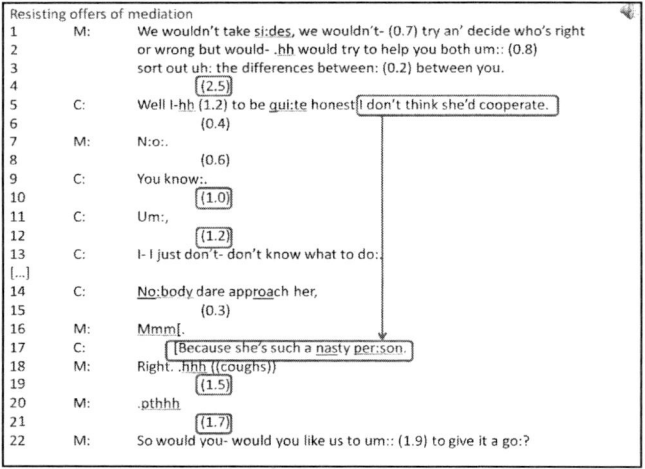

Figure 7.4 PowerPoint presentation of HC call

From this extract, participants quickly understand that 'gaps', even of 0.4 seconds (line 6), are hearable as long, awkward delays. They also understand that, when the same speaker takes successive turns (lines 9–14), there are (transition relevance) places in which the mediator could speak but does not. So, for example, they see that if the same speaker initial appears several times in succession, it is possible that the recipient is notably absent from the interaction and that trouble is emerging. From other examples, they learn that lots of square brackets means lots of overlapping talk, and while one cannot characterise an interaction on the basis of the numbers of brackets on a page, lots of overlapping talk might be indicative of animation, or conflict.

Returning to the first example, I continue to present the call, a turn at a time, until the action sequence is complete. In the next section, I provide a second example, this time developed in response to mediators' requests for help with dealing with '-isms'.

Case 2   Dealing with '-isms'

Mediators asked for specific training around how to deal with racist, sexist or homophobic callers. Because of their guiding ideology of being 'impartial', they reported that they find it challenging to respond to such callers in a way that maintains an impartial stance. The following case comes from the start of a call, in which the mediator has so far elicited permission from the caller to record their conversation

One of the first points for discussion is the caller's turn at line 4 (Figure 7.5), and whether or not it provides evidence of racism. For some workshop participants, the use of the category 'Indian' is enough to label him automatically as racist; others were more reluctant to reach this conclusion. This raises the issue of 'what counts' as racist talk, and whether or not line 4 provides for seeing the caller as 'just' *describing* his neighbour, rather than interpreting his use of the word as prejudiced. This is because the grammatical design of racial insults is based on two words: often a swear-word plus a national identity, race or ethnicity category (e.g., 'white bastard'; 'Somali bitch'). Speakers orient to this practice in various ways, including by editing one of the paired words but maintaining a *two-word* formulation (e.g., 'black this, black that' – see Stokoe and Edwards, 2007).

These ideas provide the basis for the first part of the discussion, as well as some of the prosodic features of the way the caller's turn at line 4 is delivered, with its hesitation, pause, in-breath, and speeded-up delivery of the category. I discuss with participants whether these prosodic features can be taken as evidence that the caller is oriented to his use of 'Indian' as problematic. Interestingly, things like 'ums' and pauses are categorised in the traditional role-play literature as problematic in a different way. The 'communication skills' that role-play and other forms of training are designed to assess include feature like 'active listening', 'displaying empathy', 'summarising', 'establishing rapport', 'questioning' and 'eliciting information', and non-verbal or 'paralanguage' (e.g., Caris-Verhallen, Timmermans and van Dulmenc, 2004; Maguire

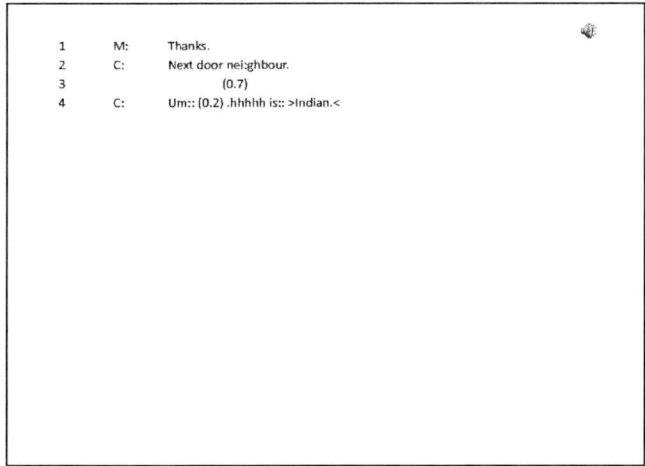

Figure 7.5 PowerPoint presentation of DC call (a)

and Pitceathly, 2002; Van Hasselt, Romano and Vecchi, 2008). However, like role-play itself, many of these skills are based on a normative sense of what 'good' communication looks like. So, for instance, Zick, Granieri and Makoul, (2007) evaluate turn components like 'um' negatively as 'disfluencies' that, if they appear in simulated interaction, would reduce participants' scores on the communication skills task. This echoes Chomsky's (1957) distinction between 'competence', which is a speaker's knowledge of how to produce grammatical sentences, and 'performance', which is actual speech. In his view, the 'performance', or natural language dimension of his theory was unworthy of scientific investigation, being too disorderly and unstructured to constitute appropriate data. In role-play training, 'good' communication should not involve the 'mess' of interaction, but be grammatical and even. However, the briefest foray into Conversation Analysis and a Jefferson transcript will quickly reveal that talk rarely conforms to Chomsky's notion of 'competence', and so role-play training that aims at such a standard is based on a flawed understanding of how talk works.

Returning to Figure 7.5, participants' next task is to role-play candidate responses to the caller's categorisation of his neighbour as 'Indian', with some suggesting an immediate challenge to its use, and others suggesting make no response except a continuer-type turn until the caller says more. Figure 7.6 provides the next turn.

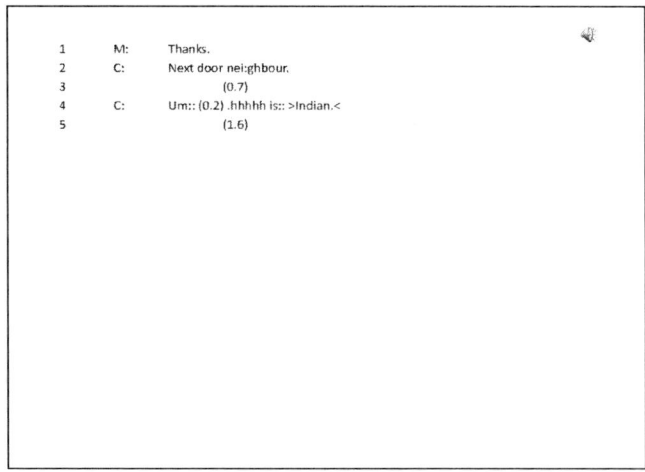

Figure 7.6 PowerPoint presentation of DC call (b)

In fact, what happens next is a lengthy gap, which can be seen as M's gap. This provides for a discussion of 'silence' as a turn, and its usefulness in such situations. Workshop participants saw silence as a valuable tool for delaying a response, waiting to hear more from the caller, and as a way of not having to challenge or accuse the caller immediately. Participants then role-play possible next turns, thinking about whether M will take a delayed turn, or whether C will orient to the gap as problematic and deal with it in his turn. This is what happens next (Figure 7.7).

After the long gap at line 5, in which there is no uptake from M, C produces a turn that both accounts for his first, starting with the disclaimer 'I've no: problem with Indians:', and frames the rest of his turn. Such disclaimers (e.g., 'I'm not racist, but') have been well-analysed by discourse analysts as methods for attending to what Edwards (2005) calls the 'subject side' of description, in which speakers attend to the possible characterological inferences that can be made about them on the basis of things that they say. Disclaimers often precede a statement that, without it, may be hearable as racist, sexist, or otherwise prejudiced. However, workshop participants immediately treated the use of a disclaimer as further evidence *in favour* of attributing racism to the caller. Again, candidate responses to C are role-played, with a continued split amongst participants between orienting and not orienting to his turns as racist. Figure 7.8 shows what happens next.

134 *Applied Conversation Analysis*

```
1    M:    Thanks.
2    C:    Next door nei:ghbour.
3          (0.7)
4    C:    Um:: (0.2) .hhhhh is:: >Indian.<
5          (1.6)
6    C:    I've no: problem with Indians: bu' unfortunately he's >lower caste< so he
7          doesn't do any work.
```

Figure 7.7 PowerPoint presentation of DC call (c)

```
1    M:    Thanks.
2    C:    Next door nei:ghbour.
3          (0.7)
4    C:    Um:: (0.2) .hhhhh is:: >Indian.<
5          (1.6)
6    C:    I've no: problem with Indians: bu' unfortunately he's >lower caste< so he
7          doesn't do any work.
8          (0.2)
9    C:    An' that's not ra:cist.
```

Figure 7.8 PowerPoint presentation of DC call (d)

As the transcript reaches line 9, the participants have another example in which C takes four turns in succession with no response from M, and 'see' from this evidence that the interaction is in troubled territory. Following another gap at line 8 – a second example of silence in which the mediator passes up the opportunity to take a turn – the caller explicitly names, and denies, what he may understand to be an unspoken assessment from the mediator ('An' that's not ra:cist.'). After more role-play discussion, the final section of the extract is presented (Figure 7.9).

As we can see, the mediator's response (lines 11–16) is to challenge the relevance of the caller's categorisation of his neighbour as 'Indian', as part of his complaint formulation. The workshop participants discuss her turn and consider possible alternative responses to what they all agree is a case of racially aggravated neighbour dispute. I also point out various interactional features of the extract, including the overlapping talk at lines 11–12, and subsequent repair initiator at line 14, both of which indicate that the caller has not, in fact, fully heard or comprehended her challenge at line 11. M's reformulation at line 16 is abandoned, as well as starting with a different footing, and C's final turn in the extract continues to explain the problem without answering either question. C continues to formulate his complaint without mentioning his neighbour's national identity.

This example prompted lengthy role-play discussion among participants, as well as a more general discussion about how best to deal with potentially racist callers to their services. I drew on findings from my study of racial abuse in neighbour disputes, one focus of which was on mediators' responses to reports of abuse, to provide further points for discussion. Mediators' responses were overwhelmingly to delete 'identity' issues from discussions, rather than issue challenges, and instead steer the discussion towards the 'material' aspects of

```
1    M:    Thanks.
2    C:    Next door nei:ghbour.
3          (0.7)
4    C:    Um:: (0.2) .hhhhh is:: >Indian.<
5          (1.6)
6    C:    I've no: problem with Indians: bu' unfortunately he's >lower caste< so he
7          doesn't do any work.
8          (0.2)
9    C:    An' that's not ra:cist.
10         (0.4)
11   M:    pt. What so: (0.6) wha' has him [being Indian got to- do: with it then. ]
12   C:                                    [W- the prob- the problem is, I mean, ]
13         (.)
14   C:    Sorry?
15         (.)
16   M:    .hhh well I'm jus- wond'[ring  why:,]
17   C:                            [(Yeh.) well]
18         (0.2)
19   C:    The pro:blem is (0.6) uh:: (some/seven) years ago:, (0.6) <I mean: he's lived
20         here since nine:teen ninety six.
```

Figure 7.9   PowerPoint presentation of DC call (e)

```
1    C:    I mean: uh- (0.4) e- ha:lf the battle of- as you u- are aware of hi:gh rise living
2          (0.4) is to get on with your nei:ghbours, [an' generally we do in this] block,
3    M:                                              [.hhh absolutely. °yeah.°    ] (0.2) I'm
4          su:re.
5    C:    There're a couple of families and uh I- I shou:ldn't sa:y this.=but I'm
6          go:in' to say because it's perfectly true:
7    M:    £uh heh.£
8    C:    They're A:sian families who seem to 'ave no control over their children.
9    M:    A:hh.
10                  (0.7)
11   M:    Y:eah.
12                  (0.3)
13   M:    .hh[hh
14   C:       [unfor:tunate but th- it's a ↓fact.
15                  (0.5)
16   M:    .hhh
17                  (0.3)
18   M:    Ye:ah so: w- well certainly whatever hh uh:- °any- any-° family if- if- if the
19         children're .hhh out of control then obviously it's going to be difficult in a:
20         (0.2) °in a° high rise flat.
21                  (0.6)
22   M:    .hhh Yh:eah: hh yeah.
23                  (1.3)
```

Figure 7.10 PowerPoint presentation of EC call

the dispute. The example below, also used in the workshops, illustrates this observation.

In this extract (Figure 7.10), I play the first seven lines, which come from the middle of a call about a noisy neighbour. At this point, I draw the workshop participants' attention towards the caller's first turn, in which he displays his understanding about how 'good' neighbours should behave towards each other (lines 1–2) and M's affiliative response (lines 3–4). C's next turn includes a disclaimer 'I shou:ldn't sa:y this.=but', which signals a potentially problematic upcoming statement. However, M's further affiliative laugh at line 7 suggests he has no idea what is coming next, and neither do the workshop participants. Then, as the interaction unfolds, the participants' role-play, then evaluate M's response to C's racially-based explanation for his neighbours' behaviour. They see, given the succession of 'M' turns and gaps (lines 9–13, 15–23) that there is trouble. In contrast to the previous example, the participants discuss this mediator's response which is to reformulate the caller's problem deleting the category 'Asian' from the reformulation and focusing on the problems 'any' family with children might cause in a high-rise block of flats.

In addition to these examples, I have provided role-play materials for instances of 'sexism' and other '-isms'. A common discussion point that emerged from such extracts was 'what counts' as sexism, and racism – a question that traditional role-play training has often focused on (e.g., Lee, Goforth and Blythe, 2009). However, in contrast to inventing examples of 'racist' or 'sexist' talk, the study of actual materials shows that categorising such talk can be a complex matter. As discourse analysts have frequently shown, 'new' and subtle forms of racist, sexist and other prejudiced talk mean that explicit forms are rarely found in public discourse (e.g., Barker, 1981; van Dijk, 1991). Furthermore, people regularly design their talk with the defeasibility of description, and hence deniability of accusations, in mind. Seeing how possibly prejudiced talk is actually formulated provides a novel empirical basis for the discussion of how to deal with it.

Interventionist Conversation Analysis

In this chapter, I have described a new approach to role-play training based in the empirical study of institutional materials, using Conversation Analysis (the 'conversation-analytic role-play method'), and contrasted it with standard types of simulated interaction for training. I end this chapter with a brief reflection on the experience of working with mediators using the materials and methods of Conversation Analysis, and consider its place as an intervention in professional practice alongside other 'applied' or 'interventionist' Conversation Analysis.

Having run numerous workshops, with several different mediation services, the participants are overwhelmingly positive about their close examination of actual mediators doing their daily work. As I mentioned earlier, the workshops provide a unique opportunity for mediators to work with live recordings and role-play through different cases. Many of the mediation centres request second and third follow-up sessions, and iterations are tailored to the specific needs of the centre. In feedback to the mediation centre directors, participants wrote that the sessions are 'very fascinating and relevant', 'inspiring', 'thought-provoking', 'raise some very difficult questions about mediation', 'excellent information and good points brought out to make you think. It challenged me!'; 'looking at the conversation was interesting for my own practice as a research interviewer'; 'the right language you use is all important'; 'the research was fascinating – the gaps and pauses having such an impact on the caller'; and 'a unique and valuable experience'.

During each workshop, I found it interesting, and a little surprising, that participants embraced both the use of technical transcription and the idea of working painstakingly with short extracts. Of course, they had no academic 'baggage' to hinder their participation, unlike student and academic audiences who sometimes respond with familiar complaints about CA's 'positivist', 'pointless' or 'apolitical' approach, and particularly to its detailed transcription (e.g., Parker, 2005). However, participants quickly saw the value in being able to study talk, in slow-motion, in a way that included every pause, perturbation and precise formulation. Indeed, several participants described seeing such materials as something of a revelation, and as providing them with some tools that would enable them to cash out their intuitions about 'how' and 'where' things 'go wrong' in their calls with clients.

Doing 'applied' or 'institutional' Conversation Analysis, in contrast to 'pure' or 'ordinary' CA, is already the subject of much discussion across the discipline, with much of the focus being on the distinguish-ability between institutional and ordinary settings, the location of institutionality in talk or setting, and the empirical value of studies of talk in applied settings over conducting 'basic' groundwork with 'ordinary' data (e.g., Benwell and Stokoe, 2006; Drew and Sorjonen, 1997; Heritage, 2005; Hester and Francis, 2001; ten Have, 1999). Making interventions in practice is a separate matter. One question that arises is whether or not using the methods and empirical findings of conversation-analytic research can be used to deliver practitioner and user interventions 'without compromise'. CA is a method which prizes its 'neutrality' and is contrasted with other explicitly political and 'interested' forms of discourse analysis. Indeed, it is often criticised for failing to engage with 'the big picture'. Furthermore, in a broader academic context where interventions are simultaneously prized by governments and funding bodies, yet often treated as less 'intellectually satisfying' and esteemed by academics themselves (e.g., von Prondzynski, 2009), the chapter raises questions about 'blue skies' vs. 'interventionist' research and the inevitable hierarchical ordering of this dichotomy.

However, conversation analysts have been making interventions in practice for some years, particularly in clinical settings and within the field of 'communication disorders', using recordings of real interactions as well as applying the cumulative findings of CA to tailor advice to speakers (e.g., Bauer and Kulke, 2004; Heritage et al., 2007; Kitzinger and Kitzinger, 2007; Wilkinson, 2006). Writing about medical settings in particular, Heritage (2009) argues that 'the examination of real data using CA is found by many to be a potent experience capable of triggering changes in attitudes and clinic practices that are beneficial for patient care'. For example, Booth and Swabey (1999) developed a communication skills programme for carers of people with aphasia, using CA to produce individually tailored advice 'using an assessment technique called the 'Conversation Analysis Profile for People with Aphasia' (Whitworth, Perkins and Lesser, 1997). Pre- and post-intervention measures included whether or not carers understood more accurately their relatives' aphasia, whether or not the severity of the communication disorder decreased, and whether or not trouble sources could be repaired more quickly, with some positive results.

The current chapter has made a novel contribution to 'interventionist CA', by developing a particular approach to role-play that uses CA's tools and techniques in ways that practitioners report are helpful to their practice. The method I have developed has the potential to work with any organisation in which interaction can be recorded and studied. From a personal perspective, my experience of working with professional mediators and, more recently, with police officers, has been very positive. Developing this role-play technique not only generates a sense of 'being useful', it does so 'without compromise'. Perhaps because CA, and its ethnomethodological roots, is the study of 'members', it is immediately of interest and accessible to 'members' whether or not they are trained conversation analysts. However, the data I present, and the discussions I steer on the basis of them, are grounded uncompromisingly in empirical findings about those data. There is no pressure to either 'dumb down' or 'theorise up': material is presented in much the same way as it might be in any CA data session. Using it for live role-play, however, allows the users of our research to engage authentically, without simulation, with their everyday professional practice.

8
Should Mandatory Jobseeker Interviews be Personalised? The Politics of Using Conversation Analysis to Make Effective Practice Recommendations[1]

Merran Toerien, Annie Irvine, Paul Drew and Roy Sainsbury

With the economic downturn of 2009, Jobcentre Plus, the UK service that gives employment advice and administers unemployment benefits, has come under increased media scrutiny. Can it deliver the *personalised* service it purports to offer, given the 90 per cent increase in number of claimants arriving at its doors? The media have been sceptical, even hostile. It is not uncommon to see stories of claimants feeling 'processed' through an impersonal and callous system, as in this horror story in *The Times:*

> A friend of mine – let's call her Gill – was one of six directors recently made redundant by a well-known UK consortium... So, like you, me or any raw school-leaver, she Googled 'job centre' and phoned the number on the website... There follows a tale of such humiliation, misunderstanding and Stalinist bureaucracy that, on reading it, the shivers will run up the spine of every white-collar worker in the land.
>
> (Reid, 2008, p. 20)

The management of Jobcentre Plus itself, on the other hand, promotes a more optimistic view, with slogans such as 'the job you want, the help you need' and success stories like the one reported below, published in the agency's in-house magazine:

> Penny Palmer is one of those lucky people who does something she enjoys. Penny grew up around horses and at 39 decided she wanted to become an equine therapist... Penny has 5 children so it wasn't easy for her to find the time to focus on what she needed to do to turn her hobby

into a business. With the help of her Jobcentre Plus adviser Jane Simpson, however, she found the drive and self-belief to get started.

(Anonymous, 2008, p. 19)

As Ruth Owen, Chief Operating Officer for Jobcentre Plus, put it in an interview: 'We've changed our service deliberately to make it a lot more personalised. We can offer much more help tailored around the individual's circumstances than ever before' (quoted by Waite, 2009).

In this chapter we look very closely at those interviews which are at the heart of this controversy: the mandatory 'New Jobseeker Interview'.[2] Scheduled to last a maximum of 40 minutes, the New Jobseeker Interview usually takes place at the claimant's local Jobcentre Plus office. Personal advisers meet claimants in open-plan offices, at workstations similar to those used by financial advisers in high street banks. A key requirement is to complete a 'Jobseeker's Agreement', a document required by law for every person claiming 'Jobseeker's Allowance' (the main state unemployment benefit in the United Kingdom). The Jobseeker's Agreement specifies the claimant's job goal(s) and the steps he or she has agreed to take each week in order to find work. Searching for the agreed jobs, and performing the agreed search activities, is a condition of receiving financial support; only those who are 'actively seeking and available for work' are legally entitled to claim Jobseeker's Allowance.

The New Jobseeker Interview has, then, two quite disparate objectives. On the one hand, advisers must administer the (impersonal) benefits system, filling in required fields on the computer, providing standardised information to claimants, and ensuring the conditions for making a claim are met. In effect, they must *process*, as efficiently as possible, the numerous claimants who pass through the Jobcentre's doors on a daily basis. On the other hand, advisers are also expected to provide *personalised guidance*, encouraging claimants to talk through their job goals and any barriers to work in order to help them take the steps needed to (re)join the labour market. Thus, although the media's rhetoric may contradict that of Jobcentre Plus, the New Jobseeker Interview is actually expected to embody both sides: claimants must be processed *and* supported.

On the frontline, the personal adviser must manage these dual requirements in real-time interaction with claimants. In this paper we examine *how* they do so. In doing the research, we were confronted with a normative question: *should* advisers be encouraged to take a more 'personalised' approach? In addressing this question within the present edited collection, we aim to go beyond the substantive issues raised by our study to open some broader debate about the role conversation analysts *ought* to play in relation to institutional change.

The study

To our knowledge this is the first study based on recordings of real Jobcentre Plus interviews, or their counterparts in equivalent services outside the United Kingdom[3] – and hence the first to focus on exactly how advisers manage the core *interactional* tasks of their working days. Most previous research on the advisory role has been indirect and retrospective: researchers have typically relied on quantitative outcome measures (e.g., numbers of claimants moving off benefits and into work) and a mix of surveys, interviews and focus groups to explore advisers' and claimants' concerns about, and satisfaction with, the service (see National Audit Office, 2006). This previous research endorses the value of the advisory role. However, we know very little about what actually happens during the adviser-claimant interactions themselves. The UK's Department for Work and Pensions' recognition of this gap in the evidence base prompted the present study.

Recruitment

Our recordings were made in eight Jobcentre Plus offices and two private sector Employment Zones across four regions of England. The sites for recording were selected in consultation with our project managers at the Department for Work and Pensions (DWP). Initial contact with Jobcentre Plus was made in writing by a DWP manager. Thereafter, the research team described the study to advisers and invited their participation on an individual, voluntary basis. Claimants were also recruited individually, shortly before their meeting with the adviser – usually by a researcher, but occasionally by the adviser, where this was the adviser's preference. All participants were given a short, accessible leaflet, which gave information about the study, including a number of confidentiality guarantees. Crucially, they were assured that raw recordings would not be made available to anyone in Jobcentre Plus or the Department for Work and Pensions. We thus avoided possible assessment of individual advisers' practices or claimants' circumstances by persons in a position of authority.

In total, 47 advisers took part. It was not possible to calculate a participation rate for advisers, but it was high for claimants: almost 80 per cent of those approached agreed to be recorded. Participants could agree to be video- and audio-recorded, or just audio-recorded; 87 per cent of the recordings were made using both. In total, 243 recordings were made between July 2007 and June 2008, covering a range of benefit interviews. In this chapter we focus on a sub-sample of our dataset: recordings of New Jobseeker Interviews. In accordance with targets agreed in advance with the Department for Work and Pensions, we gathered 42 New Jobseeker Interviews, conducted by 10 advisers.

Data collection

Over a period of 11 months, we spent one or more full or partial working days with each adviser. We did not sit in on interviews but remained in the vicinity to manage the recording equipment, including stopping recording should a participant request this; on no occasion did this occur. A camcorder mounted on a tripod enabled us to film adviser and claimant, although sometimes the angle dictated by surrounding desks meant we could not record both participants' faces. We used two uni-directional microphones (one focused on each participant) and a digital recorder to produce a high-quality soundtrack. This was crucial since there is a great deal of background noise in the open-plan Jobcentre Plus offices. Choosing, and learning to use, the equipment and related editing software involved a steep learning curve for the team. Fortunately we had funding to employ technical support. John Chatwin, a conversation analyst with specialist technical knowledge, spent time in the Jobcentre devising the recording set-up; he was also available for extensive follow-up support (for further information, see www.visibleresearch.co.uk).

The main challenge was meeting the recording targets. We found it hard to get to grips with the interview system. At the time of recording, interviews were classified according to the benefit and stage of the claim. We were only commissioned to record certain types of interview, but working out – in advance – exactly which claimants on an adviser's timetable were eligible for the study proved more complex than anticipated. Another challenge was moving the (quite cumbersome) recording equipment between advisers. Since set up was time consuming, we had to be prepared before claimants arrived. If a potential recording opportunity fell through (due to a claimant's non-attendance or decision not to take part in the study), and the adviser did not have a suitable next interview, we had to dismantle the equipment and set up with another adviser. Much time was spent negotiating with advisers about when to set up and then dashing between them, equipment in tow, to try to capture elusive interviews.

The main antidote to these difficulties was the support of advisers and their managers, who proved to be highly knowledgeable, flexible and generous with their time. We also had two sets of equipment, thereby increasing our flexibility.

Data analysis

Commissioned to use Conversation Analysis (CA) to identify 'effective practice' in Jobcentre Plus interviews, our remit was the adviser-claimant interactions alone. In accordance with the methodology of CA, we worked inductively, beginning without criteria for 'effectiveness' or any pre-classification of advisers according to training or skill. Instead, we identified the strategies that advisers in our sample were actually using, and what the interactional effects of these were.

To address the Department for Work and Pensions' concern with 'effective practice', we looked especially for indicators of which strategies met the institutional goal of moving claimants closer to the labour market. This was not a matter of linking interactional strategies with numerical outcome data (such as figures relating to job entries or periods of sustained employment). We neither had access to such data for our sample nor would it have enabled us to address the project's aims. Outcome measures like job entry only gauge the effectiveness of advisory practice indirectly. They cannot illuminate specifically what was effective about the adviser-claimant interaction itself. Instead, we looked for markers of effectiveness that were *internal* to the interviews. These included: *recruitments*, where adviser strategies lead, during the interview itself, to a claimant being signed up to a work-directed programme; *turnarounds*, where strategies lead to a clearly observable change in a claimant's outlook, such as considering a job vacancy that was initially dismissed; and the *opening up* of work-directed discussion (especially where advisers overcame 'blocks' to discussion).

Thus, while we cannot specify the relationship between adviser strategies and the ultimate goal of landing a job, we can demonstrate that some strategies were more effective at facilitating steps towards work *within the interview*. A detailed account of our methodology, and approach to identifying 'effectiveness', is available in the final project report (Drew et al., 2010; and see Irvine et al., 2010).

Findings

Completion of an official Jobseeker's Agreement – the core institutional task of the mandatory New Jobseeker Interview – was successfully accomplished in all interviews in our sample. Advisers differed significantly, however, in *how* they approached the Jobseeker's Agreement in interaction with claimants. We found two main approaches:

(i) A 'tick box' approach, where advisers focused primarily on completing the required forms and providing claimants with standardised information; and
(ii) A 'personalised' approach, where advisers focused primarily on eliciting and addressing the claimant's story.

The distinction between these is not absolute; all advisers used both approaches to some extent in all their interviews – and, as we argue below, both approaches are needed for the successful completion of any interview. However, advisers tended to favour one approach over the other, resulting in some interviews being more 'personalised' than others. We start by illustrating each approach in relation to the two fundamental tasks required of advisers: gathering and providing information. We then show how the approaches can impact on what comes to be recorded on the Jobseeker's Agreement – the document required by law for every person claiming Jobseeker's Allowance.

Gathering information: two formats for eliciting claimants' job goals

Asking claimants to identify (usually three) job goals for entry on the Jobseeker's Agreement is a key requirement of the New Jobseeker Interview. Advisers are mandated, then, to 'fill boxes' on their computer system. However, we found that advisers differed with respect to whether they *treated* the task largely as one of 'box filling' or 'talking things through' with the claimant. The former was sometimes explicitly indexed by reference to the computer, as in: '*So* (1.2) **it's got on here** (0.4) any particular work that you're going to be looking for (0.2) first of all?' [085; Oct 07].[4] But the important difference lay in the format advisers used to ask about claimants' goals. One format requests, or seeks confirmation of, the *category* of work for which the claimant is looking. Derived from the Jobseeker's Agreement itself, the question may be visibly read off the computer screen; but even if not, this format orients to the requirement to record a list of job types, as evident in the following examples:

- *So any **particular type of work** that you're looking for* [024; Jul 07]
- *What **sort of work** is it you're looking for (then)/(though)* [110; Oct 07]
- *Okay Jobseeker's Agreement u::m (2.8) okay last time you had elec- **electrical contractor=that's still the same yeah**,* [118; Oct 07]

By contrast, advisers may design the question in a way that invites a *narrative* response. In using this format, the adviser displays an orientation, not to the system requirements, but to the individual's story, as evident in the following examples:

- *So w- (1.0) I can only sympathise with you on that one ((loss of a previous job)). But **where are we now then with what you'd like to do*** [104; Oct 07]

146 *Applied Conversation Analysis*

- *So do you have erm hh .hh (0.3) °I-tee and politics.° (0.8) I mean is it- hh **what are your future plans then** [079; Sep 07]*

This distinction was particularly stark in cases where a Jobseeker's Agreement had been created during a previous claim, enabling advisers simply to seek confirmation that nothing had changed. For example, in Extract 1, below, the adviser updates the Agreement without asking the claimant about his current job goals or future plans. Except for changing his place of residence, she makes standardised amendments, typing in the kind of commitments to which most claimants are expected to agree (e.g., *prepared to travel up to an hour on public transport*, lines 9–10). Focusing on the computer rather than the claimant, she is visibly prioritising 'box filling'. Only after amending the Jobseeker's Agreement does she ask: *Is that all alright for you* (line 17) – a question which strongly prefers the *yeah* it receives. There is minimal opportunity for the claimant to contribute. Moreover, the adviser explicitly treats this as a box-filling exercise, verbally ticking off the accomplished and prospective tasks: *Okay we've done that... Ri:ght if I just run through this* (lines 20–22).

Extract 1   [120; Nov 07]

```
01   PA:     Ri::ght. (.) Jobseeker's agreement, that's how it stood
02           in:: u::m ((claimant's previous place of residence)) .hh
03   Cla?:   (°Okay°)
04           (0.2)
05   PA:     Being your main engineering, admin clerical.
06           (0.2)
07   PA:     It's exactly the same. All I've done i- he:re .hh i::s
08           u::m (0.4) amend it to the fact that you're living in
09           ((town name)) .hh (0.2) prepared to travel up to an
10           hour on public transpo::rt (0.8) you've got no
11           restrictions on your hours or da:::ys: (0.4) and that um
12           (1.2) we've given=we: give out (0.2) as a: (0.4) a list of
13           (0.2) agencies and web addresse[s.
14   Cla:                                    [Oh (yeah)
15   PA:     Oka::y?
16           (1.4)
17   PA:     Is that all alright for you::?
18   Cla:    Yeh
19           (9.4) ((PA using computer))
20   PA:     Okay we've done that.
21           (0.2)
22   PA:     .tshh Ri:ght if I just run through this I'm sure it's the
23           same as it was last time…
```

By contrast, in Extract 2, although the adviser also has a previous Jobseeker's Agreement on the screen, his first step is to ask the claimant: *Has that changed? Is there something else you want to be doing?* (lines 18–19). He thereby explicitly creates a slot for the claimant to discuss her current job goals, on the basis of which he might make tailored amendments if appropriate.

Extract 2   [050; Aug 07]

```
01  PA:    So- (0.3) what we're looking at (0.3) most importantly is
02         the Jobseekers Agreement. is what we need to look at.
03         >.hh< This is one that you did (.) ehm: .t >just over< a
04         year ago.
05         (0.7)
06  PA:    So: (0.2) (we opes) need to look at again and see- see
07         what's changed (or) >.hh< Obviously you got a bit more
08         experience since [then. you've worked with ((company))
09  Cla:                    [Mm,
10  PA:    .hhh Ehm: (1.1) .tch (0.8) °(um)° Most important part of
11         the Jobseeker's Agreement is (0.3) the job goals that
12         you're gonna be aiming for.
13         (0.4)
14  PA:    So this is where I'm hoping you going to tell me=last time
15         you were here you said you were going to be looking for
16         work as cleaner, shop assistant ('n) (check out)
17         (logger).=But that was over a year ago. You're a year
18         older now. .hhh Has that changed?=>is there something else
19         you want to be doing?<
```

All Jobseeker's Agreements are 'personal' in the sense that they contain a record of the work for which the individual has agreed to look. How advisers go about eliciting claimants' job goals, however, may create more or less opportunity for claimants to talk through – explore or negotiate – what they want to do.

Providing information: approaches to telling claimants how to look for work

Advisers are also expected to inform claimants of ways to search for job vacancies. The main options are listed on the Jobseeker's Agreement, on which the adviser must record the methods the claimant has agreed to use. Again, there are boxes to be ticked and filled. Again, however, while some advisers took a more 'tick box' approach, focusing on delivering the mandated information, others took a more 'personalised' approach, tailoring the information to what they knew about the individual.

Extract 3 illustrates a 'tick box' approach. The adviser informs the claimant about a range of generic job search strategies, which he explicitly marks as *obvious* (line 2). His tone also suggests this is a set list he is reciting. Indeed, this adviser provides almost identical information, in the same way, in the other New Jobseeker Interviews we recorded with him. This approach to information provision is largely scripted; he could be speaking to any jobseeker.

Extract 3   [026; Jul 07]
```
01  PA:  Now how you contact people is >entirely (of) yourself=I mean
02       you can obviously< pho:ne people ↑up, you can send them
03       lette:rs you can visit them, .hh you can even do it through
04       ourselves.
```

A contrasting example, in which the adviser provides more tailored information, is shown below. Here the adviser explicitly links the strategy (*registering with some agencies,* line 3) to the claimant's needs.

Extract 4   [069; Aug 07]
```
01  PA:  For the type of work you're looking for: (maybe) the butcher
02       and the factory worker in particular .h (0.3) you really
03       need to think about registering with some agencie:s:
04       [(because) (.) a l:ot of that work goes through agencie:s
05  Cla: [Yeah
```

Advisers also differed in the extent to which they explored claimants' previous job search experiences and preferences. In a more 'tick box' approach, they tended simply to provide information; in a more 'personalised' approach, they created opportunities for discussion. Extract 5 shows an example of the former. Apart from checking that the claimant knows what the job points are (computerised stations for performing searches for current vacancies), the adviser provides no slot for talking through which approach might be most appropriate. Instead, he focuses on providing the standardised information given in Extract 3, concurrently entering the agreed job search strategies on the claimant's Jobseeker's Agreement.

Extract 5   [050; Aug 07]
```
01  PA:  .hh (It'll) also have this phone number on here for the
02       Jobseekers Direct. .hh You can ring that number (0.1) it's
03       charged at local rates (0.5) ehm: (0.3) .tch they will do
04       a job search for you over the phone.
05       (0.5)
06       I can also put the(ir) website address on there for you,
07  Cla: Y[eah
08  PA:   [if you- (.) happy- happier doing that, it's up to you
```

```
09          which you use,
10   PA:    °Ehm:° (3.6) Ehm: (1.0) Do you know what the job points
11          downstairs are?
12          (0.2)
13   Cla:   >Yeah<
14   PA:    Yeah.
15          (12.3) ((adviser typing))
16   PA:    Right. So all I'm asking you is on the day you're in here
17          to sign on anyway (.) if you could use the job points:.
18          see if there's any jobs. Okay, .tchh (.) Ehm: (.) We would
19          expect that you would (.) contact at least two employers a
20          week.
21          (0.1)
22   PA:    and contact us twice a week using (those) methods he[re.
23   Cla:                                                       [Mm.
```

Extract 6 shows a contrasting example, where the adviser questions the claimant closely about his current strategies, thereby creating the Jobseeker's Agreement in collaboration with the claimant, rather than simply informing him of the standard requirements.

Extract 6   [079; Sep 07]

```
01   PA:    Er:m It sounds as though you're doing a regular internet
02          job search are you. You're on the [internet? How of- how
03   Cla:                                     [(Yeah ( )
04   PA:    often do you go on?
05   Cla:   Er:m quite a lot.
06          (.)
07   Cla:   I'm on there quite a lot.
08          (0.4)
09   PA:    So two or three times a week?
10          (.)
11   Cla:   Yeah. something like that. Ye[ah
12   PA:                                  [Okay
13          (1.6)
14   PA:    And do you have your own computer at home.
15          or a[ccess to a com [puter.
16   Cla:       [I-              [I do yeah
17   PA:    Okay
18          (0.4)
19   PA:    Erm (3.0) Do you look anywhere else at all for work.
20          or jobs. [anything-
21   Cla:            [erm Newspapers. I got- ( ) a few newspaper
22          cuttings in there.
```

```
23          (.)
24   PA:    Is that the ((names newspaper)) is it or:
25   Cla:   Er:: I think so. Ye [ah
26   PA:                       [Okay
27          (4.3)
28   Cla:   And I've er rang up companie:s and that.
29   PA:    Have you. Whi[ch-
30   Cla:                [Ask- asking if they've got apprenticeships
31          and that.
```

All Jobseeker's Agreements contain a list of what the individual has agreed to do to look for work, and in that sense are 'personalised'. How advisers go about agreeing the job search plan, however, may create more or less opportunity for claimants to talk through which job search strategies would work best for them.

Completing the Jobseeker's Agreement: how advisers' different approaches may influence what gets recorded

The two approaches identified through our empirical work map closely on to the New Jobseeker Interview's dual focus: to 'process' claimants through the system – to 'fill and tick' boxes on the computer – and to provide 'personalised' support to help claimants into work. Unsurprisingly, then, we found that advisers routinely combined the two approaches. These should not be thought of as labels to apply to individuals. They should also not be thought of as mutually exclusive, with one inherently superior; both approaches may be drawn on as resources for accomplishing different tasks. Indeed, without some attention to the 'boxes', advisers risk omitting important aspects of the interview.

However, it was common for advisers to favour a 'tick box' approach. Our findings suggest that this may be consequential, not only for the nature of the interaction, but for what comes to be recorded on the Jobseeker's Agreement itself. We illustrate this through two pairs of contrasting examples.

In the first pair, the advisers and claimants are negotiating a final job goal to add to the list on the Jobseeker's Agreement. The claimants' circumstances are not comparable – the first is trained to degree level in graphic design but has little work experience; the second has no formal qualifications and some experience of working in retail – but both have clearly stated aspirations: the first wants to work in graphic or magazine design; the second wants to move into office work. Both advisers record these primary goals. However, in line with common Jobcentre Plus practice, both pursue additional goals to widen the range of jobs for which the claimants should search. What is significant is how differently the advisers approach this common task. Both initiate some negotiation; neither accepts the additional job goals first offered by the claimants. However, in Extract 7, the adviser orients towards the institution's requirements – towards the 'boxes' he is expected to tick – while in Extract 8 the adviser orients towards the claimant's long-term aspirations.

The institutional orientation is evident (in Extract 7) in how the adviser talks about the goals themselves: as a requirement (*we need*, lines 2–3, 19 and 29, *we have to*, line 48). It is also evident in how he responds to resistance from the claimant: he spells out both his institutional mandate (lines 35–37) and government policy on unemployment (lines 43–47). He treats the additional goal, then, as a means of meeting the conditions for claiming Jobseeker's Allowance, not as a means of helping the claimant to find the work he wants. In effect, the claimant and adviser are in opposition, with the claimant pursuing job goals in line with his qualifications and interests, and the adviser treating these as unrealistic (in data not shown the claimant offers 'photography' and 'working in a gallery' as alternatives, but these are not accepted as sufficient for entry into the Jobseeker's Agreement). The disagreement, which is more extensive than we have space to illustrate here, culminates in the claimant's highly reticent agreement to record *retail* (lines 51–52).

Extract 7   [067] NJI 18–24 (Aug 07)

```
01  PA:    And this is whe::re (.) hopefully you're gonna tell me (.)
02         what type of work it is you'd like to be do:ing. We need-
03         we need to put some job goals on he::re
04  Cla:   Okay
05         (1.6)
06  Cla:   U:::m graphic design uh magazine design (0.8) u::m
07  PA:    Graphic design and magazine design ri::ght
08         (1.0)
09  Cla?:  .tch
10  PA:    A::nything else I mean yuh- (0.6) f:i:ne the graphic
11         design that's what you've worked hard to get to, you've
12         got the qualifications,
13  Cla:   Yea[h
14  PA:       [.hhhh and some experience-
15         (.)
16  Cla:   Ju[st (th's-)] [just that ]
17  PA:      [absolutely] [marvellous]
18         (0.2)
19  PA:    Yeah (.) u:::m (0.4) we would nee::d s::::omething else as
20         we::ll (0.4) u::m as a back up to that at lea:st one more
21         job goa:l.
22         (0.4)
23  PA:    I appre:ciate that's what you want to do and that's-
24         that's your main goal and that's absolutely fi::ne (0.8)
25         but obviously: (.) I'm sure you're aware (1.2) mm you
```

```
26              might not walk straight into a graphic design job,=
27              Hopefully you will.
28              (.)
29     PA:      But you might not, so we need something else as a backup
30              in the mea:n time .hhh that you could maybe try and do.
31              (1.2)
```

((lines omitted during which claimant suggests 'photography' and adviser treats this as inadequate, seeking a further goal, which the claimant does not give))

```
32     PA:      Alright, .hhh u::m what we (tr-) have to try and do is get
33              a bala::nce:: u::m of (0.4) obviously trying to achieve
34              what your long term goa:ls are (in the) graphic design and
35              photography and that's absolutely fi::ne .hhh (0.4) we also
36              have to inject u::m (0.8) .tch (0.6) a realistic approach
37              to (.) the local job market and I'm sure you're aware round
38              he:re there's not a great deal in the way of graphic design
```

((lines omitted))

```
39     PA:      .hh What I'm saying is (0.4) w- i- s- for example say it
40              took six months (0.2) to get a job as a graphic designer
41              (.) that's not- unrealistic that could well be the ca::se:
42              (.) and then you might end up with a great job and a great
43              future .hh but in the mea::n ti:me (1.0) the
44              governme[nt would rather you were working s:omewhere e:lse
45     Cla:             [Mhm
46     PA:      than claiming benefit for six months while you looked for
47              that job.
```

((lines omitted))

```
48     PA:      In the mean time (.) we have to think of something (.) #uh#
49     Cla:     Sure yea[h
50     PA:             [along a different line [yeah?
51     Cla:                                    [But- am I u::m (1.8) .tch
52              yeah just- (0.2) p- I would just go: for retail then?
53     PA:      O::kay .hhhhh (0.4) W:hat I will s:: tell you at this
54              stage is nothing here is set in sto::ne…
```

By contrast, in the following extract, the negotiation revolves around the adviser's attempts to support the claimant in achieving her long-term goal of office work. Strikingly, the adviser calls into question a job goal ('retail') that is absolutely viable in the immediate term – and would thus readily tick the institutional box. Not only are retail jobs widespread, but this claimant has experience. Yet the adviser pursues alternatives, explicitly factoring in her (uncompleted) ICT training (line 12). He encourages her to think in terms of her personal preferences (line 20) and to be aspirational (lines 21–22 and 29–32). The contrast with Extract 7 – with the adviser's emphasis on *government/institutional requirements* and his pursuit of a goal bearing no relation to the claimant's qualifications or aspirations – is stark.

Extract 8   [054; Aug 07]

```
01  PA:   So you've got call centre agent you've got trainee
02        clerical administra:tor, .hh (0.2) what about a thi:rd job
03        goal.
04  Cla:  .hhhh u::::m: hm [I could do: hh. (0.2) shop work 'cos I-
05  PA:                   [(Eh-)
06  Cla:  I'm really good at that (.) ['cos: I ada::pt really
07  PA:                                [.Tch .hhh
08  Cla:  quickly
09        (0.2)
10  Cla:  B[ut
11  PA:    [But- but you've already experienced retai:l (.) and
12        you've got your IC[T >qualifications< (.) Do you want to
13  Cla:                    [Yeah
14  PA:   do you want to fo::cus o:n developing white collar skills
15        in: .hh (0.4) in: (.) (th') clerical administration
16        (0.2)
17        'Cos don't feel as you've got to mo:ve b[ack into re:tail
18  Cla:                                          [Mm::: Huh ha
19        yea::h (h)I know   [.hh yeah
20  PA:                      [It's about what you want to be: you're
21        only eighteen (0.2) you're starting to think about
22        building a career now=
23  Cla:  =Yea:h um yeah I could do: more clerical 'cos
24  PA:   In preference to retail
25        (.)
26  PA:   Is-  [is- clerical higher up on the list than retail
27  Cla:       [Yeah
28  Cla:  It is a l[ot higher u[p
29  PA:            [.tch        [Well if it's a lot higher let's
30        not put re:tail down because [that's going back down
31  Cla:                                [Yeah
32  PA:   [the ladder o::kay?
33  Cla:  [Ha huh huh I kno:w
```

Undoubtedly, office work is more widely available than is graphic design, making it easier to accommodate the claimant's aspirations in Extract 8. Moreover, there is an institutional imperative to ensure that claimants have 'realistic' job goals. However, both advisers have an *interactional choice* in *how* they talk this through with the claimant: they can emphasise the institutional requirements or they can focus on the claimants' circumstances. In the case of the graphic design graduate, he volunteers (data not shown) that he is willing to relocate and already has a job interview later that week. Both factors suggest that his primary goals may be more realistic than the adviser has assumed. The adviser's pursuit of a more 'realistic' goal is done without initial close questioning about the claimant's situation.

The two approaches outlined in this chapter can affect, then, not only the nature of the interaction, but what job goals are recorded on the Jobseeker's Agreement. In the first (Extract 7), the adviser's interventions lead to a poorer match between recorded goals and the claimants' aspirations and qualifications; in the second (Extract 8), they lead to a better one. The same is true of what 'job search steps' get recorded, as we show in our second pair of contrasting extracts. Focusing on the institutional requirements for claiming Jobseeker's Allowance, many advisers simply recorded the minimum job search steps expected of claimants. As in Extract 9, advisers also tended to use minimising language (e.g., *just once a week,* line 5), implying that claimants need do relatively little to look for work.

Extract 9   *[152; Jan 08]*

```
01 PA:    So:: er do you use the Jobcentre Plus website for job
02        search ((claimant's name)) or have you ever used the
03        Jobcentre Plus website?
04 Cla:   No.
05 PA:    Would you have a look at it just once a week just to
06        keep an eye [on the type of work that we're offering (.)
07 Cla:               [Yeah
08 PA:    Okay. Do you use more specialised [websites
09 Cla:                                     [Yeah
10 PA:    Yeah
11        ((16 seconds))
12 PA:    I'll just put on a weekly basis I mean obviously how often
13        you go on then is entirely up to you .hhh
```

By contrast, some advisers focused on what it would actually take for claimants to achieve their job goals. For example, in Extract 10, the adviser encourages the claimant to do far more than is required to remain eligible for Jobseeker's Allowance. His focus is not on these institutional conditions, but on encouraging the claimant to land the kind of job she wants.

Extract 10   [054; Aug 07]

```
01  PA:   Now- I'm gonna make a suggestion and don't (0.8) u::m
02        panic when I say this
03  Cla:  Mhm
04  PA:   At least seven employment agencies register with .hh the
05        mo:re employment agencies your register with ((claimant
06        name)) the quicker you will be in work
07  Cla:  Ri:[ght
08         [because a lot of employers: will (.) u:m register
09        specifically with one employment agency .hh (.) example
10        being British Telecom (0.4) mainly register with Manpower
11  Cla:  Yea:[:h
12  PA:       [.hhh a::nd they've been with them for years and
13        they're happy with that rela:tionship so if you're not
14        with Re- u::m Manpower (0.6) you w- you may not hear for
15        those vacancies
```

The approach taken by advisers can, then, have concrete effects: what gets recorded on the claimant's (legally binding) action plan – the Jobseeker's Agreement – may be influenced by the extent to which the adviser focuses either on 'ticking the institutional boxes' or on the individual's circumstances. Crucially, Jobseeker's Agreements developed through a 'tick box' approach were less likely, in our sample, to be 'aspirational'; that is, they were less likely to match claimants' longer-term goals or to contain a challenging, pro-active plan for finding work.

Should advisers take a more personalised approach?

On the face of it, our findings seem to point to a clear recommendation for change: that advisers be trained in how to take a more 'personalised' approach. This accords both with the official rhetoric of Jobcentre Plus (JCP) and with the predominant view we encountered among staff at JCP and the Department for Work and Pensions (DWP). Indeed, we discovered near the end of the project that a small team, internal to DWP, was working on a review of advisory services, one aim being to reduce advisers' '"must do" and "tick lists" to enable more customer engagement' (personal communication). We were encouraged by this close alignment of perspectives, particularly since those of us most directly involved in the data analysis (PD and MT) had no prior involvement with either organisation or the related literatures; having worked inductively with what was clearly 'in the data', we were pleased to have identified an issue that was live also for policy-makers.

However, as we came to understand the complexity of the benefits system better, we recognised that the 'personalisation agenda' (see van Berkel and Valkenburg, 2007) does not necessarily apply across the board. The early stages of a claim raise particular dilemmas, which our empirical work alone cannot resolve. There are three key debates:

The first is whether it is cost effective to offer personalised support to all claimants from the start of a claim. Most people claim Jobseeker's Allowance for relatively short periods: around half leave benefit within three months, and three-quarters within six months (Department for Work and Pensions, 2008). This implies that many will find work without personalised support. It may, then, be an inappropriate use of limited resources (particularly with increased claimant numbers) to treat the New Jobseeker Interview as anything more than a means to process claimants through the system, explain its conditions, and signpost sources of support for those who need it. However, we know that the longer someone is unemployed, the harder it is to return to the labour market (Gregg, 2008), suggesting that more personalised support earlier in the claim may well prove cost effective – at least for some claimants.

The second debate revolves around the difficulty of teasing apart the factors involved in increased exit rates from benefit. For example, while the New Deal programmes targeted at those who have been out of work for longer[5] show improved exit rates from Jobseeker's Allowance, this may be attributed to the combination of increased personalised support *and* increased conditionality (Gregg, 2008). Our study shows how a more 'personalised' approach can be more effective for encouraging claimants to take steps towards work *during the interview*. It cannot, however, show which policy measures (the 'carrot' and/or the 'stick') are associated with increased exits from benefits.

Third is the question of whether advisers should be helping claimants find a job they *want* to do – and allowing them time on benefits while they do so – or focusing on moving claimants off benefits as quickly as possible. While the former may lead to greater numbers staying in work (reducing a return to benefits), it is not clear whether this is a cost-effective strategy (for a related discussion, see Dunn, 2010).

In different ways, these debates call into question the extent to which a 'personalised' approach is appropriate at the *New Jobseeker Interview* in particular. Efforts to revise Jobseeker's Allowance appear to be steering a middle course, maintaining an initial emphasis on the claimant's own efforts to find work, but increasing the support available during the first 12 months (see Bellis, Aston and Dewson, 2009). Those deemed in need of additional support may be fast-tracked to the more intensive stages of the regime, usually reserved for those who have been unemployed longer. One broad kind of solution, then, is 'targeting' – providing extra support only to those who need it.

But what about specific guidance on how advisers ought to conduct their interviews – the kind of guidance we were commissioned to provide? For interviews with the longer-term unemployed, our findings clearly support the use of a more 'personalised' approach because it is well fitted to the aims of advisory meetings at later stages of a claim: to provide tailored back-to-work support, focused around the individual's skills, experience and barriers to work. However, for New Jobseeker Interviews, the appropriate 'effective practice' recommendation is open to question precisely because the broader policy question about the purpose of these interviews is still open. If their purpose is largely to process claimants through the benefits system, then a 'tick box' approach may be defined as 'effective', since it ensures key information is gathered and provided. If, however, these interviews are meant to open up in-depth discussion of the claimant's circumstances and aspirations as a basis for individualised support, then a 'personalised' approach is to be recommended. The question of what advisers *should* be trained to do is not, then, only an empirical one; because it depends on the purpose of the interview, it is also a question of policy and politics. Our findings offer an evidence base for developing advisor training programmes; but first, a policy decision has to be made.

With respect to New Jobseeker Interviews in particular, our approach has therefore been to facilitate internal debate, not make firm recommendations. This has been accomplished through evidence-based workshops – part of a broader programme of sharing emerging findings, throughout the study, with researchers, managers and policy-makers from the Department for Work and Pensions and Jobcentre Plus. At these workshops we presented findings, and – more importantly – generated extensive discussion by playing (pixellated, anonymised) data clips. Advisers' use of a more 'tick box' or 'personalised' approach has been a recurrent theme – even when we have not raised this in the accompanying presentation. Workshop participants have been quick to identify – on the basis of the recordings – ways in which a more 'tick box' approach could be problematic. A common point, during discussions about the wider range of interviews that we studied, was that advisers could 'miss opportunities' to help claimants if they were too focused on institutional requirements. Given our cautious presentation of what we took to be highly sensitive data, we were struck by participants' forthrightness: they were significantly more critical of a 'tick box' approach than we were.

However, this general consensus did not extend to the specific context of the New Jobseeker Interview. Although some participants felt that these interviews should be more personalised, others argued that they were intended only as a mechanism for processing claims. Indeed, some suggested that the business of the New Jobseeker Interview might be accomplished *without* a one-to-one interview at all. With the programme of change being initiated by the post-2010 UK coalition government, it remains to be seen whether the purpose of early advisory interviews will be clarified. If it is, our study can provide evidence on which to base recommendations fitted to the given policy; the challenging question will be whether we agree with it.

Implications for 'applied' CA: the relationship between institutional goals and our effective practice recommendations

The goal-oriented nature of interactions in institutional settings – of which the New Jobseeker Interview is one exemplar – has been a long-running theme in the applied conversation-analytic literature (Drew and Heritage, 1992a). Indeed, Heritage lists it as one of three main features that:

> create a unique 'fingerprint' for each kind of institutional interaction – the fingerprint being made up of specific tasks, identities, constraints on conduct and relevant inferential procedures that the participants deploy and are oriented to in their interactions with one another.
> (1997, p. 164)

Analytically, then, conversation analysts working on institutional talk are interested in participants' goal orientations because they show how the parties themselves are producing, and orienting to, 'institutionality' of some kind (e.g., an advisory interview rather than a GP consultation, a police interview or salon appointment).

Practically, applied CA researchers have tended to focus on the implications of this work for developing 'effective practice' recommendations. The extent to which this is made explicit varies. The other contributions to this book show the variety, all the way from the recommendation of a very specific scripted utterance (Heritage and Robinson, Chapter 2 in this volume) to a more generalised recommendation to use CA to reflect on the collaboration between researchers and designers (Egbert, Chapter 11 in this volume). Often, the implications are stated more generally; that the findings might, in some way, be used to improve communication in the given institution.

What tends to be overlooked is how institutional goals and effective practice recommendations are *bound up*: what counts as 'effective' depends on what the goals are. This was thrown into sharp relief in our study because of debates about what the goal of the New Jobseeker Interview should be. Such questions are especially challenging because our analytic skills are insufficient for producing answers. Our empirical work can demonstrate what participants' goal orientations were at the time of recording. It alone cannot determine, however, what an institution's goals *should* be; this is an ethical and/or political question.

Most applied CA work to date has focused on institutions where the goals are directed towards an intuitively obvious social good, such as delivering emergency services, education, counselling or health care. For example, it seems self-evident that reductions in unmet patient concerns (Heritage et al., 2007; see also Heritage and Robinson, Chapter 2 in this volume) and unnecessary antibiotic prescriptions (Stivers, 2007) in primary care are valuable outcomes; there is no real policy debate to be had on these issues, for good reasons. Nevertheless, in making recommendations on how to do these things, the authors are unavoidably taking a position on the legitimate institutional goals of primary care consultations.

With regard to New Jobseeker Interviews, it is far less clear what counts as a social good. The debates, which we touch on above, are complex and unresolved. It is not our purpose here to suggest a solution to the substantive question of what New Jobseeker Interviews should achieve; indeed, we're not sure. Rather, we hope that the absence of an obvious answer might expose the ethical/political nature of making effective practice recommendations. Since what counts as 'effective' is predicated on what the institutional goal is (or should be), to make a recommendation is to take a position with respect to that goal.

Concluding comments

Explicating two approaches taken in New Jobseeker Interviews, our findings help account for both the media's horror stories of bureaucracy within Jobcentre Plus and counter-claims from within Jobcentre Plus of tailored support provided by personal advisers. When taking a predominantly 'tick box' approach, advisers focused mainly on meeting essential institutional requirements (on 'processing' claimants); but advisers sometimes took a more 'personalised' approach, treating the interview as an opportunity to focus on the claimant's story and encouraging claimants to be 'aspirational' in their job search.

Comparable distinctions have been found in medical consultations. Research in primary care and a specialist oncology clinic showed a spectrum of practitioner approaches to decision making, ranging from more 'unilateral' to more 'bilateral' (Collins et al., 2005). When taking the former approach, practitioners structured the decision-making process more independently of the patient; in the latter, it was more dependent on the patient's contributions. The researchers offer some tentative observations about ways in which a 'bilateral' approach may offer more scope for patient input.

At a more specific level, the two formats we identified for asking about job goals are akin to the question formats that primary care physicians use to elicit patients' presenting concerns. Robinson and Heritage (2006) showed that physicians typically produce either a request for confirmation (e.g., 'I see you have sinus problems', akin to: 'last time you had electrical contractor = that's still the same yeah') or a more open enquiry (e.g., 'What can I do for you today', akin to: 'what are your future plans'). Compared with the confirmation request, the open enquiry was found to be associated with significantly greater patient satisfaction with the affective/relational dimension of the physician's communication (see also Heritage and Robinson's account of 'some' versus 'any' in solicitations of patients' unmet concerns, Chapter 2 in this volume).

Together with our findings, these studies suggest that it may be common for those managing institutional interactions to favour taking either a more tailored approach, which prioritises eliciting and responding to the individual's story, or one which is more structured by the institution or its representative. Deciding which approach is most 'effective' within a given institutional interaction depends, we have argued, on the institutional goal. In turn, this raises the (potentially thorny) question of whether the goal is one worth supporting on ethical or political grounds. As the promise of an applied CA becomes more widely recognised, engagement with this question will become increasingly important if we are to be confident that our evidence base will be used for the social good.

Notes

1. The authors would like to thank the many advisers and claimants who made this study possible, and the numerous DWP and JCP managers, policy-makers and researchers who supported this new approach to exploring the advisory role.
2. The 2010 change of government in the UK meant that there were likely to be significant changes to the benefits system. However, the substantive findings discussed in this chapter are likely to remain pertinent for two reasons: the new government's rhetoric continues, at the time of writing, to favour a 'personalised approach' to working with benefits claimants; and some version of the regime of advisory interviews in place at the time of recording seems set to continue. For the purposes of this chapter, we will refer to the system that was in place at the time of recording.
3. But see doctoral work in progress by Solberg at the University of Oslo.
4. Extract labels indicate the recording ID number and date of recording.
5. At the time of our research, this was 6 months for Jobseeker's Allowance claimants aged 18–24 and 18 months for those aged 25+.

9
Giving Feedback to Care Staff about Offering Choices to People with Intellectual Disabilities

W. M. L. Finlay, Chris Walton and Charles Antaki

This chapter is about what happened when we talked to care-staff about their daily round of supporting people with learning disabilities. The idea was to share our (suitably de-jargonised) conversation-analytic observations with them, in the hope that they would reflect on their practices and, where they found them wanting, change them.

The project was an example of what Antaki (Chapter 1) terms 'interventionist' Conversation Analysis. Broadly one might identify four types of such intervention: (1) the use of findings from CA research to generate interventions which are then tested experimentally (e.g., Heritage et al., 2007; see also Heritage and Robinson, Chapter 2 in this volume); (2) the use of findings from CA to develop training packages (e.g., Gardner, 2006; see also R. Wilkinson, Chapter 5 in this volume); (3) the use of recordings and transcriptions of interactions involving unknown third parties in teaching sessions, where the relevant teaching points have been identified beforehand using Conversation Analysis (e.g., Jones, 2007); and (4) the use of recordings and transcriptions of the individuals themselves to provide feedback and the opportunity for critical reflection on their own practice (e.g., Booth and Perkins, 1999; Booth and Swabey, 1999; Bryan and Maxim, 1998; Spilkin and Bethlehem, 2003; and see also Peräkylä, Chapter 12 in this volume).

It is an example of the fourth type of applied Conversation Analysis we report here, namely our experience of providing workshops for staff and managers of residential services for people with intellectual disabilities. These workshops encouraged staff to reflect on their everyday habits in how they gave the people they worked with – who had a range of communication difficulties – opportunities for choice, and how they responded to expressions of preference and self-determination. As our core material, we used video footage of the staff members themselves and the service-users they supported, taken from everyday life. Our aim was to use our CA academic work to guide the staff members' reflections on what they saw, with the object of identifying what would, in their own terms, be better practice.

Background to the project: 'choice' as an institutional objective

The background to the feedback sessions was a two-year research project,[1] in which we video-recorded everyday interactions and collected ethnographic notes in three residential services managed by a National Health Service Trust[2] in the south of England.

What sparked our research was what welfare policy said about people with intellectual disabilities: in the United Kingdom, the imperative to increase people's control over their own lives comes from the very top (e.g., Department of Health, 2001, 2005). We were intrigued by how this might actually be played out in everyday life in residential services, and wanted to use Conversation Analysis to give us a grip on what, in social policy research, is not often recorded, still less analysed in any interactional detail. Conversation Analysis has for some twenty years been used on real-life interactions involving people with intellectual or developmental disabilities, with the pace accelerating in the last five. (For examples of that kind of research, see Antaki, 1999; Antaki, Young and Finlay, 2002; Dickerson, Rae, Stribling, Dautenhahn and Werry, 2005, Dickerson, Stribling and Rae, 2007; Jingree, Finlay and Antaki, 2006; Rapley, 2004; Rapley and Antaki, 1996; Stribling, Rae and Dickerson, 2007; Wootton, 1989). That gave us a sense that something worthwhile could be done on how people with learning disabilities were offered choices, and how they made them.

The staff we engaged with at the start weren't politicians or civil servants in the Home Office or the Department of Health, who formulate policy about 'choice' at the highest level. Rather, they were senior managers of social and health care services who oversaw local policy within and across that specific NHS Care Trust. Later, we engaged with the front-line care staff who actually delivered that policy. Our first port of call, though, was with the senior managers, who were enthusiastic about researching and evaluating their services, and it was they who suggested the three residential services we could work in (and to which we ultimately gave feedback).

We then met with the managers and staff teams in those services to discuss the research, its aims and what participation would involve. Despite intensive involvement in all three services over a number of months, no video data were collected in one site,[3] so only two of the services (two residences, which we shall call 'Ashgrove' and 'Comber Hall Way') will be discussed here. In both cases, one of the authors (Chris Walton) undertook a long series of visits, gradually getting to know the staff and the residents, gaining their trust, negotiating access, making ethnographic notes and, eventually, recording what were to be about 30 hours of video.

The residences

Both residences were ordinary-looking detached houses in residential suburbs of small English towns, neat and well-cared for, and not obviously 'institutional' at first glance. Organisationally, they differed in size and in the relative abilities of the residents. Ashgrove had a permanent staff of nine support or care workers, though over the course of the project this core team was supplemented with ten bank and agency staff. Four members of staff worked each shift. There were ten residents with ages ranging from 34–53 years old, all of whom were classed by the service as having severe to profound learning difficulties. All had little or no verbal communicative abilities, and many had multiple disabilities. Comber Hall Way had a permanent staff of eight, and two bank staff worked at the service over the course of the research; two members of staff worked each shift. There were five residents with ages ranging from 43–65 years. All were described only as having learning disabilities (mild–moderate) and all were more physically able, and more verbally communicative, than the residents of Ashgrove.

The staff

From the beginning, there was a marked difference in the attitude that the staff teams took towards the research. At Comber Hall Way – where residents were more able – the staff team was positive from the outset. At our very first meeting they outlined problems to which they hoped the research could find answers, mostly concerning difficulties in ascertaining the residents' real preferences given their communication difficulties. They saw the research as an opportunity to reflect on their practice, to get feedback on it and to improve it.

In contrast, some (although not all) members of the staff team at Ashgrove – where residents had multiple physical and learning disabilities, were less independent, and had less verbal language – were highly suspicious of our research aims. Indeed, they seemed to harbour rather sinister suspicions of their managers' motives in putting forward their site as a possible research location. In conversations, some staff members indicated that they could not see how the research might inform their practice and, in fact, saw our interest in choice as somewhat irrelevant to their service, given the lack of communicative abilities demonstrated by their residents; as far as they were concerned their residents could not understand the choice scenarios they thought we were interested in. Indeed, these staff saw the whole 'choice agenda' as somewhat idealistic – as a good idea in principle but not in practice – and basically not relevant to their everyday care concerns. As a result, some staff at Ashgrove chose not to participate in the research. That meant that they had to be left out of any recordings, which meant some limitation on taping group activities. But a number of staff at Ashgrove were happy to participate (and, in the end, even the less positive ones did at least attend the feedback sessions when they took place some months later).

Once all necessary ethical approvals and permissions had been gained, we began a three-month familiarisation period in each site to allow the staff and residents time to get used to having a researcher in their midst. This time was also used to begin the informed consent process. Ample time and opportunities were provided to the staff and residents to raise concerns about the research, to ask questions about what participation might involve, about the data that would be collected, who would have access to it and the purposes for which it would be used.

All the residents at Comber Hall Way were judged capable of giving consent to participate. The residents at Ashgrove were to be included on the basis of assent, once it had been established that participation was not contrary to their best interests and assuming no relevant parties objected to their inclusion. The parents of one resident at Ashgrove did object to him being included in the research and consequently he never appeared in any recording. Consent was sought from all those present on each occasion of recording and the responses of the residents of Ashgrove to the presence of the researcher and the camera were constantly monitored for any signs of apparent distress. It should be noted that the research took place before the publication in the United Kingdom of the Mental Capacity Act (2005) and the subsequent Code of Practice (2007), which provides new guidance for participation in research.

All the staff at Comber Hall Way consented within the three-month familiarisation period. In contrast, only four of the nine permanent members of staff at Ashgrove consented to be video recorded and, given the difficulties encountered in determining the residents' participation, recording at Ashgrove did not begin until later in the project. The small number of Ashgrove staff participating in the project imposed severe restrictions on the opportunities for recording, on the types of recording that could be made and on the kinds of interaction that were recorded. This had consequences for the feedback that we could give to the service.

A précis of some findings

We shall go into more detail below about findings that we used in the feedback, but over the 18-month period of collecting data, transcribing and analysing it, we came up with a number of observations. Not surprisingly, given that this study was the first (so far as we knew) ever to analyse video recording of everyday life in residences for people with learning disabilities, interesting phenomena came up thick and fast, and well beyond our original focus on choice. Some of these phenomena stayed tantalisingly out of reach, but others did coalesce into robust phenomena which we wrote up for an academic audience: the way that staff shaped conversational topics (Antaki, Finlay and Walton, 2007); troubles with repeat-question formats (Antaki, Finlay, Walton and Pate, 2008); staff's proposals of activities tied to named third parties (Antaki, Finlay and Walton, 2007); residents' use of the non-verbal register, ignored or overlooked by staff (Finlay, Antaki and Walton, 2007); residents' means of resisting invitations and requests (Finlay, Antaki and Walton, 2008a); the dilemmas for staff in 'playing' with residents (Finlay, Antaki, Walton and Stribling, 2008). The main line, though, was a series of papers on the recurrent difficulties of offering residents meaningful choices (Antaki, Finlay, Walton and Pate, 2008; Finlay, Antaki and Walton, 2008a). It was this last theme that gave us the most direct and liveliest data with which to engage the staff in the feedback workshops.

Workshops

The last stage of the research project was to go back to the residences and invite the staff and residents to reflect on what we had captured on video. The basic format of the workshops was to show a set of selected video clips and to encourage discussion (a procedure we've written up as a proposal for training – see Finlay, Walton and Antaki, 2008b). We chose clips carefully, including those that illustrated situations where difficulties were encountered as well as situations that seemed to go well. Although we had points we thought were important from each clip, we intended to allow the staff teams to form their own conclusions. However, if issues that we considered important were not brought up spontaneously, we meant to use questions and prompts that we had prepared for each clip to focus the discussion.

Given the differences in the staff's enthusiasm – those from one residence mostly positive, those from the other grudging at best – when the time came to give feedback to the two sites, our approach differed greatly. With Comber Hall Way we were able to select quite freely, and choose those interactions which were relevant to the issues and problems that the staff had identified (e.g., how to ask questions; how to deal with uncertainty over the residents' understanding). Further, given the staff's support for the project we were also able to highlight interactions that had interested us and which we thought might be of interest to them, but which were not specifically linked to issues they had raised (e.g., issues that arose in formal meetings involving non-verbal behaviour – see Finlay, Antaki and Walton, 2007). We were therefore able to provide opportunities for them to reflect on aspects of their practice that they had not previously had reason to question. In doing this, specifically by providing them with video evidence, we were able to provide a situation where the staff team could openly question aspects of their practice that they saw as institutionally required, such as menu-planning meetings.

With Ashgrove – where some staff had been at best indifferent, and at worst positively antipathetic, to our presence – our approach was much more cautious. Given the sensitivities, we were careful to try to avoid being seen to criticise the service or, still more importantly, the individual members of staff who had been brave enough to consent to appear in the recordings. Consequently, when it came to selecting interactions to take into the feedback sessions we chose those that seemed to demonstrate effective practice or which showed the potential of the residents to make choices or to exercise control over their lives (e.g., doing things they were not routinely given the opportunity to do, such as serving themselves food and making drinks for themselves).

Because the residents of Ashgrove demonstrated no, or limited, verbal communication, discussion was centred less on the details of verbal interaction, and more on how activities might be offered and choice/self-determination further encouraged. We wanted to challenge the belief, held by some staff, that issues of choice and control were irrelevant. We felt that there would be room to challenge that – gently – and to have some sort of dialogue about how both beliefs and practice might be changed. Given the general level of scepticism about the research at Ashgrove, we were concerned about possible resistance to our feedback. One concern was that institutional policies, accurately or inaccurately represented, or even wilfully misrepresented, might be invoked to defend existing practices and to militate against change. We had therefore also invited an area manager to the session, primarily to try to dispel some of the myths that members of staff seemed to hold and perpetuate about what was and was not institutionally permissible. However, the manager's confrontational style at one point almost derailed the feedback session and we had to do considerable work to keep the session constructive.

Before we go on to more detail, the reader may well be asking what happened with the residents – what did the people with learning disabilities make of all this? After considering what it might mean to them, we decided that the more profoundly disabled residents of Ashgrove would not be able to take part in a necessarily verbal – and perhaps challenging – exchange about relatively abstract matters. We did think, though, that the residents of Comber Hall Way might be able to participate to some degree. However, their interests seemed to lie mostly in seeing themselves, the rooms in their home and objects familiar to them on screen. Certainly their comments tended to be simple noticings: *there's Robert, that's this table, that's the dining room*, or *that's the ketchup*, or identification questions: *who's that, Chris?*. In spite of what we hoped were supportive invitations on our part, and their familiarity with Chris Walton, with whom they had developed a trusting and indeed an affectionate relationship, we were unable to involve the residents further in the details of the interactions, in who was saying what to whom and why. More can be said about engaging service-users with learning disabilities in interactional research, and Williams (1999; Williams, Symons and Swindon People First Research Team, 2005) is a pioneer in showing what can be done; but here we concentrate on our more developed dealings with the staff.

Examples of video clips used in workshops: offering choices

Our feedback sessions focused, then, on the ways in which staff offered choices to the residents. Where things went well, we would show a clip and, as it unrolled, staff would spontaneously come up with ideas as to how they should change their practice. These arose either from seeing where difficulties arose and generating solutions in the subsequent discussion, or from seeing successful interactions and discussing how this might be extended or applied elsewhere. These discussions were focused on verbal and non-verbal behaviours; rules, routines and activities; and the physical layout of the houses. At its most productive, showing a clip would lead a member of staff to say 'ah – I can see that we're confusing him there – we shan't be doing *that* again.'

Comber Hall Way

The two extracts below illustrate the type of data we presented to the staff of Comber Hall Way, and the areas the discussion covered. The first clip involved one staff member (Tim) asking a resident (Alec) which type of vegetables he would like to cook with the dinner. We selected this clip because it portrayed precisely the type of 'choice event' involving this particular resident that the staff reported struggling with. Policy directives, as we've mentioned, mandate that adults with learning disabilities be supported in making choices, and that those choices should be their own. From the very beginning of our contact with this service the staff reported experiencing difficulties in realising these directives in their everyday practice. Specifically, since Alec often chose the last item of verbal options, repeated the words spoken to him, and often appeared to 'change his mind', they reported that their greatest difficulty was in determining the validity of Alec's choices. The episode below is a good example of this dilemma.

Episode 1: Frozen Vegetables

Alec has just finished one task in the kitchen, filling the saucepans with water, putting them on the hob and fitting their lids. Tim then asks Alec an open-class question regarding the vegetables he wants for dinner. When

Alec does not give a direct answer, Tim begins to suggest options (note this follows an unsuccessful attempt ten minutes earlier, and not shown here, to offer the same options, during which Alec repeated each option).

Extract 1   CHW V08: 19.59

```
01  Tim     what did you say you want.
02          (1.0)
03  Tim     which vegetables do you want,
04          [(.9)
05          [((Tim moves out of the kitchen into back room))
06  Tim     (°from th [e°)
07  Alec              [from the GArage,
08          (2.2)
09          [((Alec follows Tim; both move out of shot))
10  Tim     which one you (li-/wa,)(.) carrots?
11          [(4.8)
12          [((camera shows Alec bending over looking at something))
13  ?Alec   (uh-)
14   Tim    carrots, there's sprouts.
15          (.3)
16  Alec    sprou:
17  Tim     >no hold on< there's not enough sprouts, so we do (.)
18          if you wan' sprou:t we're >gonna have< something else
19          as well.
20          [(0.9)
21          [((Camera shows them both looking into a freezer))
```

Figure 9.1   Staff member Tim (right) picks out a bag

```
22  Tim     right we'll get the sprouts out
23          [(1.6)      ;
24          [((Tim picks out a bag))  [Figure 9.1]
25  Tim     d'you want the sprouts.
26          [((hands Alec the packet of
27          sprouts))
28          [(2.0)
29  Alec    ((turns and shows packet to Chris,
30          holding the camera)) (where's
31          the) broccoli.
32          (.5)
33  Chris   what are they?
34  Tim     put it do:wn, an' let's go and have a look what's in
35          the other freezer
36          [(1.0)
37          [((Alec walks past Chris))
38  Chris   sprouts
```

Here we see the suggestion of carrots is not confirmed by Alec (line 11) despite a gap of 4.8 seconds in which he could respond. Alec does, however, repeat 'sprouts' after this is offered. Tim then explains that there aren't enough sprouts and Alec needs to choose something else. At this point, Alec appears to ask Chris, the researcher, where the broccoli is (line 30), though Chris seems to temporise, asking instead what Alec has in his hand (sprouts). At this point Tim and Alec go out of the back room and into the garage, where they begin to look into a large chest freezer.

Extract 2   CHW V08: 20:54

```
01  Tim     what else is in there.
02          (0.4)
03  Alec    yea:h,
04          (4.2)
05  Tim     >°do y' wan°< (1.4) BROccoli,
06          [(2.3)
07          [((holds up packet of broccoli))
08          beans- (.) 'ju you say you want' beans:.
09          (.5)
10  Alec    bea:ns
11  Tim     you want beans.
12          (.3)
13  Alec    yeah,=
14  Tim     =or d' you want (3.0) [this one,
15                                [((Tim pulls out a bag of mixed veg,
16          and reaches down again into the
17          freezer))
```

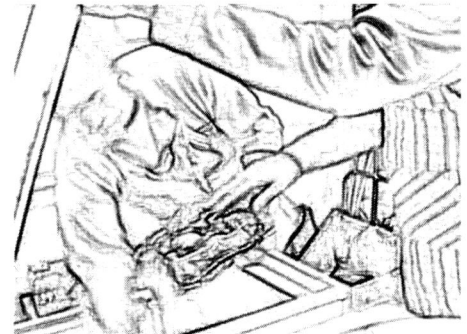

Figure 9.2 Resident Alec (right) taps the mixed veg. bag

```
18         (0.7)
19  Alec   [that one
20         [((taps the bag of mixed veg with his
21         right hand))  [Figure 9.2]
22  Tim    or [this one.=
23            [((Tim pulls out another bag, now
24         of green beans))
25  Alec   =tha    [t one that one] that one
26  Tim            [°which one.°]
27                 [((taps the bag of mixed veg twice but then
28         takes hold of the bag of green beans))]
```

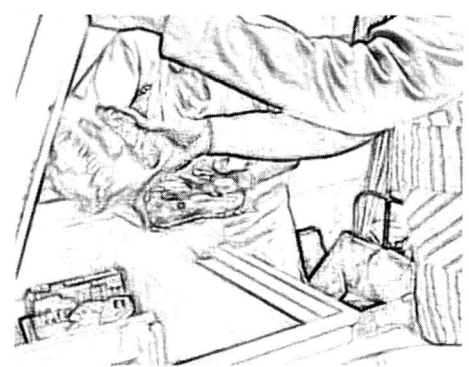

Figure 9.3 Staff member Tim (left) holds on to the green beans

```
29          (0.7)
30   Tim    [which one.
31          [(( Tim holds on to the bag of green
32          beans, withdraws it slightly))  [Figure 9.3]
33   Alec   that one ((releases hold on green beans,
34          again taps mixed veg))
35   Tim    are you su:re.
36   Alec   yeah,
37   Tim    [this one o' this one?
38          [(((right hand moves green beans forwards and
39          back)) ((left hand moves
40          mixed veg forward slightly))]
41   Alec   [that one
42          [(((hand movements mirror Tim's, reaches first for
43          green beans and then (on "that") taps mixed veg))
44   Tim    (°uh°) ((hands mixed veg bag to Alec))
```

In this extract, they are standing at the freezer, and Tim is selecting bags of frozen vegetables and offering them to Alec. First he offers broccoli, which Alec seems to have mentioned in the kitchen. However, Alec does not confirm this choice (lines 6/7). Next, Tim suggests 'beans'. Alec repeats the word 'beans' in line 10. Tim then attempts to check this by asking him again 'you want beans'; Alec confirms with a 'yeah'. At this point, instead of accepting the choice of beans, Tim offers a further option, picking up a bag of mixed vegetables (line 15). Alec appears to choose this as well by tapping it and saying 'that one'. Tim now has two possibilities, and he picks up the bag of beans and asks 'or this one'. In lines 27/28, Alec does not appear to clarify, as he taps the bag of mixed vegetables, saying *that one* but then takes hold of the bag of green beans. Subsequent attempts by Tim to clarify do not appear to produce a clearer choice.

After we played this clip, we wanted to get the staff to reflect on whether Tim's repeated offers to Alec were tendentious or not. What was clear from the outset was that the staff wanted to bring into the discussion a long and intimate familiarity with all the residents' habits, and to appeal to their understandings of what the residents could and couldn't do. It was no good – and perhaps this was right – us trying to tie them down to just what they could see on this, or any given clip.

As context for Tim's behaviour, the staff explained that Alec had predictable preferences for certain foods. For example, he usually asked for peas as a vegetable, and for peaches as dessert. The staff saw Alec's general predictability as a worry, in principle: if he (or one of the other residents) chose the same thing all the time, he might not really be choosing freely between options, and merely treading a well-worn path. It was, they said, precisely because of this that staff like Tim would go out of their way explicitly to offer alternative options, even when Alec had appeared to have already expressed a preference.

We appreciated this as a motivation for Tim embarking on his saga of offers and prompts, but nevertheless reissued our invitation to the staff to consider whether his questions were fit for their purpose. This led to a discussion of the importance of respecting people's preferences as a principle of 'person-centred' approaches to service provision. This also runs up against the issue of the staff's duty of care: unless staff ensure a balanced diet, an individual could choose to eat the same meal, potentially an unhealthy choice, each day and every day. With respect to the action in this clip, and what the staff might learn, they remained insistent that, even after watching the action twice, they were not sure what Alec wanted. However, they were able to clearly identify that the variety of different questions Tim asked, in attempting to clarify Alec's 'true' choice, were unsuccessful, and indeed seemed to generate problems in interpreting Alec's responses.

As a result of the discussion – and we felt that we had to allow the staff to talk around the issue in ways that made the exercise sensible in their own terms – the staff present decided that the kind of verbal options shown on the clip were perhaps not the best way to offer Alec choices. We were pleased to hear them spontaneously resolve to change their ways. If they were in this sort of situation again, they would, they said, ask him to go to the freezer and select a vegetable himself, without offering him options verbally. That is, they decided to change their practice, seeing that a request for *action* might be better than a request for a verbal expression of choice.

Episode 2: Pizza

The next extract we showed was of one of the regular meal-planning meetings that took place in the house. Each resident had to choose a number of meals over the coming week, and this was recorded on a checklist. Picture cards were scattered on the table during these meetings to remind the residents of what was available, to help then decide and to aid the communication of their choice.

The exchange involves Alec again, this time with two staff, Tim and Kath. Several minutes before this extract starts, Alec had picked up the pizza picture and handed it to Tim. The extract is a long one, to show how Kath circles repeatedly around the question of just what it is that Alec wants.

Extract 3a CHW V12: 24:07

```
01    Kath    Right A:lec what do you want to
02            [eat (.) on Thursday.
```

```
03   Alec   [((moves hand to touch cards))
04   Kath   [F'your supper now (.) no- not not for
05          breakfast we've done breakfast already,
06   Alec   [((picks up a picture, looking at it))
07   Tim    [°he's I think he's chosen here° (.)°th-°
08   Tim    [((picks up picture of pizza))
09   Tim    [is that is that the  one you've chosen
10   Tim    [((casts it down on table in front of Alec ))
11          (1.0)
12   Alec   ((drops card)) that one. ((points to Tim's
13          picture, looks at Kath))
14   Kath   What is [it=tell me what it is    [first
15 → Alec           [((looks down at cards)) [pi::zza.  pizza
16   Tim    Pi::zza.=
17   Kath   [=And what d'you want with it.
18   Alec   [((picks up one card, then sorts through others
19          with other hand))
20          [(1.3)
21   Kath   What would [you like with it.
22   Alec              [((picks up different picture and holds
23          up to Kath)) Tha':.
24   Kath   You can't have both dinners
25          [together or you'll bu::rst, (.4) which one
26   Alec   [((drops second card))
27   Kath   d'you want.
28   Alec   ((Points to first picture he is holding)) that one=
29   Tim    =you want chips and salad¿
30   Alec   ((looks at Tim)) salad
31   Tim    you want salad?
32   Alec   yea::h,
33   Tim    su:re?
34   Alec   uh yeah,
35   Tim    pizza [and salad
36 → Alec         [ask Chris that is
37   Alec   ((holds up original card. Resident next to him takes it))
38   Kath   ask Chris (.) Chris what is that. ((nodding at card))
39   Chris  It's pizza.
40   Kath   Do[you want pizza for (1.5)((looks down))Thursday
41   Alec     [((sorting through cards, picks up a different one))
42   Alec   (°I don't neh-°)
```

At this point Alec seems to have introduced some doubt into the proceedings, by seemingly asking (line 36) that Chris say what is on a certain card (in fact, it is the pizza card, even though the topic has moved on to what he wants to have with it). His motivation is unclear. In any case, it seems to prompt Kath to re-open the issue of what he wants for Thursday.

Extract 3b (continues immediately)

```
43    Kath     Okay (.) Alec (.3)((points to pictures on table))
44             take from here what you want for Thursday.
45    Alec     ((holds up picture he had just picked up)) That
46    Kath     Okay (.) give it to Kath:,
47    Alec     ((gives her the picture he is holding))
48    Kath     Thank you [(.)    now what else do you want (.) with salad
49    Alec               [(                ) what's that
50    Alec     ((picks up another picture and looks at it)) ri:ce (.5)
51             who' that Chris
52    Alec     (shows the picture to Chris))
53    Chris    What else you having Alec.
54    Alec     (puts card down and sorts through others))
55             [(1.5)
56    Tim      What [else do you want with the salad.
57    Tim          [((moves pictures round on the table))
58    Alec     [(((looks at Tim.))
59             [(1.0)
60    Tim      What else do you want with the salad.
61    Alec     (You got it Tim). ((points to Tim.))
62    Tim      No I haven't got anything,
63    Kath     No what do you want  [what do you want yourself,
64    Tim                           [it's on the table
65    Kath     (.3)you make the decision, (.4) you tell us what you
66             want: (.3) we can't make the decision for you
67    Alec     [(((sorting through cards on table))
68             [(.8)
69    Kath     What would you like to eat on Wednesday⁴
70             [before you go to bed?
71 →  Alec     [((picks up a picture              burgers
72    Alec     ((shows it to Kath))
73    Kath     Do you want that?
74    Alec     Yeah
75    Kath     Okay you can have burgers what do you
76             want with burgers?
```

As we warned, the printed exchange is a long one, and certainly feels so when watching it on the screen. The point that we wanted to come out from showing it to the staff is that we see Alec's apparently clear choice of *pizza* change to *burgers* by the end of the exchange.⁵ Alec seems to give his answer in line 12, and then confirms in line 15, after which Tim moves on to the question of what will go with it (chips or salad). However, given that it was Tim who appeared to suggest the pizza card in the first place (line 7), it might be that Alec is just acquiescing to Tim's suggestion rather than making a clear choice. Kath then pursues confirmation that pizza really is what Alec wants by asking a yes/no question: Do you want pizza for Thursday (line 40). When Alec does not produce a clear confirmation, she reissues the question but asks for an action instead of a yes/no response: *Take from here what you want for Thursday* (line 44). He picks up the salad card and she asks him what he wants with the salad. Similar questions are asked by Chris (line 53), then Tim (lines 56 and 60). Alec suggests Tim has the card, which he denies, then Kath continues to pursue a response from Alec. Finally, after sifting through the cards some more, Alec picks up a picture of burgers, and this is recorded as his choice.

On viewing the episode, staff again weren't sure whether this was what Alec really wanted, and identified as problems the number of options he is given, the number of picture cards on the table, and the amount of checking that staff do after pizza has been identified. Our part in the exchange was comparatively minimal: the kinds of things that the staff noted were more logistical than interactional (in so far as a clear line can be drawn between the two, in a situation like this). Firstly, it was noted that there were a lot of picture cards on the table that were merely distracting (including menu-items from breakfast as well as lunch and supper, or representing basic ingredients – a bag of flour, say – rather than dishes), and that this made it difficult for residents to find what they wanted. Certainly Alec appeared to sort through a large number of cards during this clip. The staff decided therefore to reduce the number of cards, and to separate them into breakfast, lunch and dinner piles. That, then, was a result of a kind, though not one that can be credited to Conversation Analysis as such.

Secondly, the participants noted the amount of checking that Kath engages in, and this does correspond more obviously to our intention of sensitising them to conversational practices. Recall that although Alec appears to make a choice early on, Kath, in pursuit of evidence that this is his 'true' choice, uses a catalogue of yes/no questions to insist that he identify his choice and then to select the correct card. In the workshop we looked at critical points in this interaction, such as line 44 where he is required to re-find the card among the pile, and discussed what would have happened if his choice had simply been accepted earlier in the interaction. One staff member commented: '*The point is, just accept the choice.*' The discussion also returned to the issue of whether Alec was really being offered choice if he chooses the same meals every week. It was decided that, following person-centred principles, it would be acceptable, and easier for Alec, if he was just offered a small selection of cards depicting foods he was known to like and asked to select from these.

This led to a discussion of whether a weekly meeting was the best place to offer food choice in the first place. It emerged from this discussion that the meetings were organised so as to provide evidence to the annual inspection regime (carried out by a body called the Commission for Social Care Inspection) that residents did have choice in meals. Once staff had agreed that these meetings were not the best way of offering choice, and that it was better to do it on a day-by-day basis, other ways of providing evidence to the social care inspectors were agreed on (keeping daily records of meal choices). Again, decisions were made to change practice based on close observation of video-recordings. Arguably, not much CA went into the feedback, but the very fact of seeing the video, and having on hand people like us to act as a sounding board, seemed to have been enough.

Ashgrove

All the above was at Comber Hall Way, where staff were supportive, and where residents were verbal. Matters at Ashgrove were, as we've mentioned, rather different. We approached the feedback session with some apprehension, though in the event this apprehension was misplaced.

The Ashgrove clips we showed couldn't involve such detailed inspection of talk, simply because the residents demonstrated little or no verbal communication. Instead, we showed clips aimed to provoke discussion of residents' involvement in household activities, and to illustrate situations in which residents' behaviour might be treated as expressions of choice. Although some of our analysis of data from this home was based on Conversation Analysis (Finlay, Antaki and Walton, 2008a; Finlay, Antaki, Walton and Stribling, 2008), the clips we selected for this workshop were based less often on such close analysis than they were in Comber Hall Way.

For example, we showed one clip of two residents being supported in making hot drinks (see Figure 9.4). Over the three months we spent in the house this hardly ever happened: usually the staff made the drinks and distributed them to the residents. We soft-pedalled any formal CA analysis here: what we wanted to do was merely to show the staff that the video captured the simple fact that residents could, with help, make themselves a cup of tea. We wanted to promote discussion of what staff perceived as obstacles to increasing the involvement of residents in such everyday activities. The clip generated a good deal of discussion amongst staff, with some arguing that it was not a good idea for reasons of safety. However, this led to suggestions as to safeguards and adaptations that could be put in place, and as a result several staff members resolved to encourage resident involvement in tea-making and food preparation in the future. Once again a constructive outcome, but based on the ethnographic record (and the apparently objective reality of the video recording) rather than Conversation Analysis.

Figure 9.4 Making hot drinks in the kitchen

A second example of a clip shown was one in which one resident, who had limited mobility and no observable verbal communication, was given a small jug of coffee (see Figure 9.5). It must be acknowledged that this situation occurred early in the data collection phase at Ashgrove, while staff members were still nervous of the camcorder and unsure of what it was that we wanted to observe and record. The situation depicted in the clip was therefore set up so that the resident in question could demonstrate what the staff called his 'trick'.

In part, it was the 'noteworthiness' of this phenomenon which had recommended it as suitable for recording, which also recommended it for inclusion in the workshop. Throughout the clip the resident sat at a table drinking from a mug and, at intervals, poured himself more coffee. Again, this was an occurrence that did not happen regularly. Through this clip we prompted a discussion of choice and self-determination, and explained how choice was a meaningful concept, and could be promoted, in areas as mundane as this. At the back of our minds, of course, was the commonsense notion of people doing things without help, and a sense that we could talk up what we saw in interactional terms (the resident simply got on with handling the pot and

178 Applied Conversation Analysis

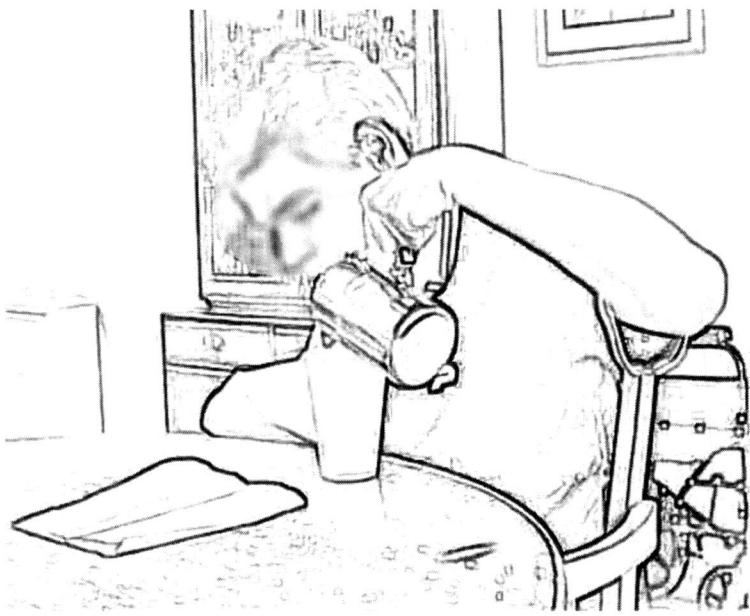

Figure 9.5 Pouring out the coffee

mug without searching around for someone to help him; his movements were, given his physical disability, as fluent and unhesitating as they could be; and his demeanour, so far as one could tell, unhurried and unruffled throughout). But we let the staff come up with observations along those lines, without labouring the point in any academic way.

The clip was useful because these sessions readily focused on conceptualising choice as a relevant concern and at appropriate levels for adults with such impairments. We showed how choice could be facilitated simply by allowing the resident to determine when, and by how much, he refilled his own cup. This led to a wider discussion of meal times, and how self-determination might be increased by the way in which food was presented on the tables. We were keen that staff members recognised that the residents in their service demonstrably possessed skills and abilities that, routinely, they were not given the opportunity to exercise. This provided for a wider discussion of how routines have the capacity to delimit opportunities to maintain and develop abilities and how even small changes to those routines can provide opportunities for choice and self-determination.

As a final example of our feedback to the Ashgrove staff, we showed a long clip of the monthly weighing session, in which residents had their body weights recorded (for a formal analysis of this, see Finlay, Antaki and Walton 2008a).

Staff weighed the residents monthly. They used ordinary bathroom scales (i.e., a flat platform, about two inches high, onto which the individual must step and balance so that their weight may be read off, Figure 9.6). During the daytime in Ashgrove, residents are usually occupied (or indeed sit or wander unoccupied) in the lounge or in other rooms. Weighing normally involves asking the residents, firstly, to come through to the dining room, or leading them into it, and then getting them to approach and stand on the scales.

While some of the residents come immediately for weighing, the recording we played shows residents who appear reluctant and are encouraged repeatedly. A couple of residents seem to be apprehensive about stepping up onto the scales, and only do so while holding onto the staff or the wall, suggesting they may be afraid of falling or have problems with balance. Through watching this extract, staff discussed the many different ways in which several of the residents appeared to resist standing on the scales, and the persistence of the staff despite these indications that they did not wish to participate. Again, we

Figure 9.6 A staff member guides a resident on to the scales

forbore to give any technical account of what we saw; it was much more appropriate to engage with the staff members in terms of choice, decision-making, resistance, gentleness and respect. To a large degree the staff volunteered the view that what they saw was indeed somewhat coercive and obviously distressing to some of the residents; but they explained that that they had to carry out these weighing sessions 'because there's a form' that they thought had to be filled in. The manager present was able to clarify that it was unnecessary, and the decision was taken to stop weighing each of the residents as a matter of routine and that the weight of individual residents would only be monitored if there was a specific reason to do so. Once more, then, a constructive result based on the ethnographic record, the vividness of the tape, and a supportive environment for discussion.

As we said above, we had come into the Ashgrove feedback session not being confident of how we would be received. The staff had been sceptical (at best) right from the beginning of the research project, unconvinced of its relevance to their service, and suspicious of the senior managers' motives in suggesting Ashgrove as a research site. However, through careful management of the workshop, by opening up space for discussion, by allowing the staff members to form their own conclusions and generate their own suggestions about how practice might be improved and, ultimately, by providing an opportunity to make our interests and intentions clear, even the most sceptical of the members of staff at Ashgrove were able to recognise that concerns about choice and control were germane to their interactions with the residents.

Concluding comments

We went into our feedback sessions ready to engage with staff about communicating with residents with learning disabilities, armed with a set of video clips. The staff interacted with the residents every day, and often had a frustrating time of it; so – hopefully – watching themselves on video might get them to reflect on what went right, and what went wrong. We found ourselves, perhaps not surprisingly, easing up on the explicitly technical language of CA, and relying on what was patently visible – with a certain amount of glossing – to get our observations across. And indeed, viewing the videos, with or without some kind of CA-informed commentary, did lead to staff reflecting critically on their practices.

With Comber Hall Way staff there was much more scope for CA because the residents were much more verbally able, and the staff were more open to the observations we made about such things as question design. With them we discussed particular conversational practices (e.g., checking answers;

pursuing choice through verbal vs. non-verbal means; non-verbal behaviours as unnoticed contributions to discussions; the problems created by asking two questions in quick succession) and ways of modifying these in order to promote the involvement of residents in decisions. However, the videos also led to wider reflections on practice, and here we relied on our ethnographic observations as well as the video recordings of staff practice. In Comber Hall Way, for example, there was discussion of the purpose and use of residents' meetings, and in Ashgrove there was discussion of how choice could be understood in the small details of everyday life (such as serving oneself food), the need for monthly weighing sessions, the involvement of residents in food preparation and the use of objects (e.g., the layout of kitchen items; the colour of jars). Discussions also arose around institutional constraints (e.g., providing evidence to inspectors that choices were being offered; the provision of day-time activities) and points of service philosophy (e.g., whether it is acceptable to engage in physical contact with people with limited verbal communication, or whether options should always be offered even when preferences are already known). It can be seen from the range of issues that were discussed that, in order to be relevant to the concerns of the services, the insights we gained from CA-based analysis of our data formed only a part of the content of the sessions. Given the nature of the services and the issues they faced around notions of choice and control, we felt this was the right decision.

We were pleased that, as a result of these discussions, staff decided to put in place a number of changes to their practice. These included less checking of residents' responses; less offering of verbal options and more reliance on objects and actions to indicate choice; less reliance on weekly meetings for meal choices; avoidance of using two versions of the same question in quick succession; having two staff members with clearly defined roles present in meetings, one of whom would monitor non-verbal contributions; more involvement of residents in food preparation; dropping weighing sessions; and providing more opportunities for residents to take control over a range of mundane aspects of their lives. In some cases, particularly in Ashgrove, there were divisions within the staff group as to whether changes would be permissible according to NHS rules and regulations, particularly for health and safety reasons, and here it was useful to have management present to reassure staff that proposed changes were not only permissible, but would improve practice. We believe that the workshops provided a rare opportunity to look at everyday practice in the two homes by engaging in the details of what actually happens, and to debate what was and was not possible. Not only did participants identify things that should change, but there was also space to acknowledge what they were doing well.

In some published accounts of using CA research and analysis for staff training and reflection on practice, the data involves people who are not present and are not known to the workshop participants (e.g., Jones, 2007). This has a number of advantages, namely participants being able to comment on the interaction without fear of giving offence and without risk of their own practice being held up for public scrutiny. However, it is a slightly less direct way of reflecting on one's practice than engaging with data collected in one's own workplace, as we did here. This did raise a number of issues. Firstly, the feedback sessions involved all staff, whether they participated in the data collection or not. Consequently, those who had consented to participate found their own practice discussed while those who did not consent to participate did not. This was not an issue in Comber Hall Way, where all staff consented, but was the case in Ashgrove. We believe there was the potential for resentment within the staff group about this, although we were very careful to check with those featured in the video clips that they were happy for their interactions to be used as examples. One unexpected issue that arose in these workshops was a number of critical comments by one manager regarding the behaviour of a staff member in a clip. Although this only happened on one occasion, about half-way through the session, it deflated the constructive and positive atmosphere to some extent.

We attempted to minimise the potential for individual criticism in several ways. Firstly, we showed clips of interactions and practice that seemed to be successful as well as those that were problematic. For those illustrating interactions that seemed less successful, we stressed that staff should not be singled out for criticism as the video extracts showed dilemmas that all staff faced, and we could have chosen other extracts involving different people facing similar dilemmas. We also reminded participants in Ashgrove that only a proportion of the staff group put themselves forward for participation and that they should not be singled out as a result. Because of our experience, however, we would think more carefully about involving management in the workshops, and when managers were involved we would brief them carefully about the principle of no criticism. Generating agreed ground rules for the whole group at the beginning of the session would also serve to reinforce the no-criticism policy.

Our experience, of conducting this research and providing feedback from it to those involved, should highlight the importance of participant investment in data collection and the value of participants having a sense of ownership over its interpretation, the importance of ethnography in shaping both our analyses and our understanding of the interpretations that the participants reach and the mechanisms for change that they generate, and it should highlight our obligation to participants to recognise the institutional, logistical and social psychological factors that shape and delimit their behaviour within such interactionally challenging and policy charged environments. Ultimately, the contribution that this research made to the services involved, to the emergent literature on 'choice' in services for adults with intellectual disabilities, as well as to the Conversation Analytic literature in general, is attributable to the generosity, patience and courage of those individuals who were willing to be recorded.

Notes

1. We're grateful to the Economic and Social Research Council for grant no. RES-148-25-0002.
2. A 'Trust' is a self-governing administrative body, often organised around a neighbouring group of hospitals, within the National Health Service (NHS) in England and Wales; it makes its own decisions, but is ultimately responsible the national NHS.
3. As sometimes happens in applied research, especially with vulnerable populations, complications to do with obtaining proper informed consent from all parties hampered our efforts to get recording permission in one residence. We did get access, and we did engage with staff and service-users there; but each time Chris Walton asked for permission to record an episode, at least one person demurred and in the end we made no recordings at all.
4. This is a slip; Kath means Thursday, as the context makes clear.
5. Although, probably unnoticed by everyone, Kath has unintentionally slipped, in line 69, and said 'Wednesday' when it is the Thursday meal that they are discussing.

10
Reflecting on Your Own Talk: The Discursive Action Method at Work

Joyce Lamerichs and Hedwig te Molder

This chapter describes how we developed a Conversation Analysis-based intervention approach, which we call the Discursive Action Method. The method aims to make people critically aware of how they talk and, on that basis, to help them shape their own practices. The method has its roots in an early statement of what Edwards and Potter termed their 'Discursive Action Model' (Edwards and Potter, 1993) and is based on insights from Conversation Analysis and Discursive Psychology[1] more generally (Edwards, 1997; Edwards and Potter, 1992; Hepburn and Wiggins, 2007; Hutchby and Wooffitt, 1998; Potter, 1996; Potter and Te Molder, 2005).

We developed the Discursive Action Method (DAM, for brevity's sake) as a systematic method in response to the needs that emerged from trying to educate young people about health and wellbeing. The framework was a four-year participatory health education project called LIFE21,[2] and our brief was to encourage adolescents to work out school-based health interventions geared towards their peers. What we developed over that period is, we think, a robust and portable set of techniques, based fundamentally on a CA reading of talk, that can be used in a variety of intervention programmes.

Before explaining the steps of the DAM in greater detail, it is important to point out that the method can fulfil different functions. The method can work with any intervention where there is engagement between trainers or facilitators and the people whose practices are to be changed (as is reported in other chapters in this volume; see for example, Kitzinger with call takers on a help line in Chapter 6, Stokoe's work with mediators in Chapter 7, or Finlay, Walton and Antaki's with care staff in Chapter 9). Depending on the key questions that are posed during the workshop by trained workshop leaders, different goals can be achieved. As such, the method can stimulate participants to improve their listening skills, raise their awareness of how they talk and act, or encourage participants to develop their own activities. In the context of the current project, the method aimed to accomplish the second and the third goal in particular. While applied here in a health context, we think the method consists of a set of generic steps that makes it a useful approach to be employed in other settings, where it can be flexibly adapted to the needs of the target group. We will discuss these matters of applicability more fully in the discussion. In the remainder of this chapter we set out to explain the method's steps and how they were applied, how the method was instrumental in raising adolescent's critical awareness of how they talk and act with their peers, as well as how it formed a basis for setting up school-based health activities.

Background to the project: a conversational turn in developing health activities

The participatory health education project that brought us into contact with young people was conducted in cooperation with the municipal health services in Eindhoven, a middle-sized city in the south of the Netherlands. The municipal health services are well-connected to the target group on many levels (see, for an overview, Lamerichs et al., 2006). LIFE21 was ultimately conducted at three secondary schools for higher education in Eindhoven. The project's aim was to invite adolescents (14 to 17 years of age) to think about the ways in which they talk about health in their everyday conversations, and to use those reflections as the basis for them to develop health interventions aimed at their peers.

There have been several attempts to apply insights from interaction analysis to the area of health communication. Initiatives that aim to improve communication in this area share a concern for: (1) working with naturally occurring talk rather than data created for the purpose of research (e.g., setting up focus groups with target group members) and (2) using taped material (often referred to as 'trigger tapes', see Jones, 2007: 2299) or transcripts as the basis to engage in a discussion about particular aspects of the unfolding talk (Koole and Padmos, 1999; Roberts, Davies and Jupp, 1992). The development of the DAM can be placed within this tradition. One of the method's most important assets is its strong basis in the interactional details of the conversational materials. But compared to other projects, our method is also innovative in two other ways. First, the input for the method – conversational data from the target group – is collected by members of the target group themselves; and second, after a preliminary analysis of the data by the researchers involved in the project, members of the target group are turned into analysts of their own data.

Setting and permission

A project that aims to involve youngsters to set up health activities at their schools cannot operate without support from the schools and the school board. Our first goal therefore was to get in touch with secondary schools in the city and introduce the project, in an attempt to raise their enthusiasm and to get permission to carry out the project at these schools. We presented the project during board meetings on four schools and explained that the project started with pupils taping conversations they had with or among their peers at the school's premises, but not in the classroom. We also explained the participative part of the project, where taped conversations were used as a starting point to develop school-based health activities, the contents of which were to be defined on the basis of the collected materials. The fact that form and content of the health activities could not be delineated at the start of the project is typical for participatory health promotion research, but is often met with some resistance by parties involved, for example because there is a need to define goals prior to committing oneself to a project (see, for an overview of dilemmas in health promotion research, Koelen, Vaandrager and Colomer, 2001; also Koelen and Van den Ban, 2004).

Members of the school board at three schools were very keen to participate, and together with the director and the municipal health services we sought a way to address the privacy issues that are involved in taping. A leaflet was prepared to hand out at school to inform the parents about the privacy issues involved and a protocol was set up for the pupils who started collecting data to ask permission when taping commenced. Additional talks were then planned with teachers who operated as a contact person in the school. During information meetings the LIFE21 project was explained in greater detail and pupils were asked if they wanted to get involved in collecting data; that is, taping conversations in their peer group.

In the weeks to follow, we had numerous talks with the fourth school to decide whether or not they could participate in the project. The school board at this school – a school for lower secondary professional education – insisted on using a topic-list to define the contents of what was to be taped beforehand, while we considered it crucial to tape conversations that resembled natural talk as much as possible. The board was also not very willing to allow pupils to develop their own initiatives for health activities, and wanted to have a say in which activities were to be carried out. Since the school board wanted to be so strongly in control of the project, we could not but conclude that this was not the best starting point for a participatory health education project. As a result, we terminated working with this school as part of the LIFE21 project.

Data

It was important to us, as of course it is to any conversation analyst, that the data be as natural as possible. Conversations were taped by youngsters themselves without a researcher nor any of the school staff present. In this way we were able to ensure that the materials were as illustrative of naturally occurring talk as possible. An important assumption was that these conversations would then display a broad range of concerns addressed in relation to a – widely defined – set of health issues. As we will discuss later, the fact that the adolescents were able to tape their own conversations, without any instructions on what to tape, and work with highly recognisable materials in the upcoming workshop, turned out to be a crucial aspect of the method.

Adolescents used digital voice recorders that operated on batteries that could be carried, or placed somewhere unobtrusive when taping took place. Pupils recorded a total of 11 hours of conversations with or among their peers. We deliberately had no control over what the pupils recorded, so perhaps inevitably the corpus of 11 hours included recordings of music, background sounds or other material not relevant to our purposes. Because of a varying set of background noises, a smaller part of the data of about 6 hours was eventually used for analysis. This is something to take into consideration when involving the target group (in this case, youngsters) in collecting data, and suggests that one should expect only about half of such free-range data to be directly useful. However, the 6 hours that could be used for analysis painted a very rich picture of the target group's life world.

As the pupils began to hand in their tapes, we started the process of transcription. All names (e.g., of classmates, parents and teachers) and other identifying information were rendered anonymous. Recordings were transcribed on the basis of a standard transcription system developed by the conversation analyst Gail Jefferson (1984; see the guide to notation on p. xi of this volume for a key to transcription). Transcription is necessary not only to establish rigour but it also makes important interactional features of the talk (e.g., overlap, pauses and laughter) visible in the transcripts. These details can be used when working with the materials. However, the level of detail of transcription that is necessary to work with the data may vary, depending on the goals that are to be accomplished and the target group. For the purpose of this project, we used a comparatively basic transcription style, so that the participants could engage as directly as possible with the text and not be put off by too much unfamiliar notation (Sneijder et al., 2007).

Action sequences as the basis for the Discursive Action Method

Our approach is conversation-analytic; we draw on CA's central principles of turn-taking, turn design and sequential positioning, as well as Discursive Psychology's concern with fact and accountability as a managed trait of various kinds of discourse (Edwards and Potter, 1992; Hutchby and Wooffitt, 1998; Pomerantz and Fehr, 1997; Potter, 1996; Sacks, Schegloff and Jefferson, 1974). The central tenet of the Discursive Action Method, shared with CA and DP, is that talk is made up of action sequences and that talk is constructed in ways 'that make things happen'. Action sequences are patterns of interaction that have identifiable and structural properties that are associated with particular social actions such as 'blaming', 'justifying', 'criticising' or 'disagreeing'. Besides fulfilling a broad range of (subtle) interactional tasks, speakers' descriptions and reports also orient to their own factual or warrantable status, say, as 'objective' renderings of events or objects being reported. In order to have youngsters consider the activities accomplished with their own discourse, we worked with two interrelated concepts, taken from discursive psychology work (Edwards and Potter, 1992) that exemplify this view on talk as oriented towards social action: *stake* and *accountability*.

Stake

One powerful way to understand the action orientation of talk is to see it as managing 'dilemmas of stake'. In their discourse, people routinely attend to how the factual status of what they say can be treated as a product of stake or interest. A blaming can be treated as rooted in jealousy and a description may be discounted by acknowledging a probable situational investment in it ('Well, people say that in these circumstances, don't they'). Speakers are found to employ a broad range of conversational resources to manage these dilemmatic instances (Potter, 1996), such as 'confessing' their stake before it threatens the factuality of their talk. Note that this way of analysing talk is different from saying that people's actions are determined by their interests; rather, it looks at how people treat one another *as if* they are entities with intentions, motives and biases (Edwards and Potter, 1992).

Accountability

A closely related, action oriented feature of talk is to what extent speakers present themselves, and hold one another accountable, for the veracity of a description and its interactional consequences (Buttny, 1993; Potter, Edwards and Wetherell, 1993; Scott and Lyman, 1968). Speakers can employ a set of different conversational resources to manage accountability: they may for example draw upon reported speech ('Paul said Lilly lacks commitment to make this a successful project') rather than presenting a statement explicitly as one's personal opinion ('I think Lilly lacks commitment to make this a successful project'). These examples show how an utterance can be attributed to different people (the speaker or a third party, Paul); variations in the basis upon which a description is offered mark the extent to which a speaker can be held personally accountable for the words he is uttering (Holt and Clift, 2007; see also Goffman, 1979 on footing). Note that with this example, the speaker may be held accountable for what is made inferentially available in the description: attributing blame or even disputing Lilly's competence.

Preliminary data analysis: identifying central concepts that inform the DAM

The Discursive Action Method was developed on the basis of a preliminary study of the conversation materials, in which we wanted to identify coarse-grained interactional patterns that would help stimulate discussion and reflection when we presented the text to the students.

During and after transcription was completed, we listened closely to the recordings and read the transcripts to see what seemed to our ears confusing, unexpected or interesting. Data was also discussed in different data sessions in which researchers from different universities took part, who all have a background in Conversation Analysis and Discursive Psychology (for accounts of Discursive Psychology, see Hepburn and Potter, 2003, and Jones, 2007).

Narratives and social exclusion

The thematic focus of our study of the conversation materials was to explore how adolescents talk about health in their everyday conversations, if and when it came up. One recurrent feature was that matters of health and wellbeing were addressed as part of larger narratives (cf. Goodwin, 1984; Jefferson, 1978) which typically culminated in negotiating the basis for inclusion or exclusion of peers. An important aspect of these narratives was that they often contained an extreme 'opinion' about a person or an occurrence (Lamerichs and Te Molder, 2009). In our initial explorations we also observed that these narratives were often followed by consecutive or second stories (cf. Arminen, 2004). Detailed inspection showed that these second stories seemed to fulfil an important interactional function: they offered a possibility to negotiate and 'readjust' what counted as an appropriate basis for presenting unequivocal opinions about themselves and their peers.

Our preliminary analysis resulted in the identification of a dominant interactional concern speakers seemed to attend to when producing these strong points of view, which we identified as: 'how to present an explicit point of view without being considered biased'. Speakers managed to counter the impression that their opinion was motivationally suspect in a number of different ways. Extract 1 illustrates one discursive strategy speakers often employed to 'solve' this prevailing interactional concern.

Extract 1   The classmate (a)

```
18   Petra:   oh Petra he says I see someone
19            it just can't be
20            he is just deformed.
```

In lines 18–19 Petra conveys her father's words via an instance of indirect reported speech. Presenting a rather overt statement about someone's physical appearance (*he is just deformed*, line 20) as the alleged (literal) words of a third party enables the speaker to minimise the extent to which she can be held personally responsible for this utterance.

Based on our preliminary analysis, a fragment was selected for the workshop that offered a canonical example of the dilemma of stake adolescents constantly oriented to when telling stories (namely: 'how to bring off an explicit point of view without being considered biased'). It also incorporated three frequently adopted discursive strategies speakers employed to resolve this interactional dilemma. Importantly, the fragment also represented a possibly controversial occurrence (voicing a strong statement about a classmate) that we expected would stimulate discussion. Selection took place on the basis of this combined set of qualities: it can therefore be considered an extreme case that offered multiple opportunities for learning. During the workshop, the fragment was presented on an anonymised handout (see Appendix A) together with a key to transcription.

The workshop: identifying action sequences in talk

With the stepwise approach of the workshop we aimed to gradually transform the pupils into analysts of their own discourse. The goals of the workshop were: (a) to make participants aware of the social functions of language; (b) to let participants explore a set of discursive strategies; and (c) to have participants discuss the results from the previous steps to develop health activities aimed at their peers. The pupils were invited to take these progressive steps:

Step 1   Adopt a non-cognitive view.
Step 2   Move from making cognitive judgments to identifying interactional effects.

Step 3   Identify the speaker's interactional problem.
Step 4   Explore discursive strategies.
Step 5   Move from analysis to eliciting critical comparisons.

Steps one to four aim to make adolescents critically aware of their talk and behaviour, whereas the fifth step is geared towards the specific goals of LIFE21, that is, to use these conversational insights to encourage thinking about possible health activities. With every step, the workshop leader used a set of key questions, the answers to which are incorporated in our description of the different stages of the workshop.[3] It is important to say here that the workshops never played the actual audio tapes to the pupils: that would have breached confidentiality, and would have probably introduced a great deal of distraction. For our purposes, the transcriptions were much more appropriate and easily manageable.

STEP 1   Adopt a non-cognitive view

Step 1 lays the foundation for the other steps. It is also closely tied to Step 2. Its aim is to get the workshop participants in the right 'frame of mind' to explore the conversational data. Importantly, this step sets out to establish a change in perspective for many. Informed by the research perspectives that lie at the basis of the DAM, this change of perspective involves a focus on conversational 'moves' as interactional accomplishments or social actions, rather than points of entry into speaker's intentions or motives.

There are many research examples that can be drawn upon to exemplify the focus on social action sequences, but this step wants to achieve more than offering illustrations alone. Relevant to the fragment used in the workshop, what we wanted to accomplish was not to have pupils engage in a discussion about the truth value of say, whether Petra really did or did not see the boy from her class previous to her dad's (alleged) remarks and laughter. Rather, we wanted to show how Petra's account, which involved a reporting of, say, surprise, may for instance account for an 'authentic' judgment (focus on action). This outlook can be described as a non-cognitive view (cf. Edwards, 1997; Edwards and Potter, 2005; Te Molder and Potter, 2005).

One can imagine that this change of perspective is not easily accomplished. Therefore, we spent some time thinking about the best way to work with this step, given that we were dealing with participants who are 14 to 17 years of age. We agreed on using a playful approach and asked everybody to wear an imaginary pair of glasses. A set of rules was put on the blackboard stating that wearing the glasses meant speakers had to withhold from passing any kind of judgment about the fragment (e.g., as to whether they thought the speaker was rude or mean; or whether they thought the story really took place as the speaker tells it). Hence, we explained that statements such as 'I just know that this person is exaggerating because she wants to impress her friends' (ascribing particular intentions to the speaker's utterance) or 'I can't imagine her father saying something like this' (determining whether the speaker's words are in accordance with reality) were not allowed.

Apart from simply installing it as a rule, we were also able to elaborate on its usefulness, because lapses did occur. When these lapses occurred we were able to show just how difficult it was to argue with statements that address the speaker's intentions ('she is just lying') since they quickly lead to a discussion in which one is inclined to pass normative judgments. Ultimately, we think that our 'working metaphor' of the glasses, coupled with the set of rules helped the pupils to acquire the analytical focus we were aiming for. It stimulated them to come up with observations that were geared towards the social effects of talk. Interestingly, they soon started to use the rules as a guiding principle to correct others and themselves (e.g., 'Okay we are imagining too much, we are acting like we are inside the speaker's head'; 'Oh I'm sorry I am not going to say this, we shouldn't comment on what we read'). An important asset of this first step was that in exploring talk's social effects, pupils could behave like 'detached observers' rather than relating their observations to the speaker or to themselves. Thus, they were discouraged from criticising the talk (and the speakers) as displayed in the fragment (cf. Hepburn and Potter, 2003).

STEP 2 Move from making cognitive judgments to identifying interactional effects

Step 1 has paved the way to work with the transcript and formulate questions that address the interactional effects of language rather than individual cognitions (beliefs, thoughts, intentions). Thus, the question 'what does the speaker mean?' (which gets at intentions) is replaced by 'what does the speaker accomplish with this utterance?'(which gets at interactional effects). Since interactional effects are accomplished between speakers, we asked our workshop participants to take a closer look at lines 21–22 and 38–39 in Extracts 2 and 3 respectively, where recipients display laughter in response to the prior speaker's story. We asked them to consider the effect of the laughter in the light of the preceding and the following turn and to consider: (1) a possible alternative uptake that could have taken place instead of the laughter that now occurs, and (2) the effect of the laughter on the next speaker's turn.

Extract 2 The classmate (b)

```
18    Petra:      oh Petra he says I see someone
19                it just can't be
```

```
20              he is just deformed.
21   Kelly:     [heheh]
22   Ilona:     [heheh]
23   Petra:     s(h)o I tu(h)rn around like
24              thi(h)s I sa(h)y he(h)is
25              i(h)n my cla(h)ss and my
26              dad really just didn't
27              believe me (.)
```

Extract 3   The classmate (c)
```
36   Petra:     He seriously thought that
37              this was a handicapped person.
38   Nico:      [*heheheheh*]
39   Ilona:     [*heheheheh*]
40   Kelly:     yeah but he is also-
41   Petra:     no but seriously (.) that
42              guy totally ehm eczema which
43              is something he just can't do
44              anything about(.)you know,
```

In looking at the transcripts and reading them out loud, pupils noted that at the instances where laughter occurred in the conversation, a different uptake could also have taken place. In elaborating on this observation, we asked them to think of some of those alternative utterances. With regard to the laughter in lines 21–22, they suggested that recipients could have expressed another type of assessment ('nobody adds something to the story except the laughter; they don't give their opinion about what is said here'). They put forward how a different kind of receipt (e.g., a marked silence, outright disagreement) may have prompted the speaker to 'change the subject' or continue with a 'negative statement' about her father's remark (lines 18–20) 'to show how she explicitly rejects it'.

In voicing these alternative utterances, pupils worked with the so-called rhetorical principle (cf. Billig, 1987; Edwards and Potter, 1992; Potter, 1996). The rhetorical principle proposes that any description is typically organised to argue against a possible contrasting version. Now that a range of different types of uptake was established, it was put forward that the first speaker may take up the recipients' laughter as indicating 'oh they like my story' and as an illustration of how recipients were 'going along' with the story as it unfolds. They glossed the laughter in lines 38–39 as possibly indicating what they described as: 'all right, my story is going okay, let's continue and take it one step further'. They discussed how the way the laughter was hearably produced (i.e., as 'guilt-stricken') potentially adds to an atmosphere in which the speaker would feel compelled (or encouraged) to continue what was taken up as being a particularly 'juicy' story.

Interestingly, rather than considering it interactionally meaningless, pupils readily glossed the laughter as a possible affiliative response that may stimulate the speaker to continue her story. They considered how it might be taken up as an invitation to produce an even bolder statement about the boy's physical appearance (see, for example, lines 26–27, line 40 and line 42), and how it clearly differed from other types of uptake, such as an overt disagreement. Pupils thus showed themselves able to deal with the laughter in terms of its interactional effects (it may be taken up as an assessment that encourages the speaker to continue her story) rather than only treating it as reflecting a mental state (what the speaker says is funny). This augured well for our aim of turning the pupils from producers into analysts of their talk.

STEP 3 Identify the speaker's interactional problem

The interactional effects of a particular utterance can be explored by using different routes. One fruitful approach is to start by identifying the speaker's central interactional problem. When able to recognise the interactional problem in a particular stretch of talk, participants are better equipped to assess how people say what they say to accomplish particular actions.

Importantly, the notion of interactional 'problem' does not refer to a thematic problem, but specifically to an interactional issue at stake[4] (not: 'why am I unpopular' but: 'How can I voice a strong statement while preventing being seen as someone who discriminates?'). A speaker's problem often 'surfaces' in talk as a dilemma of stake. As we have seen, a dilemma of stake has to do with the ways in which people generally and consciously or not, orient to how their behaviour is judged by others in the light of interests deemed to be at stake. Alternatively, speakers can refer to issues of stake and interest to undermine the credibility of another speaker's utterances (e.g., accusing someone of going for financial gain rather than providing the best service to customers). In our example used in the workshop, the speaker's dilemma of stake can be glossed as 'how do I prevent my utterances from being taken as the product of bias and interest?'.

To practice identifying a speaker's interactional problem in a conversation, in Extract 4 we explored the beginning of Petra's story. We recalled how the story begins after some work has been done in lines 2–9 to collaboratively establish the subject of the upcoming story (*Neil*, see lines 6–9). We asked the pupils to consider the following question: 'what is possibly at stake for the speaker when describing this encounter?', and more pointedly we phrased the question alternatively as 'what can the speaker be "accused of" when telling her story?'.[5]

Extract 4   The classmate (d)

```
01    Petra:      no seriously  [            ]
02    Nico:                     [about whom?]
03    Petra:      no seriously the other day-
04                the other day I walked through
05                town with my dad huh
06    Teun:       °Neil°
07    Kelly:      Neil
08    Petra:      (.) yes
09    Nico:       oh Neil
10    Petra:      and uh well (.) I was walking
11                through town with my dad- not
12                knowing who this guy is at
13                all he who who who accidentally
14                and I didn't see him and my dad
15                suddenly starts to laugh,
```

At first, the pupils glossed the beginning of Petra's story, in which she described the situation prior to her dad allegedly noticing the boy, as indicating the potentially sensitive character of what comes next ('If I told a story like this I would be very much aware of how others would react. I would present my story in a cautious way by precisely describing where I was walking and when and what I saw').

When examining Extract 4 in more detail, pupils commented upon a number of other features of the extract. They noted how the speaker presented the encounter with the boy as coincidental, as an occurrence for which the speaker seemed not particularly prepared ('it happens spontaneously'). After these first observations, we continued to discuss what describing an occurrence as unexpected, as spontaneous may accomplish in talk, in terms of its interactional effects. As a starting point for the discussion we asked participants to think of alternative descriptions Petra could have given to describe her encounter. They pointed out that describing an encounter with someone as spontaneous enabled Petra to ward off the impression that she wanted to avoid the boy, say, because she holds a bias against him or looks down on him because of the way he looks.

From this discussion it became clear that Petra's description of the situation leading up to her dad's alleged remarks about the boy, in which she portrays herself as not particularly aware or wanting to avoid running into someone, is one example of a discursive strategy that might 'solve' the speaker's interactional problem. Ultimately, on the basis of examining her strategies, Petra's interactional problem was defined as 'how can I tell a story in which I present an explicit opinion without being accused of prejudice?'.

196 Applied Conversation Analysis

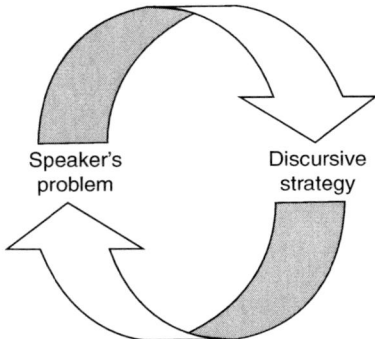

Figure 10.1 The cyclical approach to analysis

Interestingly, these kinds of observations illustrate that pointing out a discursive strategy may be one way into identifying the speaker's problem. In other instances, one may start with hypothesising the speaker's (potential) problem first, which might then enhance the ability to recognise particular strategies used to resolve the speaker's interactional problem. The way in which both speakers' strategies and speakers' problems may be taken as a point of entry into analysing talk as social action resembles the cyclical approach common to analysing data in discursive psychology (see Figure 10.1). Both routes can be used to have participants critically assess their everyday talk.

Step 4 Explore discursive strategies

In line with the speaker's problem that was identified in Step 3, we went on to explore other parts of the fragment to see what possible other discursive strategies the speaker employs. We started by taking a closer look at lines 14–22, displayed as Extract 5 below.

Extract 5 The classmate (e)

```
14    Petra:    and I didn't see him and my dad
15              suddenly starts to laugh,
16    Teun:     heheh
17    Kelly:    heheh
18    Petra:    oh Petra he says I see someone
19              it just can't be
20              he is just deformed.
21    Kelly:    [heheh]
22    Ilona:    [heheh]
```

Participants were asked to look at Extract 5 and employ the rhetorical principle to come up with alternative formulations for the stretch of talk displayed in lines 18–20. Here, we see how the speaker conveys her father's alleged words to describe the boy they saw in town. Interestingly, pupils readily observed that by conveying a quotation (*'he says* I see someone'), rather than presenting the utterance as her own words (*'I said* I see someone'), the assessment about the boy is presented as being voiced by the speaker's father. Furthermore, in the discussion the participants referred to the fact that what is presented here as the father's words might or might not have been uttered as such at all ('it might have been that her father did not utter these words at all, or said something different'). Participants also consistently glossed how drawing upon this quotation places the speaker in a position of reduced responsibility for the evaluation it contains ('using quotations is a way to prevent people from holding you responsible for that statement'; 'you're in the clear if you use quotations, you can always say, okay listen, it wasn't me'). Interestingly, in observing how quoting someone else's words may offer a 'secure basis' for voicing a strong statement, pupils touched upon the notion of accountability, which is an important principle adopted in Discursive Psychology to study the social functions of talk.

The second segment of the fragment we explored in closer detail was lines 23–37 (displayed as Extract 6 below), where the speaker describes her father's view of people with Down's syndrome. We asked the participants to consider what possible discursive strategy the speaker employs here to resolve the dominant speaker's problem, which we described as: 'how do I present an explicit viewpoint without being considered biased or interested?'.

Extract 6   The classmate (f)

```
23      Petra:      s(h)o I tu(h)rn around like
24                  thi(h)s I sa(h)y he(h)is
25                  i(h)n my cla(h)ss and my
26                  dad really just didn't
27                  believe me (.) and he just
28                  had well my dad he (.) say (0.2)
29                  my dad always likes it say people
30                  with Down syndrome and such you
31                  know. He would always watch Knoop
32                  in je zakdoek.⁶ He just loves that.
33                  And we would always laugh about
34                  that you know but apart from that
35                  well (.) he just loves that.
36                  He seriously thought that
37                  this was a handicapped person.
```

A first observation made by the participants was that the description was rather lengthy, which was glossed as 'she obviously has some explaining to do'. It was then noted that this description contained an opposing claim when compared to the statement that was allegedly made by the speaker's father earlier in the story ('stressing his liking of people with Down's syndrome here seems contrary to what he has reportedly said earlier'). In the discussion that followed, pupils came to see how drawing upon a counter-argument (stressing her dad's purported love for people with Down's syndrome) is precisely what enables the speaker to ward off the impression that her father (or she for that matter) may hold a grudge against people with Down's syndrome (cf. Potter, 1996, on stake inoculation). On the contrary, it enables the speaker to portray her father as the kind of person that *always likes* (line 29) and *just loves* (lines 32 and 35) these people.

What we see in Steps 3 and 4 is that adopting a non-cognitive view enhances the participants' abilities to work with the rhetorical principle, and explore the social actions accomplished with certain utterances. In this instance, it made them more aware of the strategies speakers may adopt to solve certain interactional problems.

Step 5 Move from analysis to eliciting critical comparisons

It has been our aim to show how the DAM provides instruments to have pupils critically reflect on how they talk to their peers. Hence, the steps that were outlined have illustrated two routes that can be used to do so. Step 5 is tailored to the goals of this participatory health education project and has a somewhat different aim than the other steps. The most important difference is that during Step 5, pupils are no longer required to behave as analysts in looking at the conversational materials, and adopt a non-cognitive view. Instead, they were asked to behave as their own interventionists; a change that was needed to facilitate the process of developing health activities.

In order to facilitate this change, we asked pupils to take off their imaginary glasses and to critically assess the discursive strategies that had come up in the discussion. The assessment consisted of answering two questions: (a) what do you think of this strategy?, and (b) would you make use of this strategy in your own conversations and why (not)? In answering these questions and explaining their answers to us, we wanted to elicit participants' views on *comparable* and *alternative* discursive strategies speakers might 'appropriately' use in talk.

Although step five has a specific function in the context of this participatory project, it also contains a more generic step, in that it connects the discussion about interactional effects of everyday talk to a critical evaluation of the strategies that are employed to fulfil these effects. In establishing this connection, Step 5 can fulfil an important agenda-setting task among youngsters to address health topics. This agenda-setting task can differ, depending on the conversation materials that are used for the DAM, and the particular strategies that are identified.

To briefly illustrate how we worked with Step 5 during this project, we will take a closer look at how the workshop participants discussed the interactional effect of the speaker (Petra) using quotations; one of the strategies that were explored in the fragment and one that was highly recognisable to the pupils. In answering the question 'what do you think of this strategy?', participants stated that it could be used for cowardly behaviour, which they claimed occurred very often at school, for instance when someone was bullied or treated unfairly ('I have seen it happen and I really think that it's so awful when people act like that'). At the same time, it was acknowledged that they also employed this strategy themselves, and used it in the same manner, thereby already addressing the second question (would you make use of this strategy in your own conversations and why (not)?). They pointed out how this strategy was often used to shift responsibility for one's words, for example when they noted: 'people use quotations to make sure that they're in the clear' and that 'they use quotations to attribute blame to others'.

Step 5 clearly enabled our target group to link their observations about the strategies to occurrences with which they were confronted in their peer groups at school ('this is what we talk about'; or 'this happened with my best friend'). Combining the roles of interventionist and analyst proved an effective stimulus for inducing reflexive awareness and it motivated youngsters to think of health activities that address topics with which they are involved in their everyday lives.

Outcomes: applying a conversational turn in designing health activities

The previous sections have described how our method was developed on the basis of a preliminary analysis of data collected by the target group and how we worked through the five steps of the workshop programme. The context in which the LIFE21 project took place meant that everyday talk on health-related matters was used as the basis to generate ideas for school-based health interventions. In this section we will report on these outcomes of the project in particular.

We organised workshops at the three schools that participated in the LIFE21 project. The workshop participants at each school decided how their observations about the conversational aspects of the materials used during the workshop were to be linked to ideas about health activities in this last stage of the workshop. We will not elaborate on how all three trajectories developed, but only highlight how one group of pupils worked with the insights from the DAM workshop in their subsequent discussions to develop a health activity of their choice. In this case, the students had already proposed writing and performing a play, since they felt that the kind of material addressed in the workshop, that is, everyday conversations between peers could very well be transformed into a stage production. The exact form and content of the play was still to be developed. On the basis of tape recordings that were made during the workshop and the subsequent meetings in which the ideas for health activities were discussed and developed further, we have identified three dimensions on which pupils linked the DAM to ideas about a play.

1 **Thematic and interactional connections based on the 'stimulus' materials (cf. Steps 2 and 3)**
Pupils discussed whether they would like to work with the thematic issues that were addressed in the data fragment (what are the 'bases' on which someone might be included or excluded from your peer group?; how can you give your opinion on matters of peer exclusion?) and/or with the interactional features that were addressed and discussed in the workshop (how to show disagreement with another speaker's point of view?; what are the interactional effects of laughter when someone tells a story?). It was interesting to see that the interactional features were considered to be very inspiring as the basis for a play ('I keep thinking about that one person, who might have wanted to say something to counter Petra's story, and doesn't find the opportunity to do so; he isn't heard by the others who keep laughing. That would be a very strong element to work with in a play.'). At the same time, the thematic issue addressed in the data fragment (negotiating the basis for excluding one of your peers, for instance on the basis of physical features) was very recognisable. Participants also linked it to bullying, which they considered as closely related to discriminating and as a next step to excluding people from one's group of friends.

2 **Determining the play's main theme from a non-cognitive and non-normative view (cf. Step 1)**
A lengthy debate followed in which the central message of the play was discussed: what would be the most suitable message to communicate to the audience? Two main views were presented: 'Do we want to develop a play

and present answers, like there are any straightforward answers about what is right and wrong in these matters? Or is it better to show that people have choices, and that these choices have an influence on the unfolding interaction?'. Ultimately the latter approach was chosen as the most rewarding way to present the play's central theme: bullying. Pupils pointed out that this decision was partly triggered by the first step of the DAM, in which they were asked to withhold from making statements that would address the veracity of Petra's story (and thus to maintain a focus on action rather than cognition). They thought that conveying a similar attitude towards the topic of bullying in the play (i.e., to withhold from making statements about who is to blame when bullying occurs), would stimulate discussion.

These ideas about how to convey the play's central message also surfaced in some of the play's most noteworthy features. For example, when proposing the use of a 'voiceover', a detached storyteller who presented the audience with one way to understand what happened on stage. The pupils (who were also the actors in the play) considered the voiceover an apt instrument that would leave more room to provoke the audience and stimulate their thoughts ('They can think about what they want to take from it themselves'), rather than 'filling in' the actors' intentions and presenting presuppositions about whether their behaviour was understandable, justified or wrong. After the play was performed, the audience was asked to fill in a questionnaire, which was part of the project's accompanying process evaluation (see, for an overview, Lamerichs et al., 2006). Interestingly, the answers that were given by the audience members suggested that the lack of a strong evaluative tone in the play did stimulate them to engage more strongly in discussions about the play's content and its characters. It also showed that the audience felt encouraged to identify with more than one character, for example, not only with the 'victim', but also with one or more of the 'bystanders', who were presented as partly guilty and partly innocent at different moments in the play.

3 Demonstrating the importance of interactional effects in different scenes of the play (cf. Steps 2 to 4)

The pupils also sought to incorporate some of the interactional effects that were discussed in the workshop into some of the scenes, and most notably, also into the closing scene. This scene incorporated the gist of the DAM, that it is not the intentions of an individual that determine the course of events but the recipient's uptake. The pupils were able to highlight the importance of these interactional effects in different ways: by including laughter in the play's dialogues, as well as silence in response to someone's story. In this way, the dialogues made apparent different effects when bullying occurred. The play's ending took up this point once again, by showing a scene that

Figure 10.2 The play as it was performed by secondary school pupils in 2004 at a symposium addressing health prevention initiatives (Photo courtesy of Jurriaan Balke)

was recognisable as the opening scene of the play, but with one slight adaptation in how the bystanders reacted. This suggested that a different outcome on events was possible. Incorporating these interactional features in the dialogues of different scenes showed how bullying can stop, depending on how people (in their roles as speakers and hearers) interact with each other. It also showed how creating interactional 'space' can accomplish change, which was something they explicitly included in their discussions about the play's central theme: 'we could show different views and how they lead to different outcomes'.

Concluding Comments

We have reported on how we developed and employed a CA- and DP-based technique, the Discursive Action Method, in a project that aimed to stimulate adolescents' awareness of how they talk about health-related topics. In this framework, the fifth step of the method was geared towards using the conversational insights as the basis for developing and implementing school-based health interventions. In this section we want to point to the most important lessons learned; discuss how the DAM relates to other attempts to work with interaction analysis to improve practice, and look at the limitations and possibilities of the method for future applications, within and beyond a health education setting.

Working with this method has taught us how important it is to start with materials that are highly recognisable to the target group. In this project, the materials were collected by the youngsters themselves, and offered a range of topics that were routinely raised in their talk. Initial analysis of the materials showed how it dealt with one aspect of their socio-emotional wellbeing in particular: negotiating what counts as a proper basis for voicing strong assessments about themselves and their peers in narratives of inclusion and exclusion. The recognisability operated not only on a thematic level, but also related to more subtle interactional features such as the use of particular discursive strategies. Starting from participants' own conversation materials may thus provide an important *point of entry* into the everyday life world of the target group.

Any reflection and/or participatory CA-based approach needs to cater for a way to address the details of your own talk in a *safe and non-threatening manner*. We have shown how this method is successful in inviting participants to 'mirror' the interactional features of their talk rather than having them focus on personal issues. They could also react without having to evaluate (or judge) the behaviour of their peers. We demonstrated how turning participants into analysts of their own discourse is instrumental in heightening the target group's attentiveness to how they talk.

The project's original aim was to stimulate pupils to develop ideas for health activities aimed at their peers. By having them change roles from 'analyst' (exploring a stretch of recognisable talk) to 'interventionist' (inviting assessments of discursive strategies to stimulate discussion about health activities), the approach is able to unlock participants' motivation to develop such activities. We refer to this as the method's catalyst function. The change of participant roles is important here because it links the conversational basis of the method to a discussion of real-life practices at school ('how can you show disagreement in your peer group?'). Further research is needed to explore the mechanisms at work that seem to link participants heightened attentiveness to talk as social action, and their motivation to develop ideas for health interventions (see, for a full discussion, Lamerichs et al., 2006).

We think the Discursive Action Method differs from other methods that have worked with interaction analysis in the area of health communication in a number of ways. The method puts a strong emphasis on having adolescents explore the conversational features of the materials *themselves*. Although they were very adept at verbalising the detailed interactional workings of talk, their explorations also included an element of surprise. Exploring these detailed interactional workings yourself, and drawing upon practical 'know-how' of how talk works, might be a strong cue for improving awareness of its social effects. In this way the method can also *reinforce* skills on which participants already draw when interacting with others.

The DAM also differs from other attempts to invite participants to reflect on conversational practices in that it explicitly facilitates the transition between reflecting on conversational features and current (or future) communicative practices. The agenda-setting function that is brought about by taking this step makes it particularly suited also to the development of communicative interventions outside the domain of health education.

Working with the method also presented some challenges, for example with regard to the workload involved. What kind of investment can people be expected to make when working with this method? This project has demonstrated that it is feasible to start from a relatively small data fragment and successfully work with the method. It is crucial, however, that participants can bring in their *own* conversation materials and that the project allows for this type of data collection.

A recent project with health professionals provides a first indication of the results that can be achieved when the DAM is applied in a different context (not geared towards participatory health education) and with another target group (see, for an overview, Sneijder et al., 2007). It would be worthwhile to further investigate the practical use of this approach for target groups in other settings as well, be it teachers, counsellors or pupils with different educational backgrounds.

APPENDIX A: FRAGMENT THAT WAS USED DURING THE DAM WORKSHOP

```
01    Petra:    no seriously-   [            ]
02    Nico:                     [about whom?]
03    Petra:    no seriously the other day-
04              the other day I walked through
05              town with my dad huh
06    Teun:     °Neil°
07    Kelly:    Neil
08    Petra:    (.) yes
09    Nico:     oh Neil
10    Petra:    and uh well (.) I was walking
11              through town with my dad- not
12              knowing who this guy is at
13              all he who who who accidentally
14              and I didn't see him and my dad
15              suddenly starts to laugh,
16    Teun:     [heheh]
17    Kelly:    [heheh]
```

```
18    Petra:    oh Petra he says I see someone
19              it just can't be
20              he is just deformed.
21    Kelly:    [heheh]
22    Ilona:    [heheh]
23    Petra:    s(h)o I tu(h)rn around like
24              thi(h)s I sa(h)y he(h)is
25              i(h)n my cla(h)ss and my
26              dad really just didn't
27              believe me (.) and he just
28              had well my dad he (.) say (0.2)
29              my dad always likes it say people
30              with Down syndrome and such you
31              know. He would always watch Knoop
32              in je zakdoek. He just loves that.
33              And we would always laugh about
34              that you know but apart from that
35              well (.) he just loves that.
36              He seriously thought that
37              this was a handicapped person.
38    Nico:     [*heheheheh*]
39    Ilona:    [*heheheheh*]
40    Kelly:    yeah but he is also-
41    Petra:    no but seriously (.) that
42              guy totally ehm eczema which
43              is something he just can't do
44              anything about(.)you know,
45              do this and everything tear-
46              falls apart (.) and say he
47              has this counterbalance
48    Kelly:    ye::(h)s heheheh
49    Ilona:    heheheh
50    Petra:    isn't it?
51    Kelly:    yes it's really wrong and his
52              jaws point really outwards=
53    Petra:    it could be that he is a nice
54              guy but he- also(.)
55              [he SMELLS because of his eczema-
53    Kelly:    [yes but he IS not nice at all
```

Notes

1. Responsibility for translating the principles of discursive psychology to the steps that ultimately form the Discursive Action Method lies solely with the authors of this chapter.

2. We are grateful to the Netherlands organisation for health research and development (ZONMw) for grant number 4010.0002.
3. For the purpose of a process evaluation, we have taped all workshops. As a result we are able to provide detailed references to the key questions asked by the workshop leader and the answers and comments made by the workshop participants.
4. Our experiences with a recent DAM workshop with health professionals (see, for an overview, Sneijder et al., 2007) has shown that this step was very difficult to take for these participants. One of the difficulties the professionals encountered was that they found it hard to work with the notion of 'interactional problem', and routinely tended to explain interactional effects as having a physical or psychological basis (e.g., 'he says this because he has not gotten over his parent's divorce'; 'he says this because he suffers from ADHD'). The adolescents we worked with during LIFE21 experienced little difficulty in maintaining their focus on the speaker's central *interactional* problem.
5. We used the formulation 'to be accused of' as a free translation to get at the speaker's dilemma of stake. Phrasing the question like this during the workshop made the participants focus strongly on the dilemmatic aspect of a description. We are well aware of the fact that this formulation suggests 'strategic' behaviour on behalf of the speaker and can carry a negative connotation (why would people specifically take into account that someone might *accuse* them of anything?). While speakers are not consciously aware of any accusations, and while these accusations not necessarily reflect any 'real' or 'legitimately' blameworthy issues, we consider the wording of this key question very effective to hypothesise about the speaker's dilemma of stake. We also discussed these aspects with the workshop participants.
6. 'Knoop in je zakdoek' is the name of a Dutch TV show that features people with Down's syndrome.

11
Conversation Analysis Applied to User-Centred Design: A Study of Who 'The User' Is

Maria Egbert

The seed of applying CA to change institutional practices may go back to the very origin of Conversation Analysis. Paul Drew mentioned in a recent personal communication that during Harvey Sacks' time at the University of California, Irvine, in the 1970s – he died in 1975 – Sacks was friends with John Seely Brown, a colleague in technological innovation at Irvine in the 1970s. Brown later served as director of the Palo Alto Research Center (first 'Xerox PARC', later 'PARC'), an interdisciplinary centre established by Xerox in 1970 for technological innovation geared towards business enterprises.[1] Curious to learn more about the relationship between Sacks and Brown, I emailed an inquiry to Brown who responded that

> ... we [Sacks and Brown] actually co-taught a course together. Gitti Jordan was also a grad student at the time with an office across the hall from me. I spent a lot of time with her and learned the ways of talking to and working with ethnoids and ethnomethodologists. It was a fantastic learning experience for me.

So it seems that the relationship between these pioneers in their respective fields may have created a fertile ground for PARC's interdisciplinary perspective and its interest in CA. In particular, Suchman's work at PARC (starting in 1979) broke new ground when she proposed to engineers to video-tape not only the technological activities of a problematic Xerox photocopying machine, but more importantly to video-tape the human users in their interaction with the machine. John Seely Brown featured Suchman's video 'When User Hits Machine' in his 1983 presentation at the *MIT Laboratory for Computer Science Distinguished Lecture Series*, thus promoting user-centred studies to an influential audience.

Suchman's seminal work has significantly contributed to an approach of technological innovation based on an understanding of the users' perspective, and at the same time it has inspired a rapidly growing body of interdisciplinary research and application involving conversation analysts/ethnographers and designers working in technology innovation (e.g., Anderson and Anderson, 1995; Bentley et al., 1992; Crabtree et al., 1998; Greatbatch et al., 1995; Heath and Luff, 1992; Heath et al., 2002; Malone, 1983; Rusinko, 1999; Sharrok and Button, 1997; Suchman et al., 1999; Szymanski et al., 2006). The interdisciplinary compatibility of CA and User-Centred Design is rooted in a shared methodological credo. To understand human interaction and the use of technologies, CA rigorously examines the participants' perspective. To gain an empirical basis for technological innovation, developers in User-Centred Design take as point of departure how the users interact with technologies.

The application of CA to design and design studies has materialised in various ways. In addition to the categorisation of CA's roles in applications set out in this volume by Antaki (Chapter 1), Heritage and Robinson (Chapter 2) and Finlay, Walton and Antaki (Chapter 9), it is useful for the purpose of this chapter to group CA applications to the field of design based on the criterion of how conversation analysts are involved (or the degree to which they intervene; see Antaki's account in Chapter 1). The following two categories group the role of conversation analysts in relation to application. All of the ensuing ways use video or audio recordings of naturally occurring interaction, and frequently other types of data such as ethnographic observations, interviews or surveys are brought in as well.

Conversation analysts collaborate with designers

The first way in which CA can work towards change is for conversation analysts to work together with designers (rather than with practitioners, as is elsewhere documented in this volume). The role of the conversation analyst can vary from describing selected interactions of interest to the design process, or the conversation analyst can go further by identifying problems, best practices, or potentials for change based on an understanding of the data. In this type of collaboration the conversation analysts move into the field of application, and may even participate directly in the design activities. Such an involvement can include conversation analysts applying their knowledge to design hypotheses, the building of prototypes, or the development of alternative practices.

An example of this type of involvement is described in Woodruff and colleagues' report 'Practical strategies for integrating a conversation analyst in an interactive design process' (2002) during a design project at PARC.

A museum in California wanted to make the experience for visitors coming with friends or family more social, something prevented by the use of electronic guides to which visitors listen individually through head phones. The Conversation Analysis of video-taped museum visits showed that visitors in interaction oriented to the electronic guide as if it were a third person. This was disturbing the social experience because the voice on the audio guide is accessible to only one of the interactants. This result, based on an analysis of turn-taking, sequence and particularities of the participation framework, triggered the idea to develop electronic guides with an additional technological function which would allow one interactant to listen in to what his co-participant is hearing through his own head set. The conversation analyst was involved in the field work, and within an iterative process also in the design activities in that the developers consulted her about design hypotheses and decisions.

Conversation analysts examine the design process

The second main way in which conversation analysts have contributed to the field of design is by analysing the design process as an interactional site with social practices and activities. This type of collaboration is based on an understanding of 'designing as a predominantly social activity' (Ylirisku and Buur, 2007, p. 34) and geared towards gaining an understanding of the interactional characteristics of a design team. In such cases the data consist of video-tapes of the design activities. For example, it has been shown how the physical environment, and in particular objects, can play a decisive role in the interaction of designers (Luff, Heath and Pitsch, 2009; Heinemann, Mitchell and Buur, ms).

The current chapter is located in this second category. As a conversation analyst, I have examined team meetings in a User-Centred Design project on hearing aid fitting. The study was motivated because a particular problem occurred during the design process. We discovered that the team of researchers and the partner from industry had divergent assumptions of who 'The User' was. The analysis suggests an explanation of how this problem came into being. Along with other conversation analysts I also participated in the team meetings (as described above in the second category of involvement), however, I will only touch on that personal role in this chapter.

The design project was carried out within the SPIRE Centre for Participatory Innovation, a federally funded research centre for innovation established at the University of Southern Denmark. The goal of SPIRE (which stands for Sønderborg Participatory Innovation Research Centre) is to promote the approach of User-Centred Design in industry and in research (cf. Buur and Bagger, 1999; Buur and Matthews, 2008; Ylirisku and Buur, 2007).[2] This is achieved in a number of innovation projects with partners from industry. Research is directed at a better understanding of human use of technologies and then applied towards innovation. Furthermore, research is conducted on the process of innovation, leading to changes in institutional practices in industry, organisations and interdisciplinary research teams. SPIRE researchers come from a variety of disciplines which all share the conviction that changes in institutional practices, in particular in technological innovation, need to be grounded in an understanding of the users' perspective, something termed differently in the respective disciplines. For conversation analysts, anthropologists and ethnographers this is the participant's perspective, for the collaborating researchers in business and management it is the customer, and for the designers it is the user. A further SPIRE partner with a tradition in promoting change in organisation is the consultancy Dacapo. They take an ethnographic approach as point of departure for using techniques from theatre to promote change in organisations (Larsen, 2005).

This methodological convergence of disciplines rooted in different traditions, in collaboration with companies interested in User-Centred Design seemed to augur well for successful cooperation. However, we did not anticipate that a misunderstanding about who 'The User' is would emerge as a focal problem. I will analyse video-taped team meetings in order to shed light on how this misunderstanding is rooted in a non-neutral relationship of the researchers towards the interactants in their video-taped hearing aid fitting sessions.

Who is 'The User'? A CA investigation

The 'Hearing in Transition' ('HinT') team that I analyse here consists of SPIRE researchers (designers and conversation analysts) collaborating with a hearing aid company in order to promote User-Centred Design, and to innovate in hearing aid use. To understand the perspective of the user is imperative because the compliance rate for hearing aid use is staggeringly low. Hearing impairment affects about every third adult above age 40 in Western countries, of whom only 5–20 per cent use hearing aids, although for most conditions it is the only help.[3] The hearing aid company who collaborated in the research project identified the interaction during selection and fitting as a barrier to hearing aid use in the early stages of the collaboration. For this reason we video-taped nine fitting sessions in a private Danish hearing clinic. The analysis showed that indeed these audiological encounters are problematic, both in respect to information transfer and social interaction (Brouwer and Day, 2009).

Research question

In discussing the analytical results and ideas for innovation with the hearing aid company, the research team encountered an unforeseen predicament. After several meetings and workshops they realised, as already noted, that the team and the hearing aid company had divergent assumptions of who 'The User' was. To the research team this was the hearing aid user, whereas to the company this was the hearing aid dispenser, that is, the audiologist who selects, fits and sells the hearing aid. The company's perspective shines through in one of the workshops where a company representative uses the term *end user* in contrast to *audiologist*. In the transcript, the speaker code 'C1' stands for 'company representative'.

Extract 1

```
01   C1:   but (these sumptionals) it's a good thing if (.)
02         it's a good thing (very) good thing if if it the:
03         end user (.) can (speak the audiologists language),
```

This discovery (not analysed here) raises the question of why the research team members assumed that the focus was on the hearing aid user (client) rather than on the hearing aid fitter (audiologist). The following analysis of video-taped research meetings proposes some reasons. By drawing on CA research on identity (Antaki and Widdicombe, 1998a) and person reference (Enfield and Stivers, 2007; Lerner and Kitzinger, 2007; Ochs, Gonzales and Jacoby, 1996; Sacks and Schegloff, 1979; Schegloff, 1996a), the analysis of HinT meetings suggests that on the one hand, the researchers analyse the interaction between the audiologist and the hearing aid user in terms of interactional achievement by focusing equally on the actions of both, yet in their discussions of the fitting sessions the researchers implicitly display an identification with, and empathy for, the hearing aid user. In their publications of the analysis the researchers show an objective stance, where in the team meetings, the researchers' take on a subjective involvement. The ensuing analysis will show how this subjective perspective becomes evident.

Person references reveal researchers' identification with and empathy for the hearing aid user

Person reference in interaction is used not only for the purpose of indicating whether the speaker refers to herself (e.g., by *I* or *we*), to her addressee (e.g., by *you*) or to non-present third parties (e.g., by *he*, *she* or *they*). Beyond doing the work of referring, person references can be employed to achieve a large number of interactional purposes (Enfield and Stivers, 2007, Schegloff, 1996). In Korean, for example, a certain overt reference form can achieve disagreement and the attribution of responsibility (Oh, 2007). A speaker can also use a third person reference form to refer to himself (instead of using *I*), thus achieving a representation of a third party position (Land and Kitzinger, 2007). A first-person reference can even be used to take on the perspective of an object. Ochs, Gonzales and Jacoby (1996) show that a speaker, such as a physicist in a research team, can employ the reference *I* to refer to an object in the physical world which the researchers are studying, thus blurring the separation between himself as a scientist and the object of inquiry. Person references belonging to the class of indexical expressions thus rely heavily on the interactional context to make sense (Antaki and Widdicombe, 1998a). The analysis of the use of person reference in the research team discussions reveals that the researchers refer to non-present third parties (the interactants in the audiological consultations they are studying) by using first-person, second-person and third-person references. The particular choices of person reference forms encode the researchers' emotional relationship to the participants in the fitting sessions and their identification with the hearing aid user rather than with the hearing aid fitter.

The analysis to be presented next draws from CA work on identity. In a review of ethnomethodological and especially CA approaches to identity, Antaki and Widdicombe (1998b) distil the following core facets, each of which is relevant to the analysis of the research meetings. The first facet entails that a person 'having an identity' implies that the particular identity is connected to a category and the features associated with this category. This is independent of whether it is the speaker, the addressee or a third person being talked about. Second, casting a person by means of identity needs to be understood as 'indexical and occasioned' (p. 5), that is, the reference forms make interactional sense in the context in which the speaker places them. As a third facet, identity and the social activity in which it occurs, are related. Likewise, 'having an identity' is consequential to the interaction (facet 4). Analytically, as noted in facet 5, these interactional aspects of identity are employed as part of the conversational structures. According to this approach, identity is:

> available for use: something that people do which is embedded in some other social activity, and not something they 'are'. This brings into sharp relief the notion that identities are put to local work ...
> (Widdicombe, 1998, p. 191)

This view is echoed by the researchers in the collection 'Person Reference' edited by Enfield and Stivers (2007). They maintain that all languages and cultures provide an array of resources for referring to people in conversation. The particular form a speaker selects is a reflection of the relationship the speaker portrays as having with the person referred to, and the perspective of that relationship. The analysis of the HinT meetings focuses on the kinds of reference forms used, the context in which they are used, and the stance the researchers take towards their object of investigation.

Differential distribution of reference forms indexing the hearing aid fitter and hearing aid user

I found that the HinT researchers – the designers and conversation analysts – did refer to both the fitter and the client with the full range of first-, second-, and third-person reference forms. But there is a striking difference in the frequency and in the choice of particular forms that the two roles attracted.

The use of third-person reference to hearing aid fitters and hearing aid users is much more frequent than the use of first- or second-person reference. The fitter is mostly referred to as the *audiologist*, and in a few instances by his first name *Stefan*. The name of the fitter is known to the researchers, but the names of the clients are not. The client is referred to with a larger array of person references, including *hearer(s), owner, the guy, the old lady, them, the patient, participant, people* and *person*. The latter three reference forms are only employed for the hearing aid user. Although these forms are so general that they could also refer to the fitter, in all cases, the context provides clear evidence that these general reference forms index the client, and that they are used in contrast to the reference *audiologist*. In the following example, a researcher refers to the hearing aid user and the hearing aid fitter in the same turn, using the third person form *participant* for the former and *the audiologist* for the latter.

Extract 2   Workshop 1

```
01   R1:  but uhm (0.5) but back to (.) establishing (.) credibility.
02        .h as a participant of that session (.) (in it).
03        ((coughs)) with the audiologist.
```

Extract 3   WS 18

```
01   R1:  but in any case. (.) the:n so there is, (.)
02        there is one thing you look at and people
03        can either be trained to better (0.3) uhm learn
04        the lingo of the audiologists?
```

These most general reference forms (*people, person*) in the researchers' talk display an implicit affiliation with hearing aid users in that they index their human aspect in contrast to the functional or institutional role of the fitter.

Even the more specific term *participant* is usually employed among CA researchers for all interactants of a participation framework, yet in these team discussions, it is only the client who is referred to by this form. This tendency of highlighting the social status of hearing aid users goes along with the researchers' affiliation with them as ultimate clients and beneficiaries of the service.

Use of the first-person form to refer to the hearing aid user and hearing aid fitter

In addition to the frequent uses of third-person reference forms, the researchers sometimes employ first-person reference forms (*I, we*) when referring to both the client and the fitter. This kind of reference, however, occurs only rarely in pointing to the fitter, and comparatively often in referring to the client. Extract 4 below furnishes an example of first-person reference to the fitter.

Extract 4   p. 16

```
01   R1:    but going in this direction too mu <we're not
02          gonna get much going> down that
03          [road of (.) ☺[discrediting people's☺
04   R2:    [(right).      [(that's),
05   R2:    right. right.
06   R1:    uh faith in their hearing,
07   R2:    exactly.
```

Note that the researcher's turn contains a negative assessment of the audiologist's work and a refusal of the effectiveness of the audiologist's action. In this way the researcher exhibits a personal stance and disaffiliates with the fitter.

In contrast, when researchers use first-person forms to refer to clients, they take an empathic personal stance and affiliate. More frequently than for referring to fitters, first-person reference forms are selected for the clients. The following segment evidences such a use. Note how the speaker switches from *I* (referring to herself) to *them* (referring to the client), and then to *I* (referring to the client) in a hypothetical piece of reported speech introduced by *like*.

Extract 5   WS 18

```
01   R3:    so wha what kind of triggered that i think is
02          [me f::freaking out about them   [coming in
03   R2:    [m.                              [ya. ((R2 nods))
04   R3:    with these kind of specifics?
05   R3:    like (.) i can't hear the fridge alarm,=
```

```
06         =and i'm thinking (.)  [°hu° that's not that big a deal.
07   R2:                          [°yes°,
08         (.)
09   R3:   [you know.
10   R4:   [m.
11   R2:   right.
12   R3:   as long as you can ((...))
```

The next data segment shows how a researcher switches from third-person reference (*the guy, he*) to impersonating the client verbally and by embodying his postures. The switch from third-person to first-person reference occurs in line 7.

Extract 6   WS 14
```
01   R2:   at the case with the guy standing up? (.) he is (.) pre
02         know uhm pre-em pre-emptory
03   R3:   mm.
04   R2:   fashion.
05         (0.2)
06   R2:   making sure. he knows this can be problematic.
07         so i keep standing up.
08         (.)
09   R2:   as long as i'm standing i have still got some sort
10         of control over where this is going. ((R2 stands up))
11   R1:   [hmm.
12   R2:   [and when he makes the big move like you (.) mentioned
13         ((R2 makes a big waving move with his hand))
14   R3:   hm.
15   R2:   he can s have some control over things.
16         (0.2)
17   R2:   so they're totally different cases they have nothing
18         to do with each other but they (0.2) they show (0.2)
19         i think credibility issues.
```

Note that in line 12 R2's body remains in a position impersonating the client while at the same time he switches in his talk back to the role of the researcher, referring to the client in third-person reference (*he*) and addressing his fellow researcher with *you*.

These extracts illustrate how researchers switch from the perspective of the self to the perspective of the non-present third party. They take on the role of the hearing aid user much more frequently than the role of the fitter. In all cases, by changing perspective, the researchers put themselves into an imagined situation in which they experience events from the perspective of the third party.

Ochs and colleagues (1996) examine this phenomenon in the physicists' team meeting where the scientists use first-person reference forms to switch perspective to the objects of their study. The physicists 'seem to blur the distinction between scientist and the physical world under scrutiny' (p. 328). In using specific interactional resources (grammar, symbolic resources and graphs) physicists identify with the physical objects they are studying. For example, the chief scientist uses the first-person reference *I* ('When I come down I'm in the domain state') to portray himself in the position of a specific magnet which can be observed to occur in different 'states', in this case the 'domain state'. The voice of the researcher is backgrounded in favour of the imagined 'voice' of the object. By means of this grammatical practice the researcher identifies with the object in an empathic way. It also pulls the other scientists into the place where the present world and the world being studied intersect.

Ochs and colleagues' conclusion of the use of first-person reference forms for objects is informative for an understanding of the HinT researchers' selection of first-person reference forms to index clients. It reveals a relationship of the researchers to clients in which they identify and empathise with the persons they are studying. This argument is strengthened by the observation that in all first-person reference forms employed for third-party reference, the researchers express a non-neutral stance in a local context where some kind of problem is topicalised. In Extract 4 above, the researcher signals disapproval of the fitter's action (*discrediting people*), and in Extract 5 above, the researcher articulates strong emotions (*me f::freaking out*). The following example serves to strengthen this point.

Extract 7   WS 22

```
01  R5:    [you know like the☺  (.)  (none of it) makes sense to say,=
02  R3:    [mm.
03  R5:    =[(how) of course hearing aids [don't always work=
04  R3:       [mm.                         [
05  R2:                                    [yea.
06  R5:    =as they should and °(that there)°.
07  R2:    right.
08  R5:    but if you just hear the fact that oh (0.4) it works
09         a bit when i wa☺ you know it (helps) quite a bit
10         when i watch te ve with that thing☺
11         and AH=YEA. [but [hearing aids don't [always work☺
12  R3:                [yea [                   [(he he he)
13  R2:                     [(ah they don't always work). ha ha ha
14  R2:    eh ya hahaha
15  R1:    (it's so many problems   [with that).
16  R2:                             [y(h)ea he he yea.
```

CA Applied to User-Centred Design   217

The connection between identifying and taking an empathic stance seems to be grounded in the researchers' perception that hearing aid users experience difficulties due to their hearing loss, the less than perfect improvement of hearing achieved through a hearing aid (*so many problems with that*, line 18), and the problems encountered during hearing aid fitting, for example when R2 impersonates a fitter as saying *hearing aids don't ah they don't always work*, lines 13–14). In one instance, a researcher even views the interaction during hearing aid fitting as a *battle* (line 11 below), an assessment his fellow researcher agrees with (line 12).

Extract 8   WS 23

```
01   R5:   oh but also (.) also have this support the, (.)
02         i mean (.) °uh° (0.3) audiologists aren't that interested in,
03         ↓or my im impression is audiologist aren't interested in this
04         but (that) how h=how the tools how (they're/can) moving the
05         patient (.) a little closer to understanding the work of the
06         audiologist.
07   R3:   hm  [m,
08   R1:       [yea.
09   R2:   [hmm.
10   R5:   [and i think that (0.2) tha that's half the (0.3)
11         half the (battle), (0.4) here.
12   R1:   yea.
```

In addition to third- and first-person reference forms, the researchers also refer to the hearing aid user and fitter in second-person *you*. This reference can also be conceived of as an indeterminate construction since it is not only employed to refer to the addressee but also to persons in general. The following data extracts provide evidence that researchers and the company representation ('C1') employ 'you' to take on the perspective of the hearing aid client (lines 2, 11, 17, 20, 21, 22, 26). In this case the boundary between C1 and the third person referred to becomes fuzzy in that C1 impersonated the client through embodiment (lines 3, 5). Shortly after, C1 uses the second-person reference *you* to refer to himself, and in the same turn, *him* to refer to the hearing aid client (line 11). The latter is achieved by means of a pointing gesture.

Extract 9   WS

```
01         ((R5 knocks two times with the model on the table.))
02   C1:   (oh) you could actually have it in your (.) shirt pocket↘
03         ((C1 takes model and holds it where his shirt pocket would be.))
04   C1:   (you know like this)?
05         ((C1 presses imaginary buttons on the model.))
```

```
06   R5:   yea,
07         (0.5)
08   R5:   yea that's great.
09         (1.2)
10   R5:   but then (.) that's right.
11   C1:   you wouldn't get behind him. ((points backwards over his shoulder))
12   R5:   no.
13         (0.2)
14   R5:   but that would be alright,
15   C1:   °yea°,
16   R5:   cause i mean really if (.) if it's an (.) a (numonic) device↓
17         if it's just to (.) [jog your memory.
18   C1:                       [yea,
19   C1:   yea=yea.
20   R5:   then all you need is a (0.3)
21   R5:   even hnhn even knowing it was in your shirt pocket ☺at the time
22         might be en(h)ough☺ he he ☺t(h)o rem(h)in(h)d you
23         [what was going on☺,
24   C1:   [y(h)e(h)(h)(h)a(h),
25   C1:   ((coughs))
26   R5:   =☺where you were standing☺,
```

In parallel to the observation that the researchers employ general reference forms to index the hearing aid client in contrast to the fitter, the researchers employ the indeterminate *you* to refer to the client (cf. above). In the following instance, this is done in contrast to the fitter, who is referred to in the third person by his first name *Stefan*.

Extract 10   p. 17

```
01   R1:   all you have: is: your stories.
02         (.)
03   R1:   as the hearer.
04         (.)
05   R1:   a:nd then you're a' the mercy of: (.) of stefan
06   to:   get you a diagnosis.
```

Note here that the researcher portrays the hearing aid client as a victim, who is dependent on the fitter. A similar stance of empathy towards the hearing aid client's hardship is expressed by R1 in a different sequence, where R1 employs *you* to refer to the client (line 1).

Extract 11   WS 1

```
01   R1:   uh (0.2) to understand (.) how you do hear.
02         (.)
03   R1:   because you °you know° ( ) how hard that is.
```

The researchers' differential use of person reference forms for the client and the fitter is evidenced in the excerpt below. The fitter is indexed by 'audiologist' (line 1). The subsequent reference to him as *he* (line 4) is self-repaired in that it is replaced by *you*. In the continuation of the turn it becomes clear that this *you* refers to the client, as well as the 'your' (line 6).

Extract 12   p. 24

```
01    R5:    cause it may be that the audiologist is better (.) at
02           interpreting ordinary stories.
03    R2:    yea. yea.
04    R5:    than he than you are (.) in self diagnosing
05    R2:    ya.
06    R5:    your experience into (.) [audiologist speak.
07    R2:                             [hm hm hm.
```

Different senses of 'The User'

Recall that our interest in looking at all these extracts has been to try and work out how different members of the project team conceived of 'The User' of the device whose development we are studying. The results were revealing.

In sum, we can see that HinT researchers' verbal and non-verbal practices of referring to the hearing aid user and the hearing aid fitter shows differential treatment in talking about the two participants in the institutional setting of hearing aid fitting. This may largely explain the misunderstanding of who 'The User' is in the series of meetings and workshops between the researchers and the collaborating company. Based on the company's suggestion that a barrier to hearing aid use lies in the interaction between client and audiologist during hearing aid fitting, the researchers assumed that the 'user' is the person with hearing loss trying to come to terms with a hearing aid. In contrast, the hearing aid company operated under the assumption that the 'user' is the audiologist who selects, adjusts and sells the hearing aid.

The realisation of this misunderstanding sparked the research question of how the researchers orient to the 'user'. The conversation-analytic study of the video-taped group meetings presented in the main part of this chapter yields that the researchers exhibit an affiliative stance towards the hearing aid user and a disaffiliative stance towards the fitter. In particular, the analysis of person-reference forms in their local context shows that the researchers empathise and identify with the hearing aid user. This differential treatment of the participants in the audiological sessions is apparent in the group discussion, while in contrast, a neutral and objective stance is assumed in publications. This result corresponds to Ochs and colleagues' (1996) findings that physicists identify with the object of their inquiry and take on an empathic position although the object is inanimate. This seems to help the physicists in talking through complicated scientific subject matter. While this may also be the case with the HinT researchers, there also seems to be a bias in that the researchers affiliate with the hearing aid user and disaffiliate with the fitter. In interpreting this finding a connection is made to the described misunderstanding of who 'The User' is. By identifying with the hearing aid user the researchers fell for the assumption that 'The User' is the person with hearing loss seeking help with their hearing aid. Since I was a researcher in the HinT team myself, I can offer my own confirmation of that mistake.

Concluding comments

This chapter has shown how CA can be applied to an interactional problem experienced by a mixed team of researchers engaged in an industrial innovation project. CA helped locate one source of the problem in the terminology which the team was using. Inspection of team talk revealed that the labels 'User-Centred Design' and 'User-Driven Innovation' implied, for some members of the team, a focus on 'The User' as the individual consumer – in this case, the hearing aid user. This sense of the term, however, was not shared by other members of the team. The team's unwitting use of the misleading term 'User' disguised the fact that the low compliance rate in using hearing aids seems to lie in different kinds of interaction between different 'Users'. The 'interaction' can be between the person with hearing loss and the hearing aid, or between the client and the hearing aid fitter as well as other representatives of the healthcare system, and it can also be the interaction between the hearing aid user and the people they meet in private contacts, at work and in public.

The innovative term 'Participatory Innovation' (Buur, 2007; Buur and Matthews, 2008) implies that beyond studying the user's perspective, users ought to be integrated into the design process in a systematic fashion. Such approaches are pioneering and have advanced both researchers' and companies' innovation practices. Based on the results of the current study, these approaches would benefit from shifting their point of departure to the space 'between' the users and the products, and the space 'between' the clients and professionals in service encounters. In order to highlight this crucial dimension, and reflecting on what has come out of the study reported in this chapter, I would like to propose the term 'Interaction Innovation'. The space 'between' clients and professionals is Interaction – jointly created and shaped, moment by moment, by social actions and by the socio-technological aspects of artefacts.

Notes

1. John Seely Brown was influential at Xerox PARC as director (1986–2000), scientific director (1986–2002), and principal scientist (1978–1984). Cf. http://www.johnseelybrown.com/cv.pdf (accessed 20 January 2010).
2. SPIRE director Buur describes the goals in the application to the Danish Council for Strategic Research as follows, '... this Centre will comparatively investigate user innovation (how people innovate) and user-driven innovation (how companies innovate through various forms of collaboration with users) as a means of advancing innovation theory and developing new methods for the integration of these theories into industrial practices' (Buur, 2007).
3. The reported figures are drawn from Christensen, 2006; Meis and Gabriel, 2006; Pelz, 2007; and Sohn, 2001. Statistics vary according to how the figures are calculated and estimated. This low compliance rate is frequently attributed to a societal taboo and the stigma associated with hearing impairment along with a strong desire to appear normal (Hetu, 1996; Pelz, 2007) or unrealistic hopes that a hearing aid will fully restore hearing once a client tries using it (Bisgaard, 2008). Other research indicates that there are great barriers in institutional healthcare encounters, in particular in hearing aid fitting (ProMatura, 2007a, b) and in otolaryngology doctor-patient interaction (Meis and Gabriel, 2006). Before the SPIRE HinT project the only CA research on interaction with hearing loss and hearing aids was by Skelt (2006, 2007), and to date, there is not a single study on the interaction between ear-nose-throat doctors and patients, despite the fact that there are over 2500 studies of doctor-patient interaction (reported by Deppermann, 2009). A recently compiled bibliography (Nowak and Spranz-Fogasy, 2010) lists over 3500 studies of medical encounters. For initial conversation-analytic studies on communication with hearing aids in Australia, Denmark, Finland, Germany and Switzerland, see Egbert and Deppermann (in preparation).

12
A Psychoanalyst's Reflection on Conversation Analysis's Contribution to His Own Therapeutic Talk[1]

Anssi Peräkylä

The topic of this chapter is almost embarrassingly self-referential. I would certainly have declined the invitation to write it, had I not agreed with the editor that the curious situation I find myself in – as academic and practitioner – fitted peculiarly well with the theme of this book. If there is a chance that a personal account of my work might advance our understanding of the applicability of Conversation Analysis, then I ought at least to try to provide one.

I started psychoanalytic training six years ago. The training is given by The Finnish Psychoanalytic Association, by a member of the International Psychoanalytic Association (IPA). My training, in other words, is in a 'Freudian psychoanalysis' (and not in some other form of psychotherapy, such as Cognitive Behavioural Therapy, Interpersonal Therapy or the like). For about five years now, I have been practising psychoanalysis, under the supervision of a senior psychoanalyst. I see one patient four times a week in 45-minute sessions. I expect my training to be finished in about a year's time. Not much will change in my practice after graduation, except that I will be free to stop going to supervision (which I will hardly want to do) and I might be able to charge higher fees from my patients (which they can't afford to pay, so that will not change).

Alongside being a candidate psychoanalyst, I am a conversation analyst. CA is my main work. My professional history as conversation analyst is longer than that as psychoanalyst: it started with a doctoral dissertation on AIDS counselling almost twenty years ago, and has continued ever since with studies on medical interactions and everyday interactions. After having studied routine medical interactions for years, I turned to psychoanalysis as a new research topic. Examining the ways in which language is used in examining mind appeared to me as an exciting extension to my earlier studies that focused on the ways in which language is used in examining body.

At the beginning part of this new project, I started to feel that it might advance my understanding if I acquired a practitioner's perspective to this new research topic of mine. And, to be honest, becoming a psychoanalyst had been my professional dream many years ago, and realising that dream now became possible.

I'm well aware of the theoretical tension, if not antagonism, between some forms of psychoanalysis and some forms of Conversation Analysis. In what might be called a social constructionist reading of Conversation Analysis, 'mind' is understood as an interactional construction, references to which serve as a resource for local accounts and justifications of social action. In what might be called a 'one person psychology reading of psychoanalysis', the processes within individual minds are the real motivational source and shaper of human action and interaction. In spite of this tension, I enjoy being where I am, as an inhabitant of both worlds.

In what follows, I will try to explicate what it means to inhabit both worlds. The chapter is divided into two parts. In the first part, using my clinical notes and ethnographic notes taken for the purposes of this study, I will describe how conversation-analytical understandings have shaped my ways of perceiving my interactions with my clients. In the latter part, I will try to explicate what kind of conceptual rethinking in my version of Conversation Analysis has been instigated by my clinical work. I shall also offer – if briefly – some thoughts on how we might solve the apparent impasse between the social constructionist and the realist account of mind, an impasse that is troubling to someone who, like me, works both with the mind's outer expression and its inner workings.

Part 1   CA informing the work of a psychoanalyst

Moments of (CA-informed) reflection during the sessions

People make myriad choices in any social interaction, but usually they are not aware of these choices. Yet the choices people make are extremely meaningful as, on the basis of those choices, ordered actions and mutual understanding is achieved. Harvey Sacks was well aware of the non-reflected or automated character of interactional choices, and he encouraged his students just to focus on what comes off in interaction, and not to worry about how can people think so fast (Sacks, 1992a, p. 11).

Psychotherapy is no exception to this: there is also that the choices participants make are largely not conscious. (This in spite of the fact that an overall goal of psychoanalysis is to make the patient more conscious about his or her mind.) Thus, as what I do as an analyst escapes my conscious attention, it is all the more difficult to account for the ways in which my training and experience as conversation analyst has shaped my doings as an analyst. But for the purposes of this book, with its commitment to showing how CA and practice intertwine, I will try.

For some months, I took ethnographic notes after my psychoanalytic sessions, with the aim of describing how my choices of action during the sessions are possibly informed by conversation-analytical considerations. I did not find myself being involved in conversation-analytical reflections *prior* to choices of action. Choices of action – for example in terms of how to respond to the patients talk – appeared to take place in a non-reflected way. What I did find, however, was that occasionally I became aware of choices that I had just made, and reflected upon those choices in what appeared to be a CA-informed way. There were two recurrent environments for this occurrence of awareness: emotional responses and responses that have to do with the maintenance of local accountability by the patient.

Recognition through response tokens

Conversation Analysis emphasises the importance of the placement and design of any utterances in interaction. I presume this has sensitised me to pay attention to the ways in which I respond to the talk of my patient. Design and placement of response tokens is a case in point (for response tokens in conversation, see Gardner, 2001; and Sorjonen, 2001; and for their use in psychotherapy, see Fitzgerald 2009). In Example 1, the patient is telling me about her latest visit to her parents' house where she does a lot of practical maintenance and repair work. In her utterance, she analyses her ambivalence. (The italicised extracts labelled 'ethnographic notes' are my own near-contemporaneous write-ups of parts of the therapeutic session; either remembered exchanges, or commentaries about my or the client's actions and motives).

Example 1 (ethnographic notes)
PA: *This thing is kind of multi-faceted, I'm quite reluctant to be there, but at the same time, I'm unable to leave.*
AN: M̲m̲:

When I produce my response token, I emphasise it in such a way that makes me hear what I say as recognising what the patient just said (cf. Voutilainen, Peräkylä and Ruusuvuori, 2010). This recognition involves both what the patient says (her ambivalence) and what she does (observes her own mental states): both the 'content' and the 'action' are treated as valid here and now. The patient is doing what she is supposed to do as a patient in psychoanalysis.

Emotion descriptions are one recurrent environment for such recognising response tokens. Example 2 is a rather straightforward case. The patient is describing a moment, a few years ago, when she was cleaning in the magnificent library that belongs to her father, who is a scholar of great eminence.

Example 2 (ethnographic notes)
PA: *I lifted my gaze up and saw all these books, and at that very moment I understood that I hate these books.*
AN: ↓Mm:

My emphasised '↓Mm:' is designed to convey recognition of the patient's experience. It treats the patient's experience as one that I can understand and consider as valid. This narrative is a nodal point in the analysis: inaccessibility of aggression appears as a key issue for this patient, and this story (which has been told a few times during the analysis) represents a moment at which she, for a short moment, felt in touch with her aggression.

Sometimes such a recognising response token may carry with it a package of orientations that link the current moment to some aspect of the history of dialogues between me and the patient. Consider Example 3. The patient is telling about a piece of academic work that she has concentrated on for a long time, and which she now wishes to complete.

Example 3 (ethnographic notes)
PA: *I want to leave this behind, this research has for such a long time been, as it were hanging in the air, in the same way as in my life things have been hanging in the air.*
AN: Mm:,
PA: ((continues))

This response token is located after the patient has drawn a parallel between her research having been unfinished ('hanging in the air'), and the many other things in her life that are unfinished. My response token is again emphasised, conveying recognition of what has been said. In this case, the recognition is targeted at the idiom 'things hanging in the air'. This idiom creates a linkage to what the patient said a few sessions earlier: when her mother fell ill, several years ago, a ball was thrown into the air, and after that, she feels that her life has been characterised by a kind of temporariness, lack of conclusiveness, as if the ball were still in the air. Now, by using the same idiom, she hearably invokes this tragic family history as a context for her current academic plans. I recognise this invocation, which is conveyed by the placement and emphasis of my 'mm:,'.

It is clear that ethnographic notes cannot convey the details concerning placement or design of utterances in any way comparable to the exactness of an audio or video recording. Therefore, the instances of interaction presented in this chapter are not research data in a CA sense. However, my notes on cases 1–3 do indicate that during the course of my daily work as psychotherapist, I have paid attention to my choice of response tokens, and especially the choice of the prosodic shape, as well as placement, of these tokens.

These tokens may stand out as exceptional in the psychoanalytic dialogue, which is normally characterised by the analyst's neutrality (and also by scarcity of any 'back-channel' items). Hence, it is possible that my awareness of my action in these particular cases has also to do with a conflict of some sort: I could have remained neutral (through different prosody in my response tokens, or by withholding response tokens altogether), but I didn't. In the following set of examples, such *'post hoc* motivational conflict' becomes apparent.

Maintenance of accountability

One of the well-known (and often criticised and/or parodied) features of psychoanalysis is the silence of the analyst. At junctures where an interlocutor in everyday interactions would take a turn at talk, the psychoanalyst often remains silent. My conversation-analytical training serves as a resource for some additional understanding in those moments when I become aware of my silence. Consider Example 4, which is from the beginning of a session.

Example 4 (ethnographic notes)
PA: I'm sorry for being late again.
      (silence)
PA: ((states a reason for being late.))
      (silence)

I choose not to respond to the apology by the patient, nor to the reason that she gives. Through my silence, I maintain the momentary accountability of the issue: should I have accepted the apology, or the reason for being late, I would also have treated the issue as closed, and 'not-any-more-accountable'. (For accountability in interaction, see, for example, Heritage, 1988; and Antaki, 1994). I *feel* my silence in myself as some kind of tension (which I think arises from the fact that acceptance is so strongly preferred in ordinary conversation in this kind of context); this feeling reveals itself as a distinct choice that I have made.

There are moments when I choose to respond to the patient's talk, and I become aware of this choice, probably because conflicting motives are involved. The response dissolves accountability, which I on the other hand would have wanted to maintain. Consider Example 5, which is from the same session as Example 4. Prior to the segment, the patient has talked about how taxing it feels to come to the sessions, and how she feels that the burden remains there throughout the day, after a session in the morning.

Example 5 (ethnographic notes)
PA: And then on the other hand, those days usually feel better, when there is no session.
AN: <u>M</u>m:

I respond to the patient's assessment with a recognising '<u>M</u>m:'. Reflecting back to this response after having produced it, it appears to me as one through which I convey to the patient that her experience is valid, and that I accept it and don't criticise her for that. And at the same time, I wonder if the recognition I gave to the patient's experience may have come too early. Did the recognition through emphasised '<u>M</u>m:' also close down the issue of taxing sessions? If I had withdrawn any response at this moment, the patient's relief on those days when she doesn't have to come to the analytic sessions might have remained an accountable issue for some time longer, and she could have elaborated more upon that very experience.

A similar question arises in my mind after a response token in Example 6 below. The note is taken after the last session of a week that has included one missed session and another one to which the patient arrived late.

Example 6 (ethnographic notes)
PA: In the events this week, there's been encapsulated the whole history of my analysis.
AN: Mm.

After having produced my acknowledgement token, I begin to doubt. Did I treat what PA said, 'understood' in a premature way?; would silence have enabled him to explore the meaning of the past week more, and also the meaning of the whole analysis to him?

A question that topicalises something that the patient talks about can raise the same doubt: did I dissolve the accountability too early. Consider Example 7.

Example 7 (ethnographic notes)
   PA tells me that she didn't come to the session yesterday morning because there was a piece of work that she needed to finish by 11 am. I ask her 'what was that

piece of work' and she tells me. My question validates the reason that PA had for not coming, and by so doing, it also halts the investigation of the very fact that PA did not come yesterday. While the conversation goes on, I am thinking whether my question, for that reason, came too early.

Maintenance of accountability involves not only the choice of withholding response or giving it – it also involves the design of the response. In Example 8, I find myself producing a 'designedly neutral' response token, through which I understand that I am trying to maintain the patient's accountability concerning her difficulty to speak freely during the analytic hour. After having come late to a number of consecutive sessions, she has at last arrived in time. Example 8 shows my recollection of her first utterance during that session.

Example 8 (ethnographic notes)
The patient says, 'It makes me laugh that when I come here in time, then I just stay silent.' I am controlling my response: It is a 'Mm:', but one that does not acknowledge the humorous tone in the patient's utterance. I understand this as an effort on my side to maintain PA's accountability, to not close the sequence PA has initiated, to maintain the state of talk where PA continues to think about what is happening right now in the consultation room.

There is a paradigmatic question that psychoanalysts use: 'what comes to your mind'. That particular question seems to have the power to *maintain* accountability on the very issue that is, through its placement and design, targeted at. Sometimes the maintenance of accountability through this question may involve a conflict of motives and the analyst becomes aware of his choices. This happened when my patient apologised for not having arrived for the session the day before. I responded to the account by asking 'what comes to your mind'. After having asked the question, I asked myself whether I had been invoking moral accountability in the disguise of an invitation to self-observation.

In all cases shown thus far, I, as the analyst, became aware of some choices of action that I made while listening and responding to the patient's talk. In the data fragments presented above, the actions of the patient and the analyst are described in a summary fashion; it is clear that these descriptions lack the level of detail of conversation-analytical transcripts. Of interest, however, are the analyst's immediate *post hoc* reflections of what he is doing or not doing. They are moments where a Conversation Analyst meets a psychoanalyst: moments during which, to make sense of the state of the talk that I shared with my patient, I used some of the sensibilities regarding interaction that I have gained through my conversation-analytical work.

Much more goes unnoticed. It is possibly *conflict* of some sort that makes us aware of choices that we make in interaction. At some moments, I will become aware of a choice that I just made in my dialogue with the patient; and these choices may involve a motivational conflict.

It should be added that I don't have any empirical evidence to indicate whether or not my actual interactions with my patients are in any systematic ways different from the practices of my psychoanalyst colleagues without conversation-analytical training. When I asked my supervisor's view, she told me that she thinks there is a difference – suggesting that I have more of a researcher's attitude to my interactions with the patient, not feeling a need to intervene therapeutically as often as the average psychoanalyst or candidate analyst does. But this difference may consist more in ways of reporting interactions (in supervision) than in the interactions themselves; and even if it concerned the very interactions, it would have more to do with the general distinction between a 'therapeutic' and a 'research' orientation, and not so much to do with CA as a specific approach to interaction. Basically, I am ready to accept that CA has not made my practice different. As the observations and reflections presented in this chapter suggest, the therapist's actual interactions with the patient are largely pre-reflective. Therefore, in my hands, CA has been a resource to enhance understanding of this practice at some particular junctures. What kind of loops these new understandings possibly have back to the shaping of these practices, in my own work and in the psychotherapeutic community, remains to be seen as our understanding grows.

Reading interaction after the sessions, in the light of research findings

After their sessions with the patients, psychotherapists typically make some notes about what happened during the session. The note taking is particularly important when the therapist is having supervision for his work, because the notes are the material that will be discussed in the supervision. In this section, I will be exploring my clinical notes from the past few years. (In the preceding section, the 'data' were ethnographic notes produced for this particular chapter.)

The clinical note taking after the session is a moment of reflection. While taking notes, I memorise what happened during the session, which inevitably creates some distance between the memorising (and writing) subject, and the events that I memorise. My notes should reveal if conversation-analytic work has had some influence on the ways in which I organise my recollections. Of particular interest, I think, are my own findings of psychoanalytic interaction (reported in Peräkylä, 2004, 2005, 2008 and 2010; see also Vehviläinen 2003 and 2008 for closely related work): have they left some impact on my way of reporting my interactions with the patient? This is a reflective, textual variant of the question that other contributors to this book have asked, namely does CA knowledge affect subsequent talk; here, my question is whether it affects subsequent writing *about* the talk.

Much of Vehviläinen's and my work revolves around what might be called an interpretative trajectory: a continuum of interactional moves which prepare for an interpretation to be given by the analyst, and after the interpretation, work on the patient's response. Only a part of the steps and interactive phases involved in this trajectory have found their expression in my own way organising my recollections from the sessions. What my notes do *not* attend to includes the *preparation of interpretation* through invoking a 'puzzle' by means of formulations, extensions and confrontations (see Vehviläinen, 2003), the patients' ways of *evading some aspects of interpretation* in their agreeing responses (Peräkylä, 2005) and analysts' ways of *shifting the perspective of description in third-position* utterances after the patients' agreeing responses to interpretations (Peräkylä, 2010). I will come back to these practices, after having shown the points at which conversation-analytic work *has* influenced the organisation of my recollections, as reflected in my post-session notes.

A point in the interpretative sequence where my clinical notes and my conversation-analytical research by and large align involves agreement, disagreement and elaboration shown in the patient's responses to interpretations. In Peräkylä 2005 (pp. 164–5), I described the variation of patients' responses as involving, as most basic types, straightforward rejections or acceptances, as well as 'in-between' responses (of the type 'I'll have to think about that'). The most interesting responses, however, were elaborations', where the patients convey their agreement and understanding of the interpretation by taking it up and by continuing talking about it. The same variation of response types can be found from my notes.

Compact agreements with interpretation have found their way into my note taking with a special symbol. In my clinical notes, I use the sign % to convey that the patient accepted an interpretation. Consider the following example. Text between double parentheses (( )) involves my summarising descriptions of topics and events, text between 'smaller than' and 'greater than' < > signs involves talk by the analyst, all other text involves talk by the patient. All talk is paraphrased on the basis of post-session recollection. Reading the extracts from the clinical notes requires some patience, because the notes are like shorthand, the text being condensed. (I have put the clinical notes in a different font, to mark them off from my ethnographic notes.)

Example 9 (clinical notes)

((talk about PA being able to at last leave things behind, not be mentally stuck in his past misfortunes)) – <what comes to your mind about leaving things behind in life?> – guilt, disappointment – guilt for X's death – external and internal in the same time – <that you are betrayed, disappointed and guilty at the same time> – % – things are not so overwhelming any more   10.8.09

In my latter utterance (see the penultimate line in the segment), I summarise the patient's experience as involving three overlapping feelings: being betrayed, disappointed and guilty. The % sign conveys my recollection at the time of the note taking that the patient agreed with this characterisation, without taking it up or further developing it. A similar kind of compact agreement is shown in Example 10. The patient is describing her recent visit abroad, comparing it to previous holiday travels. Now, unlike before, she was able to relax during the holiday.

Example 10 (clinical notes)

- no compulsive buying of things – sitting in parks, taking photos – (...) – <as if you had now more space inside yourself> – % – perhaps the best trip that I have ever done   1.11.07

The % sign indicates my recollection that the patient agreed with my characterisation of her having now had more internal freedom ('space') during the holiday. The next thing I have taken note of is her overall assessment of the trip, which, although being topically related to the previous talk, does not deal with the 'internal' perspective brought about in the interpretation.

So, in recollecting patient's responses to interpretation, I seem to have adopted the category of compact agreement that I arrived at in my CA studies on psychoanalytic interpretations. The compact agreement is different from *elaboration*, which also figures in my note-taking practices. Sometimes the word 'elaboration' is used as shorthand, to refer to a response in which the patient takes up the interpretation. Consider Example 11. The patient had recently painted walls in the living room of her flat, which she initially felt as deeply rewarding. Now, however, she has started to feel depressed again.

Example 11 (clinical notes)

- wish that painting the walls would have been part of some internal process ((not PA's words)) – it was not that – ... <disappointment that you didn't have time to paint the bedroom> – % – ((elaborates))   27.11.07

In my recollection of the session, the patient first indicates her agreement with the interpretation (coded as %), thereafter moving into elaboration. This sequence of events is very common in my CA cases of interpretations; I have used the same template to describe the course of events in my notes.

In Example 11, the patient's action after interpretation is coded as 'elaboration', but how the patient elaborates, is left unspecified. In Example 12 below, the design of the elaboration is paraphrased. The category of 'elaboration' is not used in my notes, but the action conveyed by the patient's utterance paraphrased in the notes involves an elaboration, as I have described it in my conversation-analytical work. The patient is talking about her recurrent exhaustion during the analytic sessions.

Example 12 (clinical notes)

- difficult to talk – no strength – sometimes I have the strength to continue 45 minutes, like yesterday, then again I don't have the strength – ... <it appears that talking here is taxing, it consumes your strength> – % – it's like lifting a wet cloth from water – then it falls down there again. 4.12.07

In my interpretation – which actually does not involve much more than reflecting back to patient what she already has told me, but not packaging this as a formulation of patient's words, but as my own view – I suggest that talking to me is taxing for the patient. In her response, as I have reconstructed it after the session, the patient first agrees with the interpretation, and then moves on to elaboration in which she illustrates her experience through a metaphor.

In yet another example, both agreement and elaboration are depicted by utterances that I paraphrase in my notes:

Example 13 (clinical notes)

((talking about plans regarding place where to live in future)) – ... – ((silences)) – <my feeling: not much is happening now, but you are expecting things to happen > – that was a good way to put it, I am like in traffic lights, waiting for the green – ((silence)) 22.10.09

In his response to the interpretation, the patient first agrees ('this was a good way to put it') and then elaborates with the metaphor of being in the traffic lights.

While compact agreement with interpretation is usually expressed by shorthand (%) in my notes, and elaboration is often expressed by shorthand ('elaborates'), disagreement tends to be paraphrased in full utterances. Consider the following example:

Example 14 (clinical notes)
<perhaps: the beginning of the analysis 'woke up' the good, healthy mother. Then, as the analysis goes on, the mother falls ill again. > – I cannot get hold of what you say, it may be like that – the sentences that you say would work also without the reference to mother – it woke up the good, then it falls ill.

The patient's disagreement with the interpretation is paraphrased through accounts which do not flatly reject what I suggested, but cast it as something that is subjectively inaccessible for the patient. However, in some cases, categorical descriptions are also used in my notes in paraphrasing rejections. Consider the following:

Example 15 (clinical notes)
((P tells me about having spoken with a close friend about the possibility of terminating the analysis)) – I told her that one of my feelings is that I would leave you [the analyst] with nothing in your hands. This has to do with a similar thing in my relation to other people in my life, my feeling of responsibility – ((talks further about her understandings about how long analysis should be)) – <can there be a reversed thought in the background: you are afraid that *you* will be left with nothing in your hands if you quit > – it does not feel like that ((first a straight off denial, then a reflective denial alongside which she is exploring her feelings.)) 22.9.09

In describing the patient's response to my interpretation, I first use a paraphrase ('it does not feel like that'), after which I move into categorical descriptions of two consecutive denials.

The notes shown above suggest that my work on reception of interpretations informs my way of organising my recollections of the sessions in my clinical notes: I am perceiving my interpretations as actions that invoke a response from the patient. In my clinical work, I categorise the patient's responses in a rather similar way as I have categorised them in my CA research.

Yet another practice discussed in my CA work, showing up in my notes (and also in my recollections) involves the analyst designing the interpretative utterance in specific ways that increase the plausibility of the linkages between spheres of experience that the interpretation proposes are connected (see Peräkylä, 2004). Thus, for example, when my patient described, in subdued complaining tone, that an upcoming annual January event in her workplace will nail down her life once again into the old repetitive pattern, and she will know exactly 'the course of life until next January', I suggest to her that she might be feeling that the analysis also is in a repetitive pattern, and she knows exactly 'the course of analysis until next January'. Circulation of the description 'knowing the course of X until next January' demonstrates for the patient the linkages between the two spheres of experience (working life and analysis), and serves as a means to draw the patient's attention to a feeling of stagnation in the analytic relation.

So, in designing my interpretative utterance, I find myself interacting with my patient in ways that I have first encountered in my CA work on psychoanalysis. However, in my CA work, I have also discussed a number of practices pertaining to interpretations that do *not* show up in my clinical notes. Regarding these practices, my research work has not left traces on my way to organise my recollection as a clinician. One of them, most extensively discussed by Vehviläinen (2003; see also Peräkylä, 2004), involves the invocation of a puzzle in the interaction that eventually leads up to the interpretation. My notes very seldom, if ever, show such 'projects' (see Schegloff, 2007) in which the analyst's responses to patient's talk are geared to prepare the ground for an interpretation to come. Second, the notes do not show the patients designing their elaborations of interpretation (which, by their face value, show agreement and understanding of the interpretation) in ways that make the elaborations selective *vis-à-vis* the interpretation, thereby facilitating covert resistance towards the interpretation (see Peräkylä, 2005). And third, my CA work suggests that an important facet of the interpretative work takes place in 'third position', that is, in analysts' utterances that come after the patients' responses to interpretations (Peräkylä, 2010). My clinical notes do not show any traces of such third-position interpretative work.

Why might it be that these practices that I have found by investigating psychoanalytic practice through CA do not show up in my notes on my own practice? One possibility is, of course, that my own practice is different from that of the analysts whose work I have been investigating. In principle, it is possible that I just don't do those things. That could also apply to my patients: they could be different as well, as they don't do such selective elaborations as the patients in my CA tapes do. The other possibility is that in writing up my notes, I am not able to reach these aspects of interaction. They go unnoticed while they occur, and I do not have access to them afterwards, either. Should this be the case, a further question would arise: Why is it, then, that I *do* have access to the basic sequential structure of interpretation (the adjacency pair interpretation and response) and I do perceive the patient's responses broadly along the same lines as I have analysed them in my conversation analytical work? And that I do perceive myself designing some of my interpretative utterance by circulating the words that the patient has used? Can it be the case that some interactional phenomena – perhaps the more robust ones – are available *in situ* to the practitioner, while others – perhaps the more complex and delicate ones – are not available, even if the practitioner is, like I am, highly experienced in accessing these phenomena in the role of a CA researcher?

I have no definite answers to offer, and I am ready to live without one. As a conversation analyst, I can continue my research work along the lines suggested by Sacks (1992, p. 11), by just trying 'to come to terms with how it is that that the thing comes off'. Practitioners' awareness, not even my own practitioner's awareness, is not needed as an evidence for an organisation of interaction to be there. And as a psychoanalyst, I will continue my clinical work, with the understanding that much of what I do – but not all of what I do – remains outside the scope of my reflective awareness.

Part 2   Clinical practices which prompt theoretical rethinking in CA

Understanding mind in interaction

Whereas the first part of the chapter explored the ways in which my experience as a conversation analyst has influenced my work as a psychoanalyst, this second part of the chapter will focus on the influence in the opposite direction. I will be asking how the psychoanalytic practice has influenced my conversation-analytical ideas.

We are not talking about direct and distinct consequences of clinical practice upon my conversation-analytical thinking. The influences are vague and certainly indirect. Having said this, it does appear to me that being involved in clinical training and clinical work has pushed me towards rethinking and re-explication of my own understandings regarding some central ideas of Conversation Analysis. The relation between *interaction and mind* is at the centre of this rethinking.

There are two contradicting positions on mind and interaction, both of which I find unsatisfactory. I will explain both positions in simplified terms. The traditional psychoanalytic thinking represents a position than can be characterised as *mentalist* (see Watson and Coulter, 2008, p. 1). Traditional psychoanalysis, alongside other mentalist (and 'cognitivist' and 'psychologist', Watson and Coulter, 2008, p. 1) approaches, considers human minds as entities that are linked to, but still separate from, their social environment (for a more recent psychoanalytic criticism of such positions, see, for example, Mitchell, 2000). Such entities exhibit their specific internal processes, having to do with cognition, affect, motivation or the like. Traditional psychoanalysis disagrees with, for example, cognitive psychology regarding how these processes within mind are organised, but the two approaches agree about the very distinctiveness of the individual minds. People respond to their social and other environment in ways that arise from their affects, cognitions, motivations and so on. Therefore, what people do can be explained with reference to their mental processes.

As contrast to this kind of understanding, ethnomethodologists and discursive psychologists have argued for understanding human minds as socially constructed. The object of EM and DP studies are the ways in which mental states or processes are referred to in social interaction. According to this view, any references to thinking, knowing, feeling, or the like, should be understood as public actions: as constituents of interactional processes, whereby the participants do things such as justifying, blaming, narrating or the like (see, for example, Coulter, 1989; McHoul and Rapley, 2003; Potter, 2006; Watson and Coulter, 2008). There is a strong criticism towards 'mentalism' involved in this position: internal experience, or mental processes, are considered as lay understandings, and the task of the researcher is to show how these understandings are constructed and made use of in interactions, rather than to share and use them as explanations him- or herself. Regarding one key mental concept, 'motivation', Watson and Coulter (2008, p. 12) recently wrote: 'The root phenomenon is how *members* (not analysts) attribute motive in making cultural sense of action, how members treat motives as "expressed" (i.e. avowed, exhibited) ... in real scenes of communicative interaction.' This position, shared by many ethnomethodologists, discursive psychologists and analytic philosophers, might be called 'anti-mentalism'.

Searching for a third way

Basically, my position as a conversation analyst who is involved in clinical practice of psychoanalysis has prompted me to reconsider this dichotomy between mentalism and anti-mentalism. First of all, being a conversation analyst is hardly compatible with positions that make a strong demarcation between 'inner' and 'outer' reality (mind and social interaction), and treat the individual mind as a free standing field. Seeing, through the eyes of a conversation analyst, the thoroughly dialogical character of any expressions of mental states – be they verbal descriptions or non-verbal displays – makes it impossible to justify any strong distinction between the outer and the inner. They appear as parts of the same process. Therefore, the mentalist position of traditional psychoanalysis seems to me as impossible to accept.

Let me take an example from everyday interactions. From a mentalist perspective, facial expressions are a paradigmatic case of how the internal affective states of humans shape their interactive behaviour: basic emotions (such as joy, sadness, anger or fear) have each their distinct expression in human face (see Ekman and Friesen, 2003). The face is an outlet of the mind (and the physiological emotion processes). To understand facial expression, we have to trace it back to what is happening in the inner self of the individual.

Johanna Ruusuvuori and I have in recent years examined facial expressions in everyday interactions (see Peräkylä and Ruusuvuori, 2006; Ruusuvuori and Peräkylä 2009). Basically, we show how the timing and shape of the facial expressions is thoroughly embedded in the sequential organisation of interaction. There are particular places and consequences of such expressions. Rather than being spontaneous outlets of the internal emotional state of humans, in our data facial expressions appear as interactional resources, the use of which is thoroughly interwoven with that of other such resources (word choice, syntax, prosody, gaze, gesture).

While my conversation-analytical experience alienates me from any mentalistic positions, being involved in psychoanalytic processes makes it impossible for me to sustain the claims of anti-mentalism. The EM and DP approach to mind suggests that avowal and ascription of mental predicates is a process that should be investigated in ways that are detached from any presuppositions regarding inner realities. Psychoanalysis is a practice in which the client and the analyst explore their inner experiences, and step by step either *recognise* dimensions of affect and cognition that appear for them as ones that have always been there but have not been perceived with clarity before, or *achieve* new dimensions of affect and cognition that are real but have not been possible to be experienced before the psychoanalytic process. In short, feelings, thoughts, hopes, desires appear as *real* phenomena in psychoanalytic practice – not merely as artefacts or projections produced by linguistic and interactive processes in the consultation room or elsewhere.

Hence, as a conversation analyst who is doing psychoanalysis, I have searched for an approach that would not compromise the understanding of mental phenomena as thoroughly social, but at the same time, would still accommodate the very reality of mental processes.

There are two recent conceptual developments in interaction studies that have helped me in the search for such a 'third way' between mentalism and anti-mentalism. One comes from the recent work of Enfield and Levinson (1996; Levinson, 1996a, b) and the other from the work on mother-baby interaction by Beebe and Lachman (2002; for a more extended review of these approaches, see Peräkylä, 2009). In what follows I give a sketch of those two approaches, to suggest to the reader how it is that we might begin to bridge the supposedly unbridgeable chasm between realism and social constructionism, at least as a working principle in therapy.

Mental simulation in psychotherapy

Levinson and his co-workers have brought together a key contemporary discussion in psychology on *theory of mind*, and the findings of Conversation Analysis. In result, they propose that the basic practices of social interaction involve a process of mutual 'reading' of the mental states of the co-interactants. According to Levinson and Enfield (2006, p. 1), the interactants take part in 'shared mental world'. This shared mental world involves the interactants' detailed expectations concerning each others' behaviour and their understandings regarding each other's cognitions, intentions and motives. It is a world that is shaped and maintained in and through sequentially organised action.

Theory of mind is a corner-stone of conceptualisation by Levinson and Enfield. It is not a 'researcher's theory', but a basic competence in understanding the social world, shared by normally developed humans. It involves an ability to attribute to other persons a world of inner experience that is independent from the outer world and the observer's own experience – a world consisting of states such as beliefs, desires and intentions (Premack, 1976).

According to Levinson and Enfield, theory of mind is in incessant use in social interaction. The use of theory of mind is normally automatised and non-reflected. The interactants read each others' communicative intentions and respond to these (Levinson and Enfield, 2006, p. 5; Levinson, 2006a, p. 45). Interactants do not respond to others' behaviour as such. Interaction requires interpretation of other's behaviour: 'mapping intentions or goals onto behaviour' (Levinson. 2006a, p. 45), whereby behaviour gets understood as intentional action. This process of interpretation, according to Levinson (p. 45), involves 'some kind of simulation of the other's mental world'.

Levinson (2006a, 2006b) and Enfield (Enfield and Levinson 2006), and the contributors to their recent collection (especially Schegloff, 2006) show how the practices identified by Conversation Analysis – adjacency pairs, presequences, recipient design, repair – involve reciprocal and reflexive simulation of the mental states of the participants. From here arises a new way to conceptualise psychotherapeutic interaction. Psychotherapy involves an effort to examine, recognise and modify the patient's ways of experiencing and relating to his or her experience. The mutual simulation of each other's mental world by participants to an interaction appears be a generic property of interaction that is taken into a special use in psychotherapy.

As colleagues and I proposed in the introductory article to a recent collection of CA papers on psychotherapy, '[a]ny action by the therapist ... expresses an understanding of the patient's experience' (Peräkylä et al., 2008, p. 16). Because the actions of the participants are tied together by sequential implicativeness, 'the participants inevitably have to orient to and work with the understandings that they each bring about through their actions'. The conceptualisation by Levinson provides a theoretical backing and specification for this proposal of ours. The therapist is involved in simulation of the

A Psychoanalyst's Reflection on CA's Contribution 239

patient's experience, and tries to be as aware as possible of this process. The therapist's actions convey to the patient how the therapist simulates the patient's experience, and the patient's actions convey to the therapist how (s)he simulates the therapist's experience. The therapist's actions, be they formulations (see, for example, Antaki, 2008), recognitions (Voutilainen, Peräkylä and Ruusuvuori, 2010), interpretations (Peräkylä, 2005. and 2008; Bercelli, Rossano and Viaro, 2008) involve movement in this mutual simulation.

Through the integration of Conversation Analysis and the research tradition on theory of mind suggested by Levinson and Enfield, we can thus arrive at a conceptualisation of interaction which preserves the conversation-analytical findings, and yet does not call into question the relevancy of mental processes. Another such integrative conceptual development comes from the recent work on infant-caretaker interaction by Beebe and Lachman.

Self- and interactional regulation as a system

In the past decade, much psychological research has focused on *regulation of emotion*: 'the process by which individuals influence which emotions they have, when they have them, and how they experience and express these emotions' (Gross, 1998, p. 275; see also Vandekerckhove et al., 2008). While most research on regulation of emotions focuses on this process within individual minds, Beebe and Lachman (2002) offer a perspective which integrates interactional and psychological processes of emotion regulation. They propose that there is 'an intimate connection between self and interaction regulation' (p. 22). The same behaviours that entail self-regulation also serve in interactive regulation.

A key example comes from research on baby-caretaker interaction. When playing with her mother, a baby sometimes turns her head away from the mother. In interactional terms, that entails withdrawal from mutual engagement. In a study by Field (1981), cited by Beebe and Lachman (2002, pp. 158–9), it was shown that the heart rate of babies is unusually high just prior to this withdrawal, and that it returns to normal after it, before the babies turn their heads back to their mothers. So, the turning away of gaze regulated interaction (disengagement) and at the same time, it regulated the internal state of the baby (arousal as indicated by the heart rate).

A similar connection can be found in facial expressions. Research conducted by Ruusuvuori and myself, among many other studies, indicates that the face has an important task in the regulation of interaction: the face is visually available to the other participants and has consequences for their facial expressions, talk and other behaviours (see also Goodwin, 1980; Dimberg, 1982). On the other hand, there is plenty of evidence about the impact of facial expression on the individual's *own* subjective experience and psychophysiological state (Kappas, 2008, pp. 24–7; Beebe and Lachman, 2002, p. 40). Even though the scope of validity of this facial feedback –hypothesis is still unclear (see Kappas, 2008, pp. 26–7), it opens up an exciting perspective: the same event in face regulates both the course of interaction and the subject's own state, thus influencing the affective state of the interactional system.

Like the recent work by Levinson and Enfield, so also that by Beebe and Lachman offers conceptual means to reconsider the relation between mind and interaction. These developments of research suggests that it is possible and worthwhile to consider interactive processes and mental processes as an integrated system. This is not to call into question the validity of research that focuses exclusively on the 'public' processes of avowal and ascription of mental predicates, nor research that focuses on internal cognitive and affective processes. But for a conversation analyst doing psychoanalysis, theoretical integration appears as a most attractive avenue to take.

It is not yet clear whether or not these theoretical reconceptualisations will have impact on *research practice* within CA applied in psychotherapy. It may very well be that CA's contribution to understanding psychotherapy remains primarily in its capacity to unravel the minutiae of interactive practices, and this contribution might *not* be dependent on any reconceptualisation along the lines outlined above. Then, on the other hand, it may be that the integrated, systemic views linking interaction, mind and body would lead to new research designs, for example ones that combine CA and psychophysiological measurements or neural imaging techniques. Such research could reveal new layers of organisation in, for example, the emotional interactions between therapists and patients (for non-CA exploration in this direction, see, for example, Villmann et al., 2008).

Concluding comments

Perhaps in all applied Conversation Analysis, CA is brought into contact with other social practices – be they in medicine, education, technical working environments, business or wherever. In this chapter, I have discussed a history of one contact between Conversation Analysis and psychotherapy. The distinctiveness of this particular contact is that it involves a professional, myself, adopting a dual role, as a conversation analyst and as a psychoanalyst. I have tried to show how the work of a psychoanalyst and the work of a conversation analyst are influenced by this contact.

In one sense, what I have written involves a disappointment, at least to myself: I do not have grounds to say that Conversation Analysis would have *changed* the way I practice as a psychotherapist. There are applications of Conversation Analysis that demonstrably result in changes in professional practice – the work of Heritage and colleagues (2007) on closing questions in medical encounters is a great example, well documented in Heritage and Robinson's chapter in this volume – but my personal explorations between psychoanalysis and Conversation Analysis are not among them. What CA has offered to me, as a practising psychotherapist, is means for conceptualising some of the things that I find myself doing with my patients. Besides, it has offered an understanding that much of what I do is beyond my reflexive awareness, yet ordered at all points (Sacks, 1992, p. 484) and as interactional practice, accessible to the methods of CA research.

Leaving aside my own practice, I would like to suggests that in psychotherapy, direct behavioural interventions from CA to clinical practice – for example, recommendations for practitioners to use a particular utterance design and to avoid another – may not be feasible. Apart from the fact that therapists' minutiae of behaviours are pre-reflected, this non-feasibility of direct behavioural interventions may arise from the great variability of interactions in psychotherapy. Unlike, for example, medical encounters, psychotherapy sessions (at least in psychodynamic therapies) are not organised into institutionally ascribed phases. On turn-by-turn level, the practitioners' actions are adapted to the variable actions of the individual patients. On the level of therapy processes, each patient brings in particular themes and problems, understanding of which characterises of the therapists' choices of action. Stiles, reflecting upon the lack of correlation between specific therapist behaviours and the outcome of treatment, points out that the behaviours of the therapist are (or should be) responsive to the 'emerging context, particularly including client requirements' (1999, p.6). For this reason, in psychotherapy there might not be particular clinician actions or behaviours that are beneficial for the outcome across different clients and different phases of the treatment. With each client, and at each moment, the therapist may have to assemble a particular way to proceed.

The future agenda of applied CA research on psychotherapy, therefore, probably does not involve search for distinct clinician behaviours that might be therapeutically effective, but, instead, the search for increased understanding of the means of responsiveness – that is, alignment, affiliation, as well as therapeutically meaningful non-alignment and non-affiliation – in the therapeutic interaction (cf. Voutilainen et al., 2010).

Conversation Analysis is a strong tradition and its findings are robust. It need not protect itself from other research traditions and professional practices. Being engaged in linkages like those that I have discussed in this chapter requires Conversation Analysis – and the conversation analyst to – accept methodological impurity and theoretical challenges. The reward is in the possibility of renewed understanding of the fields that get linked – and in the social, and even personal, relevance of one's work.

Note

1. The work leading to this chapter was supported by Academy of Finland grants 1131042 and 1132303. I wish to thank Charles Antaki, Doug Maynard and Liisa Voutiläinen for their helpful comments.

References

Anderson, W. L. and Anderson, S. L. (1995) *Socially Grounded Engineering for Digital Libraries*. Allerton: Allerton95.
Andresen, H. (2005) 'Role play and language development in the preschool years'. *Culture & Psychology* 11(4): 387–414.
Anonymous (2008) 'Make your hobby your job'. *Inspire: Your magazine from Jobcentre Plus* Spring issue: 18–19.
Antaki, C. (1994) *Explaining and Arguing: The Social Organisation of Accounts*. London: Sage.
Antaki, C. (1999) 'Assessing quality of life of persons with a learning disability: How setting lower standards may inflate well-being scores'. *Qualitative Health Research* 9: 437–54.
Antaki, C. (2008) 'Formulations in psychotherapy'. In A. Peräkylä, C. Antaki, S. Vehviläinen and I. Leudar (eds), *Conversation Analysis of Psychotherapy*. Cambridge: Cambridge University Press, pp. 26–42.
Antaki, C. and Widdicombe, S. (1998a) *Identities in Talk*. London: Sage.
Antaki, C. and Widdicombe, S. (1998b) 'Identity as an achievement and as a tool'. In Antaki, C. and Widdicombe, S. (eds) *Identities in Talk*, pp. 1–14.
Antaki, C., Finlay, W. M. L., and Walton, C. (2009) 'Choices for people with an intellectual impairment: Official discourse and everyday practice'. *Journal of Policy and Practice in Intellectual Disabilities* 6: 260–6.
Antaki, C., Young, N., and Finlay, W. M. L. (2002) 'Shaping clients' answers: Departures from neutrality in care-staff interviews with people with a learning disability'. *Disability & Society* 17(4): 435–55.
Antaki, C., Finlay, W. M. L., Walton, C., and Pate, L. (2008) 'Offering choices to people with intellectual disabilities: An interactional study'. *Journal of Intellectual Disability Research* 52: 1165–75.
Arminen, A. (2004) 'Second stories: The salience of interpersonal communication for mutual help in Alcoholics Anonymous'. *Journal of Pragmatics* 36(2): 319–47.
Arminen, I., and Leinonen, M. (2006) 'Mobile phone call openings: Tailoring answers to personalized summonses'. *Discourse Studies* 8(3): 339–68.
Armstrong, L., and McGrane, H. (2003) 'A Bright SPPARC'. *Speech And Language Therapy In Practice* Autumn: 8–10.
Aspinall, P.J. (2001) Operationalising the collection of ethnicity data in studies of the sociology of health and illness. *Sociology of Health & Illness* 23(6): 829–62.
Atkinson, J. M. and Drew, P. (1979) *Order in Court – The Organisation of Verbal Interaction in Judicial Settings*. Atlantic Highlands, NJ: Humanities Press.
Atkinson, J. M. (1984) *Our Master's Voices*. London: Methuen.
Atkinson, J. M. (2004) *Lend Me Your Ears*. London: Vermilion.
Auer, P. and Rönfeldt, B. (2004) 'Prolixity As Adaptation: Prosody And Turn-Taking in German Conversation With A Fluent Aphasic. In E. Couper-Kuhlen and C. E. Ford (eds), *Sound Patterns In Interaction: Cross-Linguistic Studies From Conversation*. Amsterdam, John Benjamins, pp. 171–200.

Baker, C. D., Emmison, M., and Firth, A. (eds) (2005) *Calling for Help: Language and Social Interaction in Telephone Helplines*. Amsterdam: Benjamins.
Barker, M. (1981) *New Racism: Conservatives and the ideology of the tribe*. London: Junction Books.
Bauer, A., and Kulke, F. (2004) 'Language exercises for dinner: Aspects of aphasia management in family settings'. *Aphasiology* 18(12): 1135–60.
Beckman, H., and Frankel, R. (1984) 'The effect of physician behavior on the collection of data'. *Annals of Internal Medicine* 101: 692–6.
Beebe, B., and Lachmann, F. M. (2002) *Infant Research and Adult Treatment: Co-constructing interactions*. Hillsdale, NJ: Analytic Press.
Bellis, A., Aston, J., and Dewson, S. (2009) *Jobseekers Regime Test Site Evaluation: Qualitative research*. DWP Research Report 580, Leeds: Corporate Document Services.
Bentley, R., Hughes, J., Randall, D., Rodden, T., Sawyer, P., Shapiro, D., and Sommerville, I. (1992) 'Ethnographically-informed Systems Design for Air Traffic Control'. *Proceedings of CSCW 92*, ACM, pp. 123–9.
Benwell, B., and Stokoe, E. (2006) *Discourse and Identity*. Edinburgh: Edinburgh University Press.
Bercelli, F., Rossano, F., and Viaro, M. (2008) 'Clients' responses to therapists' reinterpretations'. In A. Peräkylä, C. Antaki, S. Vehviläinen and I. Leudar (eds), *Conversation Analysis and Psychotherapy*. Cambridge: Cambridge University Press, pp. 43–61.
Billig, M. (1987) *Arguing and Thinking. A rhetorical approach to social psychology*. Cambridge: Cambridge University Press.
Bisgaard, S. (2008) *Coping with Emergent Hearing Loss: Expectations and experiences of adult, new hearing aid users. An anthropological study in Denmark*. Dissertation. University of Frankfurt/Main.
Blaxter, M. (1983) 'The causes of disease: Women talking'. *Social Science & Medicine* 17: 59–69.
Bokken, L., Rethans, J. J., van Heurn, L., Duvivier, R., Scherpbier, A., and van der Vleuten, C. (2009) 'Students' views on the use of real patients and simulated patients in undergraduate medical education'. *Academic Medicine* 84(7): 958–63.
Bolinger, D. (1957) *Interrogative Structures of American English*. Alabama: University of Alabama Press.
Bolinger, D. (1978) 'Yes-no questions are not alternative questions'. In H. Hiz (ed.), *Questions*. Dordrecht: Reidel, pp. 87–105.
Booth, S., and Perkins, L. (1999) 'The Use Of Conversation Analysis To Guide Individualised Advice To Carers And Evaluate Change In Aphasia: A Case Study'. *Aphasiology* 13: 283–304.
Booth, S., and Swabey, D. (1999) 'Group Training In Communication Skills For Carers Of Adults With Aphasia'. *International Journal Of Language And Communication Disorders* 34: 291–310.
Borkin, A. (1971) 'Polarity items in questions'. *Chicago Linguistic Society* 7: 53–62.
Boyd, E. A. (1998) 'Bureaucratic authority in the "company of equals": The interactional management of medical peer review'. *American Sociological Review* 63(2): 200–24.
Boyd, E., and Heritage, J. (2006) 'Taking the History: Questioning During Comprehensive History Taking'. In J. Heritage and D. Maynard (eds), *Communication in Medical Care: Interactions between Primary Care Physicians and Patients*. Cambridge: Cambridge University Press, pp. 151–84.

Braun, V., and Clarke, V. (2006) 'Using thematic analysis in psychology'. *Qualitative Research in Psychology* 3: 77–101.
Brouwer, C. E., and Day, D. (2009) *Interaction in the Audiologic Consultation*. Paper presented at the 10th NNDR Conference 2009: *Challenging Positions in Disability Research: Normativity, Knowledge, Praxis*, 2 April 2009.
Brown, J. S. (1983) 'When User Hits Machine'. In *MIT Laboratory for Computer Science Distinguished Lecture Series*. Cambridge, MA.
Brown, P., and Levinson, S. C. (1987) *Politeness: Some Universals of Language Use*. Cambridge: Cambridge University Press.
Bryan, K., and Maxim, J. (1998) 'Enabling staff to relate to older communication disabled people'. *International Journal of Language and Communication Disorders* 33: 121–5.
Burch, K., Wilkinson, R., and Lock, S. (2002) 'A Single Case Study Of Conversation-Focused Therapy For A Couple Where One Partner Has Aphasia'. *British Aphasiology Society Therapy Symposium Conference Proceediings*. British Aphasiology Society.
Burns, A., and Moore, S. (2008) 'Questioning in simulated accountant–client consultations: Exploring implications for ESP teaching'. *English for Specific Purposes* 27: 322–37.
Buttny, R. (1993) *Social Accountability in Communication*. London, Sage.
Button, G., and Casey, N. J. (1984) 'Generating a topic: The use of topic initial elictors'. In J. M. Atkinson and J. Heritage (eds), *Structures of Social Action: Studies in Conversation Analysis*. Cambridge: Cambridge University Press, pp. 167–90.
Buur, J. (2007) *The Participatory Dynamics of User-Driven Innovation (Participatory Innovation)*. Application to the Danish Council for Strategic Research, Programme Commission on Creativity, Innovation, New Production Forms and the Experience Economy (KINO)/User-Driven Innovation.
Buur, J., and Bagger, K. (1999) 'Replacing usability testing with user dialogue'. *Communications of the ACM* 42(5): 63–6.
Buur, J., and Matthews, B. (2008) 'Participatory Innovation'. *International Journal of Innovation Management*. 12(3): 255–73.
Callahan, E., Stange, K., Zyzanski, S., Goodwin, M., Flocke, S., and Bertakis, K. (2004) 'Physician-elder interaction in community family practice'. *Journal of the American Board of Family Practice* 17(1): 19–25.
Cameron. D. (1997) 'Demythologizing sociolinguistics. In N. Coupland and A. Jaworski (eds), *Sociolinguistics: A coursebook and reader*. Basingstoke: Macmillan – now Palgrave Macmillan.
Cameron, D. (2008) 'Talk from the top down'. *Language and Communication* 28: 143–55.
Campanelli, P., and Sturgis, P. (1997) 'Can You Hear Me Knocking: An Investigation into the Impact of Interviewers on Survey Response Rates'. Great Britain: The Survey Methods Centre at SCPR.
Caris-Verhallen, W., Timmermans, L., and van Dulmen, S. (2004) 'Observation of nurse-patient interaction in oncology: Review of assessment instruments'. *Patient Education and Counseling* 54(3): 307–20.
Chomsky, N. (1957) *Syntactic Structures*. The Hague: Mouton de Gruyter.
Christensen, V. T. (2006) *Nedsæt hørelse og føretidig tilbagetrækning, Socialpolitik og velfærdsydelser*. Denmark: Social Forsknings Institut.
Clayman, S. E. (1988) 'Displaying neutrality in television news interviews'. *Social Problems* 35: 474–92.

Clayman, S. E., and Whalen, J. (1988) 'When the medium becomes the message: The case of the Bush-Rather encounter'. *Research on Language and Social Interaction* 22: 241–72.

Clayman, S. E., Heritage, J., Elliott, M. N., and McDonald, L., (2007) 'When Does the Watchdog Bark?: Conditions of Aggressive Questioning in Presidential News Conferences'. *American Sociological Review* 72: 23–41.

Code, C. (2010) 'Aphasia'. In J. Damico, N. Müller and M. Ball (eds), *The Handbook Of Language And Speech Disorders*. Oxford: Blackwell.

Collins, S., Drew, P., Watt, I., and Entwistle, V. (2005) '"Unilateral" and "bilateral" practitioner approaches in decision-making about treatment'. *Social Science & Medicine* 61: 2611–27.

Coulter, J. (1989) *Mind in Action*. Polity Press, Cambridge.

Couper, M. P., and Groves R. M. (2002) 'Introductory Interactions in Telephone Surveys and nonresponse'. In D. W. Maynard, H. Houtkoop-Steenstra, N. C. Schaeffer, and H. v. d. Zouwen (eds), *Standardization and Tacit Knowledge: Interaction and Practice in the Survey Interview*. New York: Wiley Interscience, pp. 161–77

Crabtree, A., Nichols, D., O'Brien, J., Rouncefield, M., and Twidale, M. (1998) *The Contribution of Ethnomethodologically Informed Ethnography to the Process of Designing Digital Libraries*. Lancaster University: Sociology and Computing Departments.

Curl, T. S., and Drew, P. (2008) 'Contingency and action: A comparison of two forms of requesting'. *Research on Language and Social Interaction* 41(2): 129–53.

Davis-Floyd, R. (1992) *Birth as an American Rite of Passage*. Berkeley: University of California Press.

De la Croix, A., and Skelton, J. (2009) 'The reality of role-play: Interruptions and amount of talk in simulated consultations'. *Medical Education* 43: 695–703.

Department for Work and Pensions (2008) *Raising Expectations and Increasing Support: Reforming welfare for the future*. London: The Stationery Office.

Department for Work and Pensions, Research Report 633. Available at: http://php.york.ac.uk/inst/spru/pubs/1742/

Department of Health (UK) (2001) *Valuing People*. London: HMSO.

Department of Health (UK) (2005) *Independence, Well-Being and Choice: Our vision for the future of social care for adults in England*. Green Paper – Consultation Document. London: HMSO.

Deppermann, A. (2009) *Understanding and Cooperation in Doctor-Patient Interaction: Negotiations about a hearing problem*. Presentation at the workshop 'Hearing Aids Communication', Centre for Interdisciplinary Research, Bielefeld.

Dickerson, P. Stribling, P., and Rae, J (2007) 'Tapping into interaction: How children with autistic spectrum disorders design and place tapping in relation to activities in progress'. *Gesture* 7(3): 271–303.

Dickerson, P., Rae, J., Stribling, P., Dautenhahn, K., and Werry, I. (2005) 'Autistic children's co-ordination of gaze and talk: Re-examining the "asocial' autist"'. In K. Richards and K. Seedhouse (eds), *Applying Conversation Analysis*. Basingstoke: Palgrave Macmillan.

Dijkstra, W., and Smit, J. H. (2002) 'Persuading Reluctant Recipients in Telephone Surveys'. In R. Groves, D. Dillman, J. Eltinge and R. Little (eds), *Survey Nonresponse,*. New York: John Wiley & Sons, pp. 135–48.

Dimberg, U. (1982) 'Facial reactions to facial expressions'. *Psychophysiology* 19(6): 643–7.

Drew, P. (1997) '"Open" class repair initiators in response to sequential sources of troubles in conversation'. *Journal of Pragmatics* 28: 69–101.

Drew, P. (2005) 'Foreword: Applied linguistics and Conversation Analysis'. In K. Richards and P. Seedhouse (eds), *Applying Conversation Analysis*. Basingstoke: Palgrave Macmillan, pp. xiv–xxx.

Drew, P. (2010) 'Commentary'. *Journal of Asian Pacific Communication* 20: 303–5.

Drew, P., and Heritage, J (1992a) *Talk at Work: Interaction in institutional settings*. Cambridge: Cambridge University Press.

Drew, P., and Heritage, J. (1992b) 'Analyzing talk at work: An introduction'. In P. Drew and J. Heritage (eds), *Talk at Work: Interaction in institutional settings*. Cambridge: Cambridge University Press, pp. 3–65.

Drew, P., and Holt, E. (1988) 'Complainable Matters: The Use of Idiomatic Expressions in Making Complaints'. *Social Problems* 35: 398–417

Drew, P., and Sorjonen, M. (1997) 'Institutional dialogue'. In T. A. van Dijk (ed.), *Discourse as Social Interaction*. London: Sage.

Drew, P., Toerien, M., Irvine, A., and Sainsbury, R. (2010) *A study of language and communication between advisers and claimants in Work Focused Interviews: Research Report No 633*. London: Department of Work and Pensions. http://research.dwp.gov.uk/asd/asd5/report_abstracts/rr_abstracts/rra_633.asp

Dunn, A. (2010) 'The "dole or drudgery" dilemma: Education, the work ethic and unemployment'. *Social Policy & Administration* 44(1): 1–19.

Edwards, D. (1997) *Discourse and cognition*. London: Sage.

Edwards, D. (2005) 'Moaning, whinging and laughing: The subjective side of complaints'. *Discourse Studies* 7(1): 5–29.

Edwards, D. (ed.) (2007) *Calling for Help*. Special issue of *Research on Language and Social Interaction* 40(1): 1–144.

Edwards, D., and Potter, J. A. (1992) *Discursive Psychology*. London: Sage.

Edwards, D., and Potter, J. (1993) 'Language and causation: A discursive action model of description and attribution'. *Psychological Review* 100(1): 23–41.

Edwards, D., and Potter, J. (2005) 'Discursive Psychology, mental states, and description'. In H. te Molder and J. Potter (eds), *Conversation and Cognition*. Cambridge: Cambridge University Press.

Edwards, D., and Stokoe, E. (2007) 'Self-help in calls for help with problem neighbours'. *Research on Language and Social Interaction* 40(1): 9–32.

Egbert, M., and Deppermann, A. (eds) (in preparation) 'Hearing Aids Communication'. *Zeitschrift für Gesprächsforschung*.

Ekman, P., and Friesen, W. V. (2003) *Unmasking the Face. A Guide to Recognizing Emotions from Facial Clues*. Cambridge, MA: Malor Books.

Enfield, N. J., and Levinson, S. C. (eds) (2006) *Roots of Human Sociality: Culture, cognition and interaction*. New York: Berg.

Enfield, N. J., and Stivers, T. (2007) (eds) *Person Reference in Interaction: Linguistic, Cultural and Social Perspectives*. Cambridge: Cambridge University Press.

Field, T. (1981) 'Gaze behaviour of normal and high-risk infants during early interactions'. *Journal of the Academy of Child Psychiatry* 20(2): 308–17.

Finlay, W. M. L., Antaki, C., and Walton, C. (2007) 'On not being noticed: Intellectual disabilities and the non-vocal register'. *Intellectual and Developmental Disabilities* 45: 227–45.

Finlay, W. M. L., Antaki, C., and Walton, C. (2008a) 'Saying no to the staff: An analysis of refusals in a care home for people with intellectual disabilities'. *Sociology of Health and Illness* 30: 55–75.

Finlay, W. M. L., Walton, C., and Antaki, C. (2008b) 'A manifesto for the use of video in service improvement and staff development in residential services for people with learning disabilities'. *British Journal of Learning Disabilities* 36: 227–31

Finlay, W. M. L., Antaki, C., Walton, C., and Stribling, P. (2008) 'The dilemma for staff in "playing a game" with a person with profound intellectual disabilities: Empowerment, inclusions and choice in interactional practice'. *Sociology of Health and Illness* 30(4): 531–49.

Fizgerald, P. (2009) *The Use of Response Tokens in Person-Centred Solution-Focused Therapy*. Unpublished manuscript.

Francis, D. (1989) 'Game identities and activities: Some ethnomethodological observations. In D. Saunders and D. Crookall (eds), *Communication and simulation: From two fields to one theme*. London: Multilingual Matters, pp. 53–68.

Gafaranga, J., and Britten, N. (2005) 'Talking an institution into being: The opening sequence in general practice consultations'. In K. Richards and P. Seedhouse (eds), *Applying Conversation Analysis*. Basingstoke: Palgrave/Macmillan, pp. 75–90.

Gardner, H. (2006) 'Training others in the art of therapy for speech sound disorders: An interactional approach'. *Child Language Teaching and Therapy* 22: 27–46.

Gardner, R. (2001) *When Listeners Talk: Response tokens and listener stance*. Amsterdam: Benjamins.

Gardner, R. (2007) 'The *right* connections: Acknowledging epistemic progression in talk'. *Language in Society* 36: 319–41.

Garfinkel, H. (1967) *Studies in Ethnomethodology*. Englewood Cliffs, NJ: Prentice-Hall.

Gill, V. T. (1998) 'Doing Attributions in Medical Interaction: Patients' Explanations for Illness and Doctors' Responses'. *Social Psychology Quarterly* 61: 342–60.

Glenn, P. (2003) *Laughter in Interaction*. Cambridge: Cambridge University Press.

Goffman, E. (1979) 'Footing'. *Semiotica* 25(1–2): 1–29.

Goodglass, H., Kaplan, E., and Barresi, B. (2001) *The Boston Diagnostic Aphasia Examination (BDAE)*, 3rd edn. Baltimore, MD: Lippincott Williams & Wilkins.

Goodwin, C. (1984) 'Notes on Story Structure and the Organization of Participation'. In M. Atkinson and J. Heritage (eds), *Structures of Social Action*. Cambridge: Cambridge University Press, pp. 225–46.

Goodwin, C. (1987) Forgetfulness As An Interactive Resource. *Social Psychology Quarterly* 50, 115–130.

Goodwin, C. (1995) 'Co-Constructing Meaning in Conversations with an Aphasic Man'. *Research On Language And Social Interaction* 28: 233–60.

Goodwin, C. (2003a) 'Conversational frameworks for the accomplishment of meaning in aphasia'. In C. Goodwin (ed.), *Conversation and Brain Damage*. New York: Oxford University Press, pp. 90–116.

Goodwin, C. (ed.) (2003b) *Conversation and Brain Damage*. New York: Oxford University Press.

Goodwin, C. (2007) 'Language, Culture, Social Organization and the Material Word: Why a Five Field Approach is Necessary'. *Teaching Anthropology: SACC Notes* 13(2): 5–9, 34.

Goodwin, C., and Goodwin, M. H. (1987). 'Concurrent Operations on Talk: Notes on the Interactive Organization of Assessments'. *IPrA Papers in Pragmatics* 1(1): 1–52.

Goodwin, C., and Goodwin, M. H. (1990) 'Interstitial Argument'. In A. Grimshaw (ed.), *Conflict Talk*. Cambridge: Cambridge University Press, pp. 85–117.

Goodwin, M. H. (1980) 'Processes of mutual monitoring implicated in the production of description sequences'. *Sociological Inquiry* 50(3–4): 303–17.

Greatbatch, D. (1988) 'A turn talking system for British news interviews'. *Language in Society* 17: 401–30.
Greatbatch, D., Heath, C., Campion, P., and Luff, P. (1995) 'How do desk-top computers affect the doctor-patient interaction?' *Family Practice* 12: 32–6.
Gregg, P. (2008) *Realising Potential: A vision for personalised conditionality and support*. An independent report to the Department for Work and Pensions.
Grice, H. P. (1975) 'Logic and Conversation'. In P. Cole and J. L. Morgan (eds), *Syntax and Semantics: Volume 3, Speech Acts*. New York: Academic Press, pp. 43–58.
Griffin, C. (2007) 'Being dead and being there: Research interviews, sharing hand cream and the preference for analysing "naturally occurring data"'. *Discourse Studies* 9(2): 246–69.
Gross, J. J. (1998) 'The Emerging field of emotion regulation: An integrative review'. *Review of General Psychology* 2(3): 271–99.
Groves, Robert M., and Couper, M. P. (1996) 'Contact Level Influences on Cooperation in Face-to-Face Surveys'. *Journal of Official Statistics* 12: 63–83.
Groves, Robert M., and Couper, M. P.(1998) *Nonresponse in Household Interview Surveys*. New York: Wiley.
Hauser, R. M. (2005) 'Survey Response in the Long Run: The Wisconsin Longitudinal Study'. *Field Methods* 17: 3–29.
Heath, Christian (1981) 'The opening sequence in doctor-patient interaction'. In P. Atkinson and C. Heath (eds), *Medical Work: Realities and Routines*. Farnborough: Gower, pp. 71–90
Heath, C. (1986) *Body Movement and Speech in Medical Interaction*. Cambridge: Cambridge University Press
Heath, C., and Luff, P. (1992) 'Collaboration and Control Crisis Management and Multimedia Technology in London Underground Line Control Rooms'. *Computer Supported Cooperative Work (Cscw)* 19: 69–94.
Heath, C., Sanchez Svensson, M., et al. (2002) 'Configuring awareness'. *Computer Supported Cooperative Work* 11(3–4): 317–47.
Heeschen, C., and Schegloff, E. A. (1999) 'Agrammatism, Adaptation Theory, Conversation Analysis: On The Role Of So-Called Telegraphic Style In Talk-In-Interaction'. *Aphasiology* 13: 365
Heeschen, C., and Schegloff, E. A. (2003) 'Aphasic Agrammatism As Interactional Artifact And Achievement'. In C. Goodwin (ed.), *Conversation And Brain Damage*. New York: Oxford University Press.
Heinemann, T, Mitchell, R., and Buur, J. (ms) *Co-Constructing Meaning with Materials in Innovation Workshops*.
Heinemann, T. (2006) '"Will You or Can't You?": Displaying Entitlement in Interrogative Requests'. *Journal of Pragmatics* 38: 1081–104.
Hepburn, A. (2004) 'Crying: Notes on description, transcription and interaction'. *Research on Language and Social Interaction* 37(3): 251–90.
Hepburn, A., and Potter, J. (2003) 'Discourse analytic practice'. In C. Seale, D. Silverman, J. Gubrium, and G. Bobo (eds), *Qualitative Research Practice*. London: Sage, pp. 180–96.
Hepburn, A., and Wiggins, S. (eds) (2007) *Discursive Research in Practice. New approaches to psychology and interaction*. Cambridge: Cambridge University Press.
Heritage, J. (1984a) *Garfinkel and Ethnomethodology*. Oxford: Polity Press.
Heritage, J. (1984b) 'A Change-of-State Token and Aspects of its Sequential Placement'. In J. M. Atkinson and J. Heritage (eds), *Structures Of Social Action: Studies In Conversation Analysis*. Cambridge: Cambridge University Press.

Heritage, J. (1988) 'Explanations as accounts: A conversation analytic perspective'. In C. Antaki (ed.), *Analysing Everyday Explanation: A casebook of methods*. London: Sage, pp. 127–44.

Heritage, J. (1995) 'Conversation Analysis: Methodological Aspects'. In U. M. Quasthoff (ed.), *Aspects Of Oral Communication*. Berlin: Walter De Gruyter.

Heritage, J. (1997) 'Conversation analysis and institutional talk'. In D. Silverman (ed.), *Qualitative Research: Theory, method and practice*. London: Sage, pp. 161–82.

Heritage, J. (1998) '*Oh*-prefaced responses to inquiry'. *Language in Society* 27:291–334.

Heritage, J. (2005) 'Conversation analysis and institutional talk'. In K. L. Fitch and R. E. Sanders (eds), *Handbook of Language and Social Interaction*. Mahwah, NJ: Lawrence Erlbaum.

Heritage, J. (2009) 'Conversation analysis as an approach to the medical encounter'. In J. B. McKinlay and L. Marceau (eds), e-Source: *Behavioral and Social Science Research Interactive Textbook*. www.esourceresearch.org (accessed 10.01.10).

Heritage, J. (2010a) 'Conversation Analysis: Practices and Methods'. In D. Silverman (ed.), *Qualitative Sociology*, 3rd edn. London: Sage, pp. 208–30.

Heritage, J. (2010b) 'Questioning in Medicine'. In A. Freed and S. Ehrlich (eds), *'Why Do You Ask?': The Function of Questions in Institutional Discourse*. New York: Oxford University Press, pp. 42–68.

Heritage, J. (2011) 'The Interaction Order and Clinical Practice: Some Observations on Dysfunctions and Action Steps.' *Patient Education and Counseling*.

Heritage, J. C., and Atkinson, J. M. (1984) Introduction. In J. M. Atkinson and J. Heritage (eds), *Structures of Social Action: Studies in conversation analysis*. Cambridge: Cambridge University Press, pp. 1–16.

Heritage, J., and Clayman, S. E. (2010) *Talk in Action: Interactions, Identities and Institutions*. Oxford: Blackwell-Wiley.

Heritage, J., and Maynard, D. W. (2006) *Communication in Medical Care*. Cambridge: Cambridge University Press.

Heritage, J., and Raymond, G. (frth) 'Navigating Epistemic Landscapes: Acquiescence, Agency and Resistance in Responses to Polar Questions'. In J.-P. De Ruiter (ed.), *Questions: Formal, functional and interactional perspectives*. Cambridge: Cambridge University Press.

Heritage, J., and Robinson, J. D. (2006a) 'Accounting for the visit: Giving reasons for seeking medical care'. In J. Heritage and D. Maynard (eds), *Communication in Medical Care: Interactions between Primary Care Physicians and Patients*. Cambridge: Cambridge University Press, pp. 48–85.

Heritage, J., and Robinson, J. (2006b) 'The Structure of Patients' Presenting Concerns: Physicians' Opening Questions'. *Health Communication* 19(2): 89–102.

Heritage, J., and Sorjonen, M-L. (1994) 'Constituting and maintaining activities across sequences: *And*-prefacing as a feature of question design'. *Language in Society* 27: 291–334.

Heritage, J., Elliott, M., Stivers, T., Richardson, A., and Mangione-Smith, R. (2010) 'Reducing antibiotics prescribing: The role of online commentary'. *Patient Education and Counseling*.

Heritage, J., Robinson, J. D., Elliott, M., Beckett, M., and Wilkes, M. (2007) 'Reducing patients' unmet concerns: The difference one word can make'. *Journal of General Internal Medicine* 22: 1429–33.

Hesketh, A., and Sage, K. (eds) (1999) *Aphasiology Special Issue: Conversation Analysis* 13(4–5).

Hester, S., and Francis, D. (2001) 'Is institutional talk a phenomenon? Reflections on ethnomethodology and applied conversation analysis'. In A. McHoul and M. Rapley (eds), *How to Analyse Talk in Institutional Settings*. London: Continuum.
Hetu, R. (1996) 'The stigma attached to hearing impairment'. *Scandinavian Audiology* 25, suppl. 43: 12–24.
Hillbrand, M., Hawkins, D., Howe, D. M., and Stayner, D. (2008) 'Through the eyes of another: Improving the skills of forensic providers using a consumer-informed role-play procedure'. *Psychiatric Rehabilitation Journal* 31(3): 239–42.
Hindmarsh, J., and Pilnick, A. (2002) 'The tacit order of teamwork: Collaboration and embodied conduct in anaesthesia'. *The Sociological Quarterly* 43: 139–64.
Hollander, M. (2008) *The Interactional Organization of Telephone Survey Openings*. Unpublished MA Diss. Department of Sociology. Madison: University of Wisconsin.
Holstein, J. A. (1988) 'Court-Ordered Incompetence: Conversational Organization in Involuntary Commitment Hearings'. *Social Problems* 34: 458–74.
Holt, E., and Clift, R. (2007) *Reporting Talk: Reported speech in interaction*. Cambridge: Cambridge University Press.
Horn, L. R. (1978) 'Some aspects of negation'. In J. H. Greenberg, C. A. Ferguson, E. A. Moravscik (eds), *Universals of Human Language, Vol. 4: Syntax*. Stanford, CA: Stanford University Press, pp. 127–210.
Houtkoop-Steenstra, H. (2000) *Interaction and the Standardized Interview: The living questionnaire*. Cambridge: Cambridge University Press.
Houtkoop-Steenstra, H., and van-den Bergh, H. (2002) 'Effects of Introductions in Large Scale Telephone Survey Interviews'. In D. W. Maynard, H. Houtkoop-Steenstra, N. C. Schaeffer and H. v. d. Zouwen (eds), *Standardization and Tacit Knowledge: Interaction and Practice in the Survey Interview*. New York: Wiley Interscience, pp. 205–18.
Hutchby, I., and Barnett, S. (2005) 'Aspects of the sequential organization of mobile phone conversation'. *Discourse Studies* 7(2): 147–71.
Irvine, A., Sainsbury, R., Drew, P., and Toerien, M. (2010) *An exploratory comparison of the interactions between advisers and younger and older clients during work focused interviews*. London: Department for Work and Pensions. Research Report 634. Available at: http://php.york.ac.uk/inst/spru/pubs/1744/.
James, D., and Clarke, S. (1993) 'Women, men, and interruptions: A critical review. In D. Tannen (ed.), *Gender and Conversational Interaction*. Oxford: Oxford University Press.
James, D., and Drakich, J. (1993) 'Understanding gender differences in amount of talk: A critical review of research. In D. Tannen (ed.), *Gender and Conversational Interaction*. Oxford: Oxford University Press.
Jefferson, G. (1978) 'Sequential aspects of story telling in conversation'. In J. N. Schenkein (ed.), *Studies in the Organization of Conversational Interaction*. New York: Academic Press, pp. 13–48.
Jefferson, G. (1984) 'Transcription notation'. In J. M. Atkinson and J. Heritage (eds), *Structures of Social Action: Studies in conversation analysis*. Cambridge: Cambridge University Press, pp. ix–xvi.
Jefferson, G. (1988) 'On the Sequential Organization of Troubles-Talk in Ordinary Conversation'. *Social Problems* 35: 418–41.
Jefferson, G. (2004) 'Glossary of transcript symbols with an introduction'. In G. Lerner (ed.), *Conversation Analysis: Studies from the first generation*. Amsterdam: John Benjamins.

Jefferson, G., and Lee, J. R. E. (1981) 'The rejection of advice: Managing the problematic convergence of a "troubles-telling" and a "service encounter"', *Journal of Pragmatics* 5: 399–422.

Jingree, T., Finlay, M., and Antaki, C. (2006) 'Empowering words, disempowering actions: An analysis of interactions between staff members and people with learning disabilities in residents' meetings'. *Journal of Intellectual Disability Research* 50: 212–26.

Jones, A. (2007) 'Putting practice into teaching: An exploratory study of nursing undergraduates' interpersonal skills and the effects of using empirical data as a teaching and learning resource'. *Journal of Clinical Nursing* 16: 2297–307.

Kagan, A., Black, S. E., Duchan, J. F., Simmons-Mackie, N., and Square, P. (2001) 'Training Volunteers as Conversation Partners Using "Supported Conversation for Adults with Aphasia" (SCA): A Controlled Trial'. *Journal Of Speech, Language And Hearing Research* 44: 624–38.

Kappas, A. (2008) 'Psssst! Dr. Jekyll and Mr. Hyde are actually the same person! A tale of regulation and emotion'. In M. M.P. Vandekerckhove, C. von Scheve, S. Ismer and S. Kronast (eds), *Regulating Emotions: Social necessity and biological inheritance*. Oxford: Blackwell, pp. 15–38.

Kitzinger, C. (2000) 'Doing feminist conversation analysis'. *Feminism & Psychology* 10: 163–93.

Kitzinger, C. (2003) 'Feminist approaches to qualitative research practice'. In C. Seale, J. Gubrium and D. Silverman (eds), *Qualitative Research Practice*. London: Sage, pp. 125–40.

Kitzinger, C. (2005a) 'Heteronormativity in action: Reproducing the heterosexual nuclear family in "after hours" medical calls'. *Special Section: Language Interaction and Social Problems, Social Problems* 52(4): 477–98.

Kitzinger, C. 2005b. 'Flashbacks, nightmares, panic attacks: why?' *Royal College of Obstetricians and Gynaecologists and British Maternal and Fetal Medicine Society Course on Management of the Labour Ward*, London: 3–7 October.

Kitzinger, C. (2008a) 'Developing feminist conversation analysis'. *Human Studies* 31: 179–208.

Kitzinger, C. (2008b) 'Keynote Address: Calling the helpline'. *Pelvic Partnership Annual Conference: PGP/SDP – A dynamic approach*, 11 October. Tara Towers Hotel, Dublin.

Kitzinger, C. (2008c) 'Conversation analysis: Technical matters for gender research'. In K. Harrington, L. Litosseliti, H. Saunston and J. Sunderland (eds), *Gender and Language Research Methodologies*. Basingstoke: Palgrave Macmillan.

Kitzinger, C., and Frith, H. (1999) 'Just Say No? The Use of Conversation Analysis in Developing a Feminist Perspective on Sexual Refusal'. *Discourse and Society* 10(3): 293–316.

Kitzinger, C., and Rickford, R. (2007) 'Becoming a "bloke": The construction of gender in interaction'. *Feminism & Psychology* 17: 214–22.

Kitzinger, C., and Wilkinson, S. (1997) 'Validating women's experience? Dilemmas in feminist research'. *Feminism & Psychology* 7: 566–74.

Kitzinger, C., and Kitzinger, S. (2007) 'Birth trauma: Talking with women and the value of conversation analysis'. *British Journal of Midwifery* 15(5): 256–64.

Kitzinger, S. (2006) *Birth Crisis*. London: Routledge.

Koelen, M. A., and Van den Ban, A. (2004) *Health Education and Health Promotion*. Wageningen, The Netherlands: Wageningen Academic Publishers.

Koelen, M. A., Vaandrager, L., and Colomer, C. (2001) 'Health promotion research: Dilemmas and challenges'. *Journal of Epidemiology and Community Health* 55(4): 257–62.
Koole, T., and Padmos, H. (1999) 'Gesprekstraining en gespreksanalyse: Een literatuurstudie' [Conversation skills training and conversation analysis: A review of the literature]. *Tijdschrift voor Taalbeheersing* 1: 49–62.
Kreuter, M. W., Lezin, N. A., and Young, L. A. (2000) 'Evaluating community-based collaborative mechanisms: Implications for practitioners'. *Health Promotion Practice* 1(1): 49–63.
Laakso, M., and Klippi, A. (1999) 'A Closer Look At The "Hint And Guess" Sequences In Aphasic Conversation'. *Aphasiology* 13: 345–64.
Lakoff, R. (1973) 'Language and woman's place'. *Language in Society* 2: 45–79.
Lamerichs, J., and te Molder, H. F. M. (2009) '"And then I'm really like...": The role of fuzzy self-quotations in adolescent talk'. *Discourse Studies* 11(4): 369–87.
Lamerichs, J., Koelen, M., te Molder, H. F. M., and van Nierop, P. (2006) *De discursieve actie methode: Jongeren ontwikkelen gezondheidsinterventies [The discursive action method: Adolescents develop health interventions]*. Wageningen, The Netherlands: Communication Strategies, Wageningen UR, and Municipal Health Services Eindhoven, The Netherlands.
Land, V., and Kitzinger, C. (2007) 'Some uses of third-person reference forms in speaker self-reference'. In G. Lerner and C. Kitzinger (eds), *Person-reference in conversation analytic research*. Special issue of *Discourse Studies* 9(4): 493–525.
Lane, C., and Rollnick, S. (2007) 'The use of simulated patients and role-play in communication skills training: A review of the literature to August 2005'. *Patient Education and Counseling* 67: 13–20.
Lane, C., Hood, K., and Rollnick, S. (2008) 'Teaching motivational interviewing: Using role-play is as effective as using simulated patients'. *Medical Education* 42: 637–44.
Larsen, H. (2005) *Spontaneity and Power: Theatre Improvisations as Processes of Change in Organizations*. Dissertation, University of Hertfordshire, England.
Lawson, R., and Fawcus, M. (1999) 'Increasing Effective Communication Using a Total Communication Approach'. In S. Byng, K. Swinburn and C. Pound (eds), *The Aphasia Therapy File*. Hove: Psychology Press.
Lee, E. K. O., Goforth, K., and Blythe, B. (2009) 'Can you call it racism? An educational case study and role-play approach'. *Journal of Social Work Education* 45(1): 123–30.
Leising, D., Rehbein, D., and Sporberg, D. (2007) 'Validity of the inventory of interpersonal problems (IIP-64) for predicting assertiveness in role-play situations'. *Journal of Personality Assessment* 89(2): 116–25.
Lerner, G. (2004) 'Introductory remarks'. In G. Lerner (ed.), *Conversation Analysis: Studies from the first generation*. Amsterdam and Philadelphia: John Benjamins, pp. 1–12
Lerner, G., and Kitzinger, C. (eds) (2007) *Person-reference in conversation analytic research*. Special issue of *Discourse Studies* 9(4).
Levinson, S. C. (1983) *Pragmatics*. Cambridge University Press.
Levinson, S. C. (2006a) 'On the human "interaction engine"'. In N. J. Enfield and S. C. Levinson (eds), *Roots of Human Sociality: Culture, cognition and interaction*. New York: Berg, pp. 39–69.
Levinson, S. C (2006b) 'Cognition at the heart of human interaction'. *Discourse Studies* 8(1): 85–93.

Levinson, S. C., and Enfield, N. J. (2006) 'Introduction: Human sociality as a new interdisciplinary field'. In N. J. Enfield and S. C. Levinson (eds), *Roots of Human Sociality: Culture, cognition and interaction*. New York, Berg, pp. 1–38.

Lim, E. C. H., Oh, V. M. S., and Seet, R. C. S. (2008) 'Overcoming preconceptions and perceived barriers to medical communication using a "dual role-play" training course'. *Internal Medicine Journal* 38(9): 708–13.

Lindström, A. (2005) 'Language as Social Action: A Study of How Senior Citizens Request Assistance with Practical Tasks in the Swedish Home Help Service'. In A. Hakulinen and M. Selting (eds), *Syntax and Lexis in Conversation: Studies on the Use of Linguistic Resources in Talk-in-Interaction*. Amsterdam: Benjamins, pp. 209–30.

Linell, P., and Thunqvist, D. P. (2003) 'Moving in and out of framings: Activity contexts in talks with young unemployed people within a training project'. *Journal of Pragmatics* 35: 409–34.

Lock, S., Wilkinson, R., and Bryan, K. (2001) *Supporting Partners of People with Aphasia in Relationships and Conversation (SPPARC): A Resource Pack*. Bicester: Speechmark.

Luff, P., Heath, Ch., and Pitsch, K. (2009) 'Indefinite precision: The use of artefacts-in-interaction in design work'. In C. Jewitt (ed.), *The Routledge Handbook of Multimodal Analysis*. London: Routledge, pp. 213–24.

Maguire, P., and Pitceathly, C. (2002) 'Key communication skills and how to acquire them'. *British Medical Journal* 325: 697–700.

Malone, T. (1983) 'How Do People Organize Their Desks? Implicaitons for the Design of Office Information Systems'. *ACM Transactions of Office Information Systems* 1(1): 99–112.

Mangione-Smith, R., Elliott, M. N., Stivers, T., McDonald, L. L., and Heritage, J. (2006) 'Ruling out the need for antibiotics: Are we sending the right message?' *Archives of Pediatric and Adolescent Medicine* 160: 945–52.

Marvel, M. K., Epstein, R. M., Flowers, K., and Beckman, H. B. (1999) 'Soliciting the patient's agenda: Have we improved?' *Journal of the American Medical Association* 281(3): 283–7.

Mates, A .W., Mikesell, L., and Smith M. S. (eds) (2010) *Language, Interaction and Frontotemporal Dementia: Reverse engineering the social mind*. London and Oakville, CT: Equinox.

Maynard, D. W. (1988) 'Language, Interaction, and Social Problems'. *Social Problems* 35: 311–34.

Maynard, D. W. (2003) *Bad News, Good News: Conversational Order in Everyday Talk and Clinical Settings*. Chicago: University of Chicago Press.

Maynard, D. W., Freese, J., and Schaeffer, N. C. (2010) 'Calling for Participation: Requests, Blocking Moves, and Rational (Inter)action in Survey Introductions'. *American Sociological Review* 75: 791–814.

Maynard, D. W., and Hollander, M. M. (2010) 'Asking to Speak with Another: An Everyday Skill for the Telephone and Obtaining Survey Participation'. Madison WI: Department of Sociology, University of Wisconsin.

Maynard, D. W., Houtkoop-Steenstra, H., Schaeffer, N. C., and Zouwen, J. van der (eds) (2002) *Standardization and Tacit Knowledge: Interaction and Practice in the Survey Interview*. New York: Wiley Interscience.

Maynard, D. W., and Schaeffer, N. C. (1997) 'Closing the Gate: Declinations of the Request to Participate in a Telephone Survey Interview'. *Sociological Methods & Research* 26: 34–79.

Maynard, D. W., and Schaeffer, N. C. (2000) 'Toward a Sociology of Social Scientific Knowledge: Survey Research and Ethnomethodology's Asymmetric Alternates'. *Social Studies of Science* 30: 264–312.
Maynard, D. W., and Schaeffer, N. C. (2002) 'Refusal Conversion and Tailoring'. In D. W. Maynard, H. Houtkoop-Steenstra, N. C. Schaeffer and H. v. d. Zouwen (eds), *Standardization and Tacit Knowledge: Interaction and Practice in the Survey Interview*. New York: Wiley Interscience, pp. 219–39.
McGuire, P., and Pitceathly, C. 2002. 'Key communication skills and how to acquire them'. *British Medical Journal* 325 (28 September): 697–700.
McHoul, A. (1978) 'The organization of turns at formal talk in the classroom'. *Language in Society* 7: 183–213.
McHoul, A., and Rapley, M. (2003) 'What can psychological terms actually do? (Or: if Sigmund calls, tell him it didn't work)'. *Journal of Pragmatics* 35: 507–22.
McKay, S., and Smith, S. Y. (1993) 'What are they talking about? Is something wrong? Information sharing during the second stage of labor'. *Birth* 20(3): 142–7.
Mehan, H., and Wills, J. (1988) 'MEND: A Nurturing Voice in the Nuclear Arms Debate'. *Social Problems* 35(4): 363–83.
Meis, M., and Gabriel, B. (2006) 'Barriers in the supply with hearing systems: The view of the customer'. *Proceedings of the 51st International Congress on Hearing Aid Acousticians*, 10–20 October 2006 in Frankfurt/Main.
Mikesell, L. (2009) 'Conversational practices of a frontotemporal dementia patient and his interlocutors'. *Research on Language and Social Interaction* 42: 135–62.
Mitchell, S. A. (2000) *Relationality: From attachment to intersubjectivity*. Hillsdale, NJ: The Analytic Press.
Mjaaland, T. A., and Finset, A. (2009) 'Communication skills training for general practitioners to promote patient coping: The GRIP approach'. *Patient Education and Counseling* 76: 84–90.
Mondada, L. (2003) 'Working with video: How surgeons produce video records of their actions'. *Visual Studies* 18: 58–73.
Mondada, L. (2009) 'Emergent focused interactions in public places: A systematic analysis of the multimodal achievement of a common interactional space'. *Journal of Pragmatics* 41: 1977–97.
Morton-Williams, J. (1993) *Interviewer Approaches*. Brookfield, VT: Dartmouth Publishing.
Morton-Williams, J., and Young, P. 1987. 'Obtaining the Survey Interview – An Analysis of Tape Recorded Doorstep Introductions'. *Journal of the Market Research Society* 29: 35–52.
Mounsey, A. L., Bovbjerg, V., White, L., and Gazewood, J. (2006) 'Do students develop better motivational interviewing skills through role-play with standardised patients or with student colleagues?' *Medical Education* 40(8): 775–80.
Müller, F, E. (1996) 'Affiliating and Disaffiliating with Continuers: Prosodic Aspects of Recipiency'. In E. Couper-Kuhlen and M. Selting (eds), *Prosody in Conversation: Interactional Studies*. Cambridge: Cambridge University Press, pp. 131–76.
National Audit Office (2006) *Jobcentre Plus: Delivering effective services through personal advisers*. Report by the Comptroller and Auditor General; HC 24 Session 2006–2007.
Nevile, M. (2004) *Beyond the Black Box: Talk-in-interaction in the airline cockpit*. Aldershot: Ashgate.
Nickels, L. (2002) 'Therapy For Naming Disorders: Revisiting, Revising And Reviewing'. *Aphasiology* 16: 935–79.

Niewenhuis, R. (2005) 'SPPARC In Action'. *Bulletin Of The Royal College Of Speech And Language Therapists* May: 5.
Nolen, J. (2008) *Entitlement, Contingency, and Presumption in the Request for Survey Participation*. Unpublished MA Diss. Department of Sociology. Madison: University of Wisconsin.
Novak, P., and Spranz-Fogasy, Th. (2010) *Literatur zur Arzt-Patient-Kommunikation*. Institut für deutsche Sprache. http://hypermedia.ids-mannheim.de/gais/pdf/Bibliografie_zur_Arzt-Patient-Kommunikation.pdf (accessed July 2010).
O'Baugh, J., Wilkes, L. M., Sneesby, K., and George, A. (2009) 'Investigation into the communication that takes place between nurses and patients during chemotherapy'. *Journal of Psychosocial Oncology* 27(4): 396–414.
Oakley, A. (1980) *Women Confined: Towards a Sociology of Childbirth*. Oxford: Martin Robertson.
Ochs, E., Gonzales, P., and Jacoby, S. (1996a) 'When I come down I'm in the domain state: Grammar and graphic representation in the interpretive activity of physicists'. In E. Ochs, E., Schegloff and S. Thompson (eds), *Interaction and Grammar*. Cambridge: Cambridge University Press.
Ochs, E., Schegloff, E., and Thompson, S. (eds) (1996b) *Interaction and Grammar*. Cambridge: Cambridge University Press.
Office for National Statistics website: http://www.ons.gov.uk/census/ (Accessed 10 July 2010)
Oh, S.-Y. (2007) 'Overt reference to speaker and recipient in Korean'. In G. Lerner and C. Kitzinger (eds), *Person-Reference in Conversation Analytic Research*. Special issue of *Discourse Studies* 9: 462–92.
Okada, Y. (2010) 'Role-play in oral proficiency interviews: Interactive footing and interactional competencies'. *Journal of Pragmatics* 42: 1647–68
Palmieri, G., Margison, F., Guthrie, E., Moorey, J., Hardy, G., Evans, C., Barkham, M., and Rigatelli, M. (2007) 'A preliminary study of a measure of role-play competence in psychodynamic interpersonal therapy'. *Psychology and Psychotherapy-Theory Research and Practice* 80: 327–31.
Parker, I. (2005) *Qualitative Psychology: Introducing radical research*. Buckingham: Open University Press.
Pelz, C. (2007) *Das Stigma Schwerhörigkeit – Empirische Studien und Ansätze zur Erhöhung der Akzeptanz von Hörgeräten*. Germany: Median Verlag.
Peräkylä, A. (1995) *AIDS Counselling: Institutional Interaction and Clinical Practice*. Cambridge: Cambridge University Press.
Peräkylä, A. (2004) 'Making links in psychoanalytic interpretations: A conversation analytic view'. *Psychotherapy Research* 14(3): 289–307.
Peräkylä, A. (2005) 'Patients' responses to interpretations: A dialogue between conversation analysis and psychoanalytic theory'. *Communication & Medicine* 2(2): 163–76.
Peräkylä, A. (2008) 'Conversation analysis and psychoanalysis: Interpretation, affect and intersubjectivity'. In A. Peräkylä, C. Antaki, S. Vehviläinen and I. Leudar (eds), *Conversation Analysis and Psychotherapy*. Cambridge: Cambridge University Press, pp. 100–19.
Peräkylä, A. (2009) 'Mieli ja sosiaalisessa vuorovaikutuksessa'. *Sosiologia* 46(4): 251–68.
Peräkylä, A. (2010) 'Shifting the perspective after the patient's response to an interpretation'. *International Journal of Psychoanalysis* 91(6): 1363–84.
Peräkylä, A., and Ruusuvuori, J. (2006) 'Facial expression in an assessment'. In H. J. Knoblauch, B. Schnettler, J. Raab and H.-G. Soeffner (eds), *Video-Analysis: Methodology*

and methods. *Qualitative audiovisual data analysis in sociology*. Frankfurt: Peter Lang, pp. 127–42.
Peräkylä, A., and Vehviläinen, S. (2003) 'Conversation analysis and the professional stocks of interactional knowledge'. *Discourse & Society* 14: 727–50.
Peräkylä, A., Antaki, C., Vehviläinen, S., and Leudar, I. (2008) 'Analysing psychotherapy in practice'. In A. Peräkylä, C. Antaki, S. Vehviläinen and I. Leudar (eds), *Conversation Analysis and Psychotherapy*. Cambridge: Cambridge University Press, pp. 5–25.
Pieterse, A. H., van Dulmen, A. M., Beemer, F. A., Ausems, M. G. E. M., and Bensing, J. M. (2006) 'Tailoring communication in cancer genetic counseling through individual video-supported feedback: A controlled pretest-posttest design'. *Patient Education and Counseling* 60: 326–35.
Pomerantz, A. (1986) 'Extreme case formulations: A way of legitimizing claims'. *Human Studies* 9: 219–29.
Pomerantz, A. M. (1988a) 'Offering a Candidate Answer: An Information Seeking Strategy'. *Communication Monographs* 55: 360–73.
Pomerantz, A. (1988b) 'Telling my side'. *Sociological Inquiry* 50: 186–98.
Pomerantz, A., and Fehr, B. J. (1997) 'Conversation Analysis: An Approach to the Study of Social Action as Sense Making Practices'. In T. A. van Dijk (ed.), *Discourse as Social Interaction*. London: Sage Publications, pp. 64–91.
Potter, J. (1996) *Representing Reality: Discourse, rhetoric and social construction*. London: Sage.
Potter, J. (2002). 'Two kinds of natural'. *Discourse Studies* 4(4): 539–42.
Potter, J. (2006) 'Cognition and conversation'. *Discourse Studies* 8(1): 131–40.
Potter, J., and Hepburn, A. (2005) 'Qualitative interviews in psychology. Problems and possibilities'. *Qualitative Research in Psychology* 2: 38–55.
Potter, J., Edwards, D., and Wetherell, M. (1993) 'A model of discourse in action'. *American Behavioral Scientist* 36: 383–401.
Premack, D. (1976) 'Language and intelligence in ape and man'. *American Scientist* 64(6): 674–83.
ProMatura (2007a) *Exploring the Consumer's Journey: A Report of an In-Depth Survey with Hearing Aid Users to Learn What Impacts Their Sense of Delight with Their Hearing Aid*. February, Hearing Industries Association.
ProMatura (2007b) *Report of Four Focus Groups with Hearing Aid Users to Define the Best Practices for Dispensing Hearing Instruments that will Improve the Success Rate*. 21 August, Hearing Industries Association.
Rapley, M. (2004) *The Social Construction of Intellectual Disability*. Cambridge: Cambridge University Press.
Rapley, M., and Antaki, C. (1996) 'A conversation analysis of the acquiescence of people with learning disabilities'. *Journal of Community and Applied Psychology* 6: 371–91.
Rapley, T. (2001) 'The art(fullness) of open-ended interviewing: Some considerations on analyzing interviews'. *Qualitative Research* 1(3): 303–23.
Raymond, G. (2003) 'Grammar And Social Organization: Yes/No Interrogatives and the Structure of Responding'. *American Sociological Review* 68: 939–67.
Raymond, G., and Zimmerman, D. H. (2007) 'Rights and responsibilities in calls for help: The case of the Mountain Glade fire'. *Research on Language and Social Interaction* 36: 197–240.
Reid, M. (2008) 'Close encounter with planet Jobcentre'. *The Times*, 30 December: 20.

Reuber, M., et al. (2009) 'Using interactional and linguistic analysis to distinguish between epileptic and psychogenic nonepileptic seizures: a prospective, blinded multirater study'. *Epilepsy Behaviour* 16(1): 139–44.

Richards, K. (2005a) Introduction. In K. Richards and P. Seedhouse (eds), *Applying Conversation Analysis*. Basingstoke: Palgrave Macmillan, pp. 1–15

Richards, K., and Seedhouse, P. (eds) (2005b) *Applying Conversation Analysis*. Basingstoke: Palgrave Macmillan.

Roberts, C., Davies, E., and Jupp, T. (1992) *Language and Discrimination: A study of communication in multi-ethnic workplaces*. London: Longman.

Robinson, J. D. (2001) 'Closing medical encounters: Two physician practices and their implications for the expression of patients' unstated concerns'. *Social Science and Medicine* 53(5): 639–56.

Robinson, J. D. (2006) 'Soliciting patients' presenting concerns'. In J. Heritage, and D. W. Maynard (eds), *Communication in Medical Care*. Cambridge: Cambridge University Press, pp. 22–47.

Robinson, J. D. (2007) 'The role of numbers and statistics within conversation analysis'. *Communication Methods and Measures* 1: 65–75.

Robinson, J., and Heritage, J. (2005) 'The Structure of Patients' Presenting Concerns: The Completion Relevance of Current Symptoms'. *Social Science and Medicine* 61: 481–93.

Robinson, J. D., and Heritage, J. (2006) 'Physicians' Opening Questions and Patients' Satisfaction'. *Patient Education and Counseling* 60: 279–85.

Robinson, J. D., and Stivers, T. (2001) 'Achieving activity transitions in primary-care encounters: From history taking to physical examination'. *Human Communication Research* 27(2): 253–98.

Rogers, S., and Evans, J. (2007) 'Rethinking role play in the Reception class'. *Educational Research* 49 (2): 153–67.

Roose, H., Lievens, J., and Waege, H. (2007) 'The Joint Effect of Topic Interest and Follow-Up Procedures on the Response in a Mail Questionnaire: An Empirical Test of the Leverage-Saliency Theory in Audience Research'. *Sociological Methods & Research* 35: 410–28.

Rosenbaum, M. E., and Ferguson, K. J. (2006) 'Using patient-generated cases to teach students skills in responding to patients' emotions'. *Medical Teacher* 28(2): 180–2.

Roter, D. (2008) 'RIAS: Roter Interaction Analysis System Web site': http://www.rias.org/articles

Rothman, B. K. (1982) *In Labour: Women and Power in the Birthplace*. Junction: London.

Rothman, B. K. (1996) 'Bearing witness: Representing women's experiences of prenatal diagnosis'. *Feminism & Psychology* 6: 52–5.

Rusinko, C. A. (1999) 'Exploring the Use of Design-Manufacturing Integration (DMI) to Facilitate Product Development: A Test of Some Practices'. *IEEE Transactions on Engineering Management* 46(1): 56–71.

Ruusuvuori, J., and Peräkylä, A.(2009) 'Words and facial expression in assessing stories and topics'. *Resarch on Language and Social Interaction* 42(4): 377–94.

Sacks, H. (1987) 'On the Preferences for Agreement and Contiguity in Sequences in Conversation'. In G. Button and J. R. E. Lee (eds), *Talk and Social Organisation*. Clevedon: Multilingual Matters: 54–69.

Sacks, H. (1992a, b) *Lectures on Conversation*, Volumes 1 and 2, ed. Gail Jefferson, with an introduction by Emanuel A. Schegloff. Oxford: Blackwell.

Sacks, H., and Schegloff, E. A. (1979) 'Two Preferences in the Organization of Reference to Persons in Conversation and Their Interaction'. In G. Psathas (ed.), *Everyday Language: Studies in Ethnomethodology*. New York: Irvington, pp. 15–21.

Sacks, H., Schegloff, E. A., and Jefferson, G. (1974) 'A Simplest Systematics for the Organization of Turn-Taking in Conversation'. *Language* 50: 696–735.

Sandhu, H., Dale, J., Stallard, N., Crouch, R., and Glucksman, E. (2009) 'Emergency nurse practitioners and doctors consulting with patients in an emergency department: A comparison of communication skills and satisfaction'. *Emergency Medicine Journal* 26: 400–4.

Sandvik, M, Eide, H., Lind, M., Graugaard, P. K., Torper, J., and Finset, A. (2002) 'Analyzing medical dialogues: Strengths and weakness of Roter's interaction analysis system'. *Patient Education & Counseling* 46: 235–41.

Schaeffer, N. C. (1991) 'Conversation with a purpose – or conversation?' In P. P. Biemer, R. M. Groves, L. E. Lyberg, N. A. Mathiowetz and S. Sudman (eds), *Measurement Error in Surveys*. New York: Wiley & Sons, pp. 367–91.

Schaeffer, N. C., Garbarski, D., and Freese, J. (2010) 'Beyond the Paradigmatic Opening: Sample Members' Questions and Their Placement in the Call for Participation'. Madison WI: Department of Sociology, University of Wisconsin.

Schegloff, E. A. (1968) 'Sequencing in Conversational Openings'. *American Anthropologist* 70: 1075–95.

Schegloff, E. A. (1979) 'Identification and Recognition in Telephone Openings'. In G. Psathas (ed.), *Everyday Language*. New York: Erlbaum, pp. 23–78.

Schegloff, E. A. (1980) 'Preliminaries to preliminaries: "Can I ask you a question"'. *Sociological Inquiry* 50: 104–52.

Schegloff, E. A. (1982) 'Discourse as an interactional achievement: Some uses of "uh huh" and other things that come between sentences'. In D. Tannen (ed.), *Analyzing Discourse*. Washington: Georgetown University Press, pp. 71–93.

Schegloff, E. A. (1986) 'The Routine as Achievement'. *Human Studies* 9: 111–51.

Schegloff, E. A. (1988) 'Goffman and the analysis of conversation'. In P. Drew and A. Wootton (eds), *Erving Goffman: Exploring the Interaction Order*. Cambridge: Polity Press.

Schegloff, E. A. (1992a) Introduction. In H. Sacks, *Lectures on Conversation*, Volume 1. Oxford: Basil Blackwell, pp. ix–lxii

Schegloff, E. A. (1992b) Introduction. In H. Sacks, *Lectures on Conversation*, Volume 2. Oxford: Basil Blackwell, pp. ix–lii

Schegloff, E. A. (1992c) 'To Searle on conversation: A note in return'. In J. R. Searle, H. Parret and J. Verschueren (eds), *(On) Searle on Conversation*. Amsterdam and Philadelphia: John Benjamins, pp. 113–28.

Schegloff, E. A. (1993) 'Reflections on Quantification in the Study of Conversation'. *Research On Language And Social Interaction* 26: 99–128.

Schegloff, E. A. (1996a) 'Some Practices for Referring to Persons in Talk-in-Interaction: A Partial Sketch of a Systematics'. In B. Fox (ed.), *Studies in Anaphora*. Amsterdam: John Benjamins, pp. 437–85.

Schegloff, E. A. (1996b) 'Turn Organization: One Intersection of Grammar and Interaction'. In E. Ochs, E. A. Schegloff and S. Thompson (eds), *Interaction and Grammar*. Cambridge: Cambridge University Press.

Schegloff, E. A. (1996c) 'Confirming allusions: Toward an empirical account of action'. *American Journal of Sociology* 102(1):161–216.

Schegloff, E. A. (2002) 'Beginnings in the Telephone'. In J. E. Katz and M. Aakhus (eds), *Perpetual Contact: Mobile communication, private talk, public performance*. Cambridge: Cambridge University Press, pp. 284–300.

Schegloff, E. A. (2003) 'Conversation analysis and communication disorders'. In C. Goodwin (ed.), *Conversation and Brain Damage*. New York: Oxford University Press.

Schegloff, E. A. (2006) 'Interaction: The Infrastructure for social institutions, the natural ecological niche for language, and the arena in which culture is enacted'. In N. J. Enfield and S. C. Levinson (eds), *Roots of Human Sociality: Culture, cognition and interaction*. New York: Berg, pp. 70–98.

Schegloff, E. A. (2007) *Sequence Organization in Interaction: A Primer in Conversation Analysis*, Volume 1. Cambridge: Cambridge University Press.

Schegloff, E. A., Jefferson, G., and Sacks, H. (1977) 'The Preference for Self-Correction in the Organization of Repair for Conversation'. *Language* 53: 361–82.

Schwabe, M., Howell, S. J., and Reuber, M. (2007) 'Differential diagnosis of seizure disorders: A conversation analytic approach'. *Social Science & Medicine* 65: 712–24

Schwartz, N., and Hippler, H.-J. (1991) 'Response alternatives. In P. P. Biemer, R. M. Groves, L. E. Lyberg, N. A. Mathiowetz and S. Sudman (eds), *Measurement Error in Surveys*. New York: Wiley & Sons, pp. 41–56.

Scott, M. B. and Lyman, S. M. (1986) 'Accounts'. *American Sociological Review* 33(1): 46–62.

Seale, C., Butler, C., Hutchby, I., Kinnersley, P., and Rollnick, S. (2007) 'Negotiating frame ambiguity: A study of simulated encounters in medical education'. *Communication & Medicine* 4(2): 177–87.

Searle, J. R. (1969) *Speech Acts: An Essay in the Philosophy of Language*. Cambridge: Cambridge University Press.

Searle, J. R. (1975). 'Indirect Speech Acts'. In P. Cole and J. L. Morgan (eds) *Syntax and Semantics: Volume 3, Speech Acts*. New York: Academic Press, pp. 59–82.

Searle, J. R. (1986) 'Introductory essay: Notes on conversation'. In D. Ellis and W. Donohue (eds), *Contemporary Issues in Language and Discourse Processes*. Hillsdale, NJ: Lawrence Erlbaum Associates, pp. 7–19.

Shakespeare, P. (1998) *Aspects of Confused Speech*. Mahwah, NJ: Erlbaum.

Sharrock, W., and Button, G. (1997) 'Engineering Investigations: Practical Sociological Reasoning in the Work of Engineers'. In G. Bowker, S. Star, W. Turner and L. Gasser (eds), *Social Science, Technical Systems, and Cooperative Work*. Mahway, NJ: Lawrence Erlbaum, pp. 79–104.

Sharrock, W. W., and Watson, D. R. (1985) '"Reality construction" in second-language-learning (L2) simulations'. *System* 13: 195–206.

Shaw, R., and Kitzinger, C. (2005) 'Calls to a homebirth helpline: Empowerment in childbirth'. *Social Science and Medicine* 61: 2374–83.

Shaw, R., and Kitzinger, C. (2007) 'Memory in interaction: An analysis of repeat calls to a home birth helpline'. *Research on Language and Social Interaction* 40(1): 117–44.

Silverman, D. (1997) *Discourses of Counselling*. London: Sage.

Silverman, D. (1998) *Harvey Sacks: Social Science and Conversation Analysis*. Oxford: Polity Press .

Silverman, J., Kurtz, S., and Draper, J. (2005) *Skills for Communicating with Patients*, 2nd edn. Oxford: Radcliffe Publishing.

Simmons-Mackie, N., Elman, R. J., Holland, A. L., and Damico, J. S. (2007) 'Management of Discourse in Group Therapy for Aphasia'. *Topics In Language Disorders* 27: 5–23.

Skelt, L. (2006) *See What I Mean: Hearing Loss, Gaze and Repair in Conversation*. PhD Dissertation, Canberra, The Australian National University.
Skelt, L. (2007) 'Damage Control: Closing problematic sequences in hearing-impaired interaction'. *Australian Review of Applied Linguistics* 30(3): 34.1-34.15.
Sneijder, P., Lamerichs, J., te Molder, H. F. M., Koelen, M., and van Nierop, P. (2007) *Handleiding discursieve actie methode [Manual of the discursive action method]*. Wageningen, The Netherlands: Communication Strategies, Wageningen UR, and Municipal Health Services Eindhoven, The Netherlands.
Sohn, W. (2001) 'Schwerhörigkeit in Deutschland. Repräsentative Hörscreening-Untersuchung bei 2000 Probanden in 11 Allgemeinpraxen'. *Zeitschrift für Allgemeinmedizin* 77. Stuttgart: Hippokrates-Verlag, pp. 143–7.
Sorjonen, M.-L. (2001) *Responding in Conversation: A study of response particles in Finnish*. Amsterdam: Benjamins.
Speer, S. (2002) '"Natural" and "contrived" data: A sustainable distinction'. *Discourse Studies* 4(4): 511–25.
Speer, S. A. (2005) *Gender Talk: Feminism, discourse and conversation analysis*. London: Routledge
Speer, S. A., and Stokoe, E. (eds) (2010) *Conversation and Gender*. Cambridge: Cambridge University Press.
Spilkin, M.-L., and Bethlehem, D. (2003) 'A Conversation Analysis approach to facilitating communication with memory books'. *Advances in Speech and Language Pathology* 5: 105–18.
Stiles, W. B. (1999) 'Signs and voices in psychotherapy'. *Psychotherapy Research* 9(1): 1–21.
Stivers, T. (2002) 'Presenting the problem in pediatric encounters: "Symptoms only" versus "Candidate Diagnosis" Presentations'. *Health Communication* 14(3): 299–338.
Stivers, T. (2007) *Prescribing under Pressure: Parent-physician conversations and antibiotics*. Oxford: Oxford University Press.
Stivers, T. (2008) 'Stance, Alignment, and Affiliation During Storytelling: When Nodding is a Token of Affiliation'. *Research on Language & Social Interaction* 41: 31–57.
Stivers, T., Mangione-Smith, R., Elliott, M. N., McDonald, L., and Heritage, J. (2003) 'Why do physicians think parents expect antibiotics? What parents report vs. what physicians perceive'. *The Journal of Family Practice* 52(2): 140–8.
Stivers, T., Enfield, N. J., Brown, P., Englert, C., Hayashi, M., Heinemann, T., Hoymann, G., Rossano, F., De Ruiter, J. P., Kyung-Eun Yoon, K.-E., and Levinson, S. C. (2009) 'Universals and cultural variation in turn-taking in conversation'. *Proceedings of the National Academy of Sciences* 106(26): 10587–92.
Stokoe, E. (2010) '"I'm not gonna hit a lady": Conversation Analysis, membership categorization and men's denials of violence towards women'. *Discourse & Society* 21(1): 1–24.
Stokoe, E., and Edwards, D. (2007) '"Black this, black that": Racial insults and reported speech in neighbour complaints and police interrogations'. *Discourse & Society* 18(3): 337–72.
Stokoe, E., and Edwards, D. (2010) 'Accomplishing social action with identity categories: Mediating neighbour complaints'. In M. Wetherell (ed.), *Theorizing Identities and Social Action*. London: Sage.

Stribling. P., Rae, J., and Dickerson, P. (2007) 'Two forms of spoken repetition in a girl with autism'. *International Journal of Language & Communication Disorders* 42(4): 427–44.
Suchman, L., Blomberg, J., Orr, J., and Trigg, R. (1999) 'Reconstructing Technologies as Social Practice'. In P. Lyman and N. Wakeford (eds), *Special issue of the American Behavioral Scientist on Analysing Virtual Societies: New Directions in Methodology* 43(3), November/December: 392–408.
Szymanski, M. H., Aoki, P. M., Vinkhuyzen, E., and Woodruff, A. (2006) 'Organizing a remote state of incipient talk: Push-to-talk mobile radio interaction' *Language in Society* 35(3): 393–418.
te Molder, H. F. M., and Potter, J. (eds) (2005) *Conversation and Cognition*. Cambridge: Cambridge University Press.
ten Have, P. (1999) *Doing Conversation Analysis: A practical guide*. London: Sage.
Turner, S., and Whitworth, A. (2006) 'Clinicians Perceptions of Candidacy for Conversation Partner Training in Aphasia: How Do We Select Candidates for Therapy and Do We Get it Right?' *Aphasiology* 20: 616–43.
Van Berkel, R., and Valkenburg, B. (eds) (2007) *Making it Personal: Individualising activation services in the EU*. Bristol: Policy.
Van Dijk, T. (1987) *Communicating Racism: Ethnic prejudice in thought and talk*. London: Sage.
Van Dijk, T. (1991) *Racism and the Press*. London: Routledge.
van Hasselt, V. B., Romano, S. J., and Vecchi, G. M. (2008) 'Role playing: applications in hostage and crisis negotiation skills training'. *Behavior Modification* 32(2): 248–63.
Vandekerckhove, M. M. P., Scheve, C. von, Ismer, S., and Kronast, S. (eds) (2008) *Regulating Emotions: Social necessity and biological inheritance*. Oxford: Blackwell.
Vehviläinen, S. (2003) 'Preparing and delivering interpretations in psychoanalytic interaction'. *Text* 23: 573–606.
Vehviläinen, S. (2008) 'Identifying and managing resistance in psychoanalytic interaction'. In A. Peräkylä, C. Antaki, S. Vehviläinen and I. Leudar (eds), *Conversation Analysis and Psychotherapy*. Cambridge: Cambridge University Press, pp. 120–38
Villmann, T., Liebers, C., Bergmann, B., Gumz, A., and Geyer, M. (2008) 'Investigation of psycho-physiological interactions between patient and therapist during a psychodynamic therapy and their relation to speech using in terms of entropy analysis using a neural network approach'. *New Ideas in Psychology* 26: 309–25
Vinkhuyzen, E., and Whalen, J. (2007) 'Expert System Technology in Work Practice'. In S. Hester and D. Francis (eds), *Orders of Ordinary Action*. Aldershot: Ashgate Publishing, pp. 135–58.
Vinkhuyzen, E., and Szymanski, M. H. (2005) 'Would You Like to do it Yourself? Service Requests and Their Non-Granting Responses'. In K. Richards and P. Seedhouse (eds) *Applying Conversation Analysis*. New York: Palgrave Macmillan, pp. 91–106.
von Prondzynski, F. (2009) 'A university blog: Diary of a university president'. http://universitydiary.wordpress.com/2009/07/09/pure-or-applied (accessed 06.01.10).
Voutilainen, L., Peräkylä, A., and Ruusuvuori, J. (2010) 'Recognition and interpretation: Responding to emotional experience in psychotherapy'. *Research on Language and Social Interaction* 43(1): 85–107.
Waite, J. (2009) 'Jobcentre Plus – Not Working'. *Face the Facts*, Radio 4 documentary, 16 August (http://www.bbc.co.uk/programmes/b00m0k5f)
Wannan, G., and York, A. (2005) 'Using video and role-play to introduce medical students to family therapy: Is watching better than appearing?' *Journal of Family Therapy* 27(3): 263–71.

Watson, D. R., and Sharrock, W. W. (1988) 'Some social-interactional aspects of a business game for special purposes in the (L2) teaching of English'. In D. Crookall (ed.), *Simulation-Gaming in Education and Training*. Oxford: Pergamon, pp. 177–86.
Watson, R., and Coulter, J. (2008) 'The debate over cognitivism'. *Theory, Culture and Society* 25(2): 1–17.
Watts, R. J. (2003) *Politeness*. Cambridge: Cambridge University Press.
Weathersbee, T. E. (2009) 'Dialling for Donations: Practices and Actions in the Telephone Solicitation of Human Tissues'. *Sociology of Health & Illness* 31: 803–16.
Wetherell, M., and Potter, J. (1992) *Mapping the Language of Racism: Discourse and the legitimation of exploitation*. Hemel Hempstead: Harvester Wheatsheaf.
Whalen, J., and Bobrow, D. (2010) 'Communal Knowledge Sharing: The Eureka Story'. In J. Whalen and M. Szymanski (eds), *Making Work Visible: Ethnographially Grounded Case Studies of Work Practice*. Cambridge: Cambridge University Press.
Whalen, M. R., and Zimmerman, D. H. (1987) 'Sequential and institutional contexts in calls for help'. *Social Psychology Quarterly* 50: 172–85.
White, C. H., and Agne, R. R. (2009) 'Communication practices of coaches during mediator training: Addressing issues of knowledge and enactment'. *Conflict Resolution Quarterly* 27(1): 83–105.
White, J., Levinson, W., and Roter, D. (1994) '"Oh, by the way …": The closing moments of the medical visit'. *Journal of General Internal Medicine* 9(1): 24–8.
White, J., Rosson, C., Christensen, J., Hart, R., and Levinson, W. (1997) 'Wrapping things up: A qualitative analysis of the closing moments of the medical visit'. *Patient Education and Counseling* 30: 155–65.
Whitworth, A., Perkins, L., and Lesser, R. (1997) *Conversation Analysis Profile for People with Aphasia*. London: Wiley.
Widdicombe, S. (1998) 'Identity as an analysts' and a participants' resource'. In C. Antaki and S. Widdicombe (eds), *Identity in Talk*. London: Sage, pp. 191–207.
Wieder, D. L. (1988) 'From resource to topic: Some aims of conversation analysis'. In J. Anderson (ed.), *Communication Yearbook 11*. Beverly Hills: Sage.
Wielaert, S. M., and Wilkinson, R. (in prep.) *Partners van Afasiepatienten Conversatie Training (PACT)*. Houten: Bohn Stafleu van Loghum.
Wilkinson, R. (1999) 'Sequentiality As a Problem and Resource for Intersubjectivity in Aphasic Conversation: Analysis and Implications for Therapy'. *Aphasiology* 13: 327–43.
Wilkinson, R. (2004) 'Reflecting on Talk in Speech and Language Therapy: Some Contributions Using Conversation Analysis'. *International Journal Of Language & Communication Disorders* 39: 497–503.
Wilkinson, R. (2006) 'Applying conversation analysis to aphasic talk: From investigation to intervention'. *Revue Francaise de Linguistique Appliquée* 11(2): 99–110.
Wilkinson, R. (2007) 'Managing Linguistic Incompetence as a Delicate Issue in Aphasic Talk-in-Interaction: On the Use of Laughter in Prolonged Repair Sequences'. *Journal Of Pragmatics* 37: 542–69.
Wilkinson, R., Beeke, S., and Maxim, J. (2003) 'Adapting to Conversation: On the Use of Linguistic Resources by Speakers with Fluent Aphasia in the Construction of Turns at Talk'. In C. Goodwin (ed.), *Conversation And Brain Damage*. New York, Oxford University Press.
Wilkinson, R., Bryan, K., Lock, S., and Sage, K. (2010) 'Implementing and Evaluating Aphasia Therapy Targeted at Couples' Conversations: A Single Case Study'. *Aphasiology* 24(6): 869–86.

Wilkinson, R., Gower, M., Beeke, S., and Maxim, J. (2007) 'Adapting To Conversation as a Language-Impaired Speaker: Changes in Aphasic Turn Construction Over Time'. *Communication And Medicine* 4: 79–97.

Wilkinson, R., Lock, S., Bryan, K. and Sage, K. (2011) 'Interaction-focused intervention for acquired language disorders: Facilitating mutual adaptation in couples where one partner has aphasia'. *International Journal of Speech and Language Pathology* 13(1): 74–87.

Wilkinson, R., Bryan, K., Lock, S., Bayley, K., Maxim, J., Bruce, C., Edmundson, A., and Moir, D. (1998) 'Therapy Using Conversation Analysis: Helping Couples Adapt to Aphasia in Conversation'. *International Journal Of Language And Communication Disorders (Supplement)* 33: 144–9.

Wilkinson, S. (2010) 'Gender, routinization and recipient design'. In S. Speer and E. Stokoe (eds), *Conversation and Gender*. Cambridge: Cambridge University Press.

Wilkinson, S. (2011) 'Constructing ethnicity statistics in talk-in-interaction: Producing the "White European"'. *Discourse and Society* 22(3): 343–61.

Wilkinson, S., and Kitzinger, C. (2006) 'Surprise as an interactional achievement'. *Social Psychology Quarterly* 69(2): 150–82.

Wilkinson, S., and Kitzinger, C. (frth) 'Surprise and repair'.

Williams, V. (1999) 'Researching Together'. *British Journal of Learning Disabilities* 27(2): 48–51.

Williams, V., Simons, K., and Swindon People First Research Team (2005) 'More Researching Together'. *British Journal of Learning Disabilities* 32: 1–9.

Wolf, M. H., Putnam, S. M., James, S. A., and Stiles, W. B. (1978) 'The medical interview satisfaction scale: Development of a scale to measure patient perceptions of physician behavior'. *Journal of Behavioral Medicine* 1: 391–401.

Woodruff, A., Szymanski, M. H., Grinter, R. E., and Aoki, P. (2002) 'Practical strategies for integrating a conversation analyst in an interactive design process'. *Proceedings 4th ACM Conference on Designing Interactive Systems*. London, pp. 19–28.

Wootton, A. (1989) 'Speech to and from a severely retarded young Down's syndrome child'. In M. Beveridge, G. Conti-Ramsden and I. Leudar (eds), *The Language and Communication of Mentally Handicapped People*. London: Chapman-Hall.

Yearley, S., and Brewer, J. (1989) 'Stigma and conversational competence: A conversation analytic study of the mentally handicapped'. *Human Studies* 12: 97–115

Ylirisku, S., and Buur, J. (2007) *Designing with Video: Focusing the user-centred design process*. Including DVD with 34 video samples. New York: Springer.

Yoo, M. S., Son, Y. J., Kim, Y. S., and Park, J. H. (2009) 'Video-based self-assessment: Implementation and evaluation in an undergraduate nursing course'. *Nurse Education Today* 29: 585–9.

Zick, A., Granieri, M., and Makoul, G. (2007) 'First-year medical students' assessment of their own communication skills: A video-based, open-ended approach'. *Patient Education and Counseling* 68(2): 161–6.

Zimmerman, D. H. (2005) 'Introduction: Conversation Analysis and Social Problems'. *Social Problems* 52: 445–8.

Author Index

Agne, R.R., 125, 126
Anderson, W.L., 208
Anderson, S.L., 208
Andresen, H., 119
Antaki, C., 1, 4, 12, 16, 32, 97, 161, 162, 165, 176, 179, 184, 208, 211, 212, 226, 239, 242
Arminen, I., 16, 189
Armstrong, L., 52
Aspinall, P.J., 88
Aston, J., 156
Atkinson, J.M., 7, 10, 14, 15, 32, 122
Auer, P., 35

Bagger, K., 210
Baker, C.D., 97, 115
Barker, M., 137
Barresi, B., 39
Barnett, S., 16
Bauer, A., 138
Bellis, A., 156
Bentley, R., 208
Beckman, H.B., 17
Beebe, B., 237, 239, 240
Beeke, S., 35
Benwell, B., 138
Bercelli, F., 239
Bethlehem, D., 161
Billig, M., 193
Bisgaard, S., 221
Bobrow, D., 16
Bolinger, D., 19
Booth, S., 53, 138, 161
Bokken, L., 120
Borkin, A., 19
Boyd, E., 16, 20, 22
Braun, V., 100
Brewer, J., 5
Britten, N., 107
Brouwer, C.E., 210
Brown, J.S., 207, 221
Brown, P., 56, 62

Bryan, K., 32, 33, 35, 36, 37, 43, 48, 51, 53, 161
Burch, K., 32, 53
Burns, A., 122
Buttny, R., 188
Button, G., 107, 208
Buur, J., 209, 210, 220, 221

Callahan, E., 17
Cameron, D., 85, 121
Campanelli, P., 54
Caris-Verhallen, W., 131
Casey, N., 107
Chomsky, N., 132
Christensen, V.T., 221
Clarke, V., 100, 121
Clayman, S.E., 7, 15, 16
Clift, R., 189
Code, C., 34
Collins, S., 159
Colomer, C., 186
Coulter, J., 235, 236
Couper, M.P., 54, 74
Crabtree, A., 208
Curl, T.S., 56, 58, 59, 97

Damico, N., 52
Dautenhahn, K., 162
Davies, E., 185
Davis-Floyd, R., 98
Day, D., 210
De la Croix, A., 121, 122
Deppermann, A., 221
Dewson, S., 156
Dickerson, P., 162
Dijkstra, W., 54
Dimberg, U., 239
Drakich, J., 121
Draper, J., 16, 31
Drew, P., 4, 6, 7, 10, 13, 15, 16, 26, 36, 56, 58, 59, 81, 97, 99, 135, 138, 140, 144, 158, 207
Dunn, A.,156

265

Author Index

Edwards, D., 3, 4, 97, 115, 125, 127, 128, 131, 133, 184, 188, 191, 193
Egbert, M., 158, 207, 221
Ekman, P., 236
Elman, R.J., 52
Emmison, M., 97, 115
Enfield, N.J., 211, 212, 237, 238, 239, 240

Fawcus, M., 34
Fehr, B.J., 188
Ferguson, K.J., 119
Field, T., 239
Finlay, W.M.L., 12, 161, 162, 165, 176, 179, 184, 208
Finset, A., 104
Firth, A., 97, 115
Fitzgerald, P., 224
Francis, D., 123, 138
Frankel, R. 17
Freese, J., 54, 55, 72
Friesen, W.V., 236
Frith, H., 4

Gabriel, B., 221
Garbarski, D., 72, 73
Gardner, H., 161
Gardner, R., 108, 112, 113, 224
Gafaranga, J., 107
Garfinkel, H., 15
Gill, V.T., 59, 61
Glenn, P., 95
Goffman, E., 189
Gonzales, P., 211, 212
Goodglass, H., 39
Goodwin, C., 5, 6, 12, 34, 35, 36, 189
Goodwin, M., 12, 239
Granieri, M., 117, 132
Greatbatch, D., 7, 208
Gregg, P., 156
Grice, H.P., 56
Griffin, C., 122
Gross, J.J., 239
Groves, R.M., 54, 74

Hauser, R.M., 55, 73
Heath, C., 7, 25, 107, 208, 209
Heeschen, C., 35
Heinemann, T., 58, 73, 209

Hepburn, A., 3, 106, 109, 122, 184, 189, 192
Heritage, J., 6, 10, 14, 15, 16, 19, 20, 22, 32, 41, 46, 56, 59, 67, 79, 81, 87, 104, 109, 110, 117, 122, 125, 138, 158, 159, 160, 161, 208, 226, 241
Hester, S., 138
Hetu, R., 221
Hillbrand, M., 122
Hindmarsh, J., 7
Hippler, H.J., 87
Holland, A., 52
Hollander, M., 71, 72, 73
Holstein, J.A., 7
Holt, E., 4, 189
Hood, K., 120
Horn, L.R., 19
Houtkoop-Steenstra, H., 56, 61, 70, 93, 97
Hutchby, I., 16, 184, 188

Irvine, A., 13, 140, 144, 207

Jacoby, S., 211, 212
James, D., 121
Jefferson, G., 4, 35, 41, 43, 49, 55, 69, 90, 113, 117, 121, 126, 129, 132, 187, 188, 189
Jingree, T., 162
Jones, A., 161, 182, 185, 189
Jupp, T., 185

Kagan, A., 34
Kaplan, E., 39
Kappas, A., 240
Kitzinger, C., 4, 9, 93, 97, 98, 99, 100, 102, 103, 107, 108, 114, 117, 121, 125, 138, 184, 211, 212
Kitzinger, S., 98, 99, 103, 107
Klippi, A., 35
Koelen, M.A., 186
Koole, T., 185
Kulke, F., 138
Kurtz, S., 16, 31

Laakso, M., 35
Lachman, F.M., 237, 239, 240
Lakoff, R., 122

Lamerichs, J., 184, 185, 189, 201, 203
Land, V., 100, 212
Lane, C., 120
Larsen, H., 210
Lawson, R., 34
Lee, E.K.O., 113, 117, 136
Leinonen, M., 16
Leising, D., 119
Lerner, G., 14, 100, 211
Lesser, R., 138
Levinson, S., 3, 17, 56, 62, 237, 238, 239, 240
Lievens, J., 60
Lindström, A., 58, 73
Linell, P., 123
Lim, E.C.H., 120
Lock, S., 32, 33, 35, 36, 37, 43, 48, 51, 53, 55, 58, 71, 72, 136, 144, 203
Luff, P., 7, 208, 209
Lyman, S.M., 188

Makoul, G., 117, 132
Maguire, P., 104, 131
Malone, T., 208
Mangione-Smith, R., 16
Marvel, M.K., 17
Mates, A.W., 6
Matthews, B., 210, 220
Maxim, J., 35, 161
Maynard, D.W., 3, 4, 54, 55, 56, 59, 60, 68, 71, 72, 97, 117, 242
McGrane, H., 52
McHoul, A., 7, 236
McKay, S., 117
Mehan, H., 4
Meis, M., 221
Mikesell, L., 6
Mitchell, S.A., 209, 235
Mjaaland, T.A., 104
Mondada, L., 7, 13
Moore, S., 122
Morton-Williams, J., 61, 70
Mounsey, A.L., 120
Müller, F.E., 73
Muybridge, E., 2

Nevile, M., 7
Nickels, L., 34
Niewenhuis, R., 52

Nolen, J., 72, 73, 74
Novak, P., 221

Oakley, A., 98
O'Baugh, J., 117
Ochs, E., 3, 211, 212, 216, 219
Oh, S.Y., 120, 212
Okada, Y., 122, 124

Padmos, H., 185
Palmieri, G., 119
Parker, I., 137
Pate, L., 165
Pelz, C., 221
Peräkylä, A., 8, 12, 115, 116, 161, 222, 224, 230, 233, 234, 237, 238, 239
Perkins, L., 53, 138, 161
Pieterse, A.H., 104, 117
Pilnick, A., 7
Pitceathly, C., 104, 132
Pitsch, K., 209
Pomerantz, A., 19, 91, 110, 188
Potter, J., 3, 122, 184, 188, 189, 191, 192, 193, 198, 236
Premack, D., 238
ProMatura (Company), 221

Rae, J., 162
Rapley, T., 122, 162, 236
Raymond, G., 19, 20, 40, 41, 109
Rehbein, D., 119
Reid, M., 140
Reuber, M., 6
Richards, K., 1, 5, 7
Rickford, R., 100, 117
Roberts, C., 185
Robinson, J.D., 15, 16, 17, 22, 31, 32, 107, 109, 110, 158, 160, 161, 208, 241
Rogers, S., 119
Rollnick, S., 120
Romano, S.J., 119, 120, 132
Rönfeldt, B., 35
Roose, H., 60
Rosenbaum, M.E., 119
Rossano, F., 239
Roter, D., 17, 104
Rothman, B.K., 98, 103

Rusinko, C.A., 208
Ruusuvuori, J., 224, 237, 239

Sacks, H., 2, 3, 15, 17, 18, 19, 35, 41, 43, 49, 55, 69, 90, 99, 119, 121, 188, 207, 211, 223, 235, 241
Sage, K., 32
Sainsbury, R., 13, 140
Sandhu, H., 104, 117
Sandvik, M., 117
Schaeffer, N.C., 54, 55, 56, 60, 68, 72, 87, 97
Schegloff, E. A., 3, 5, 6, 14, 15, 16, 19, 32, 35, 41, 43, 44, 46, 49, 55, 56, 64, 69, 71, 77, 79, 90, 93, 97, 104, 107, 108, 111, 114, 117, 121, 188, 211, 234, 238
Schwabe, M., 6
Schwartz, N., 87
Scott, M.B.,188
Seale, C., 123
Searle, J.R., 56, 121
Seedhouse, P., 5, 7
Seet, R.C.S., 120
Shakespeare, P., 6
Sharrock, W., 123
Shaw, R., 102, 114, 117
Silverman, D., 2, 8, 14, 16, 31
Simmons-Mackie, N., 52
Skelt, L., 221
Skelton, J., 121, 122
Smit, J.H., 54
Smith, S.Y., 117
Sneijderet, P., 187
Sohn, W., 221
Sorjonen, M.L., 79, 81, 138, 224
Speer, S.A., 4, 121, 122
Spilkin, M.L., 161
Sporberg, D., 119
Spranz-Fogasy, T., 221
Stiles, W.B., 241
Stivers, T., 11, 16, 18, 73, 159, 211, 212
Stribling, P., 162, 165, 176
Sturgis, P., 54
Stokoe, E., 4, 119, 122, 127, 131, 138, 184
Suchman, L., 207, 208
Swabey, D., 53, 138, 161

Swindon People First Research Team, 167
Symons, K., 167
Szymanski, M.H., 58, 208

Te Molder, H.F.M., 184, 189, 191
ten Have, P., 138
Thompson, S., 3
Thunqvist, D.P., 123
Timmermans L., 131
Toerien, M., 13, 140
Turner, S., 53

Vaandrager, L., 186
Van den Ban, A., 186
van-den Bergh, H., 56, 61, 70
Van Dijk, T., 122, 137
van Dulmenc, S., 131
Vandekerckhove, M.M.P., 239
Van Hasselt, V.B., 119, 120, 132
Vehviläinen, S., 230, 234
von Prondzynski, F., 138
Voutilainen, L., 224, 239, 241, 242
Vecchi, G.M., 119, 120, 132
Vehviliainen, S., 12
Viaro, M., 239
Villmann, T., 240
Vinkhuyzen, E., 16, 58

Waege, H., 60
Waite, J., 141
Walton, C., 12, 161, 162, 165, 167, 176, 179, 183, 184, 208
Wannan, G., 120
Watson, D.R., 123
Watson, R., 235, 236
Watts, R.J., 62
Weathersbee, T.E., 73
Werry, I., 162
Wetherell, M., 188
Whalen, J., 7, 16
White, C.H., 125, 126
White, J., 17
Whitworth, A., 53, 138
Widdicombe, S., 4, 211, 212
Wieder, D.L., 123
Wielaert, S.M., 52
Wilkes, M., 23, 25
Williams, V., 10, 167

Wilkinson, R., 6, 9, 32, 33, 35, 37, 42, 43, 48, 51, 52, 53, 138, 161
Wilkinson, S., 4, 33, 35, 36, 41, 50, 75, 87, 90, 93, 100, 103, 108, 116
Wills, J., 4
Wiggins, S., 3, 184
Wolf, M.H., 26
Woodruff, A., 208
Wooffitt, R., 184, 188

Wootton, A., 162

Yearley, S., 5
Ylirisku, S., 209, 210
Yoo, M.S., 117
York, A., 120
Young, P., 70, 162

Zick, A., 117, 132
Zimmerman, D.H., 4, 7, 109

Subject Index

Action, 2, 16, 48
  Requesting actions, 58 (*see also* Requests)
AIDS counselling, 8, 222
Aligning responses, 18–20, 22, 41
Antibiotics (prescription), 11
Anti-Mentalism, 236–7 (*see also* Mentalism)
Aphasia, 5–6, 9, 32–53
  Aphasic/Non-Aphasic Dyad, 32–53
  Definition, 34
  Intervention in Aphasia: Design, 36–8, 51; Facilitating Change, 33–4; Handout (example), 45; Intervention types, 34; Repair in Aphasia, 35, 39, 40, 43, 47–8; Sequence Organisation in Aphasia, 35, 39, 41; Supporting Partners of People with Aphasia in Relationships and Conversation (SPPARC), 33, 51, 52; Turn Formats, 42, 46; Turn Taking, 35, 41, 44
Autism, 5
Applied CA, 1–14, 15–16, 138
  Ethics, 116, 159–60
  Types of applied CA: Foundational, 1, 3; Social-problem oriented, 1, 3–4; Communicational, 1, 5–6; Diagnostic, 1, 6; Institutional, 1, 6–8; Interventionist, 1, 8–13, 119–20, 136–9, 161
  Obstacles for researchers, 12
  Themes in interventionist applied CA, 10–13

Call monitoring (*see* Ethnic Monitoring)
Care homes, 12–13
Childbirth helplines, 98–118 (*see also* Helplines)
Choices, 32
Cognition, 56, 235

Collaboration with Agencies/Organisations, 9, 99–100
Complaints, 58
Context, 56
Continuers ('mm hm'), 44, 108–9
Conversation Analysis (CA) (*see also* Applied CA)
  Arguments for using CA methods, 96
  and change, 8, 9, 12, 13–14
  and Linguistics, 3, 121, 132
  and multi-modal work, 13
  and Pragmatics, 3
  and Psychology, 3, 235–37
  and Psychoanalysis, 223–42
  and Sociology, 3
  Definition of CA, 1–2, 15–16, 32
  Feminist CA, 4, 99–100
  Limitations of using CA, 13, 96, 98, 115, 171
  Theoretical principles, 104; versus other theoretical frameworks, 104–5

Delays, 18–19
Dementia, 5, 9
Discourse Analysis, 4
Discursive Action Method (DAM), 184–206
  Accountability, 188–90, 197–9
  Action Sequences, 188
  Applications, 184–5
  Cyclical Approach to Analysis, 196
  DAM in different settings, 204
  Facilitating Change, 198, 202
  Interactional Problems, 194–8
  Narratives, 189
  Non-Cognitive View, 191–2, 198, 200–1
  Playful approach, 191–2
  Reflexive Awareness, 199
  Rhetorical Principle, 193, 197–8
  Stake, 188–190, 194–5

270

Subject Index   271

Workshops, 190, 199–202
Discursive Action Model, 184
Discursive Psychology, 3, 184, 236
  and cognitions (cognitivism), 235–7
  and memory, 3
  and motivation, 236
Disordered talk, 5
Doctor-Patient Interaction, 10, 15–31
  Prescribing antibiotics, 11, 16

Entitlement, 58, 59
Epilepsy, 6
Ethnic Monitoring Questions, 75–97
  Accents, 86–7, 90–3
  Category labels, 87–8
  Failing to ask the question, 83–5
  Inaccurate answers, 87–90
  Not asking the question, 82–3, 85–6
  Offense, 75–6, 90, 94
  Pre-designated responses, 78–9
  Problematic asking of, 79–82, 87–90
  Recipient design, 90–3, 95–6
  Survey-type questions, 87–90
  Topicalisation, 93–6
  Training, 96
  Unproblematic asking of, 77–8
Ethno-methods, 3
Ethnography, 9, 59, 162–3
  Ethnographic Notes, 223–9
  Successful use of ethnographic methods, 176, 180–3, 223
Ethnomethodology, 236, 237
Evaluation, 36, 46–7, 120, 198–9, 201, 206
Everyday methods, 2
Experimental methods, 12, 31

Feedback to staff, 17, 43, 99, 101, 103, 104, 109, 111–15, 116, 120, 125, 137, 161, 162, 163, 164, 165, 166, 167, 176, 182–3
Facial Expressions, 236–7
Field experiment (see 'Some/Any')
Focus Groups, 142

Gender, 4
Generalised vs. Individualised Intervention, 32–3

Gesture, 12
Ground Up vs. Top Down approaches, 16

Hearing aids, 209–21
Health-related charity helpline, 75–97 (see Helplines)
Helplines, 9, 75–97, 98–118 (see also Ethnic Monitoring)
  Active Listening, 108
  Call openings, 107–8; Closings, 77, 79, 84, 85
  Feedback to call-takers, 111–15
  'Interactional asynchrony', 113
  Repeat Callers, 113–15
  Validating Experiences, 109–11
Humour, 48 (see also Laughter)

Identity, 211–12
  Categories, 212
Inductive approach, 144, 155
Intellectual disabilities, 161–83
  Gaining Consent, 164
  Residential services: Feedback with staff, 164–82; No-Criticism Policy, 182; Problems, 182; Resistance from staff, 166, 176; Workshops, 165–82
  Inspections, 16
  Policy directives, 167, 176, 182–3
  Staff/service-user interactions, 161, 163, 165, 167–83
Interaction order, 4, 32
Interviews, 46, 48, 54–74, 122, 140–60
  Critique of interview material, 122

Jobseeker interviews, 140–60
  Completing the Jobseeker's Agreement, 150
  Effectiveness of advisor-claimant interaction, 144
  Gathering information from claimants: Question design, 145–7; Preference, 146
  Personalised service, 140–1, 144–50, 155–9
  Providing information to claimants: Tailoring information, 147–50, 160; 'Tick box' approach, 144–55, 157

Subject Index

Jobcentres, 140–60 (*see also* Interviews, Jobseeker Interviews)
Processing claimants 140–1, 150, 156–7

Laughter, 48, 95, 192–4, 200–1
Learning disabilities, 5, 10, 163 (*see also* Intellectual Disabilities)
Linguistics, 56

Medical Consultations (*see* Physicians' Consultations)
Medical Diagnosis, 6
Mental Retardation (*see* Intellectual Disabilities)
Mentalism, 235–7
Mind, 222–3, 228, 235–7
Multi-methods (Eclecticism), 12, 20–1, 31, 46, 50, 51, 54, 98–100, 162–3, 223–35, 241–2
Mundane Conversation, 32, 49
Museums, 209
Electronic Guides, 209

National Ambulatory Medical Care Survey, 17, 24
Natural practices, 17
Naturally occurring data, 21, 46, 98–9, 138, 142, 185, 187, 208
Neighbour disputes, 125, 127–9
Normative expectations, 2
Normal Conversation, 33, 35
Non-CA methods, 115–16
Nuclear deterrence, 4

Offers, 56, 57
Pre-emptive offers, 58
Ordinary Talk, 10, 15

Palo Alto Research Center (PARC), 207, 208
Patients' Unmet Concerns, 15–31, 159–60
Physicians' solicitation of issues, 17
Policy, 100, 151, 155, 156, 157, 158, 159, 162, 167, 183
Pragmatics, 56
Practitioner-Client encounters, 10

Preference organisation, 15, 56, 72
Dispreferred actions, 56–7, 64
Pilots, 10
Political speeches, 7, 32
Politeness Theory, 56
Problems, 42
Interactional problems, 8, 9
Management of problems, 8
Practical problems, 16
Presentation of problems, 16–17
Psychoanalysis and CA, 222–42
CA and Changes to Practice, 229, 240–1
CA Reflection of Own Talk during Therapy Sessions, 223–9; Choices of Action, 223–4, 226, 228, 241; Responding to patients talk, 224–6
CA Reflection of Notes made during Therapy Session, 229–35; CA Interpretative Practices not Evident in Notes, 234; Patient's Responses to Interpretations, 230; Emerging Context, 241; Client Requirements, 241
Practices which Prompt Rethinking of CA, 235–40; Implications for Psychotherapy, 240; Emotion, 239; Mind, 235–7; Theory of Mind, 237–8

Quantitative outcome measures, 142
Questions:
'Anything else' questions, 19–22, 25–30, 32
Opening questions, 17
'Pandora's Box' effect, 23, 26, 28
Placement, 26
Polar questions (yes/no), 18–23, 28, 30–1, 32, 41; Preference, 18–20, 41; Stance, 19
Sensitive Questions, 75–97
Soliciting information, 110–11
'Some' version questions, 22–3, 25–30

Race, 4
Rape Myths, 4 (*see also* Sexual Violence)
Reaction tokens, 108–9, 111–13
Recipient design, 71, 122

Subject Index 273

Recordings, 2
  Audio, 9, 54, 76–7, 98–9, 101, 125, 142–3, 185–6, 191, 200, 208, 226
  Video, 9, 37, 125–6, 142–3, 164, 207, 208, 209, 210, 211, 219, 226; As a tool for intervention, 42–4, 46; Restrictions, 164
  Used for training, 25, 30, 50, 51, 103–4, 106, 115–16, 119, 125–39, 157, 161–2, 165–80, 185–6, 191, 200
Reflecting on Own Talk (*see* Discursive Action Method)
Repair Sequences, 64
Requests, 56, 58
  Acceptance, 67, 70, 71
  Agreeing, 65–6
  Ambiguous environments, 67, 68, 71–2; Encouraging and discouraging indicators, 68
  Blocking, 55, 58, 71, 72–3; 'Who is calling?', 72
  Call openings, 70–1
  Casual topics, 56
  'Context-shaped and context renewing', 59
  Context sensitivity, 69
  Contingency, 62, 66–7, 70, 71
  Continuum of requests, 62–3
  Presumptive requests, 63, 65–6, 70
  Cautious requests, 63, 65
  Cues, 55, 61, 63–5, 70, 71
  Declinations, 70, 71
  Deferred requests, 56
  Discouraging environments, 63–4, 65, 71, 72
  Embellishing requests, 65
  Encouraging environments, 65–6, 68, 71, 72
  Entitlement, 61–2, 65, 66, 68, 70, 71
  For antibiotics, 11
  For participation, 54–74
  Ill-fitted requests, 69–70
  In institutional settings, 58
  Introductory scripts, 60–1
  Mitigators, 62, 65, 67, 68, 71
  'Oh-prefaced' responses, 67
  Politeness terms, 58, 71
  Pre-emption, 62, 68
  Prefaces, 58–9; 'Wondering' prefaces, 61
  Pre-requests, 71
  Presumptive requests, 63, 68, 71
  Refusal, 70, 72
  Refusal conversion, 72
  Self-identification, 72
  Stance, 59, 64, 65
  'Tailoring', 54–5, 69, 70, 71, 72
  Task Partitioning, 62, 65, 67, 68, 70, 71
  Timing, 65, 66, 68, 70
  Training, 55
  Turned down, 65
Resistance:
  Clients', 63–4, 87, 89, 90, 129, 151, 234
  Patients', 10
  Participants', 165, 179–80
  Physicians', 11
  Staff members', 12, 105, 166, 186
Response Tokens, 109, 111–14
Role-play, 16, 43, 46, 105, 119–39
  Authenticity of, 120–5
  CA and role-play, 123–39; Conversation analytic role-play method (CARM), 119, 125–37
  Definition, 119
  Doctor-patient consultations, 121–2
  Identities, 123
  Managing interaction, 126
  Police Interrogations, 122, 124
  Stake, 121–2
  Uses, 119

Sampling, 23–5, 46
Second languages, 5, 6, 124
Sequential organisation, 2
Sexuality, 4
Sexual Violence, 122
Simulated Interaction, 119–39 (*see also* Role Play)
  Action formation, 124
  Repair, 124
  Sequence Organisation, 124
  Transition relevance, 124
  Turn-taking, 121, 124
Social Effects of Talk, 192
Social Problems, 3, 4

Subject Index

Social Justification, 11
'Some/any' experiment, 15–31
Sønderborg Participatory Innovation Research Centre (SPIRE), 209–10
Speech-acts, 3, 56
Stance, 11, 19, 59, 69
Supporting Partners of People with Aphasia in Relationships and Conversation (SPPARC), 33, 51, 52
Surveys, 12, 26, 31, 57, 59, 69, 72, 73, 142
  Scripts, 70, 71
  Tendency toward optimism, 68
  Wisconsin Longitudinal Study (WLS), 54–5, 59–62, 70
Suspicion of Research Aims, 163–4, 180

Teachers, 10
Telephone calls:
  Helplines (see Helplines)
  Interviews, 54–74
  Mediation Services, 127–37; Call openings, 129; Category use, 131–7; Resisting mediation, 129–30; Silence, 133–4; Stance, 13–18
  Telephone Surveys, 54
  To the doctor, 4
Thematic analysis:
  Suggestions for the use of, 99–103
Transcripts, 43, 187
  For training purposes, 50, 51, 126, 129–37; Arguments against, 106
  Level of detail, 187, 228
  Problems, 52
Training:
  CA group training workshops, 104–11
  Feedback to call-takers, 111–15
  Mediation Training, 125–37
  Role-play (see Role-play)
  Use of PowerPoint slides 128–36
  Use of Roter Interaction Analysis System (RIAS), 104, 108, 109
Turns:
  Turn-constructional units (TCUs), 44, 49, 50
  Turn design, 2, 31
  Turn taking, 5

Unmet Patient Concerns (see Patient Concerns)
User-Centred Design, 207–9, 220
  CA collaboration with Designers, 208–209
  Change, 207, 209
  Design as a predominantly social activity, 209
  Hearing Aids: Fitting of, 209, 210; 'Hearing in Transition' (HinT), 210, 211, 213, 216, 219; Hearing Impairment, 210
  Human Users Interacting with Photocopiers, 207
  Technological Innovation, 208–11; Interaction Innovation, 220; Participatory Innovation, 220; The Participants Perspective, 208–9

Video (see Recordings)

Wisconsin Longitudinal Study (WLS), 54–74